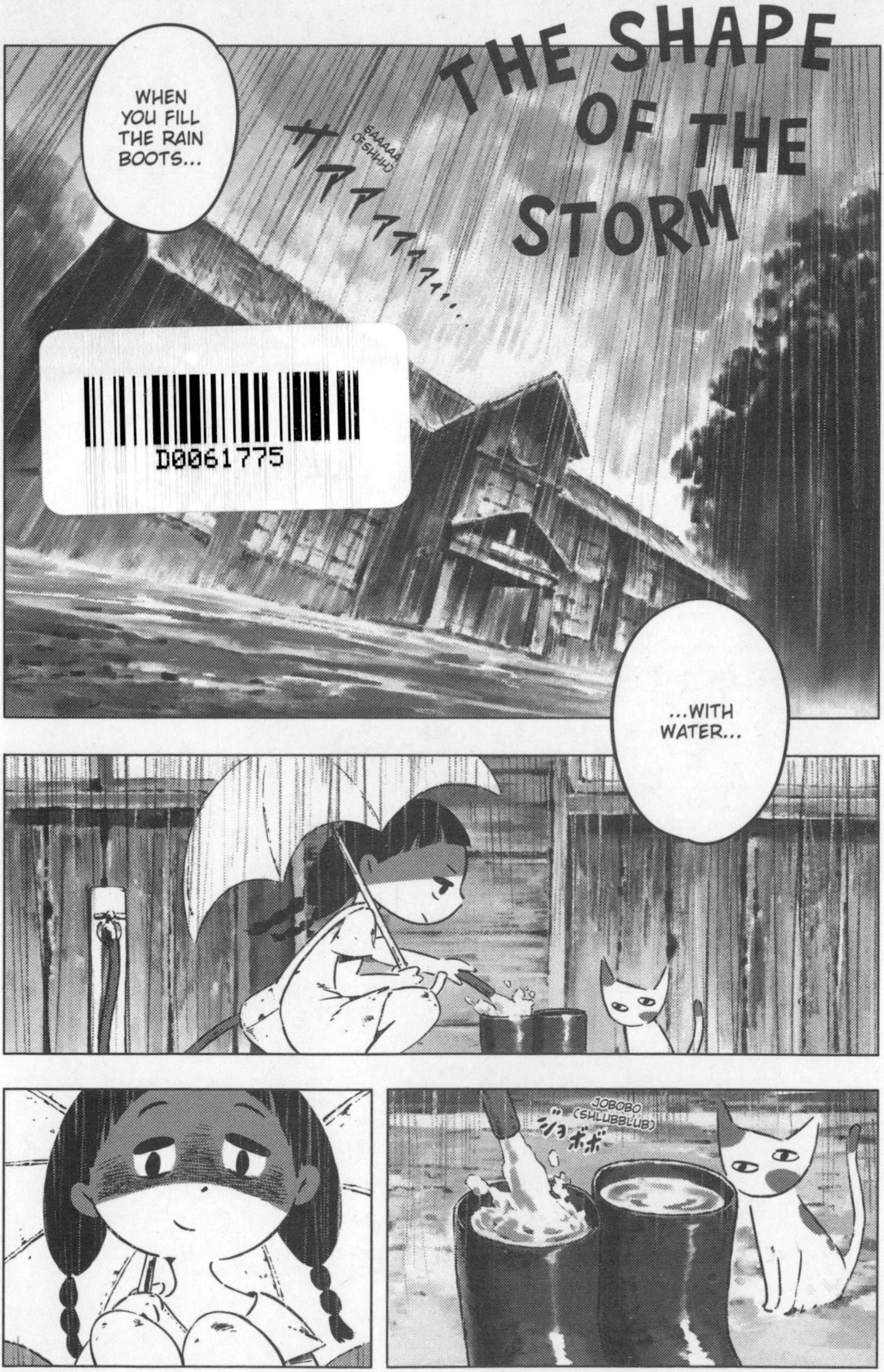
THE SHAPE OF THE STORM
SAAAAA (FSHHH)
WHEN YOU FILL THE RAIN BOOTS...
...WITH WATER...
JOBOBO (SHLUBBLUB)

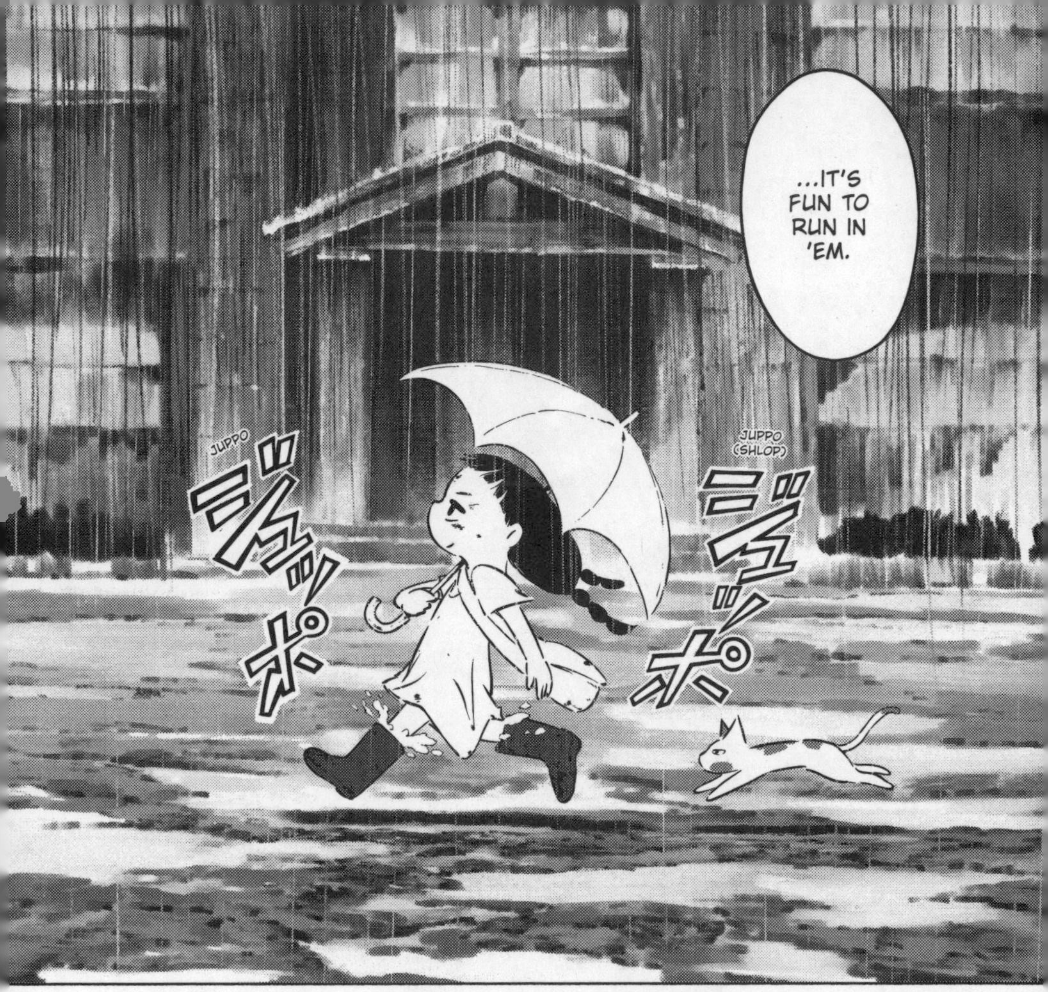
...IT'S FUN TO RUN IN 'EM.
JUPPO (SHLOP)
JUPPO

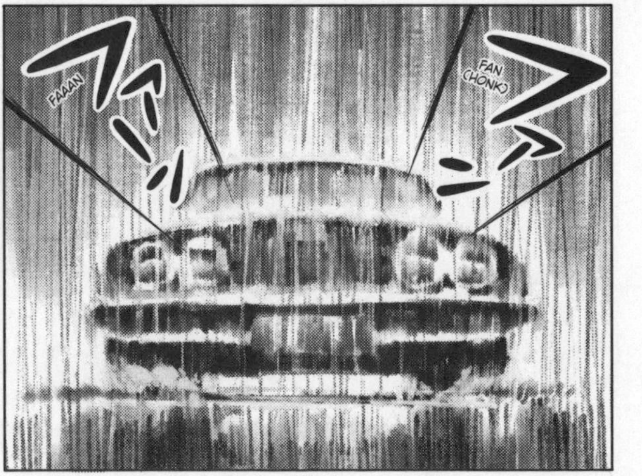
FAN (HONK)
FAAAN

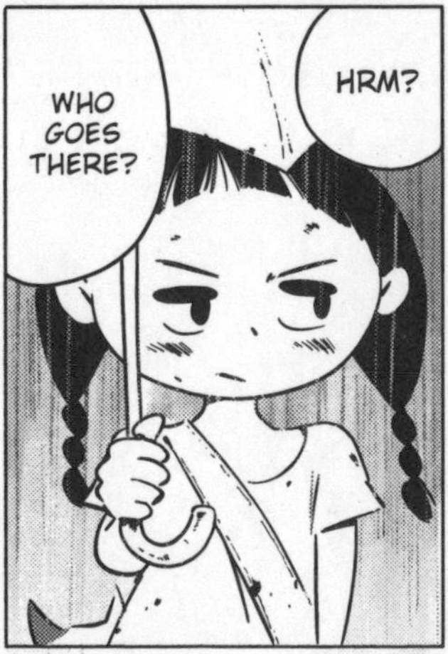
HRM?
WHO GOES THERE?

Hana-chan
and the Shape of the World

Ryotaro Ueda

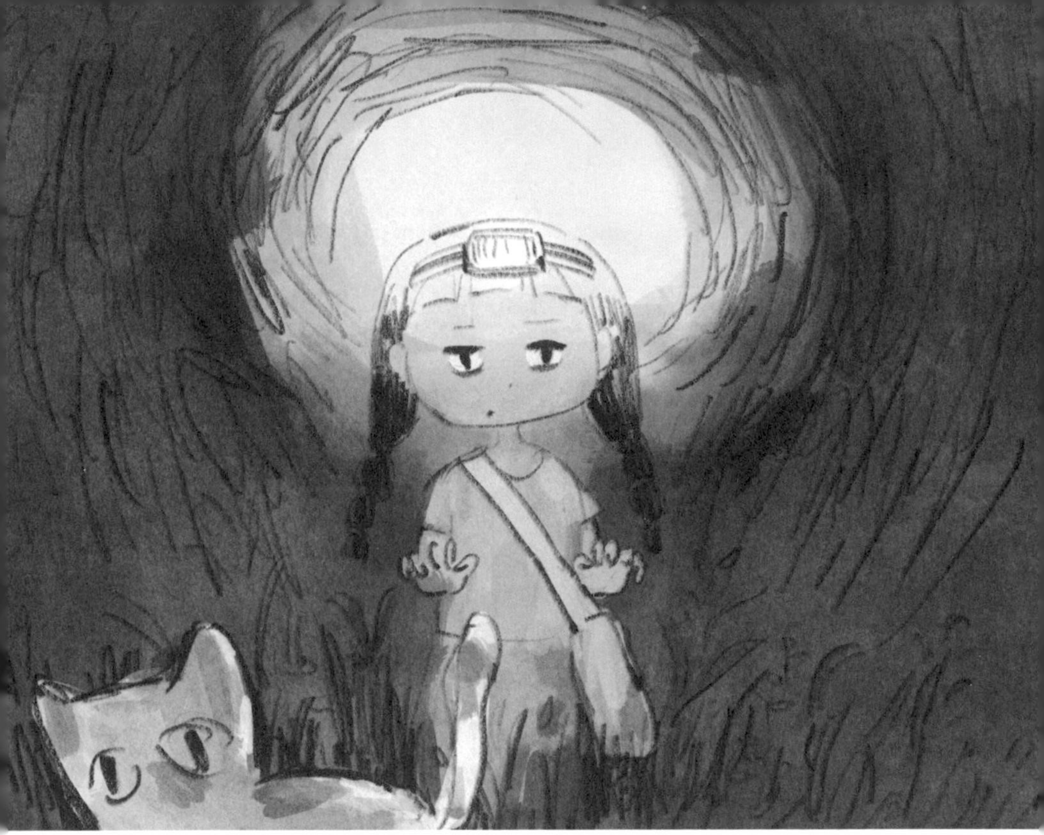

CONTENTS

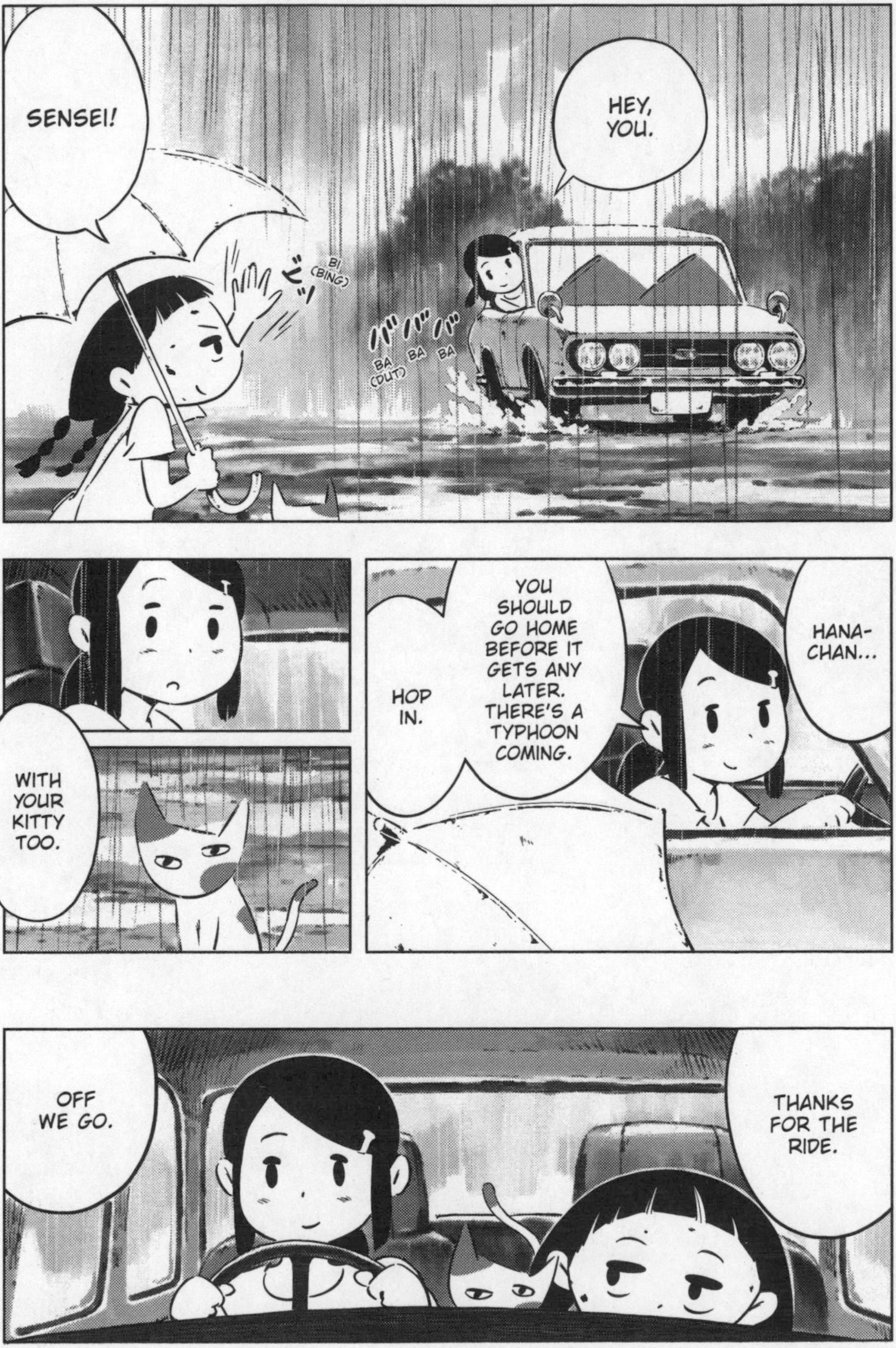
HEY, YOU.
BI (BING)
BA BA BA (DUT)
SENSEI!
HANA-CHAN...
YOU SHOULD GO HOME BEFORE IT GETS ANY LATER. THERE'S A TYPHOON COMING.
HOP IN.
WITH YOUR KITTY TOO.
THANKS FOR THE RIDE.
OFF WE GO.

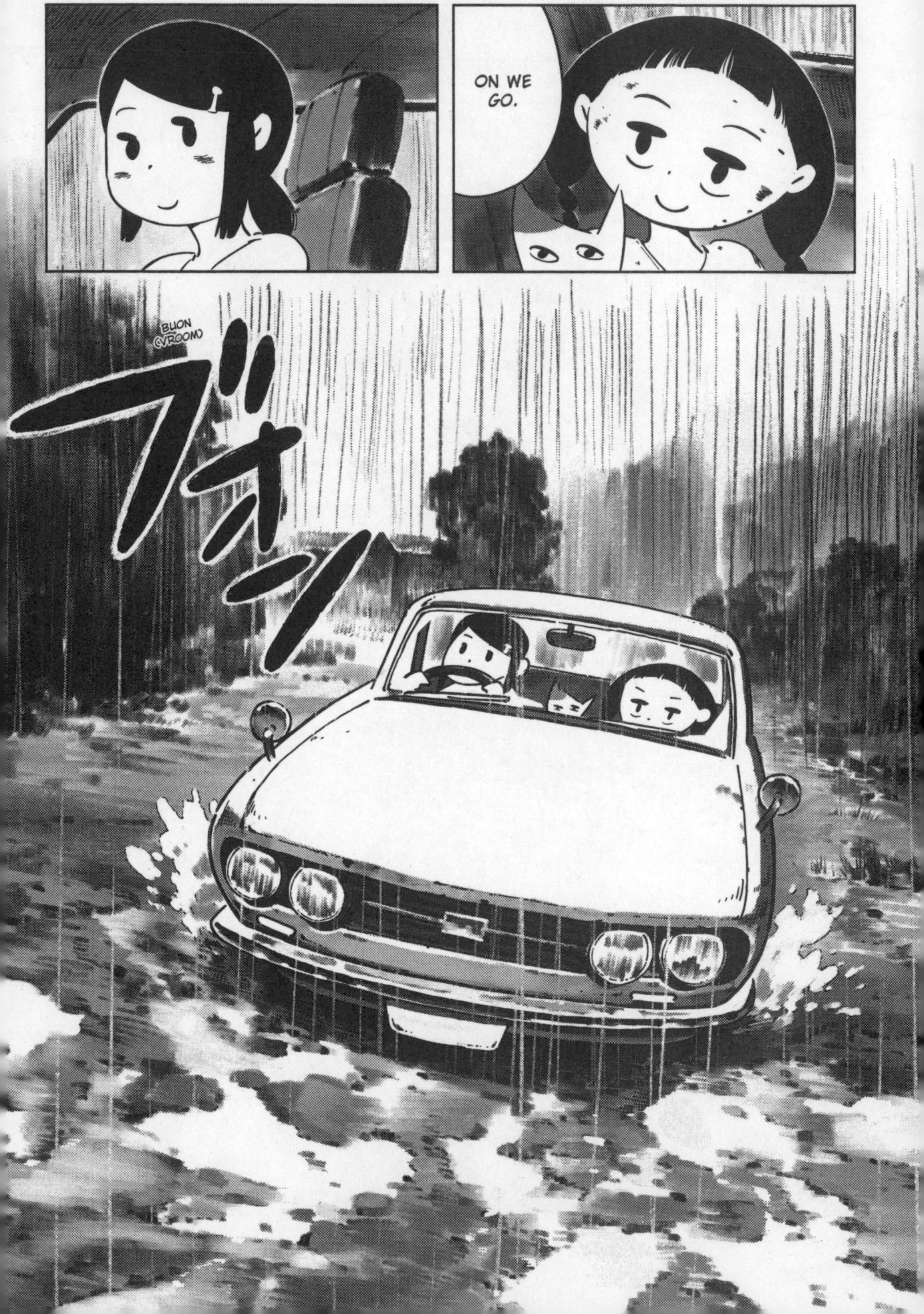
ON WE GO.
BUON (VROOM)
ブオン

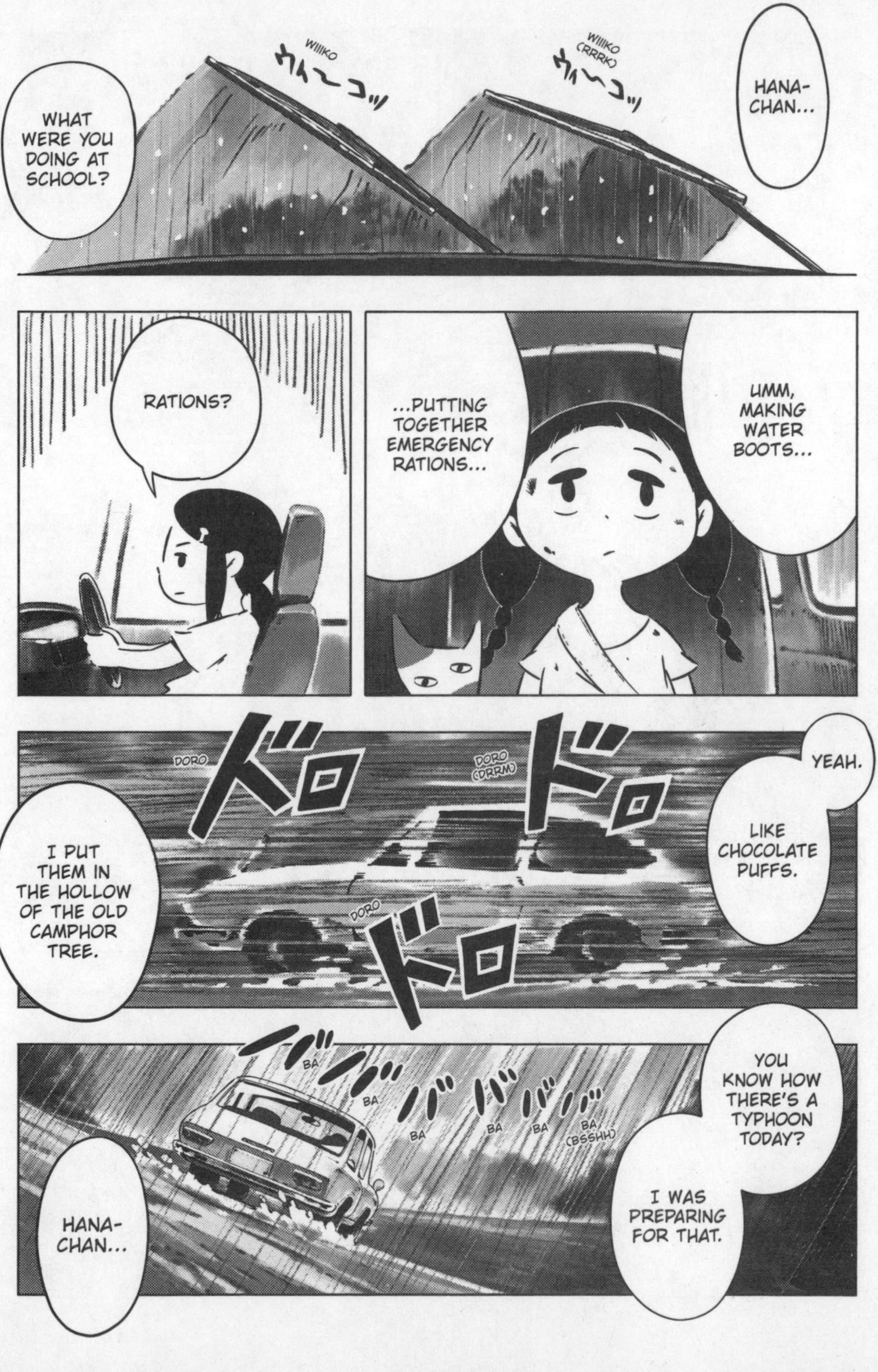
HANA-CHAN...
WIIIKO (RRRK)
WIIIKO
WHAT WERE YOU DOING AT SCHOOL?
UMM, MAKING WATER BOOTS...
...PUTTING TOGETHER EMERGENCY RATIONS...
RATIONS?
YEAH.
LIKE CHOCOLATE PUFFS.
DORO (DRRM)
DORO
DORO
I PUT THEM IN THE HOLLOW OF THE OLD CAMPHOR TREE.
YOU KNOW HOW THERE'S A TYPHOON TODAY?
I WAS PREPARING FOR THAT.
BA
BA
BA
BA
BA
BA (BSSHH)
HANA-CHAN...

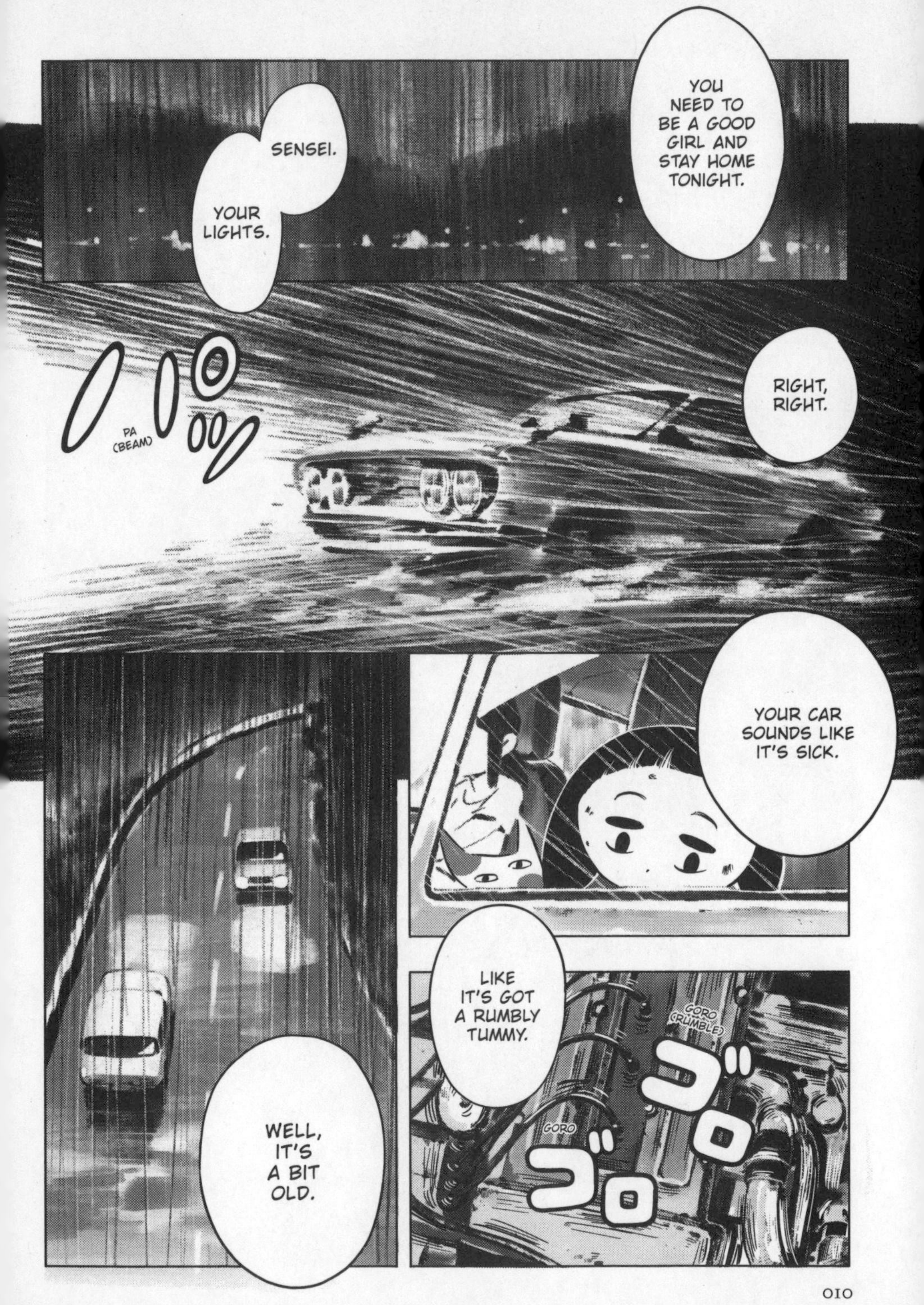
YOU NEED TO BE A GOOD GIRL AND STAY HOME TONIGHT.
SENSEI.
YOUR LIGHTS.
RIGHT, RIGHT.
PA (BEAM)
YOUR CAR SOUNDS LIKE IT'S SICK.
LIKE IT'S GOT A RUMBLY TUMMY.
GORO (RUMBLE)
ゴロ
GORO
ゴロ
WELL, IT'S A BIT OLD.

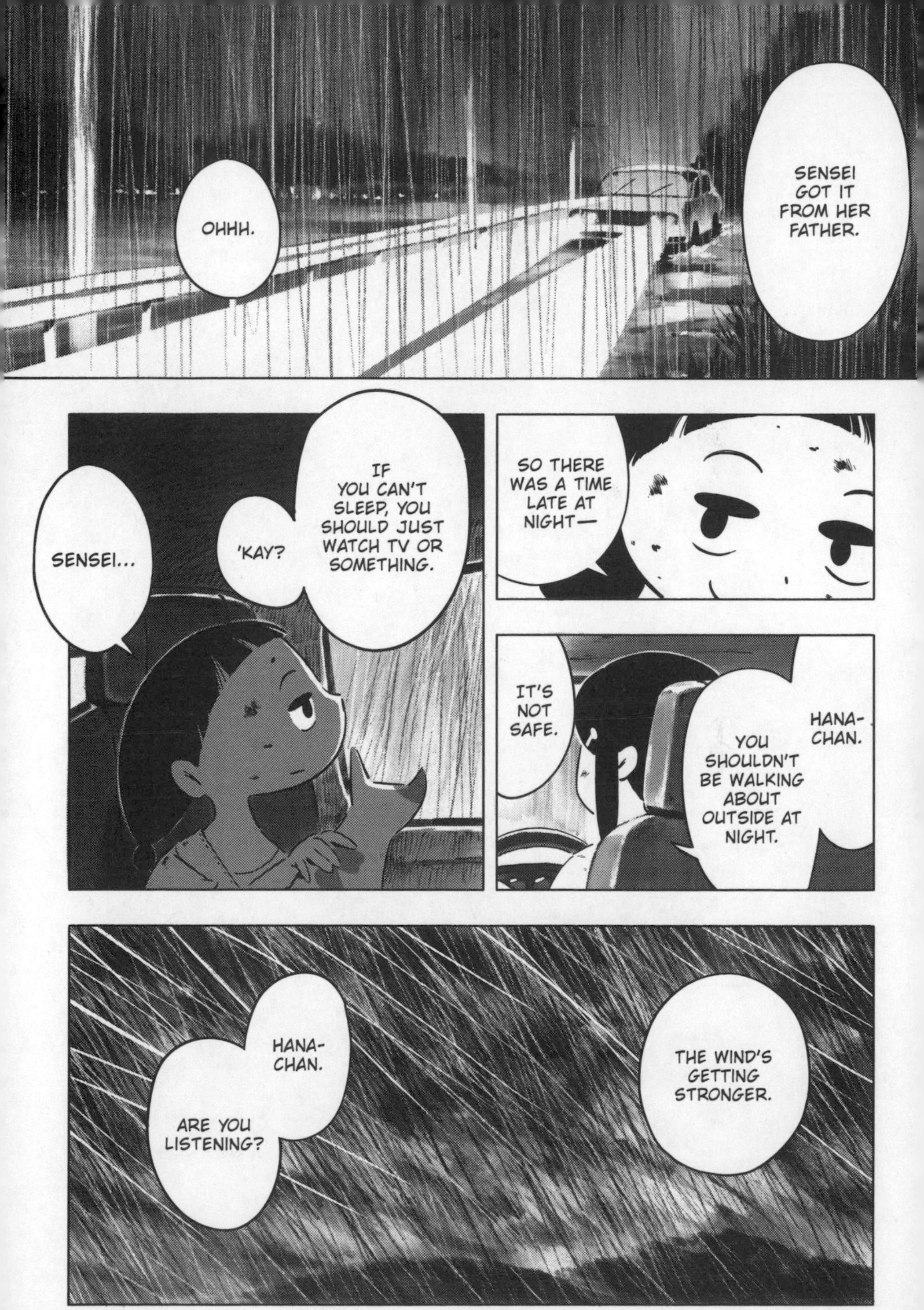
SENSEI GOT IT FROM HER FATHER.
OHHH.
SO THERE WAS A TIME LATE AT NIGHT—
HANA-CHAN.
YOU SHOULDN'T BE WALKING ABOUT OUTSIDE AT NIGHT.
IT'S NOT SAFE.
IF YOU CAN'T SLEEP, YOU SHOULD JUST WATCH TV OR SOMETHING.
'KAY?
SENSEI...
THE WIND'S GETTING STRONGER.
HANA-CHAN.
ARE YOU LISTENING?

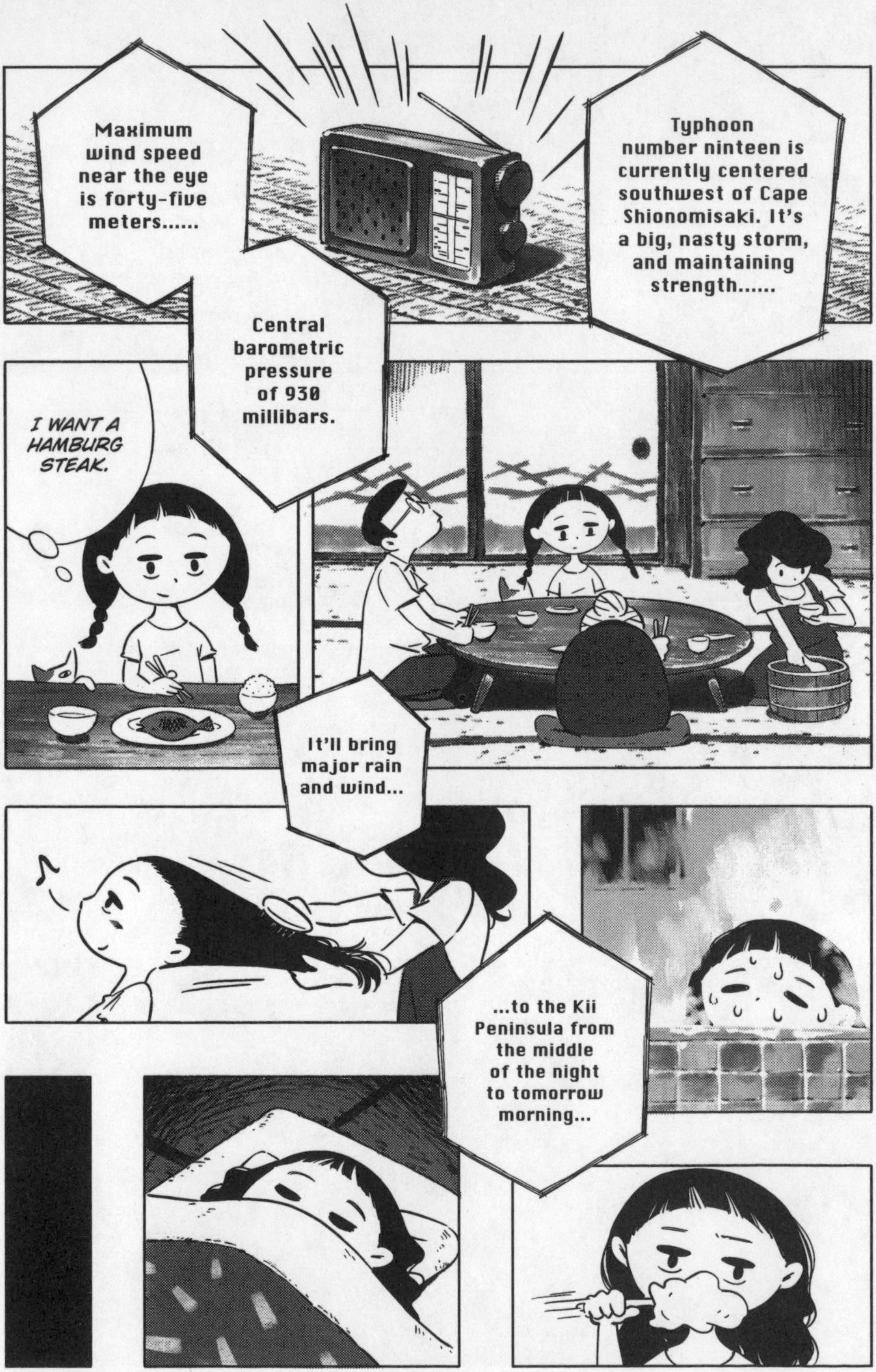
Typhoon number ninteen is currently centered southwest of Cape Shionomisaki. It's a big, nasty storm, and maintaining strength......
Maximum wind speed near the eye is forty-five meters......
Central barometric pressure of 930 millibars.
I WANT A HAMBURG STEAK.
It'll bring major rain and wind...
...to the Kii Peninsula from the middle of the night to tomorrow morning...

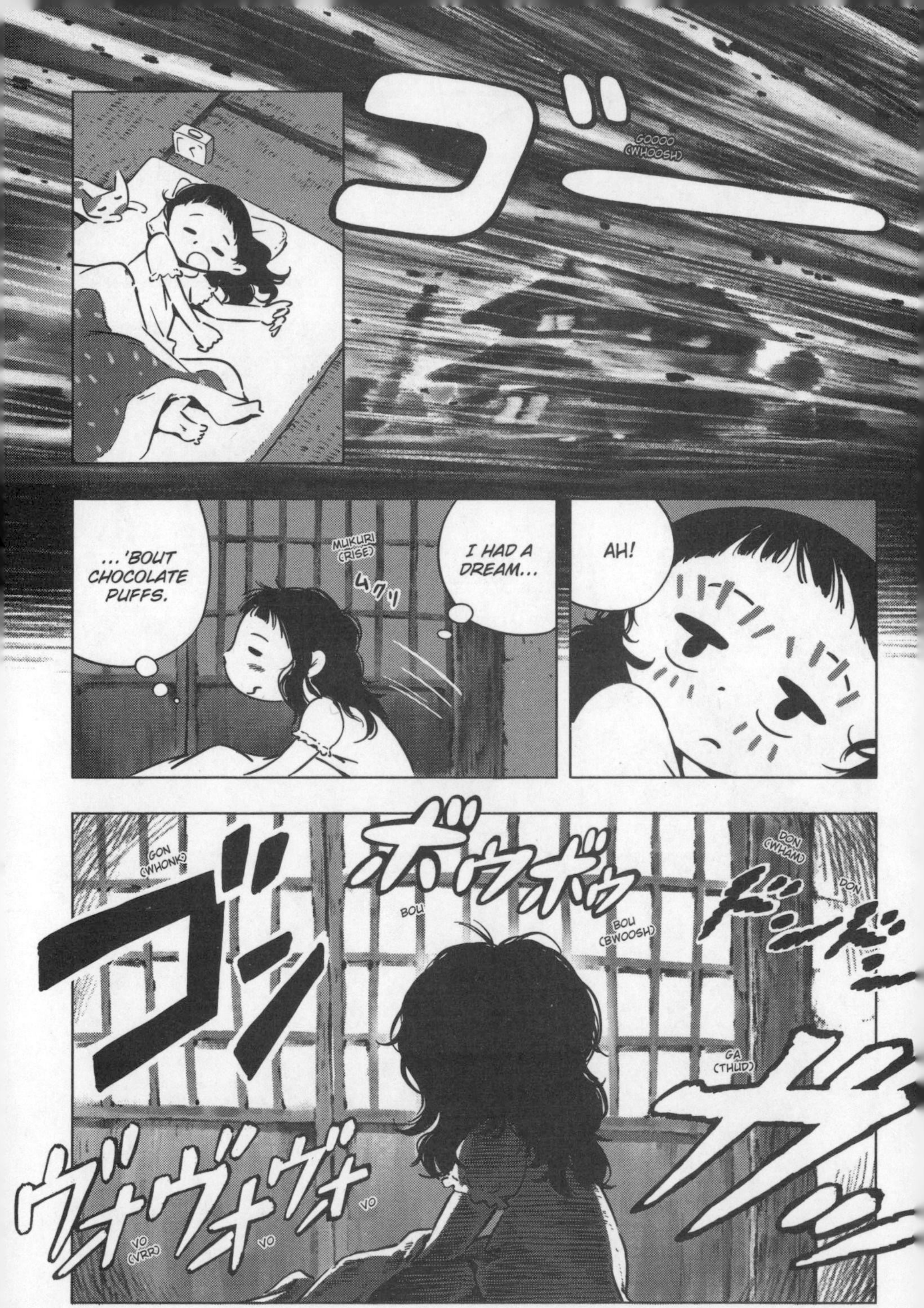
ゴー
GOOOO (WHOOSH)
AH!
I HAD A DREAM...
MUKURI (RISE)
ムクリ
...'BOUT CHOCOLATE PUFFS.
DON (WHAM)
DON
GA (THUD)
BOU (BWOOSH)
BOU
ボウボウ
GON (WHONK)
ゴン
ヴォウヴォウヴォ
VO
VO
VO (VRR)

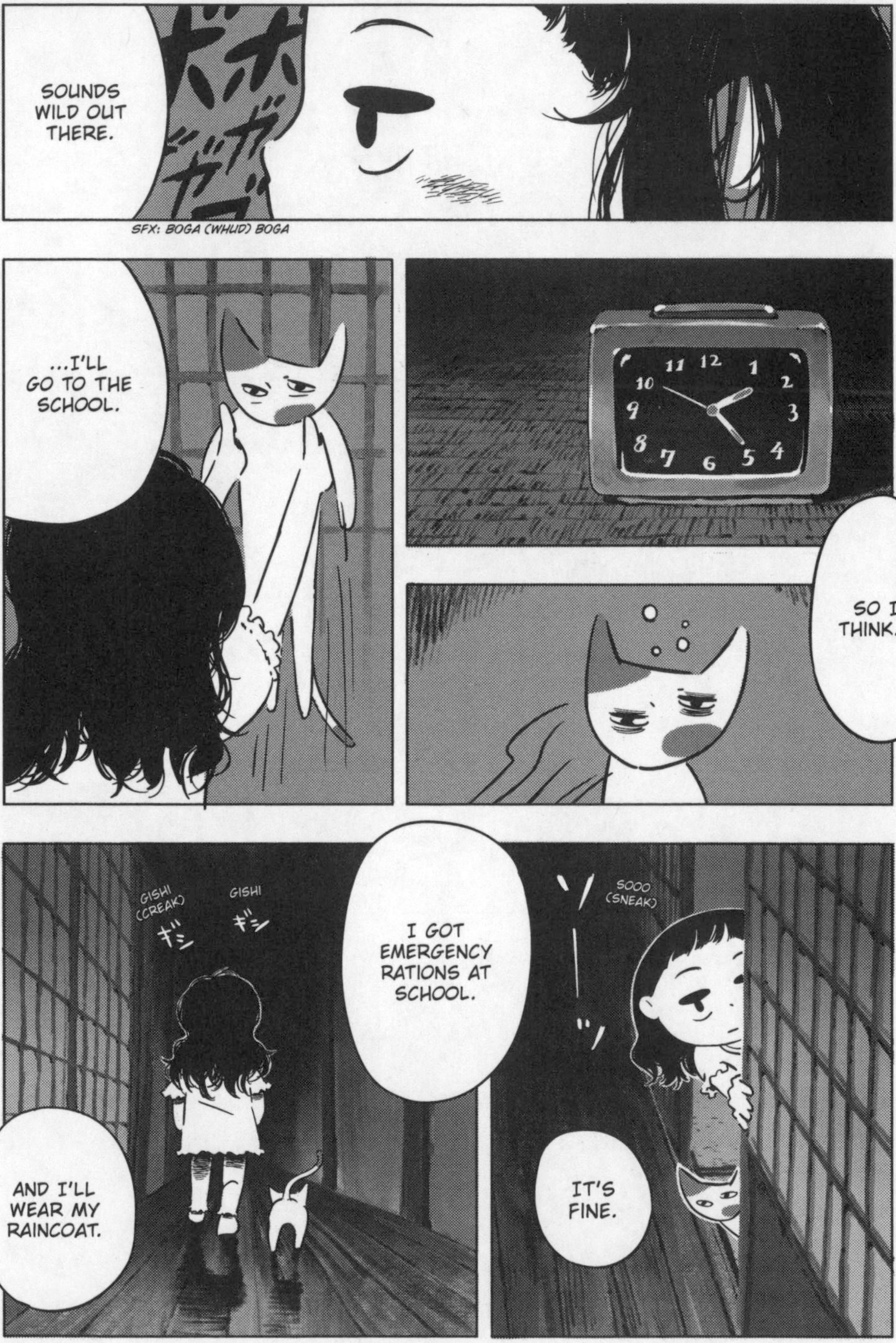
SOUNDS WILD OUT THERE.
SFX: BOGA (WHUD) BOGA
SO I THINK...
...I'LL GO TO THE SCHOOL.
SOOO (SNEAK)
IT'S FINE.
I GOT EMERGENCY RATIONS AT SCHOOL.
GISHI (CREAK)
GISHI
AND I'LL WEAR MY RAINCOAT.

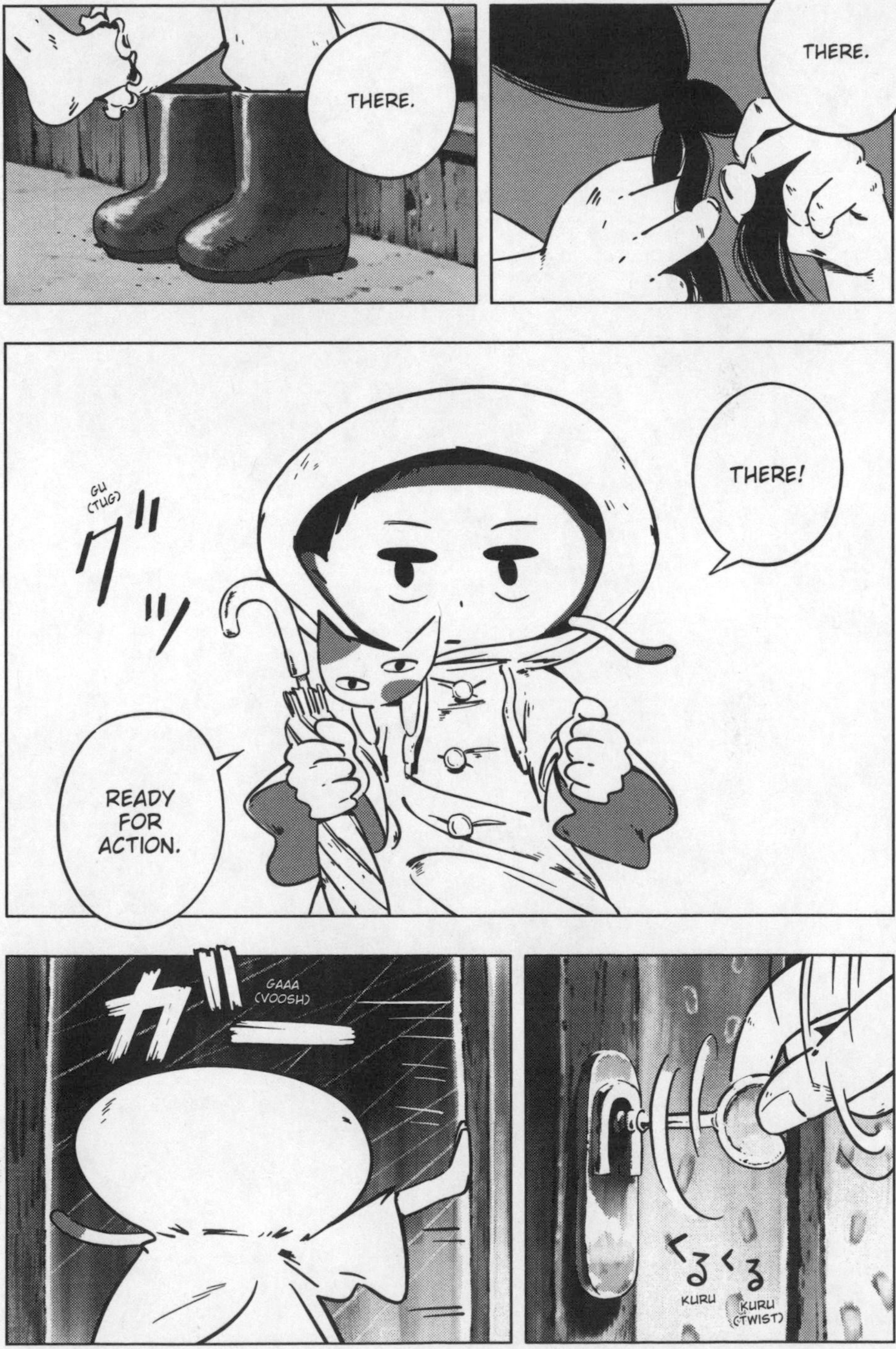
THERE.
THERE.
THERE!
GU (TUG)
グッ
READY FOR ACTION.
くるくる
KURU KURU (TWIST)
ガー
GAAA (VOOSH)

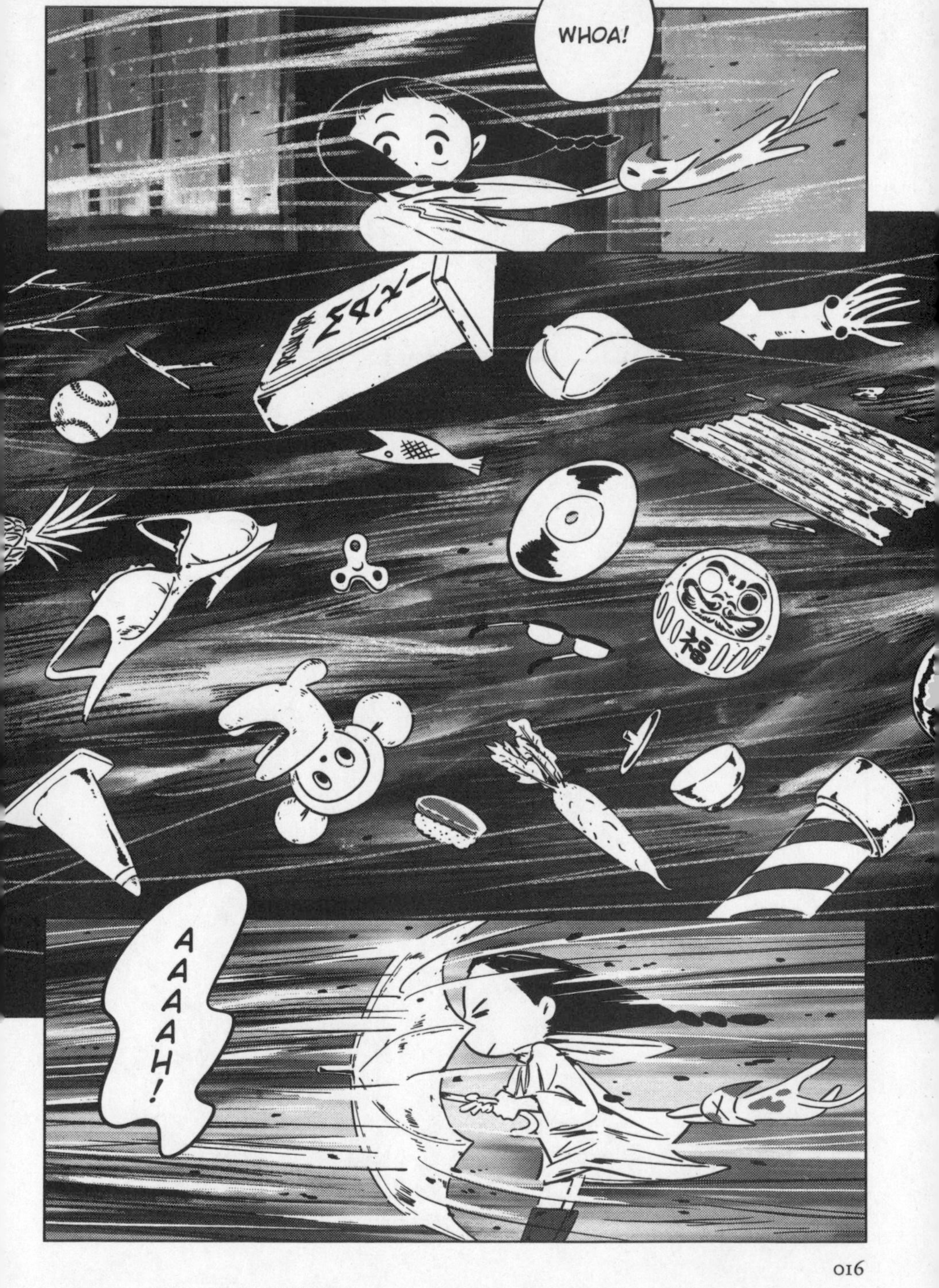
WHOA!
福
AAAAAH!

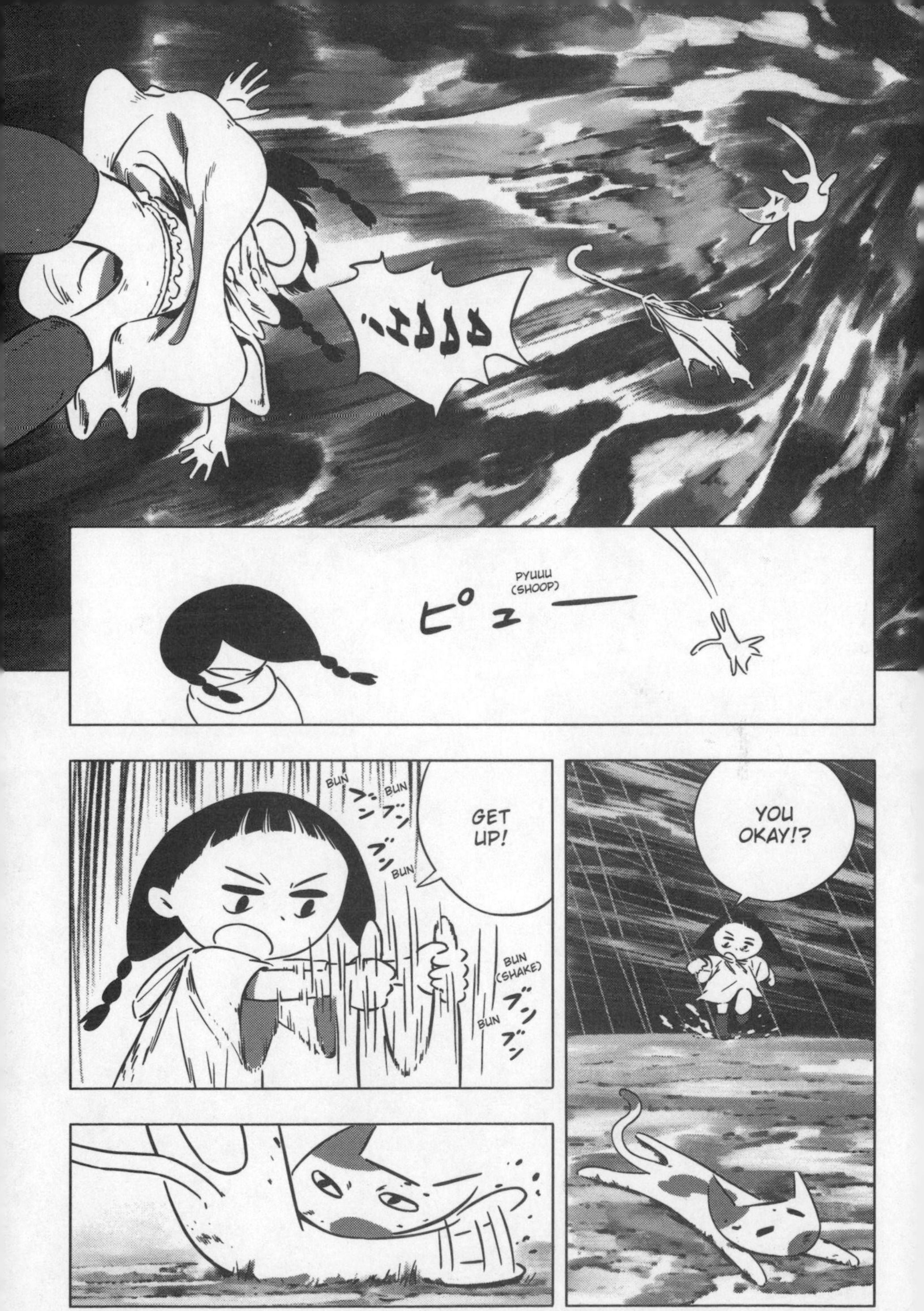
PYUUU
(SHOOP)
ピュー
YOU OKAY!?
BUN
ブン
BUN
ブン
ブン
BUN
GET UP!
BUN
(SHAKE)
ブン
BUN
ブン

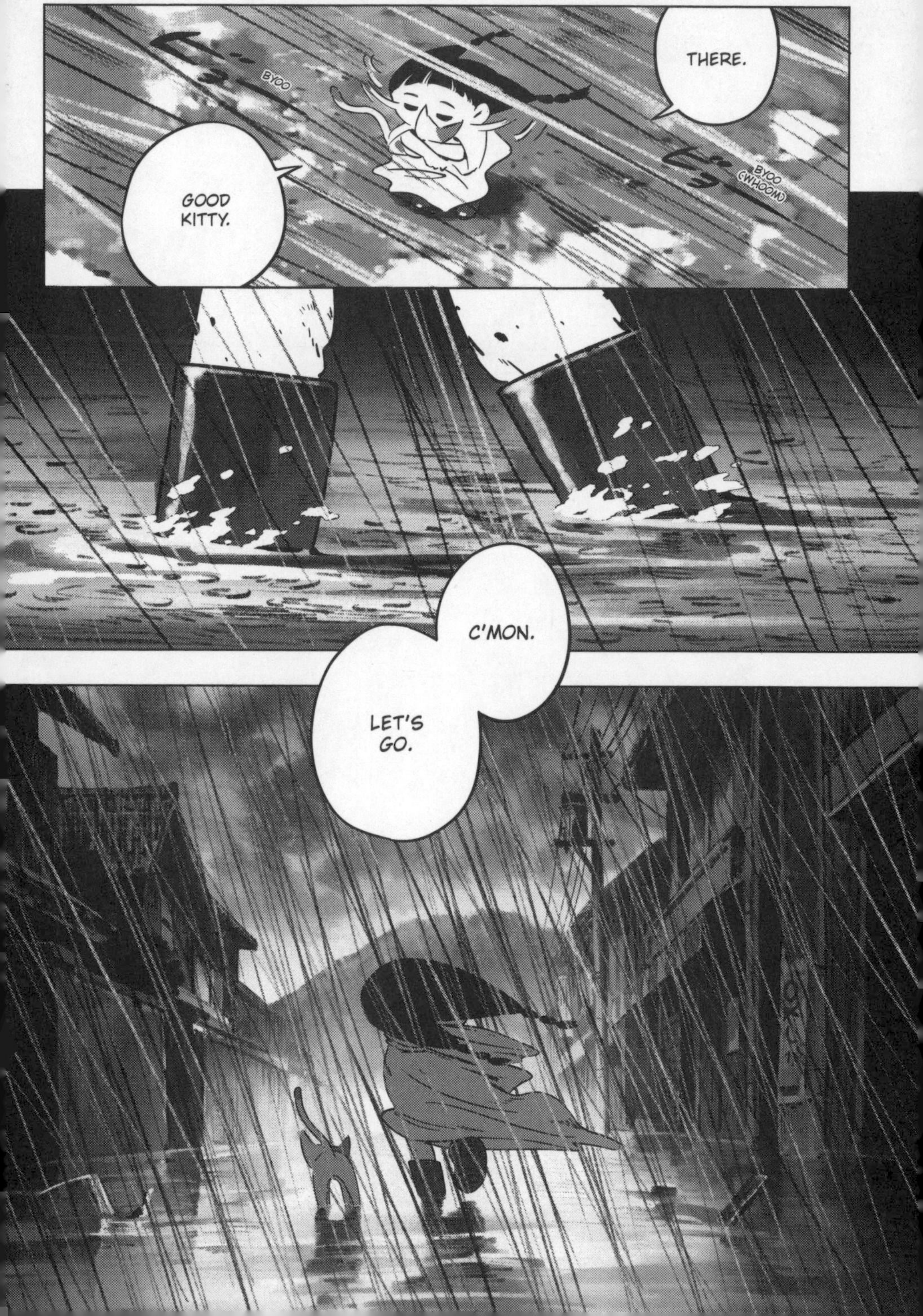
THERE.
BYOO (WHOOM)
BYOO
GOOD KITTY.
C'MON.
LET'S GO.

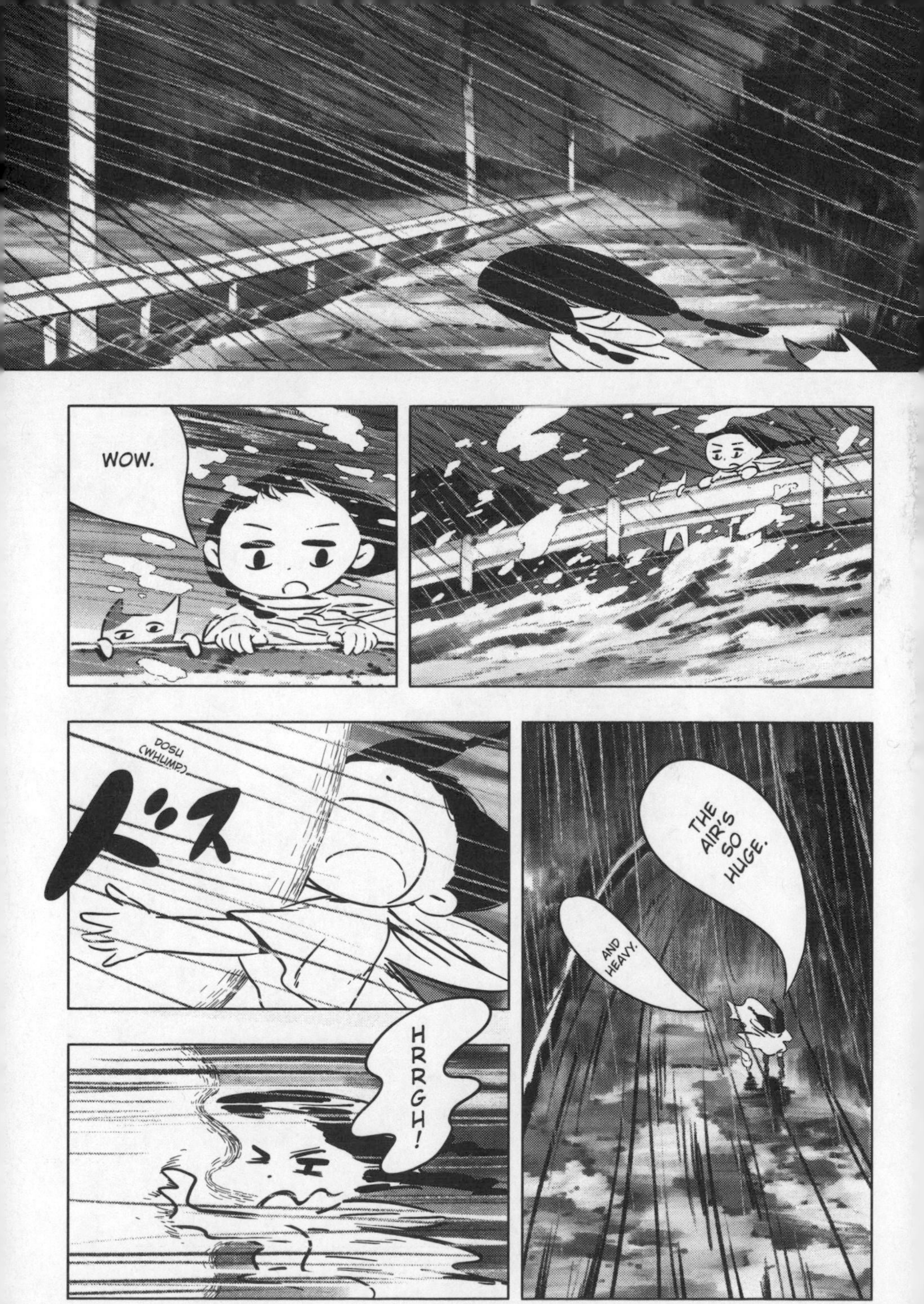
WOW.
THE AIR'S SO HUGE.
AND HEAVY.
DOSU (WHUMP)
ドス
HRRGH!

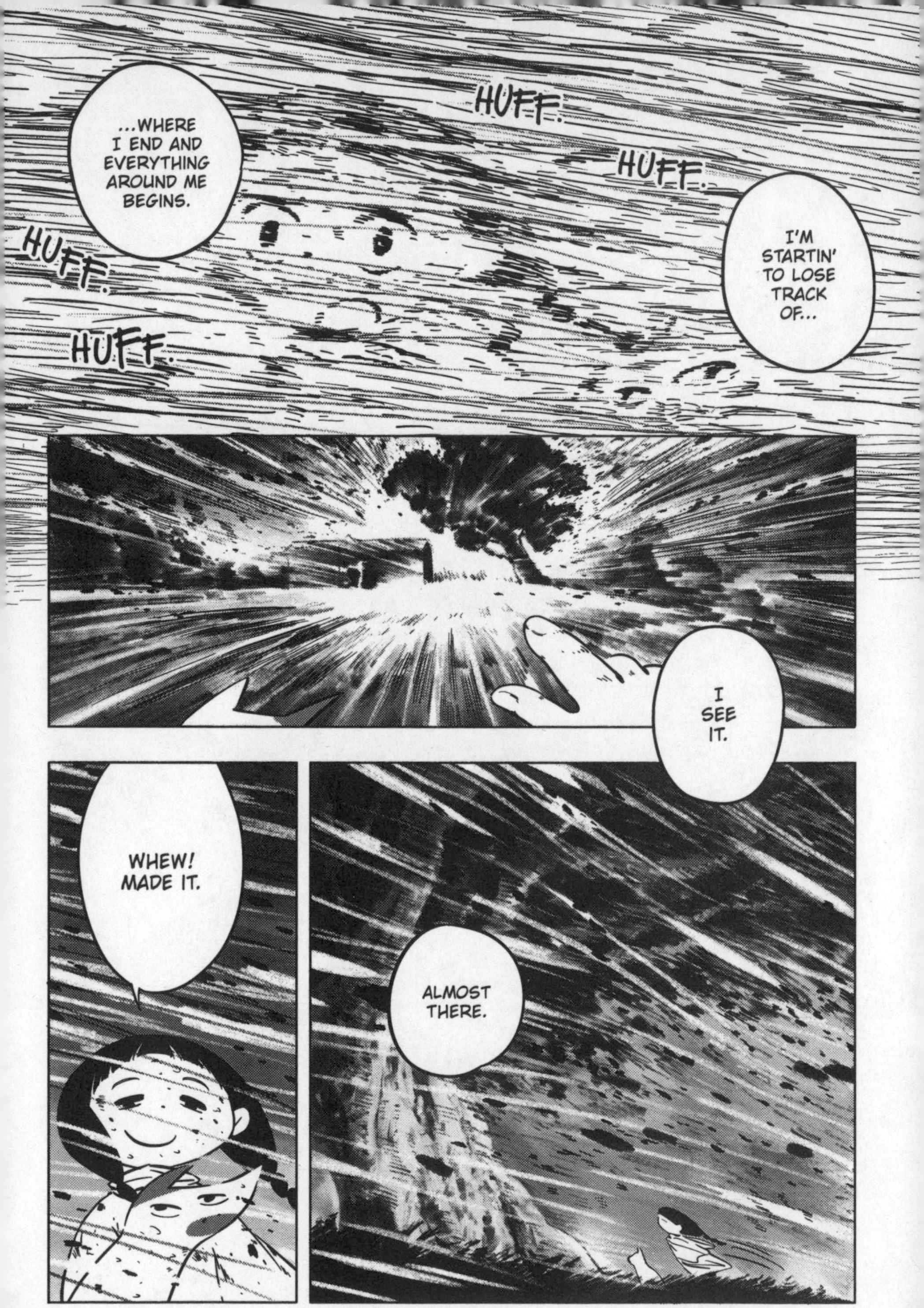
HUFF.
HUFF.
I'M STARTIN' TO LOSE TRACK OF...
...WHERE I END AND EVERYTHING AROUND ME BEGINS.
HUFF.
HUFF.
I SEE IT.
ALMOST THERE.
WHEW! MADE IT.

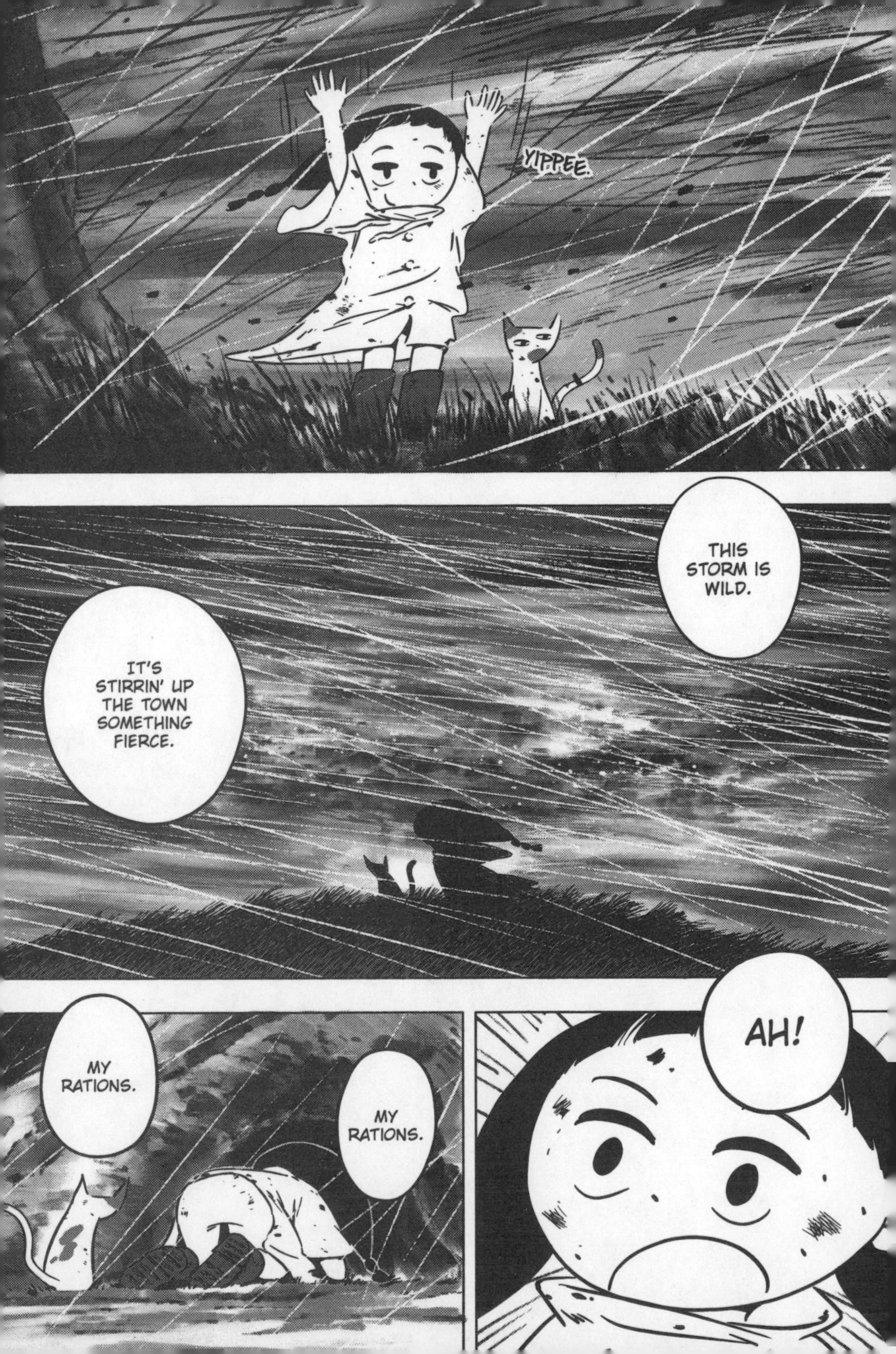
YIPPEE.
THIS STORM IS WILD.
IT'S STIRRIN' UP THE TOWN SOMETHING FIERCE.
AH!
MY RATIONS.
MY RATIONS.

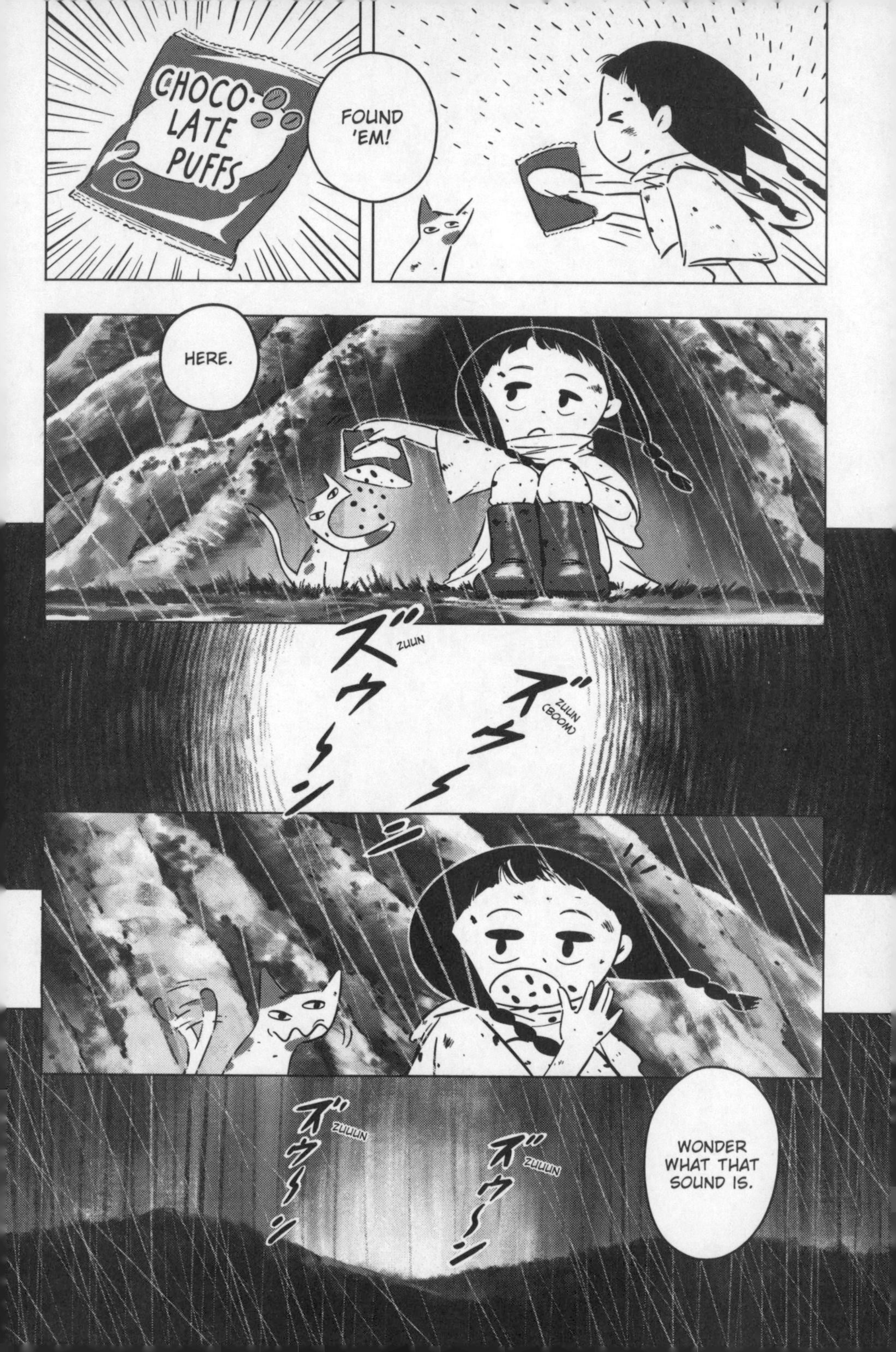
FOUND 'EM!
CHOCO-LATE PUFFS
HERE.
ZUUN (BOOM)
ZUUN
WONDER WHAT THAT SOUND IS.
ZUUUN
ZUUUN

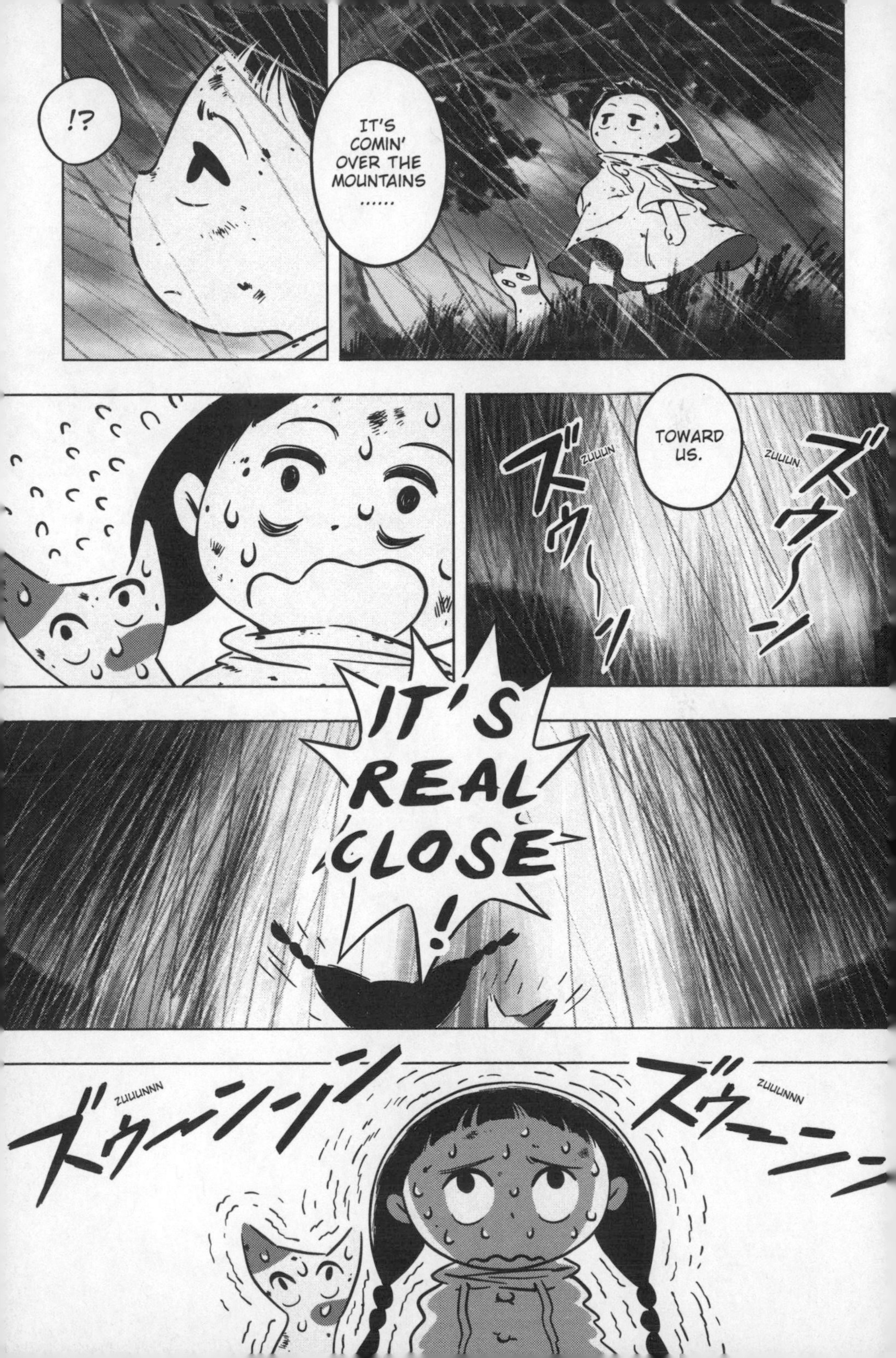
IT'S COMIN' OVER THE MOUNTAINS ......
!?
ズゥーン
ZUUUN
TOWARD US.
ズゥ〜ン
ZUUUN
IT'S REAL CLOSE!
ズゥーン
ZUUUNNN
ズゥ〜ン
ZUUUNNN

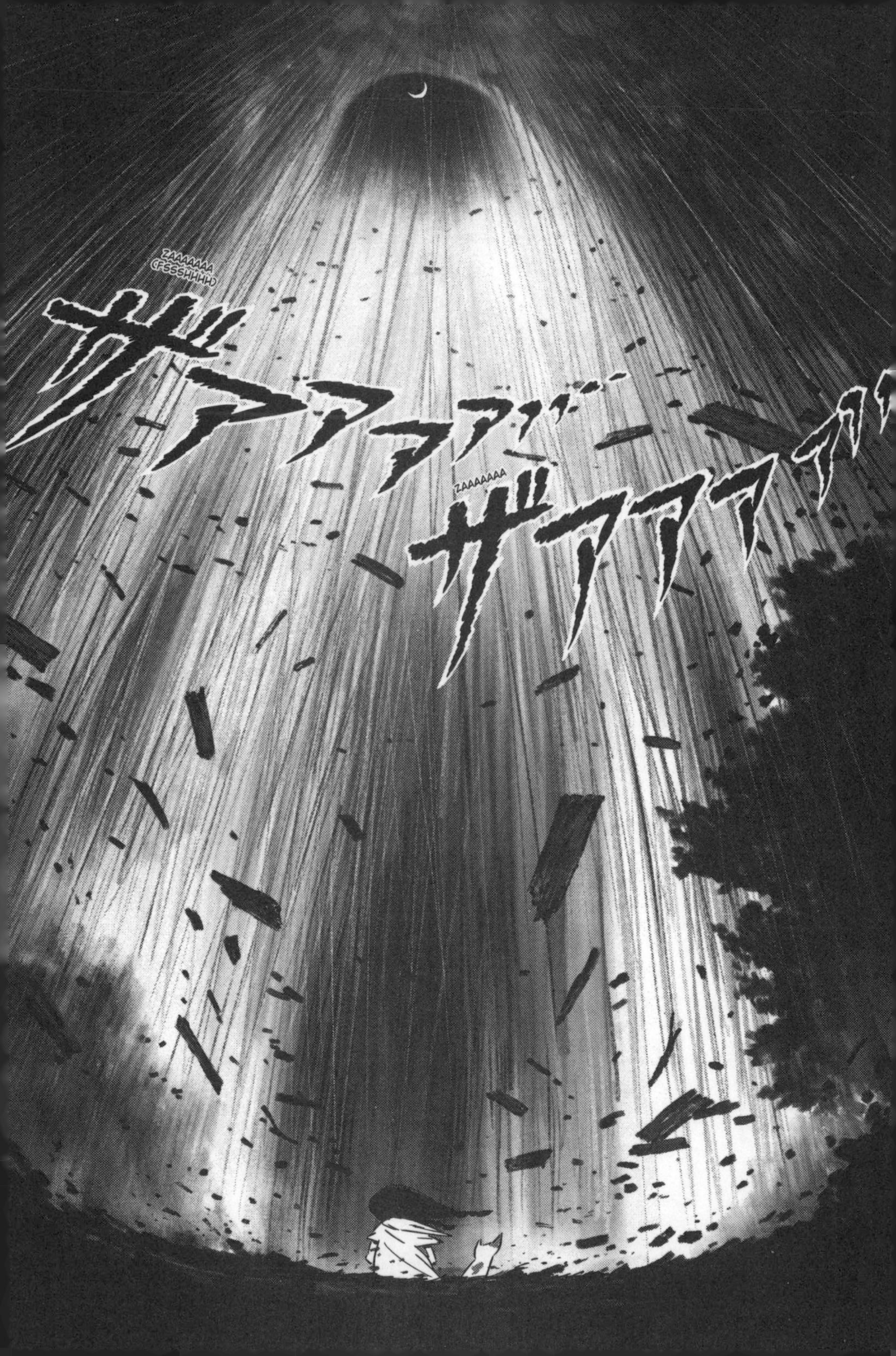
ZAAAAAAA (FSSSHHHH)
ザァァァ
ZAAAAAAA
ザァァァァ

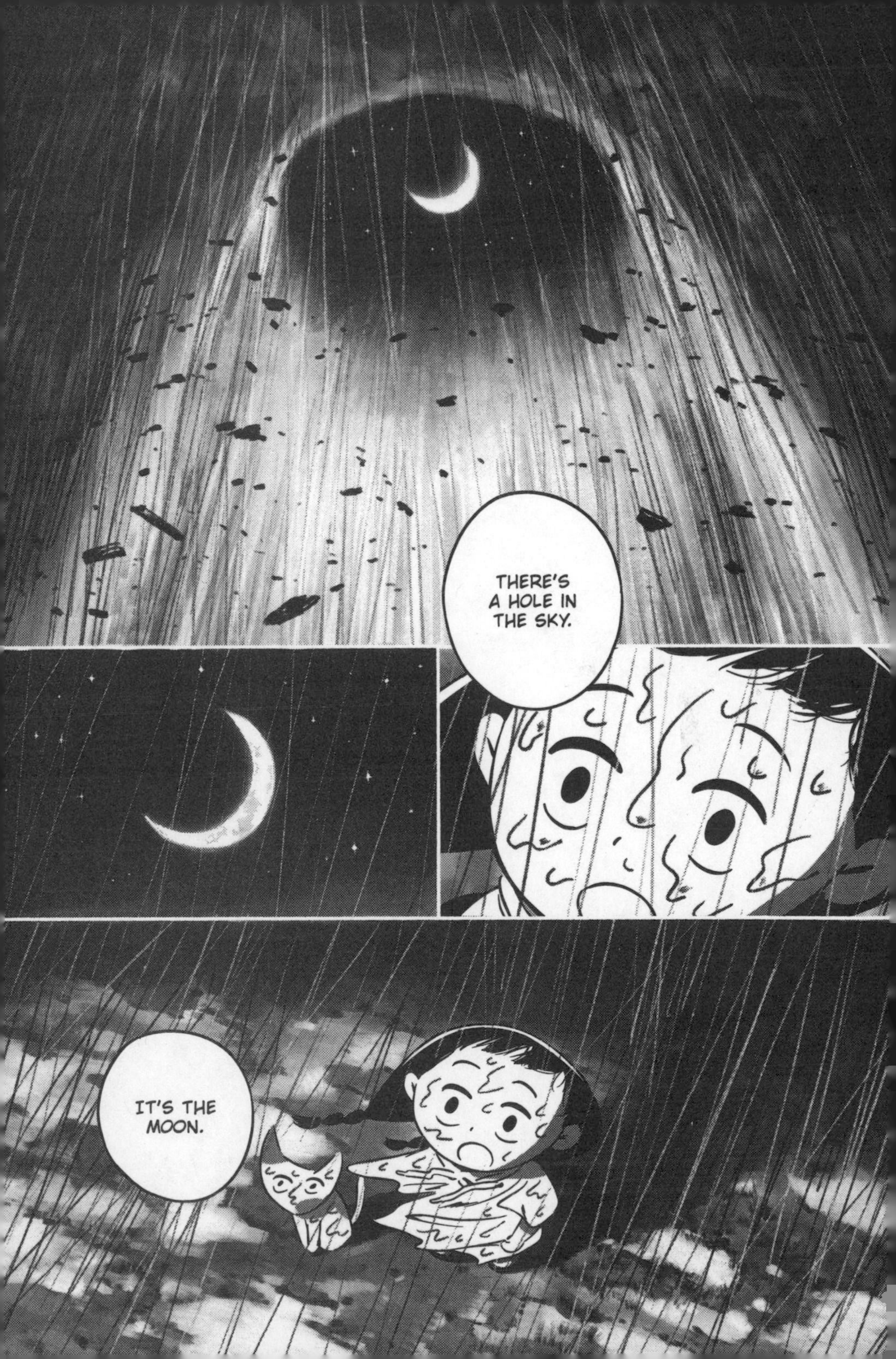
THERE'S A HOLE IN THE SKY.
IT'S THE MOON.

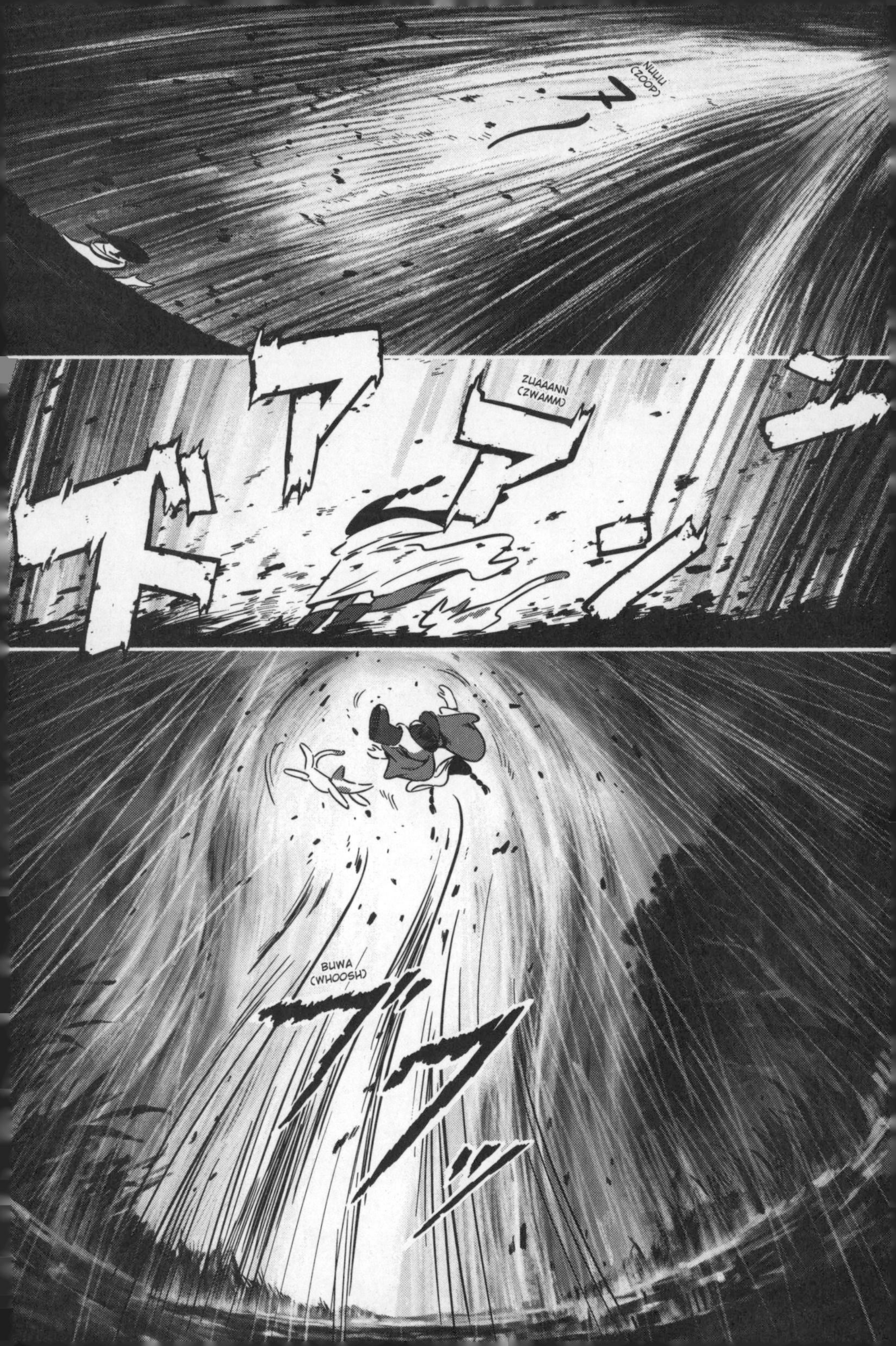
NUUU
(ZOOP)
ZUAAANN
(ZWAMM)
BUWA
(WHOOSH)

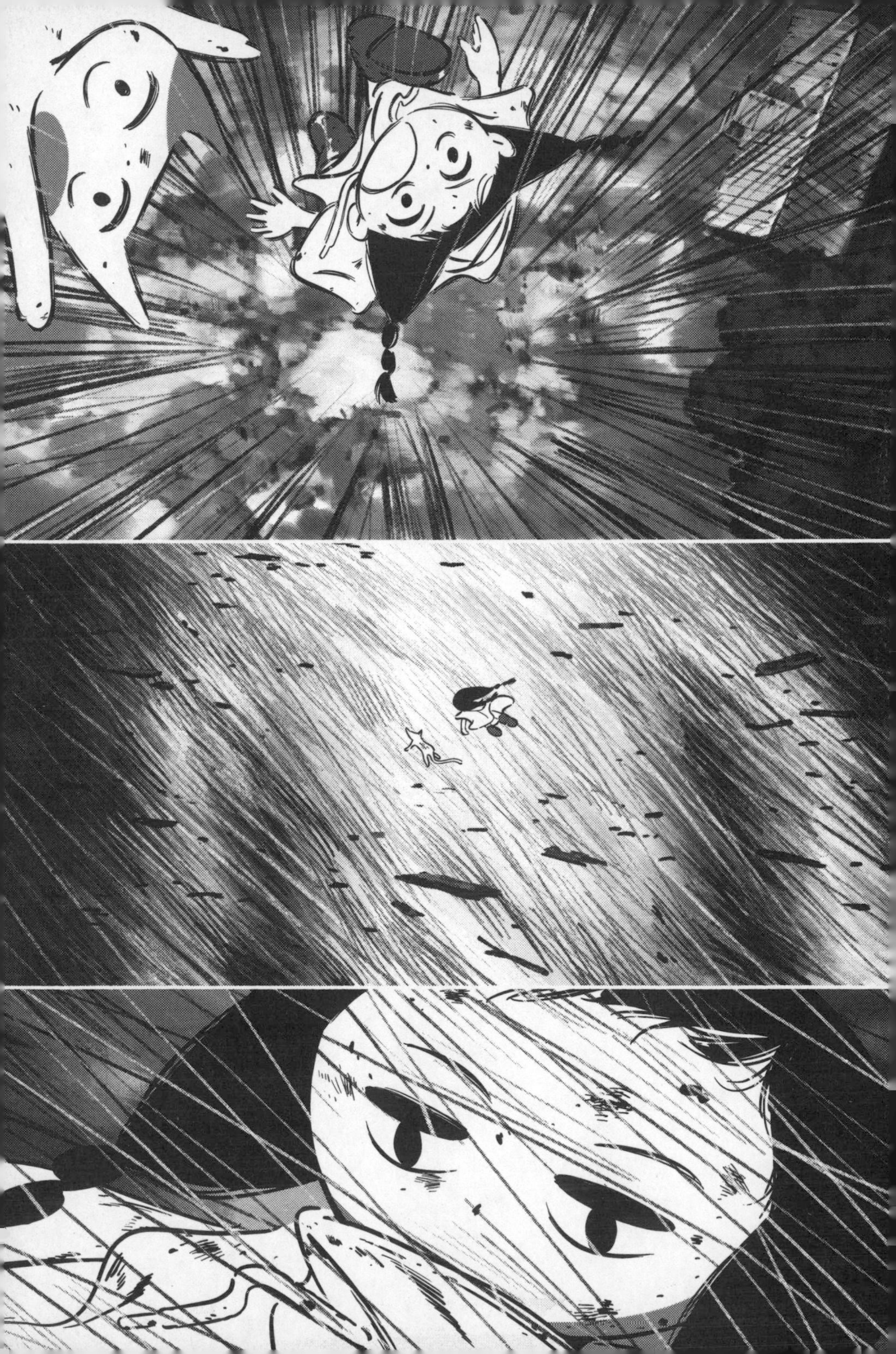

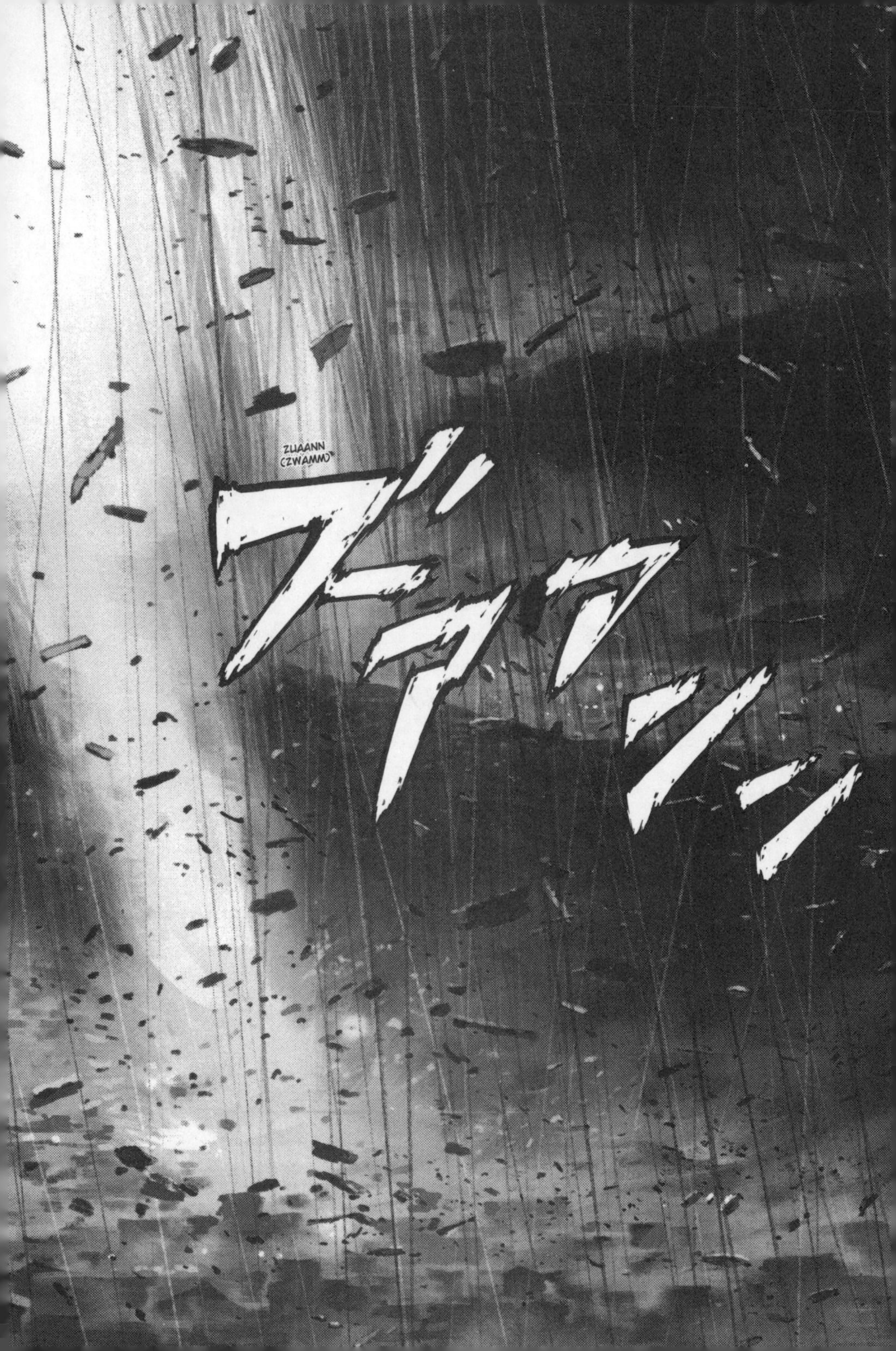
ズアアンッ
ZUAANN (ZWAMM)

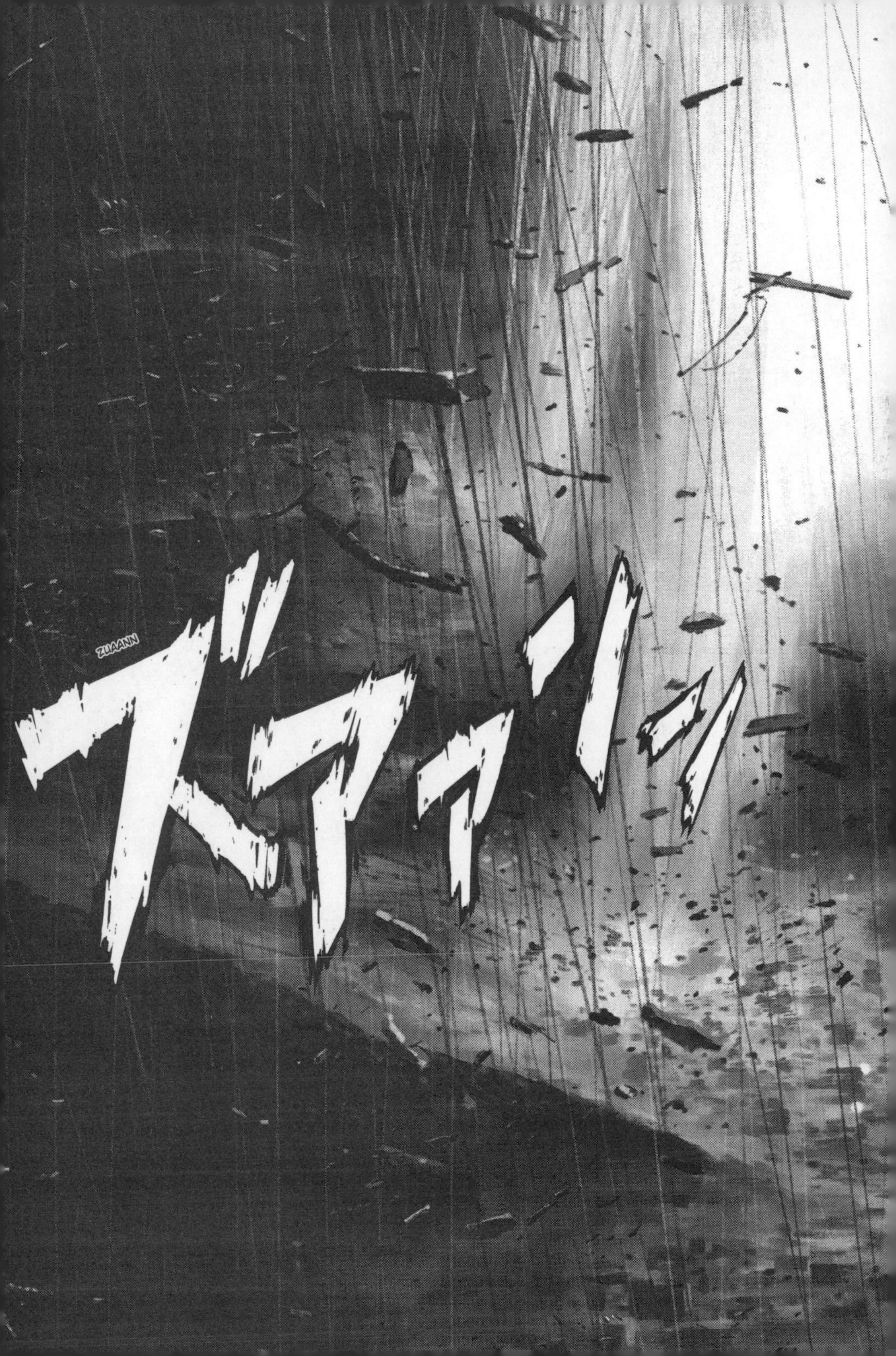
ズァーッ
ZUAANN

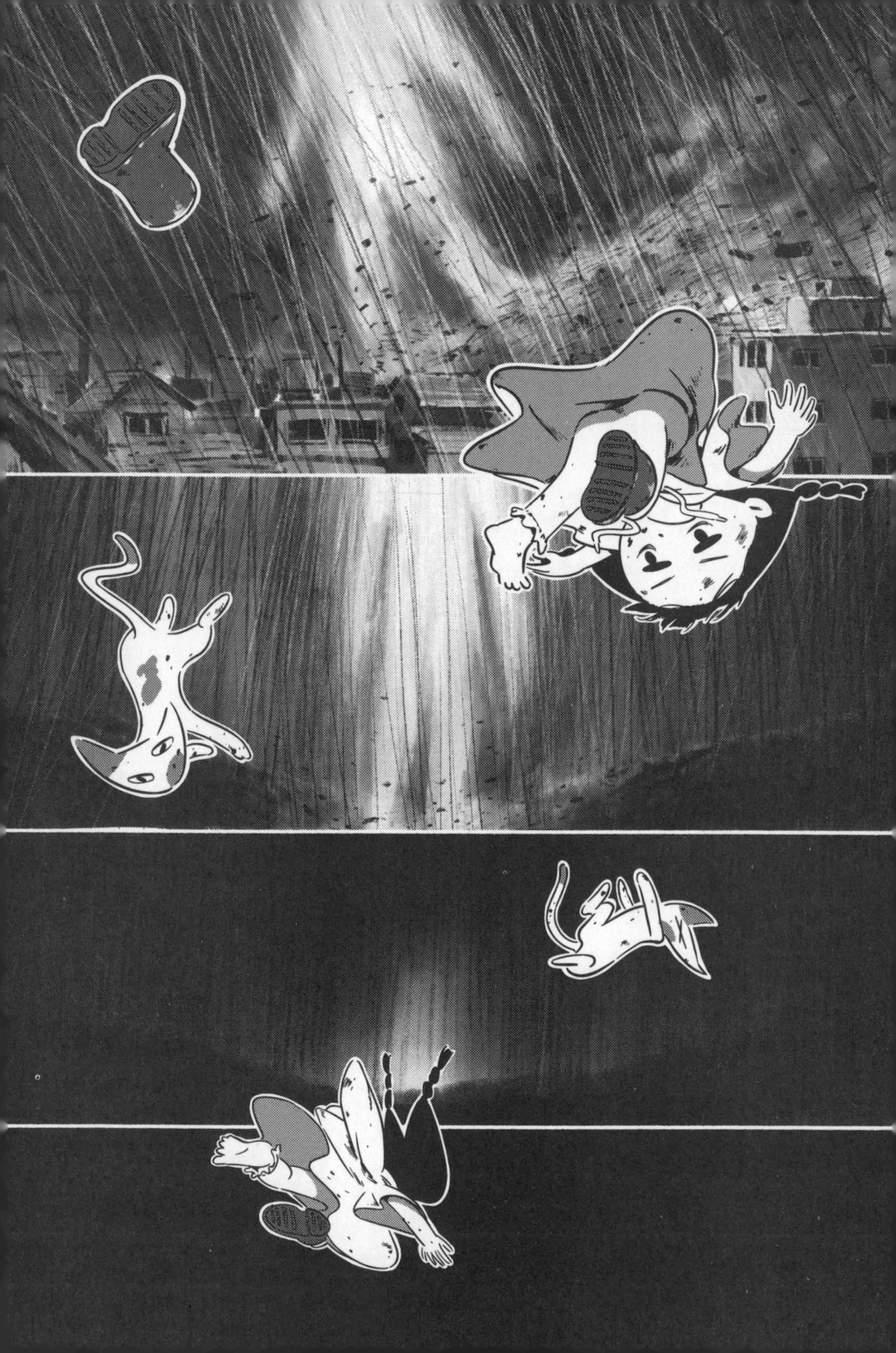

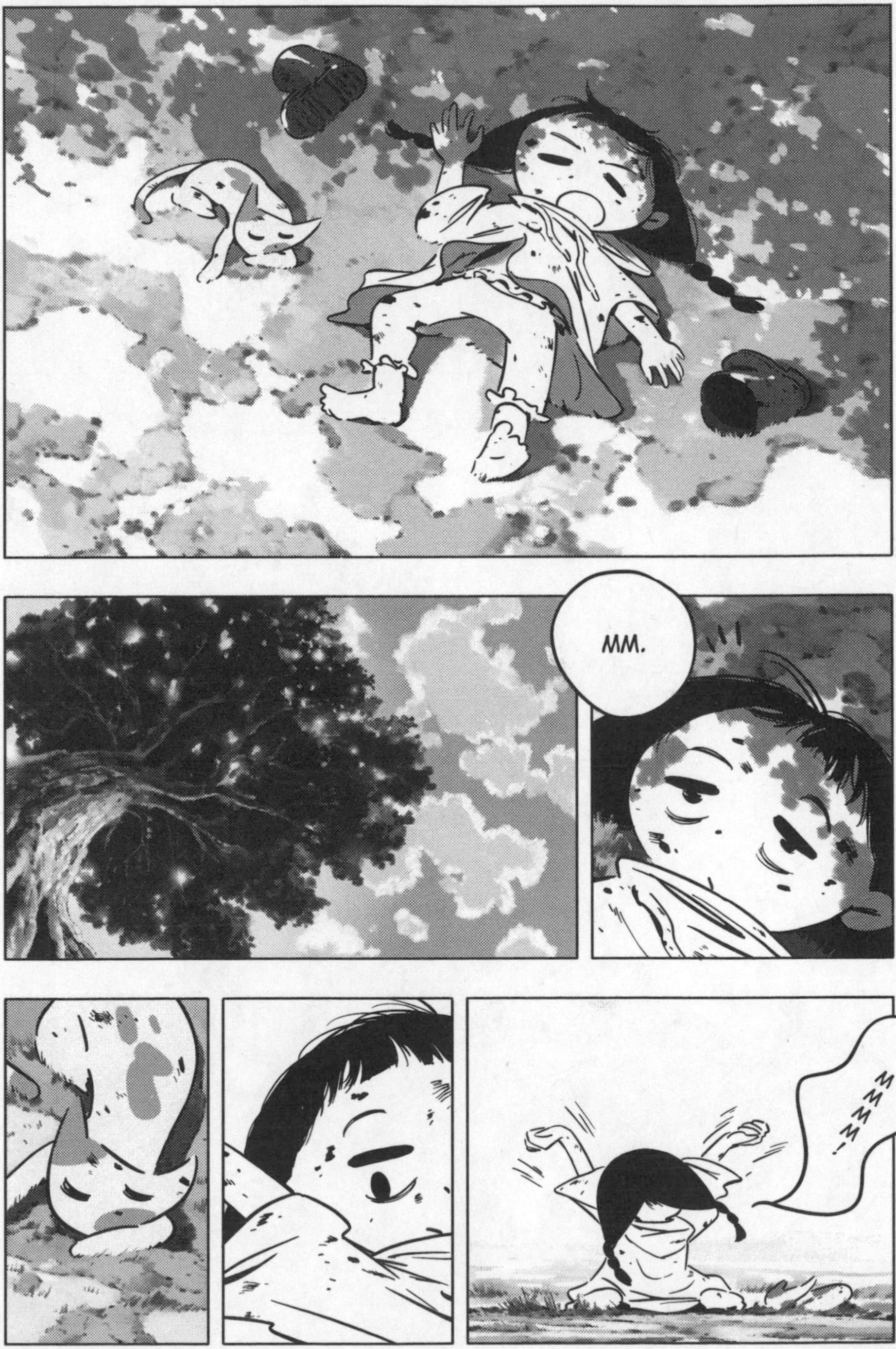
MM.
MMMM!

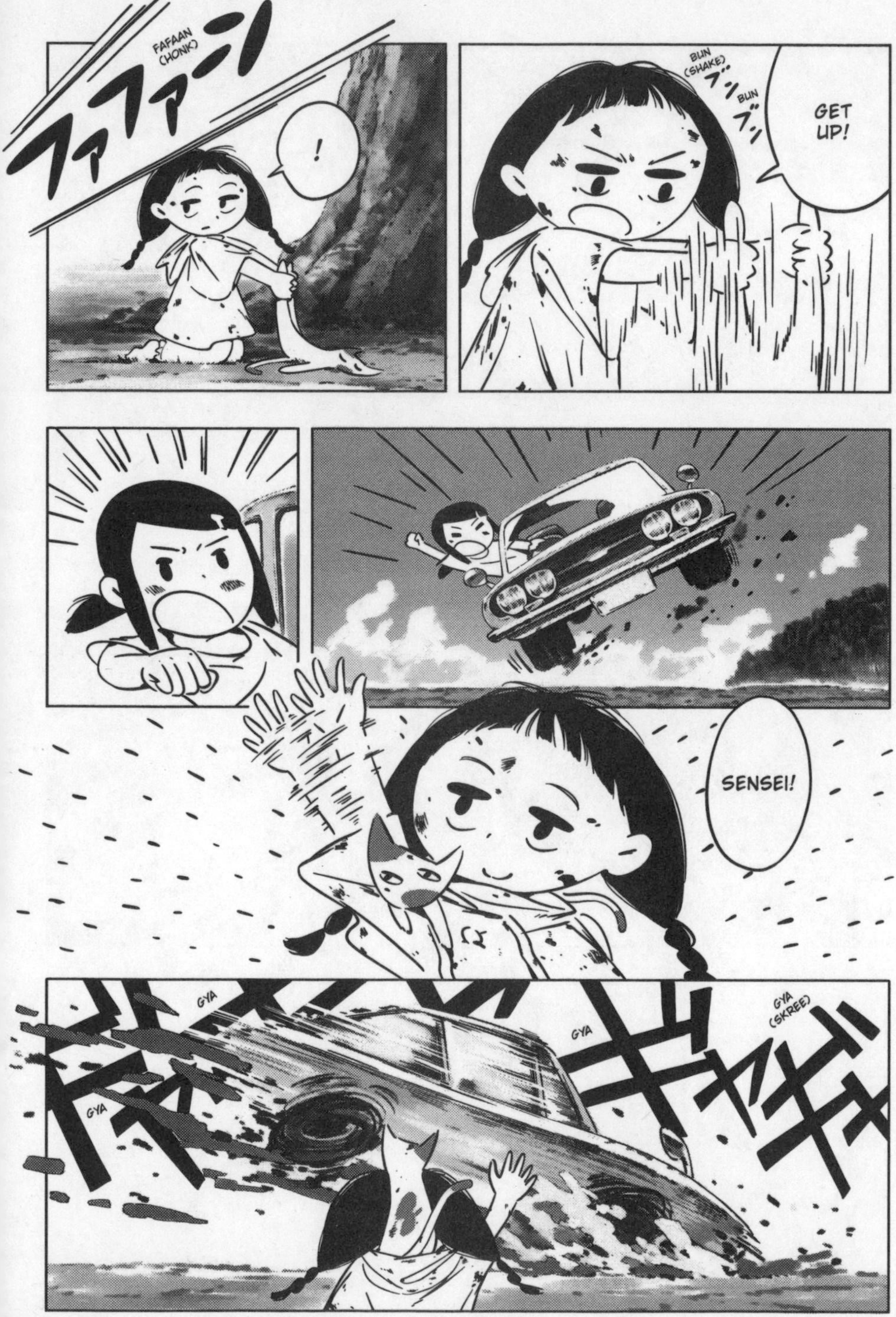
BUN (SHAKE)
ブン
BUN
ブン
GET UP!
FAFAAN (HONK)
ファファーン
!
SENSEI!
GYA (SKREE)
GYA
GYA
GYA

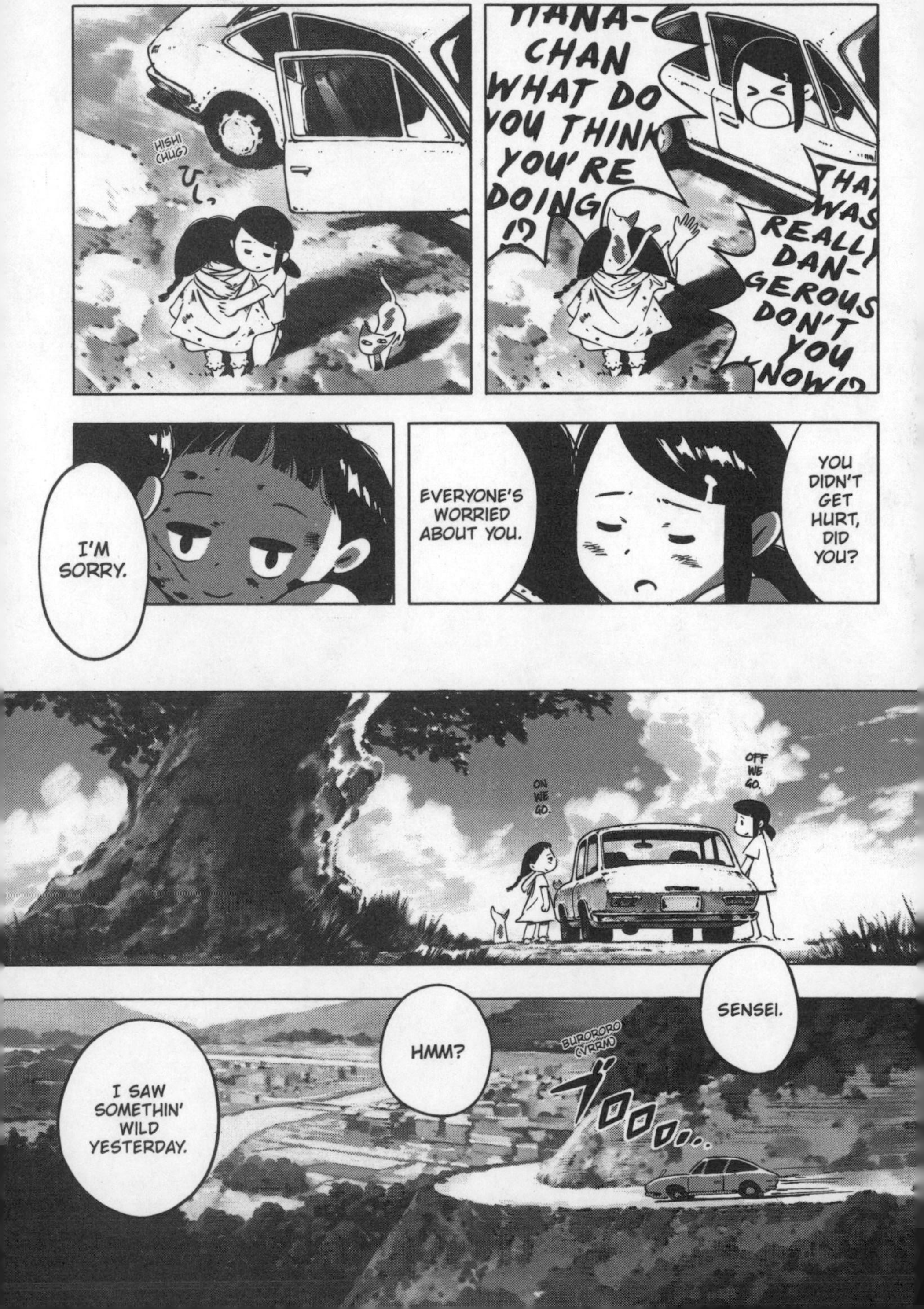

HANA-CHAN WHAT DO YOU THINK YOU'RE DOING!?
THAT WAS REALLY DANGEROUS DON'T YOU KNOW!?
HISHI (HUG)
ひし
YOU DIDN'T GET HURT, DID YOU?
EVERYONE'S WORRIED ABOUT YOU.
I'M SORRY.
OFF WE GO.
ON WE GO.
SENSEI.
BURORORO (VRRM)
ブロロロ...
HMM?
I SAW SOMETHIN' WILD YESTERDAY.

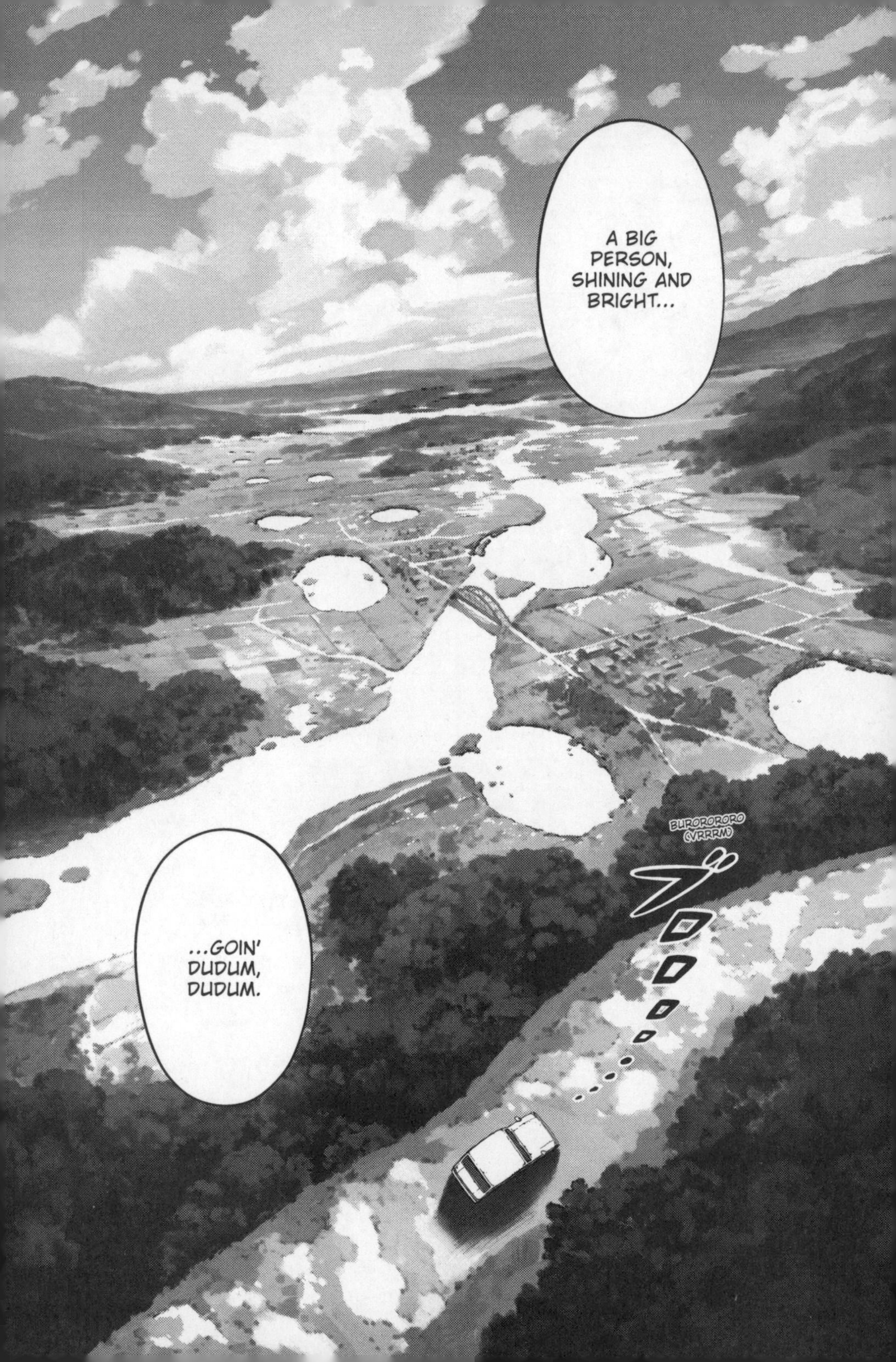
A BIG PERSON, SHINING AND BRIGHT...
BUROROROROOO (VRRRM)
...GOIN' DUDUM, DUDUM.

Hana-chan
and the Shape of the World

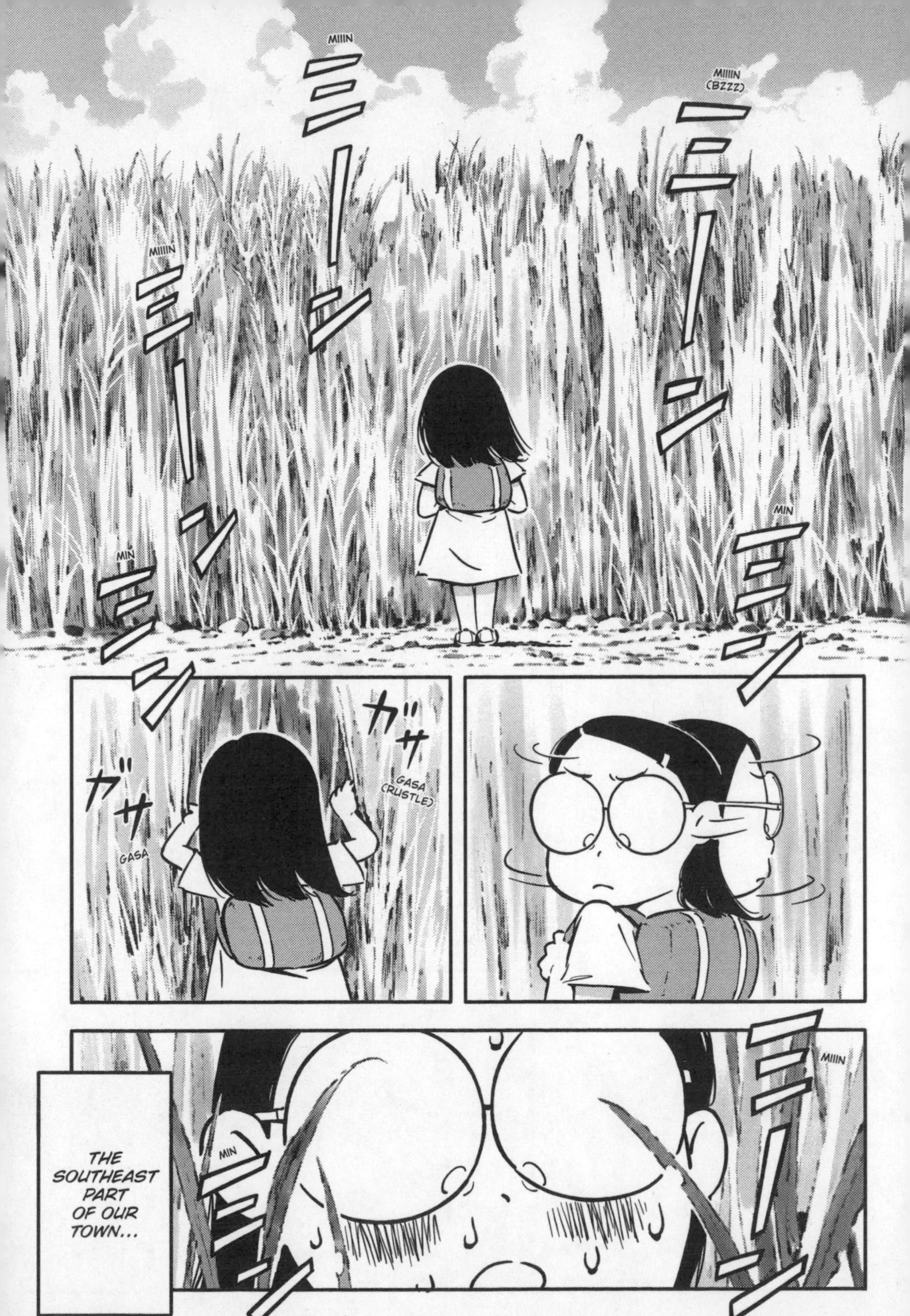

MIIIN (BZZZ)
MIIIN
MIIIN
MIN
MIN
GASA (RUSTLE)
GASA
MIIIN
MIN
THE SOUTHEAST PART OF OUR TOWN...

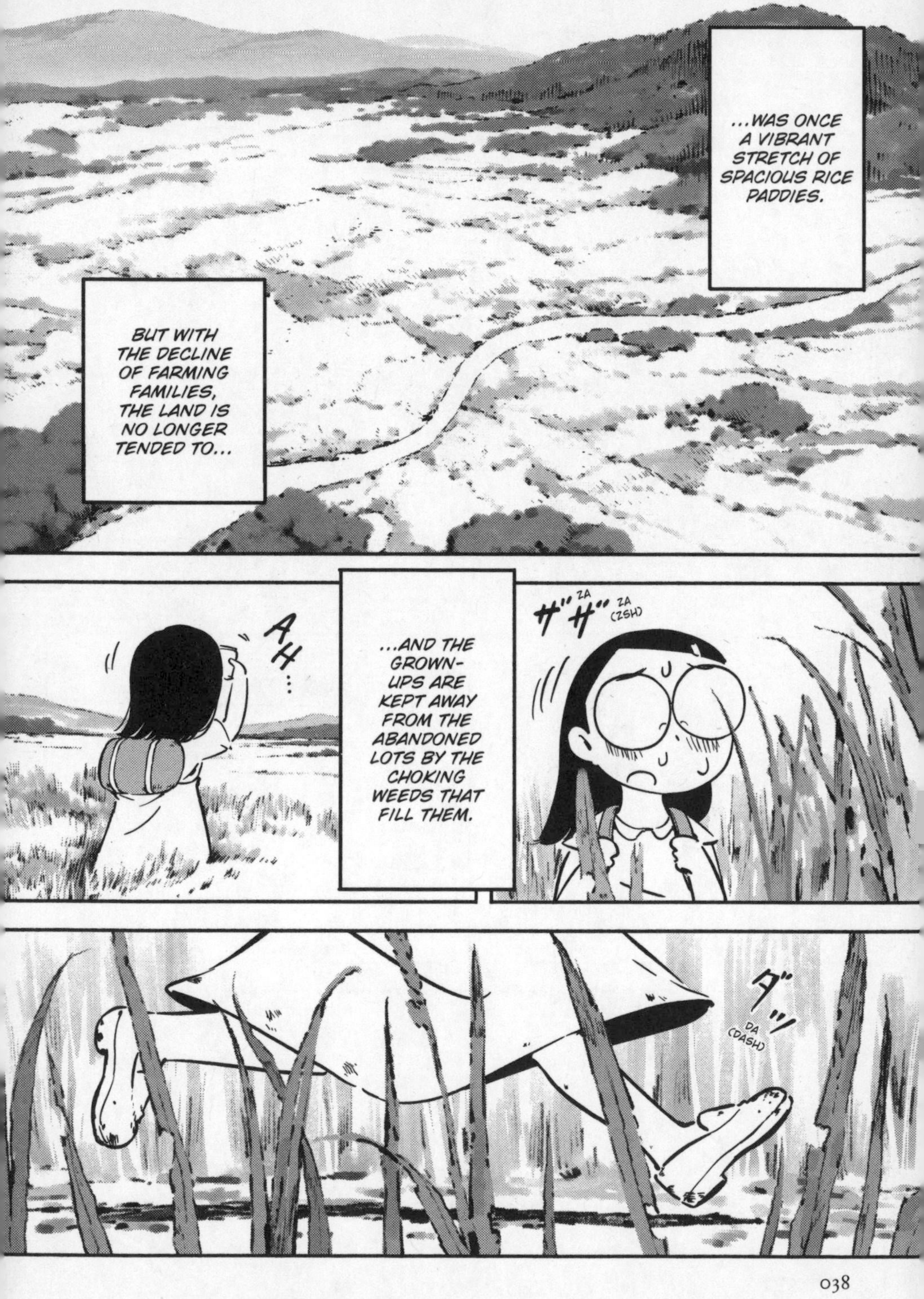
...WAS ONCE A VIBRANT STRETCH OF SPACIOUS RICE PADDIES.
BUT WITH THE DECLINE OF FARMING FAMILIES, THE LAND IS NO LONGER TENDED TO...
ZA ZA (ZSH)
...AND THE GROWN-UPS ARE KEPT AWAY FROM THE ABANDONED LOTS BY THE CHOKING WEEDS THAT FILL THEM.
AH...
DA (DASH)

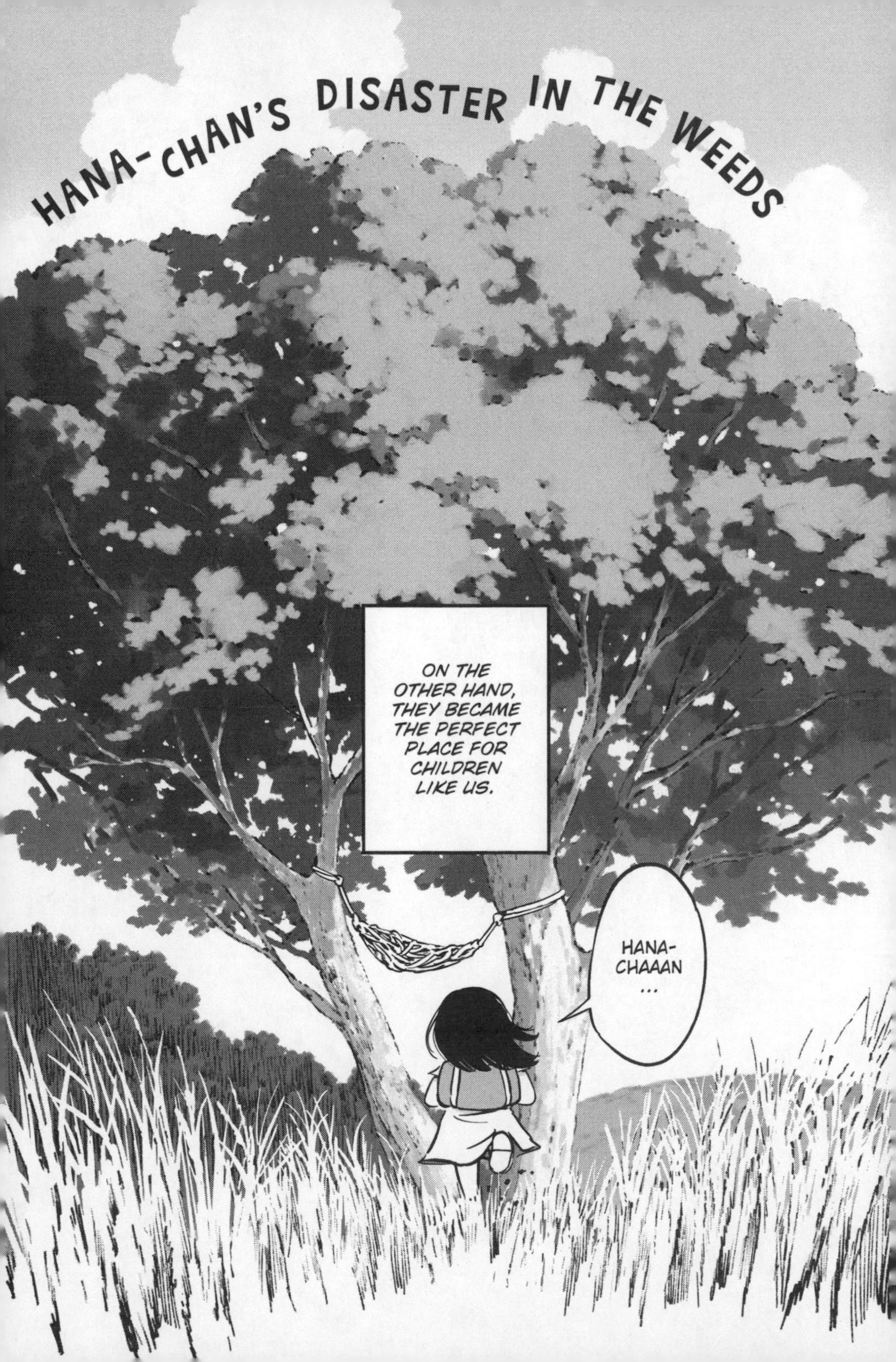
HANA-CHAN'S DISASTER IN THE WEEDS
ON THE OTHER HAND, THEY BECAME THE PERFECT PLACE FOR CHILDREN LIKE US.
HANA-CHAAAN ...

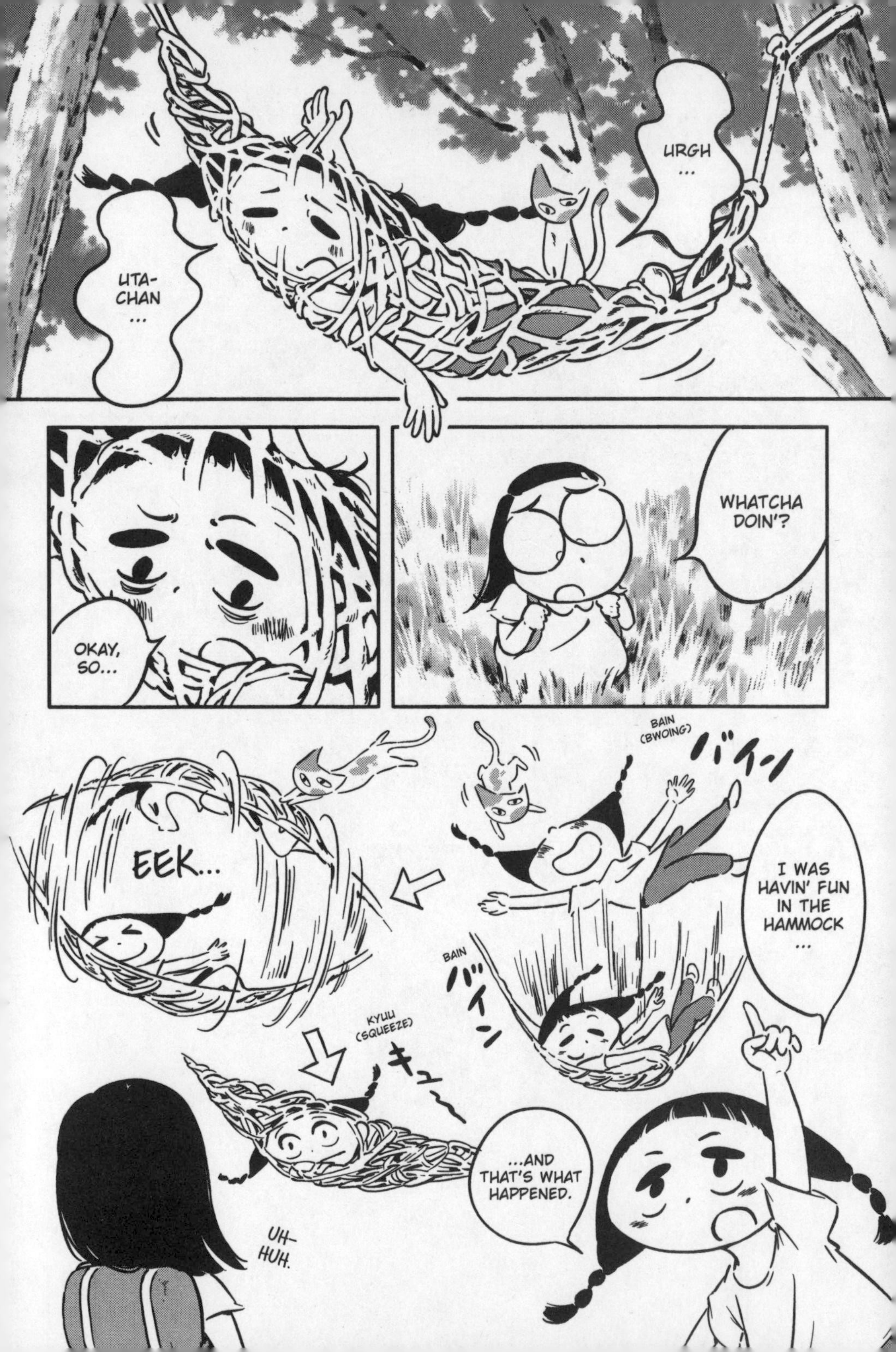
URGH ...
UTA-CHAN ...
WHATCHA DOIN'?
OKAY, SO...
BAIN (BWOING)
バイ〜ン
I WAS HAVIN' FUN IN THE HAMMOCK ...
BAIN
バイ〜ン
EEK...
KYUU (SQUEEZE)
キュ〜
...AND THAT'S WHAT HAPPENED.
UH-HUH.

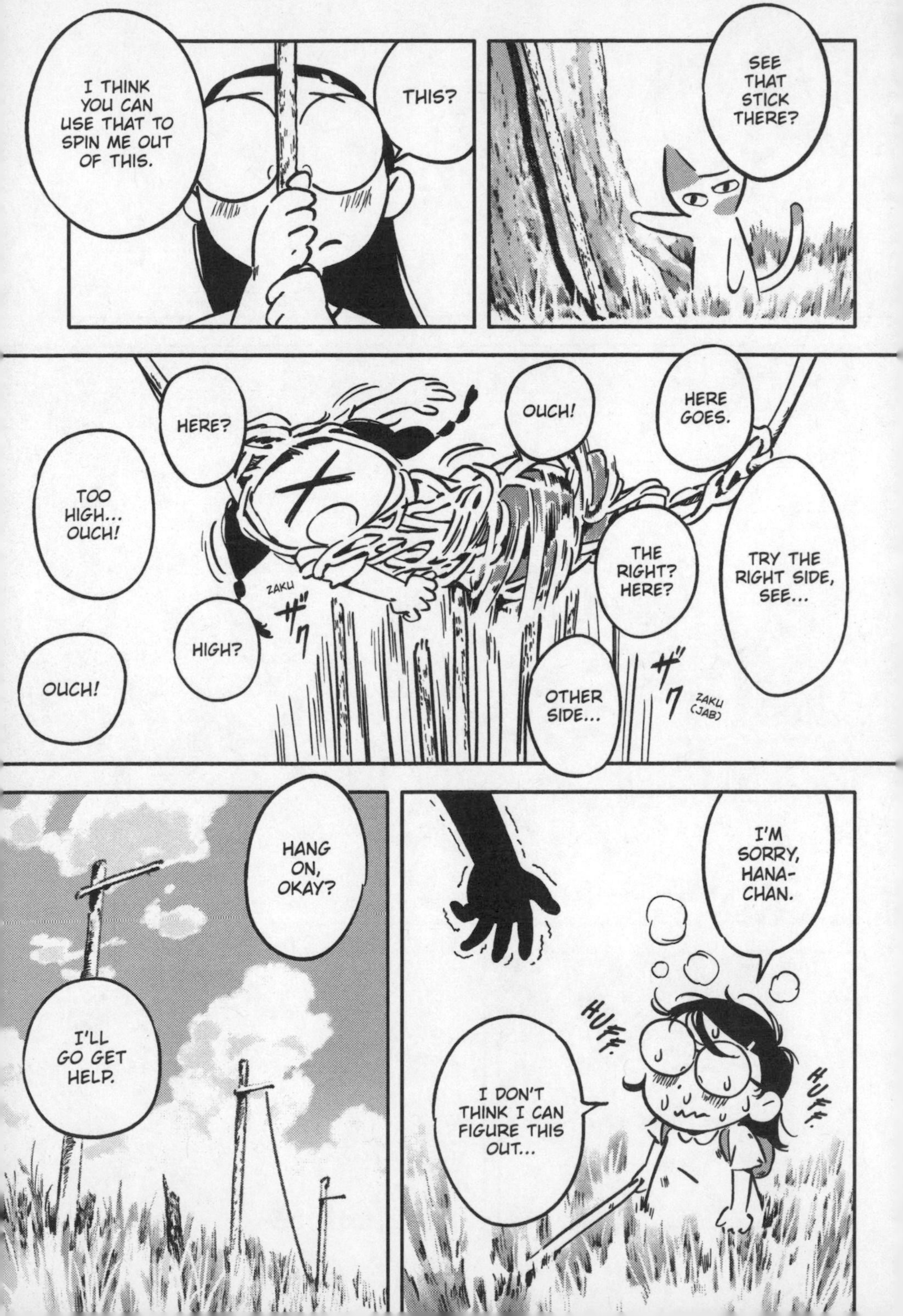
SEE THAT STICK THERE?
THIS?
I THINK YOU CAN USE THAT TO SPIN ME OUT OF THIS.
HERE GOES.
OUCH!
TRY THE RIGHT SIDE, SEE...
THE RIGHT? HERE?
ZAKU (JAB)
OTHER SIDE...
HERE?
TOO HIGH... OUCH!
ZAKU
HIGH?
OUCH!
I'M SORRY, HANA-CHAN.
HUFF
HUFF
I DON'T THINK I CAN FIGURE THIS OUT...
HANG ON, OKAY?
I'LL GO GET HELP.

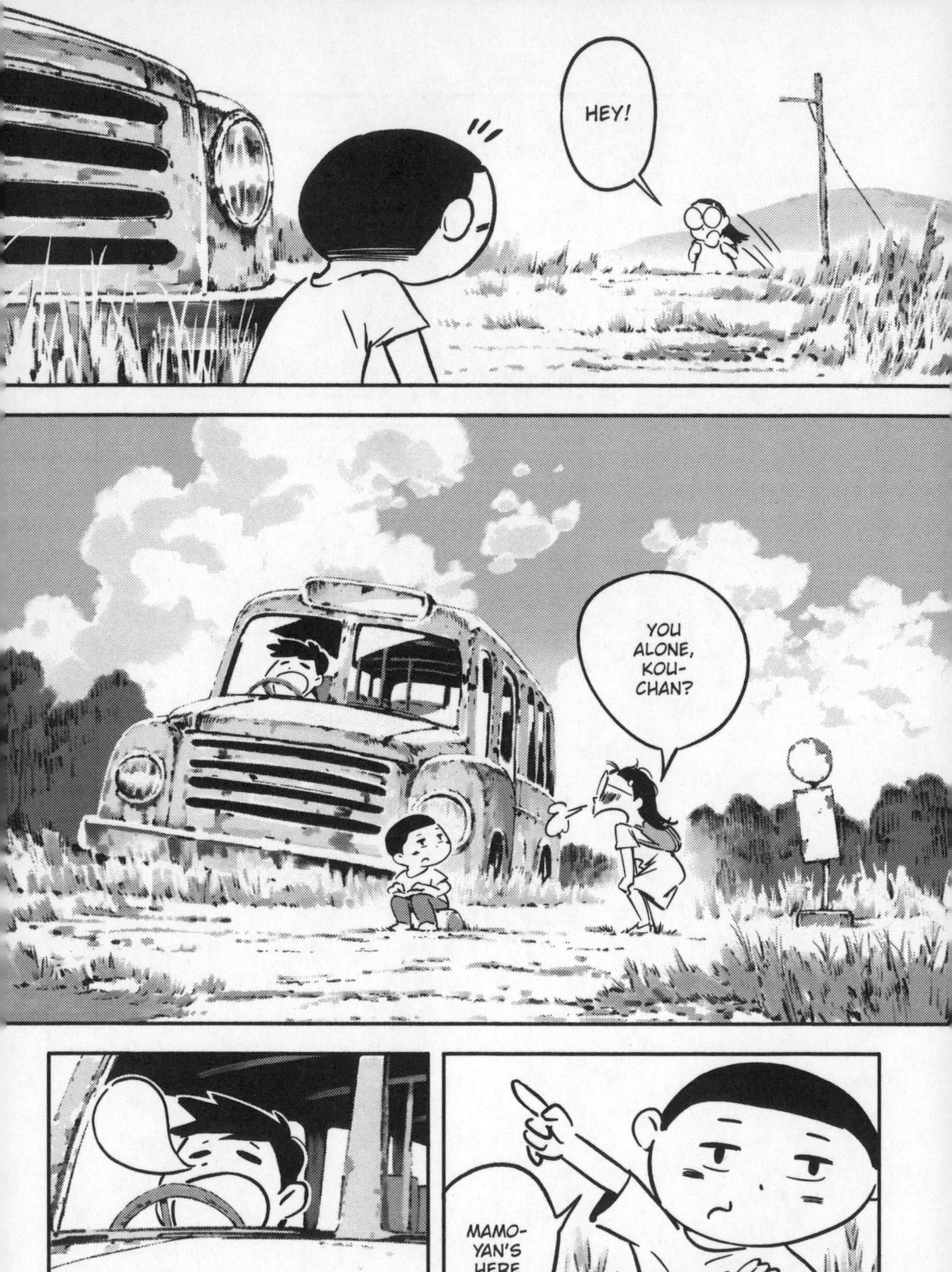
HEY!
YOU ALONE, KOU-CHAN?
MAMO-YAN'S HERE TOO.

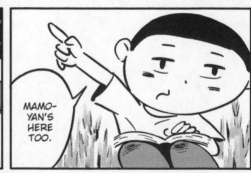

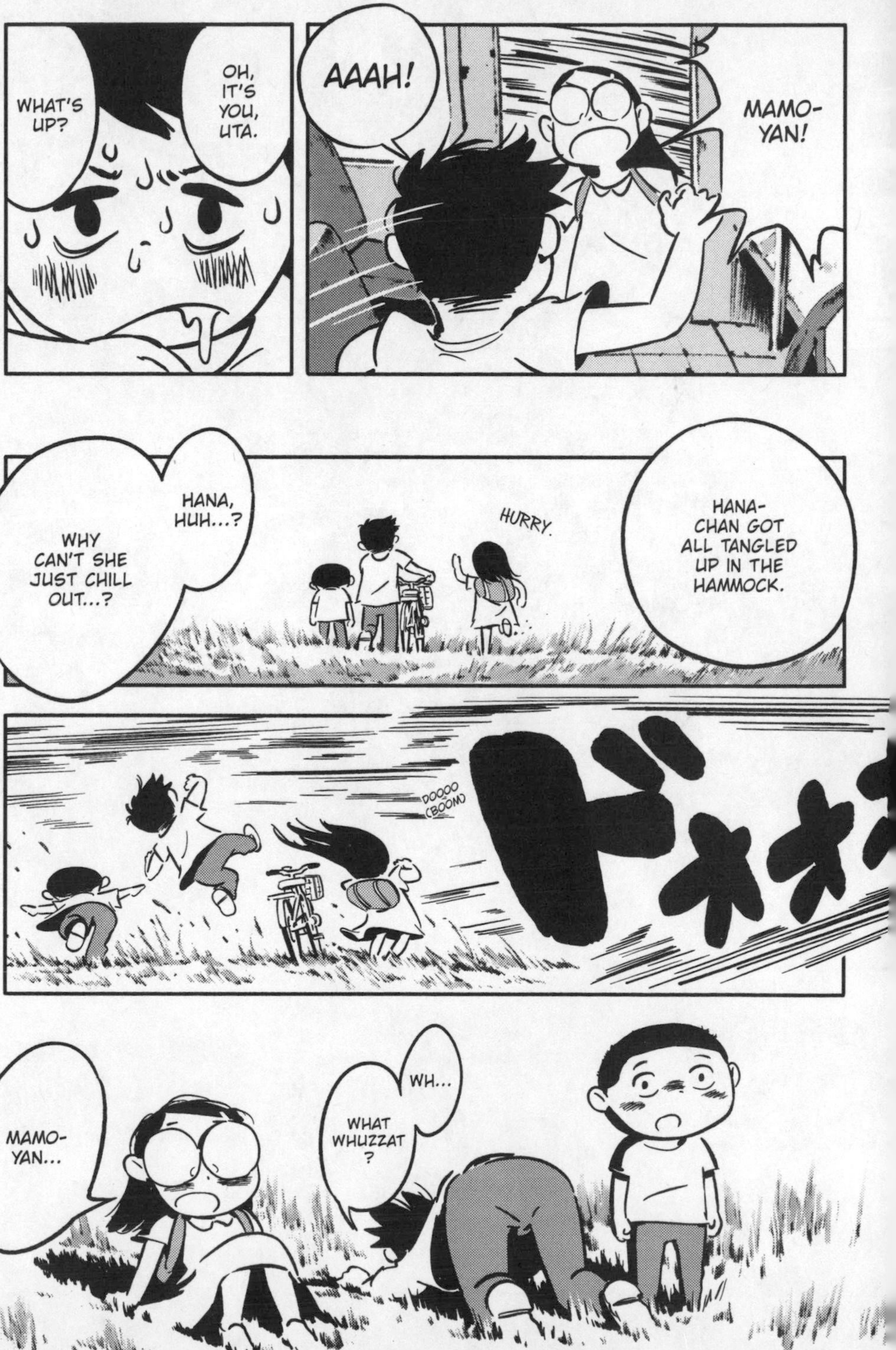
MAMO-YAN!
AAAH!
OH, IT'S YOU, UTA.
WHAT'S UP?
HANA-CHAN GOT ALL TANGLED UP IN THE HAMMOCK.
HURRY.
HANA, HUH...?
WHY CAN'T SHE JUST CHILL OUT...?
DOOOO (BOOM)
WH...
WHAT WHUZZAT?
MAMO-YAN...

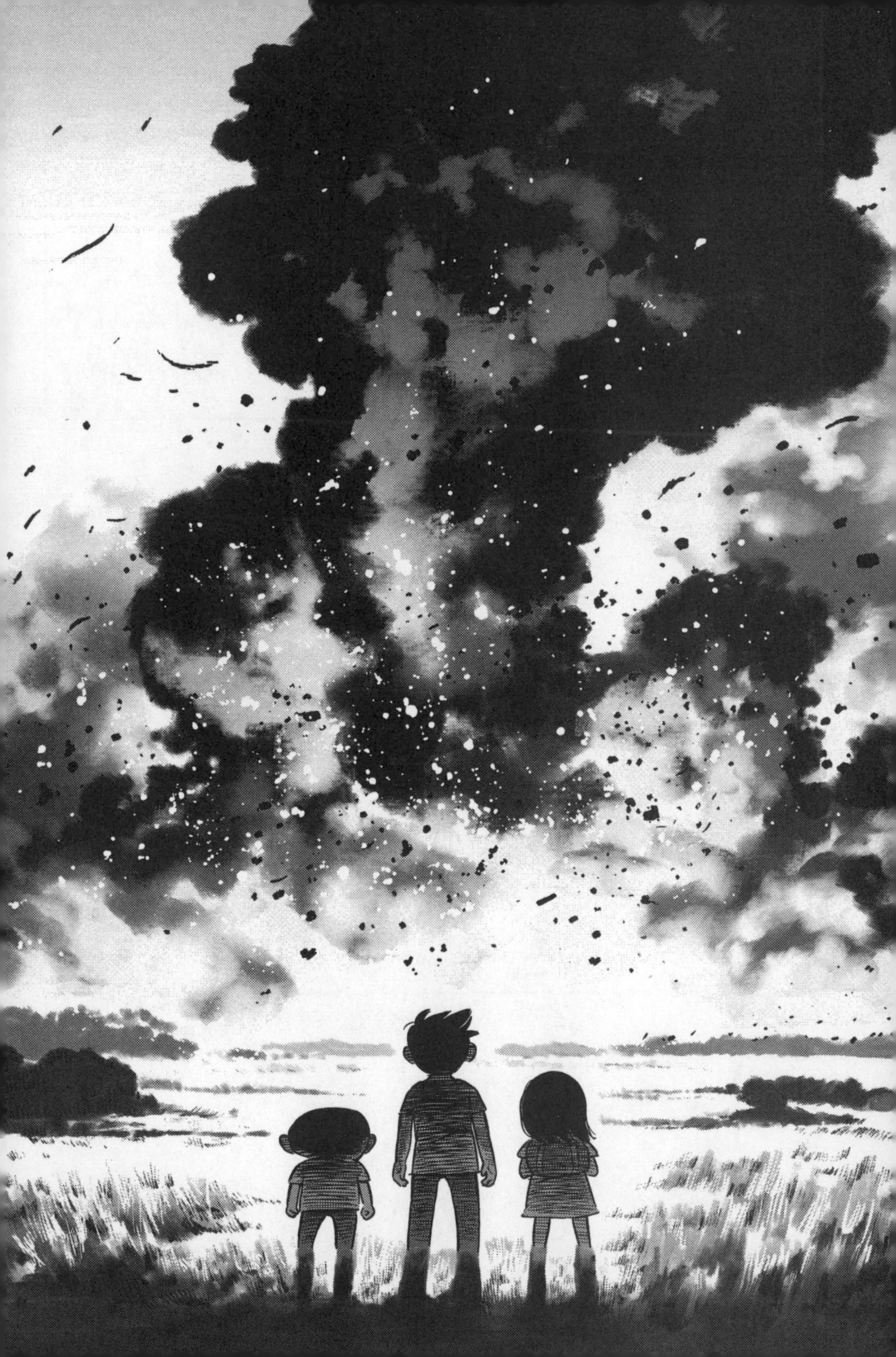

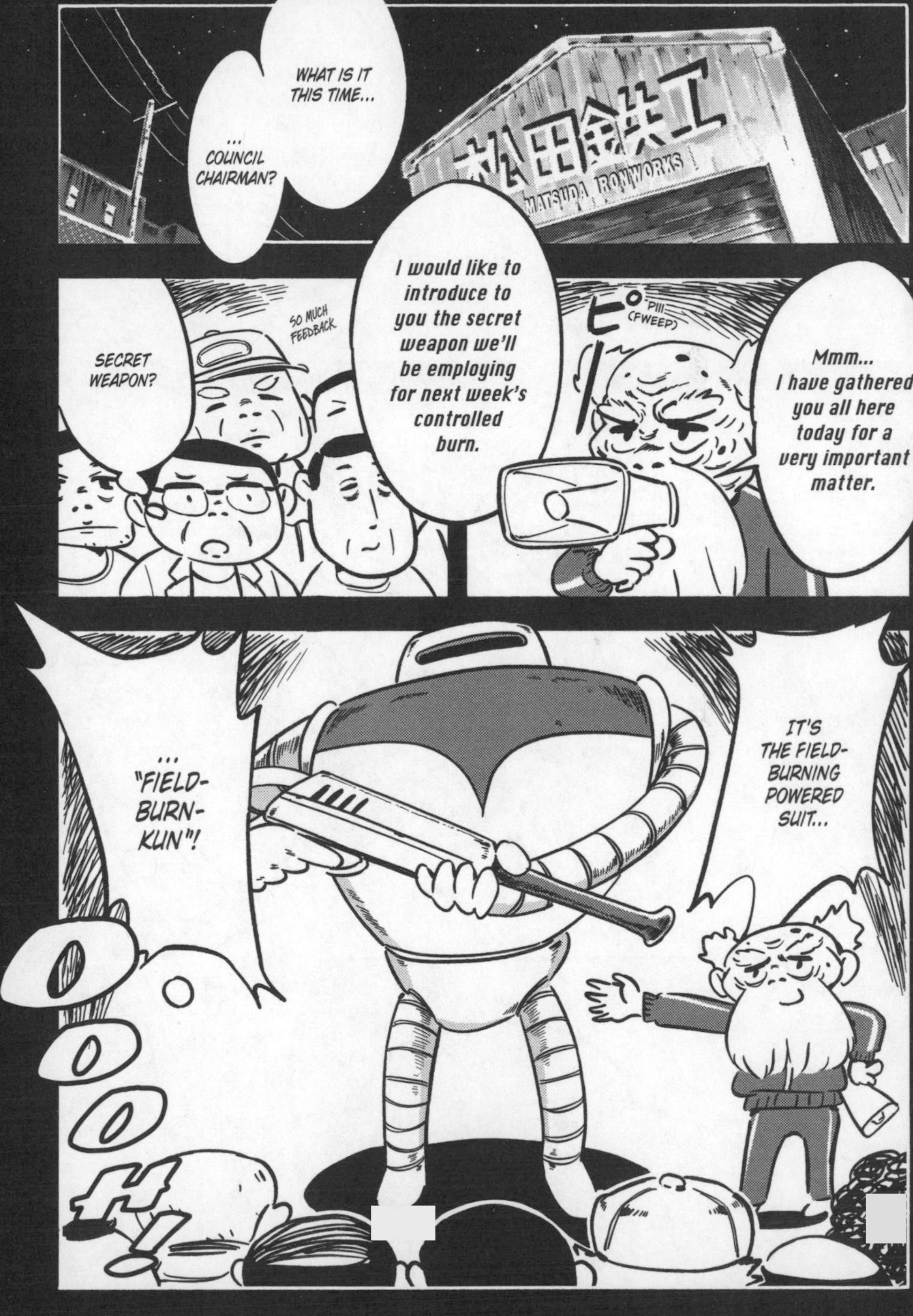
松田鉄工
MATSUDA IRONWORKS
WHAT IS IT THIS TIME...
... COUNCIL CHAIRMAN?
ピ
PIII (FWEEP)
Mmm... I have gathered you all here today for a very important matter.
I would like to introduce to you the secret weapon we'll be employing for next week's controlled burn.
SO MUCH FEEDBACK
SECRET WEAPON?
IT'S THE FIELD-BURNING POWERED SUIT...
... "FIELD-BURN-KUN"!
OOOOOH!

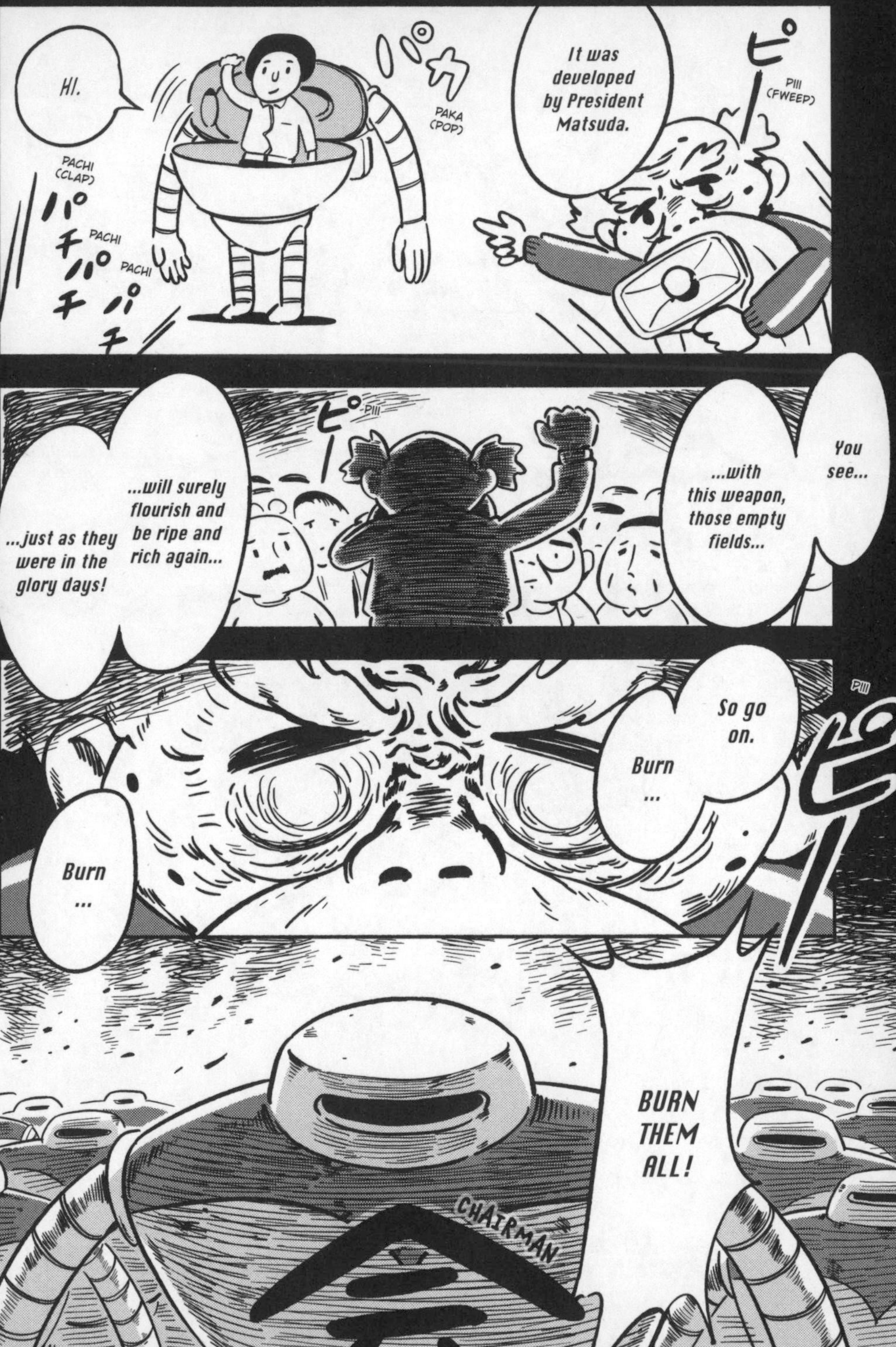

It was developed by President Matsuda.
ピ
PIII (FWEEP)
パカ
PAKA (POP)
HI.
PACHI (CLAP)
パチパチ
PACHI
パチパチ
PACHI
You see...
...with this weapon, those empty fields...
ピ
-PIII
...will surely flourish and be ripe and rich again...
...just as they were in the glory days!
So go on.
Burn ...
ピ
PIII
Burn ...
BURN THEM ALL!
CHAIRMAN

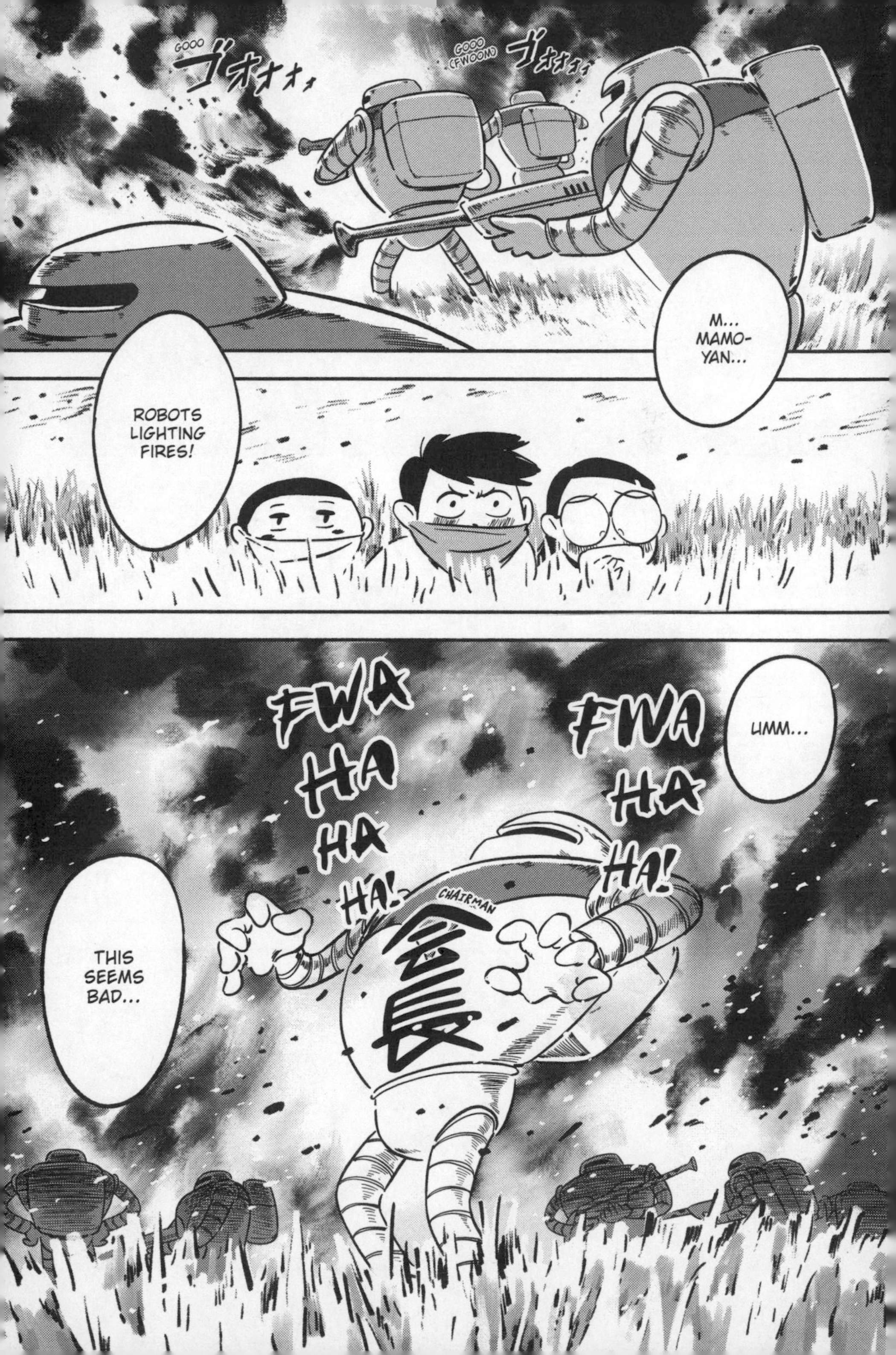
GOOO (FWOOM)
ゴオオオォ
GOOO
ゴオオオォ
M... MAMO-YAN...
ROBOTS LIGHTING FIRES!
UMM...
FWA HA HA HA!
FWA HA HA HA!
CHAIRMAN
会長
THIS SEEMS BAD...

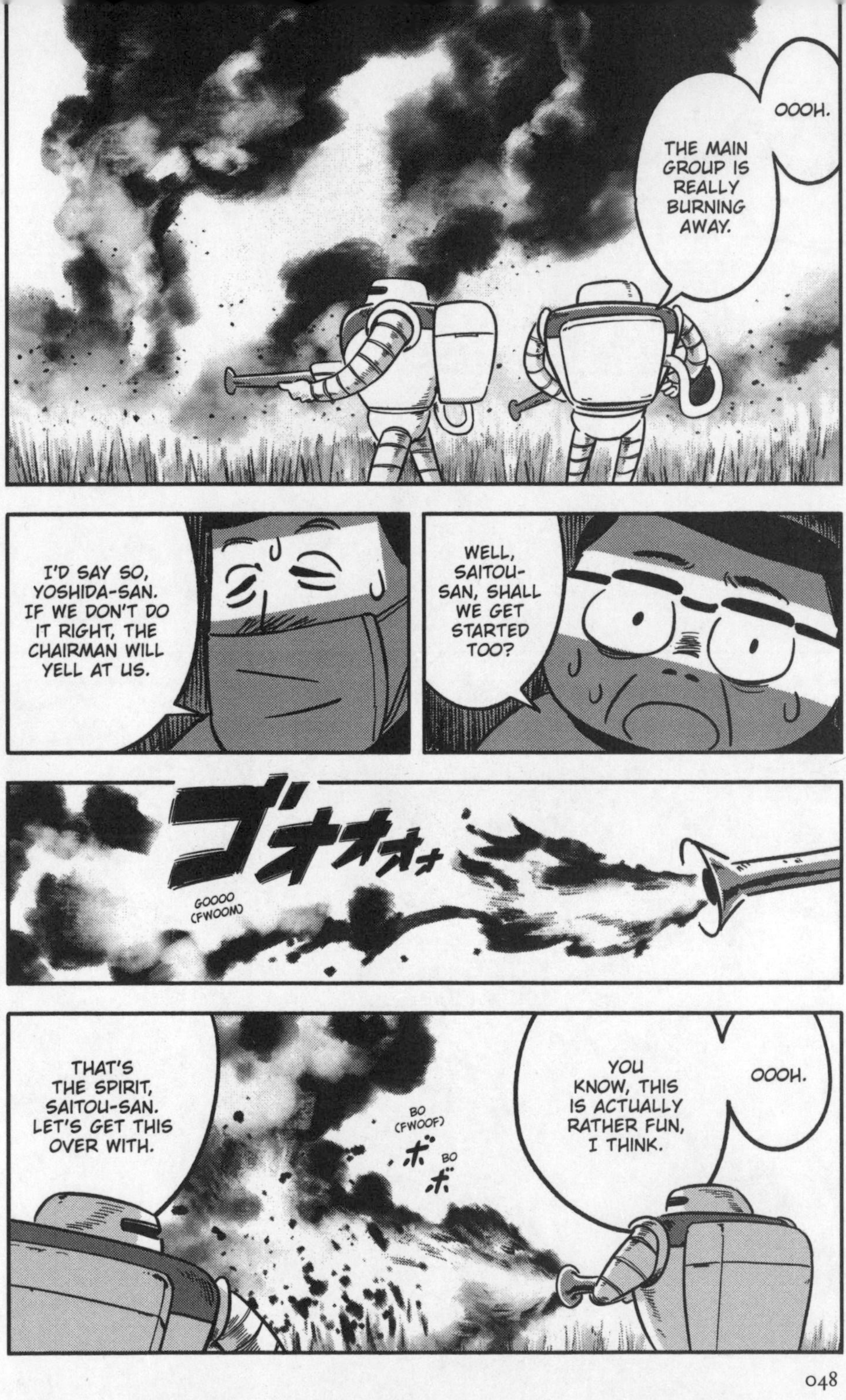
OOOH.
THE MAIN GROUP IS REALLY BURNING AWAY.
WELL, SAITOU-SAN, SHALL WE GET STARTED TOO?
I'D SAY SO, YOSHIDA-SAN. IF WE DON'T DO IT RIGHT, THE CHAIRMAN WILL YELL AT US.
ゴオオオォ
GOOOO (FWOOM)
OOOH.
YOU KNOW, THIS IS ACTUALLY RATHER FUN, I THINK.
ボ
BO (FWOOF)
ボ
BO
THAT'S THE SPIRIT, SAITOU-SAN. LET'S GET THIS OVER WITH.

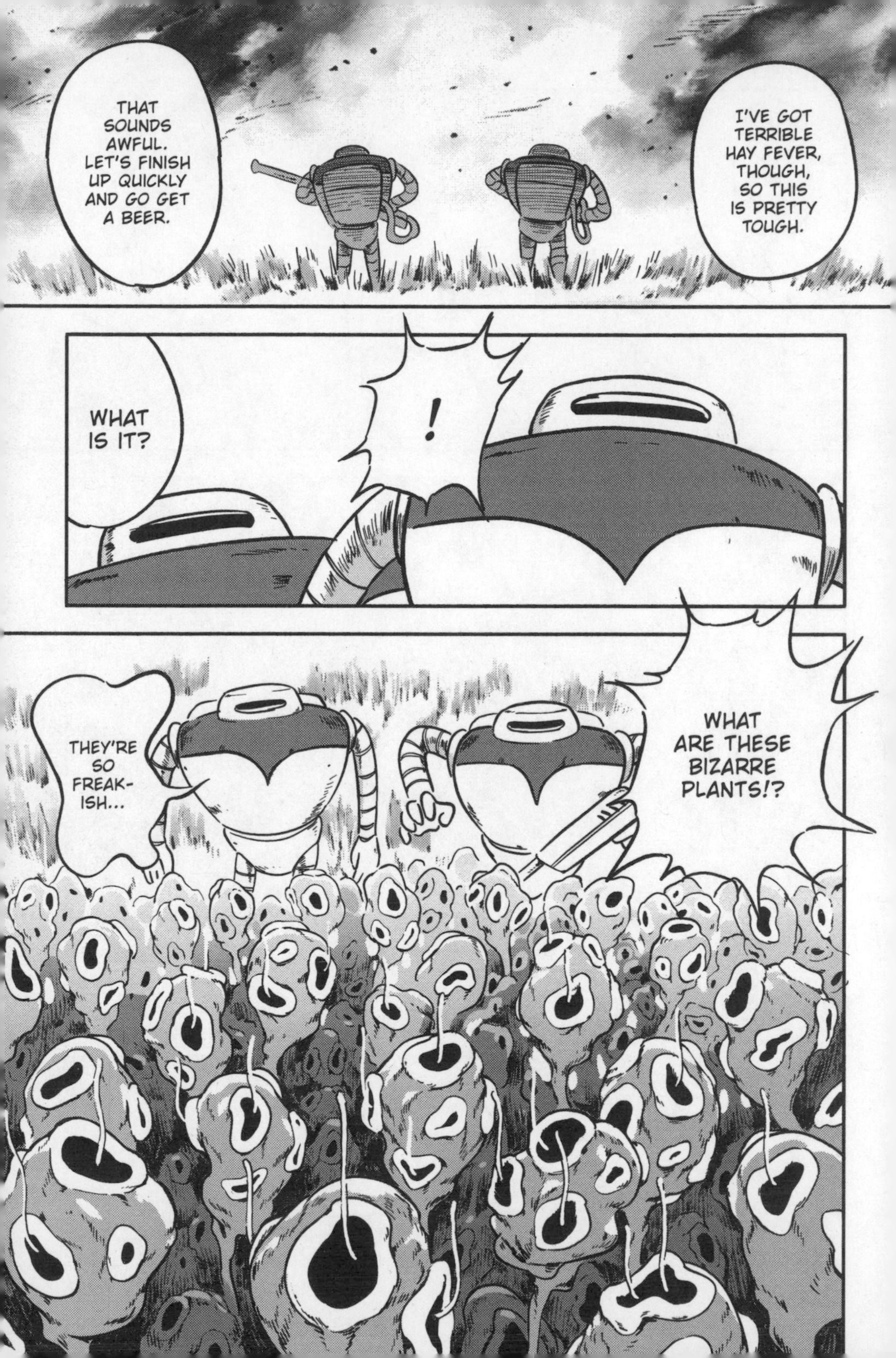
I'VE GOT TERRIBLE HAY FEVER, THOUGH, SO THIS IS PRETTY TOUGH.
THAT SOUNDS AWFUL. LET'S FINISH UP QUICKLY AND GO GET A BEER.
!
WHAT IS IT?
WHAT ARE THESE BIZARRE PLANTS!?
THEY'RE SO FREAK-ISH...

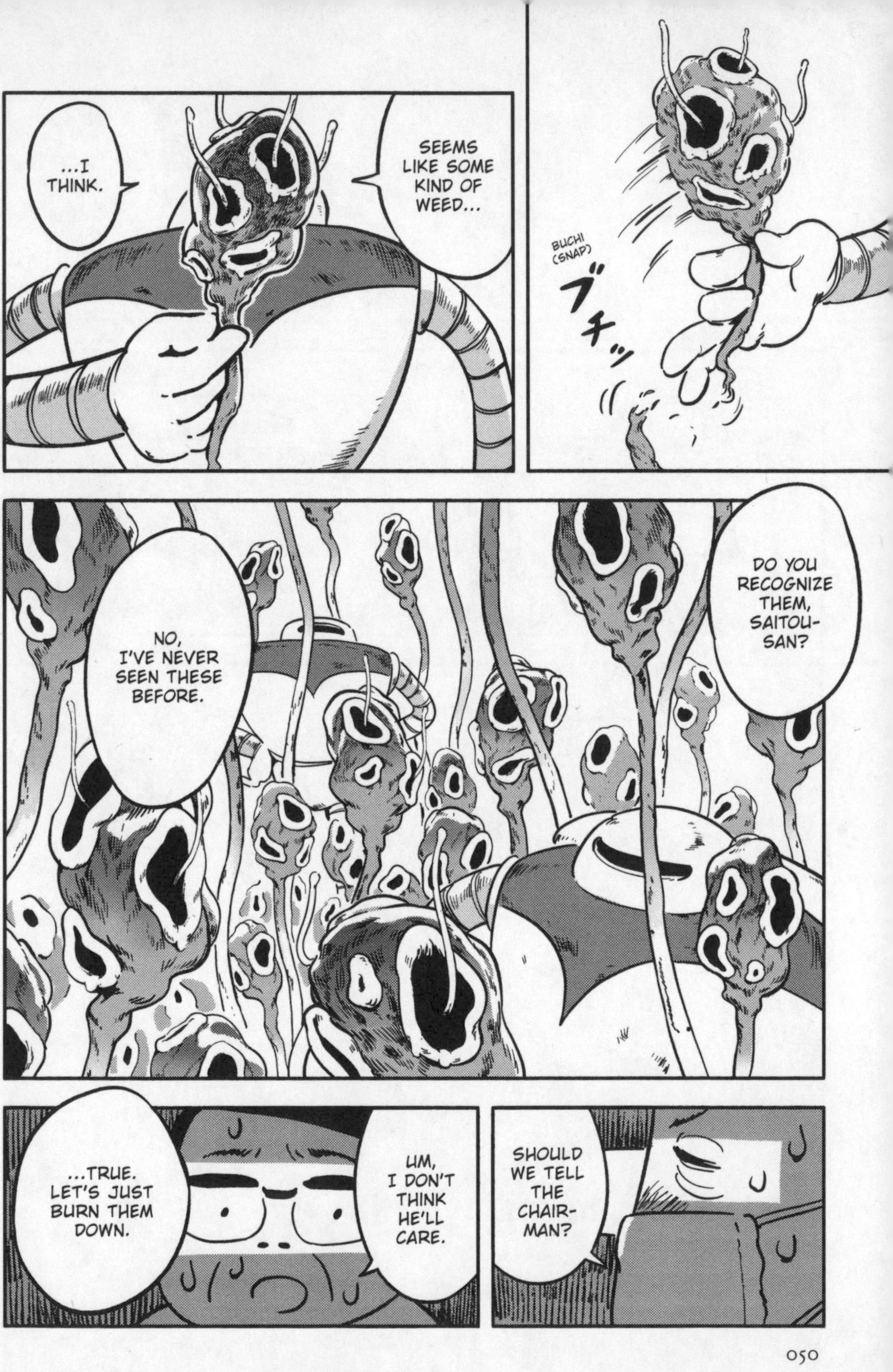
BUCHI (SNAP)
ブチッ
SEEMS LIKE SOME KIND OF WEED...
...I THINK.
DO YOU RECOGNIZE THEM, SAITOU-SAN?
NO, I'VE NEVER SEEN THESE BEFORE.
SHOULD WE TELL THE CHAIR-MAN?
UM, I DON'T THINK HE'LL CARE.
...TRUE. LET'S JUST BURN THEM DOWN.

GOBOO (FWOOSH)
GOBOBOOO
SHUUU (FSSS)
?
SOMETHING STRANGE'S COMING OUT OF THEM.
WHAT IS THIS STUFF?

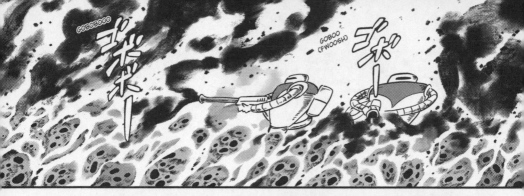

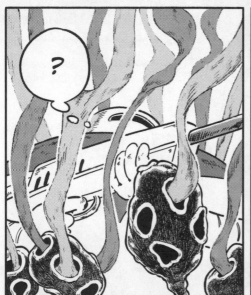

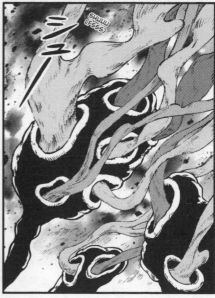

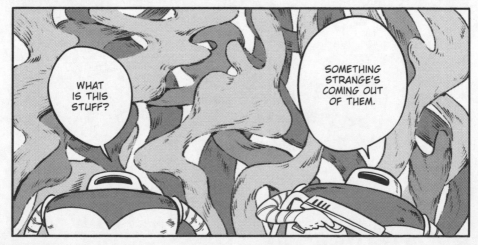

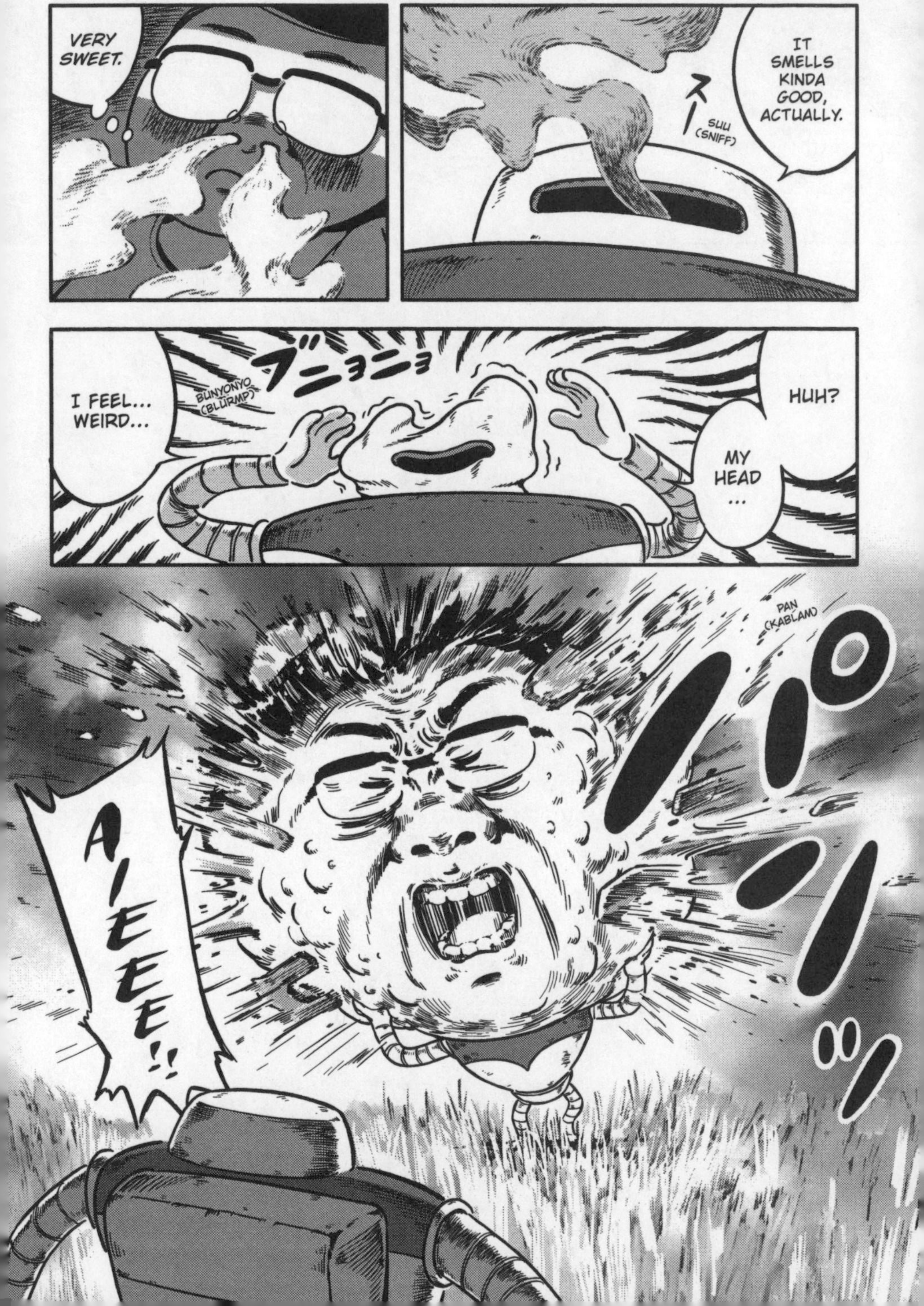
SUU (SNIFF)
IT SMELLS KINDA GOOD, ACTUALLY.
VERY SWEET.
HUH?
MY HEAD ...
BUNYONYO (BLURMP)
I FEEL... WEIRD...
PAN (KABLAM)
AIEEEE!!

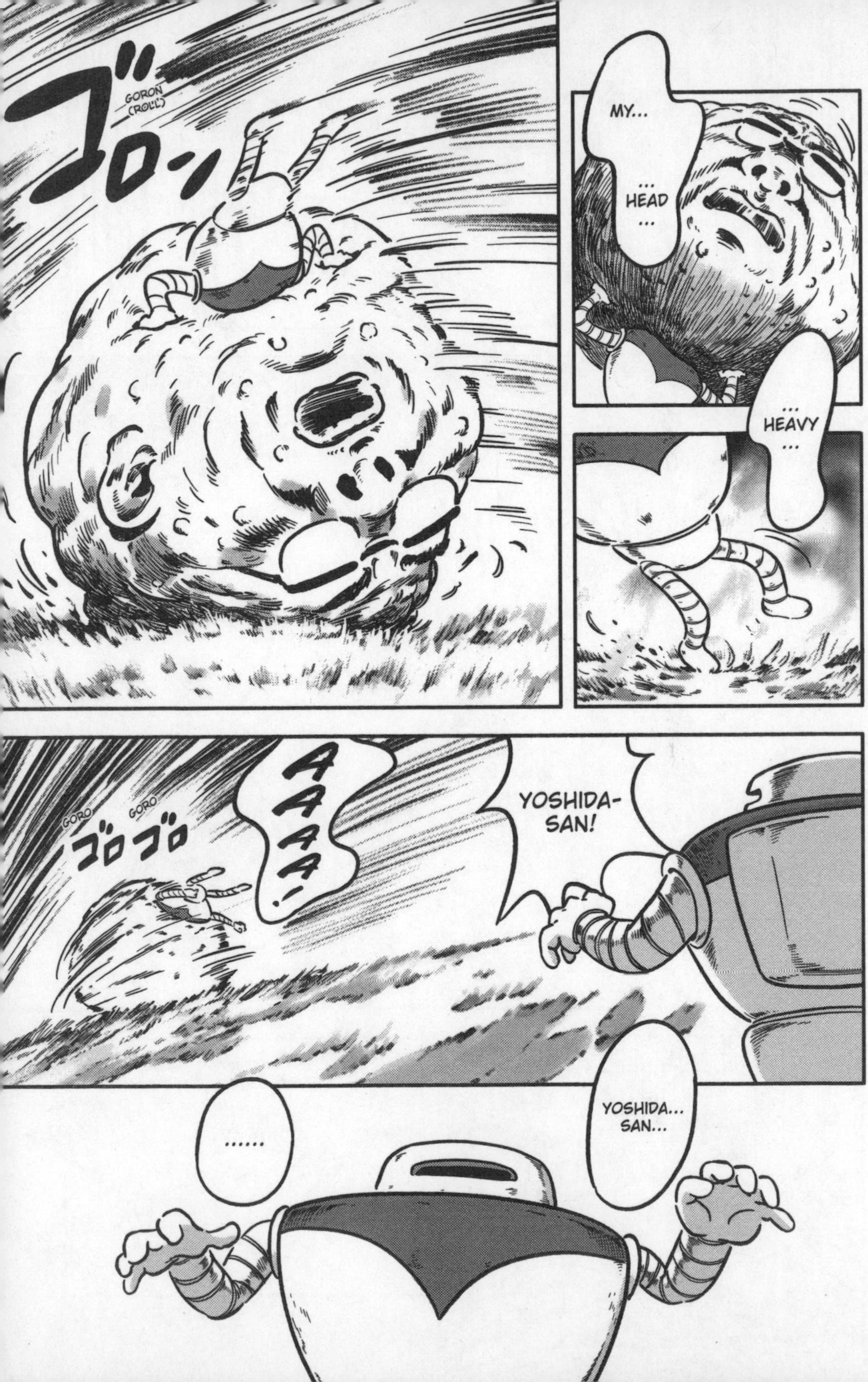
MY...
...HEAD...
...HEAVY...
ゴロン
GORON (ROLL)
YOSHIDA-SAN!
AAAAA!
ゴロゴロ
GORO GORO
YOSHIDA... SAN...
......

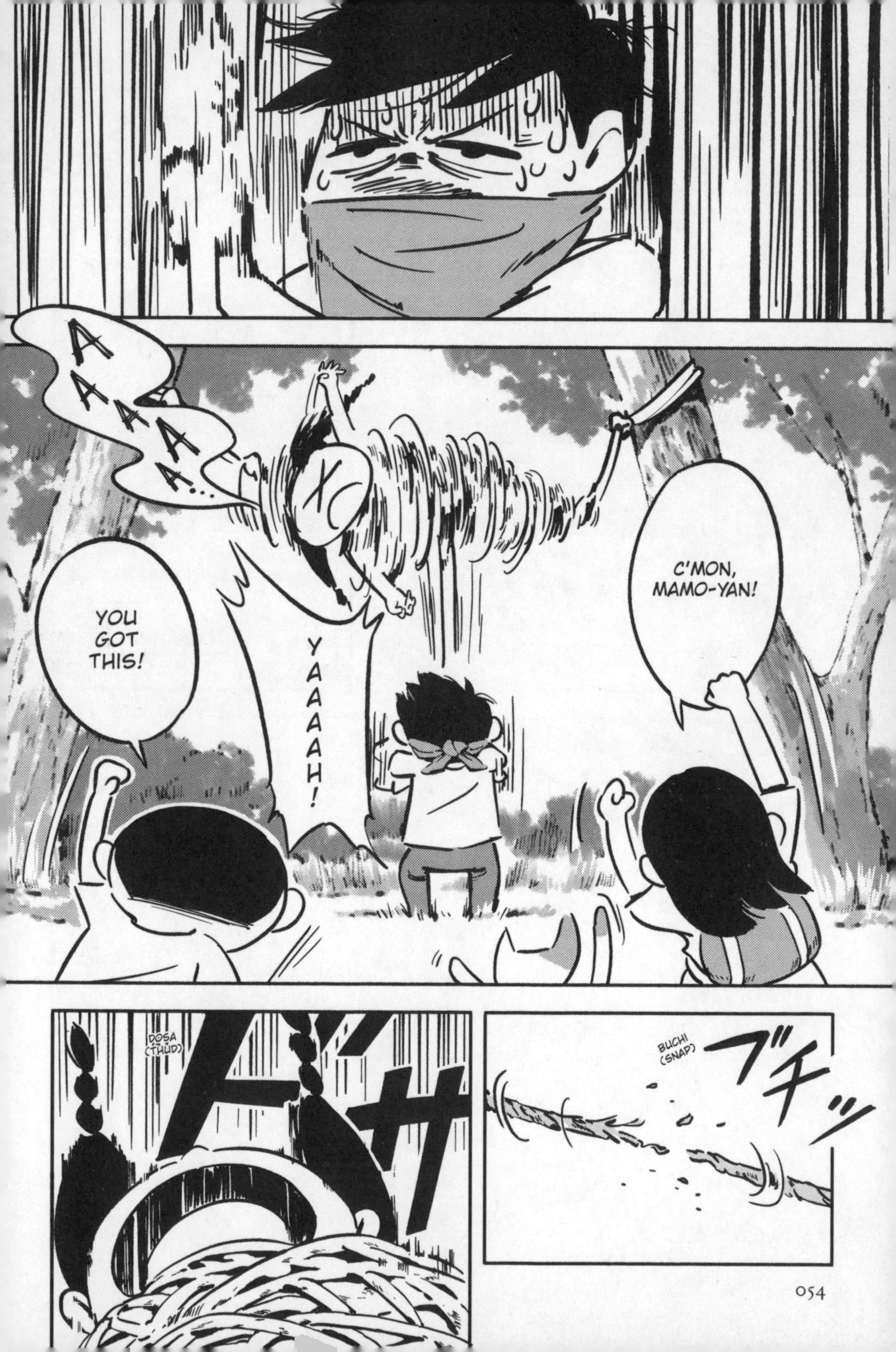
C'MON, MAMO-YAN!
AAAAA...
YAAAAAH!
YOU GOT THIS!
BUCHI (SNAP)
ブチッ
DOSA (THUD)
ドサ

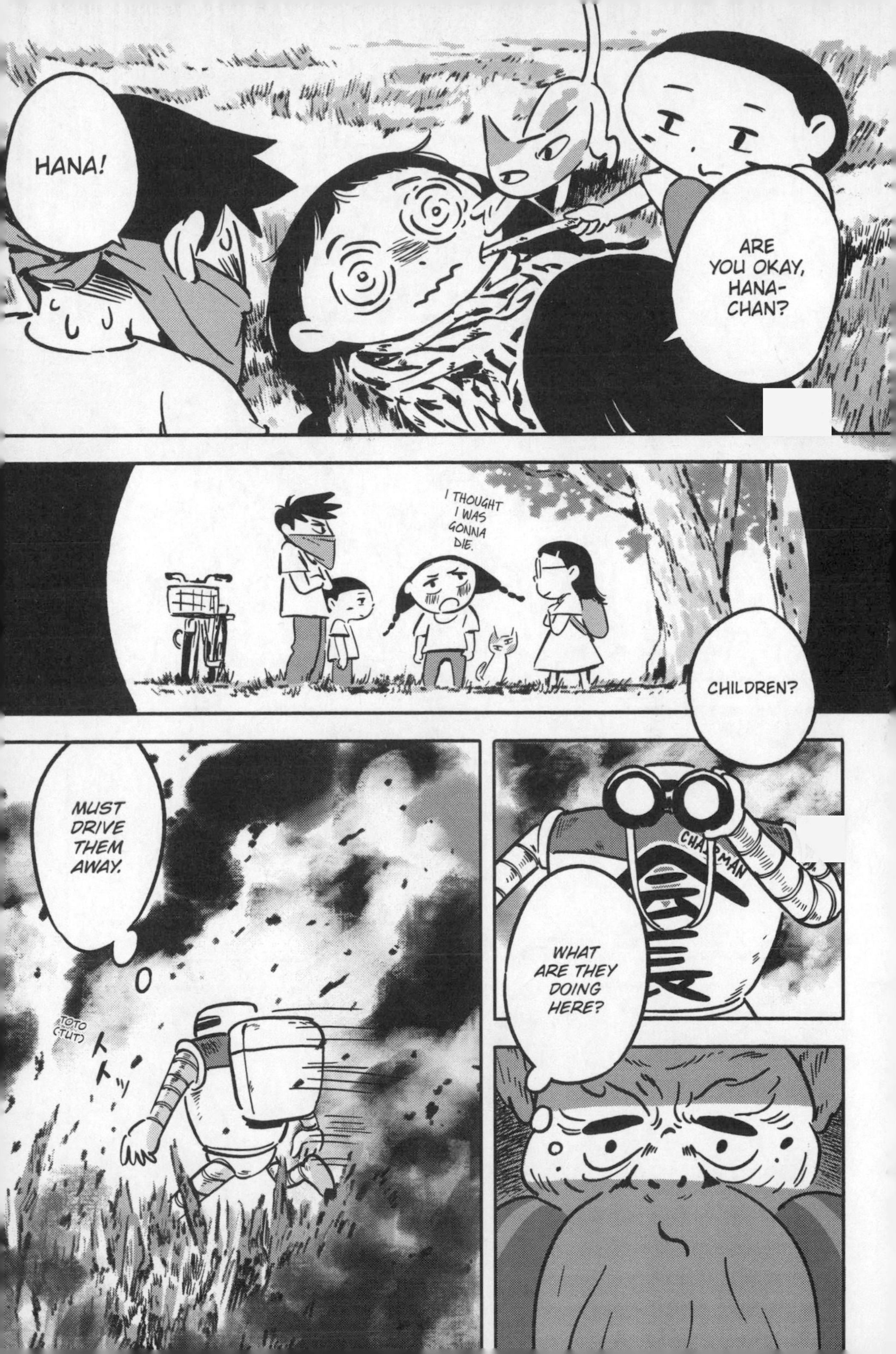
ARE YOU OKAY, HANA-CHAN?
HANA!
I THOUGHT I WAS GONNA DIE.
CHILDREN?
WHAT ARE THEY DOING HERE?
MUST DRIVE THEM AWAY.
TOTO (TUT)
トトッ

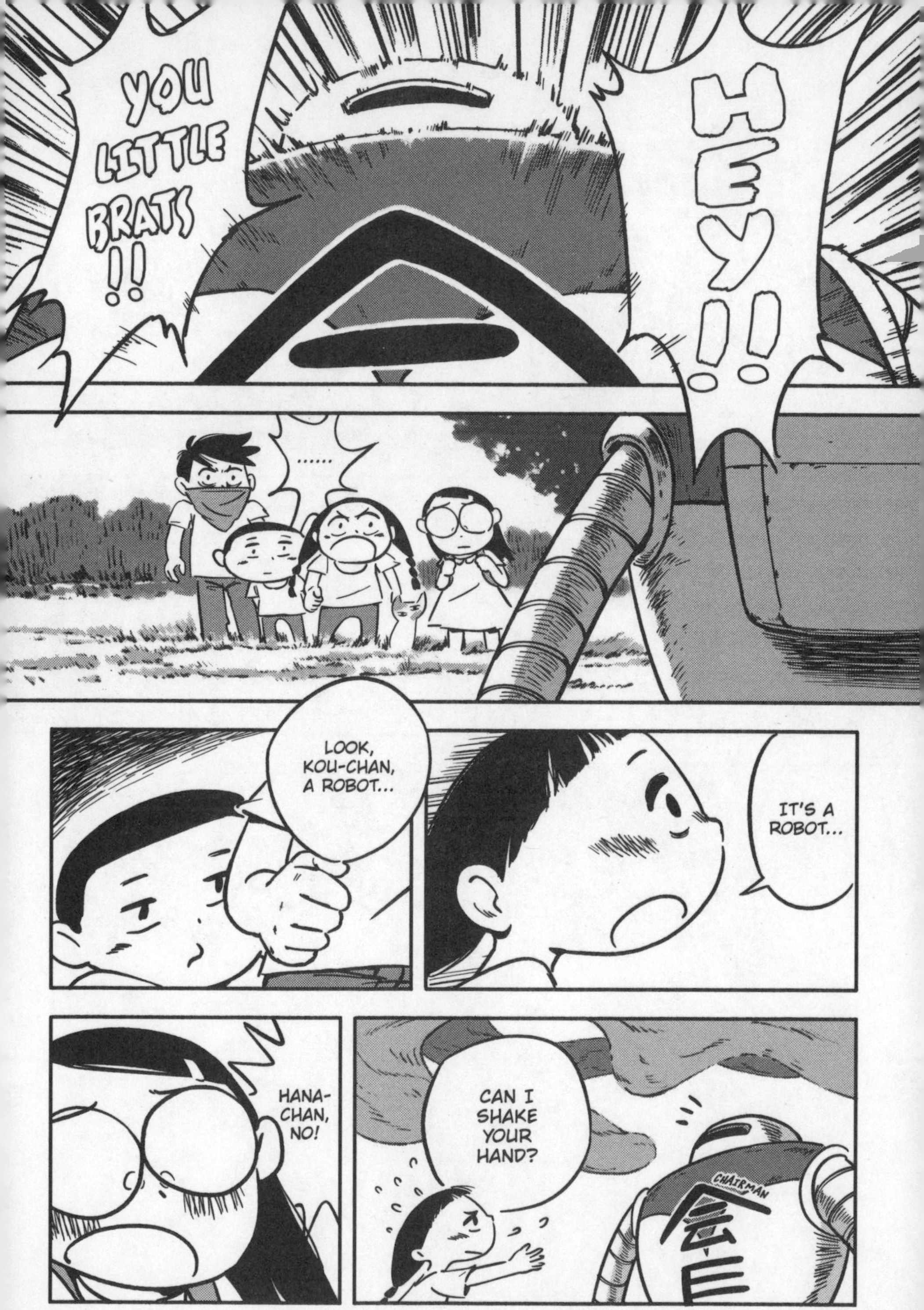
HEY!!
YOU LITTLE BRATS!!
......
IT'S A ROBOT...
LOOK, KOU-CHAN, A ROBOT...
CAN I SHAKE YOUR HAND?
CHAIRMAN
HANA-CHAN, NO!

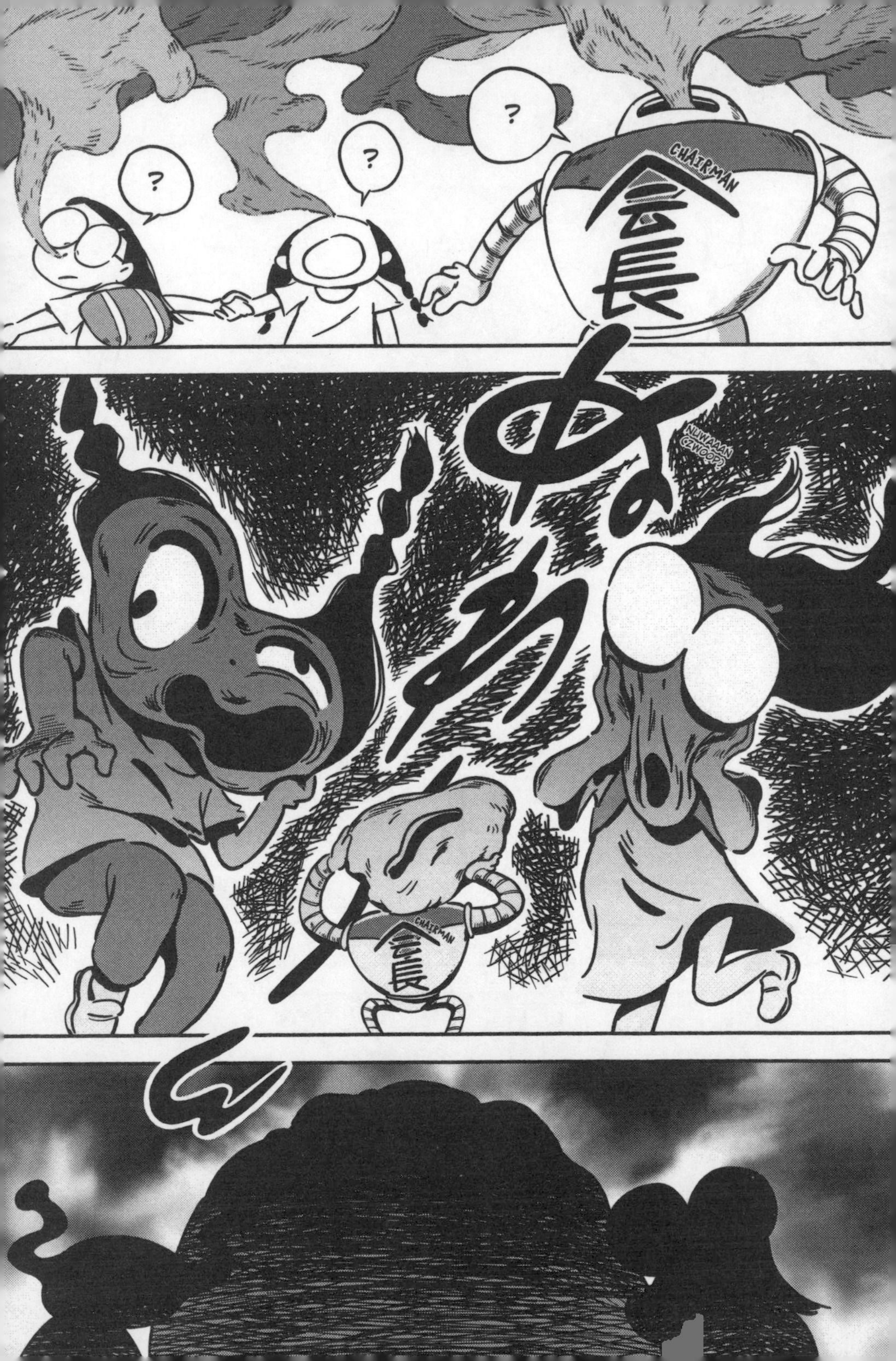
?
?
?
CHAIRMAN
会長
NUWAAAN (ZWOOP)
CHAIRMAN
会長

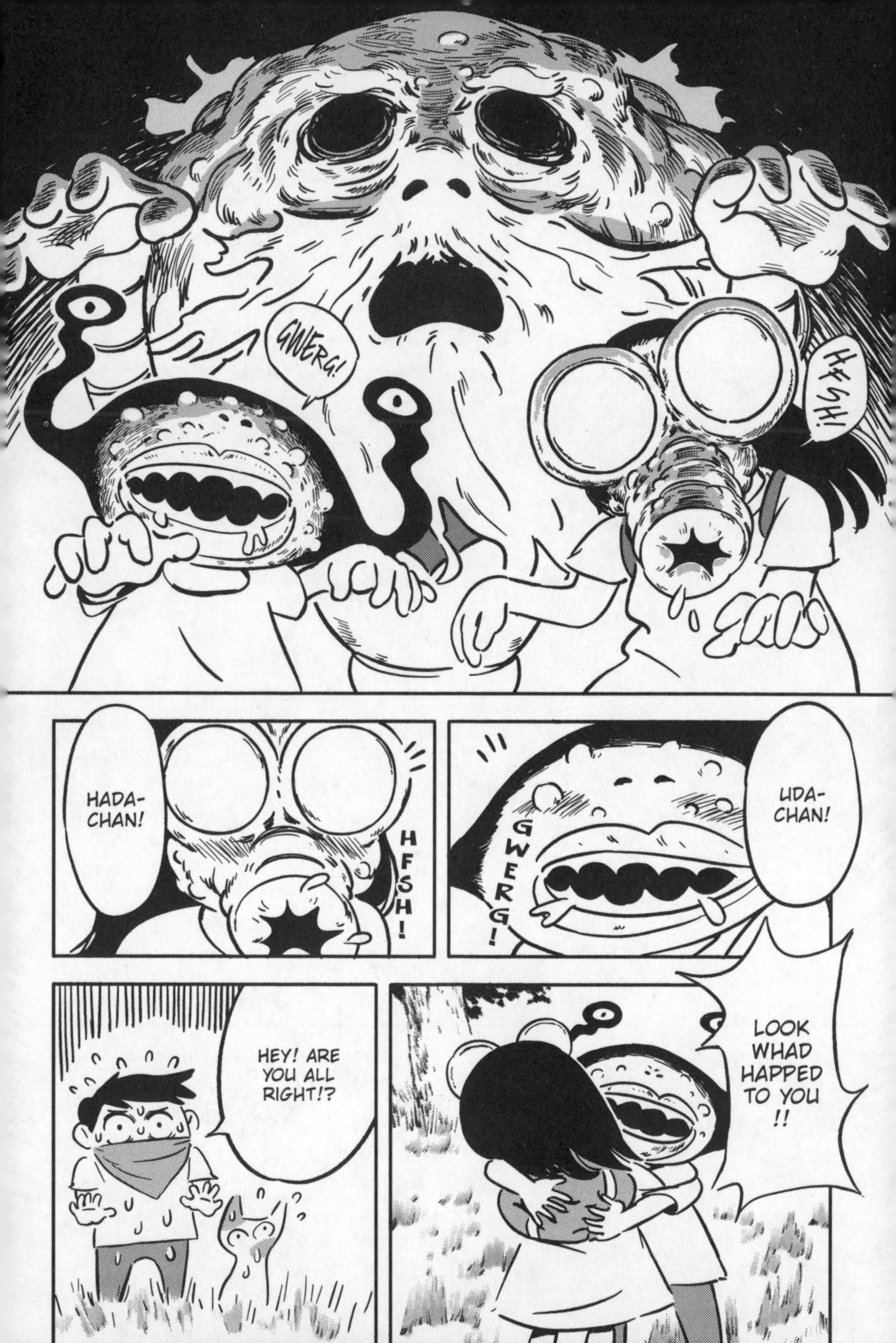
HFSH!
GWERG!
UDA-CHAN!
GWERG!
HADA-CHAN!
HFSH!
LOOK WHAD HAPPED TO YOU!!
HEY! ARE YOU ALL RIGHT!?

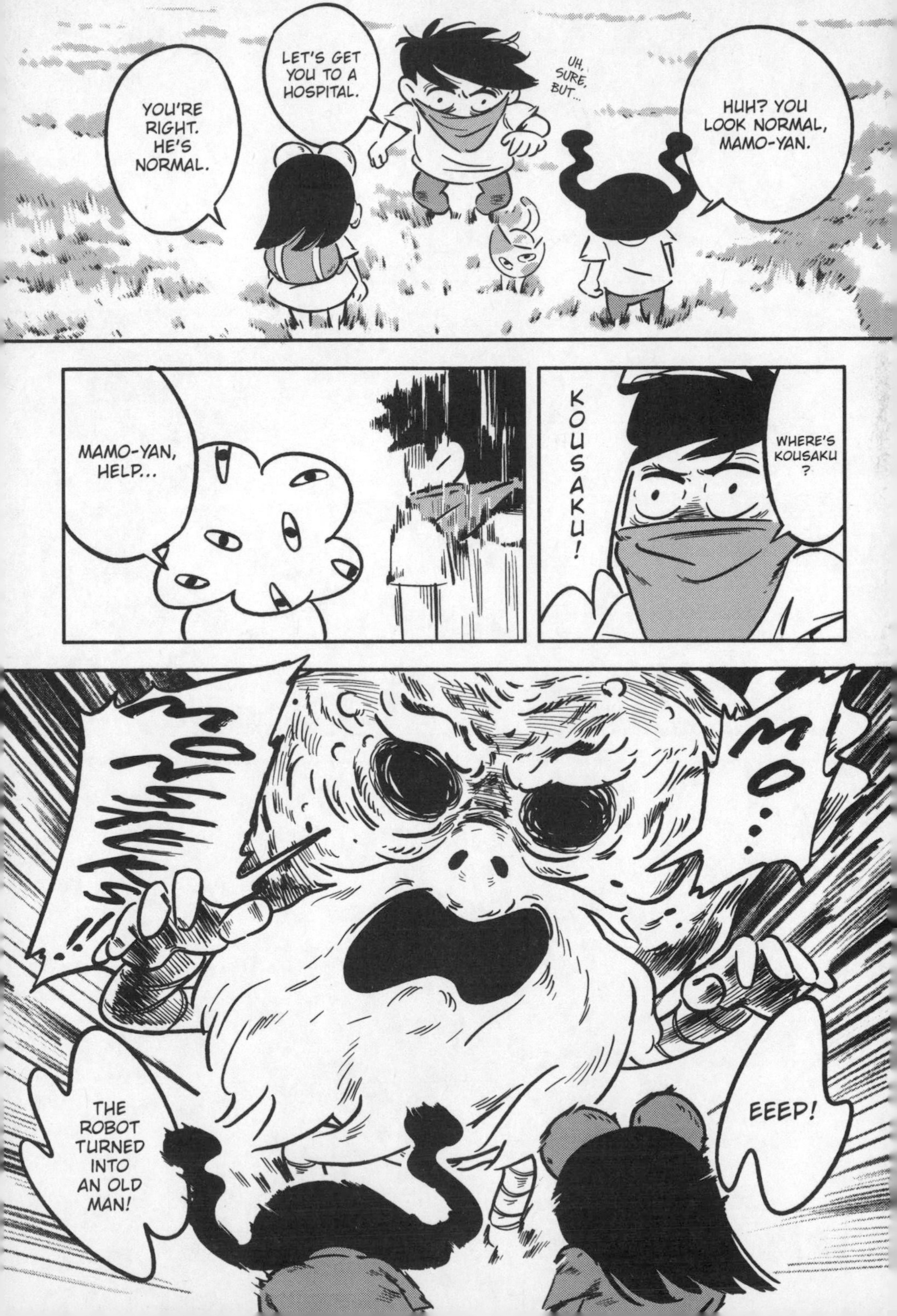
HUH? YOU LOOK NORMAL, MAMO-YAN.
UH, SURE, BUT...
LET'S GET YOU TO A HOSPITAL.
YOU'RE RIGHT. HE'S NORMAL.
WHERE'S KOUSAKU?
KOUSAKU!
MAMO-YAN, HELP...
MO...
MOSHUKS!!
EEEP!
THE ROBOT TURNED INTO AN OLD MAN!

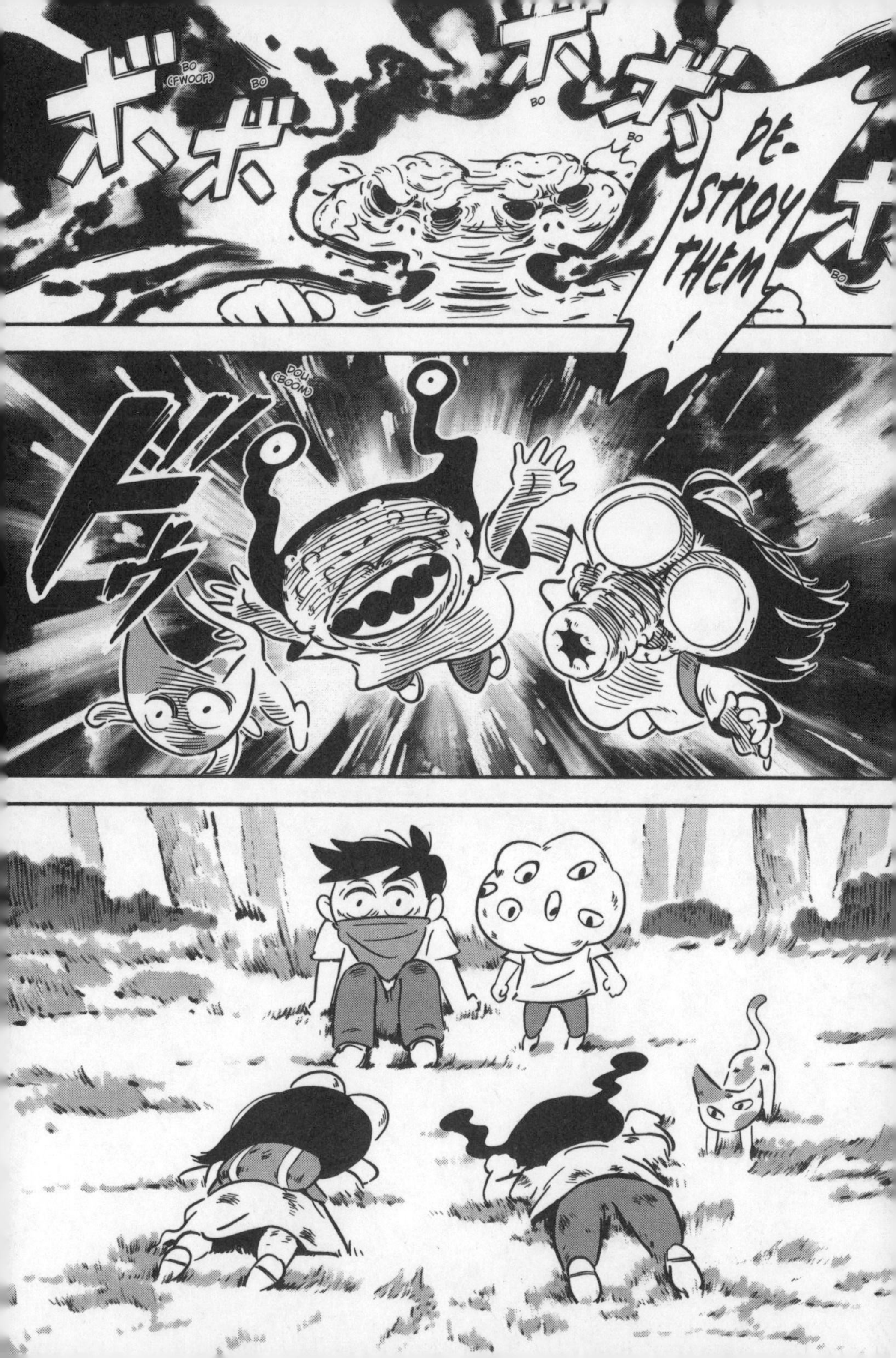
BO
DE-STROY THEM!
BO
BO
BO
BO (FWOOF)
DOU (BOOM)

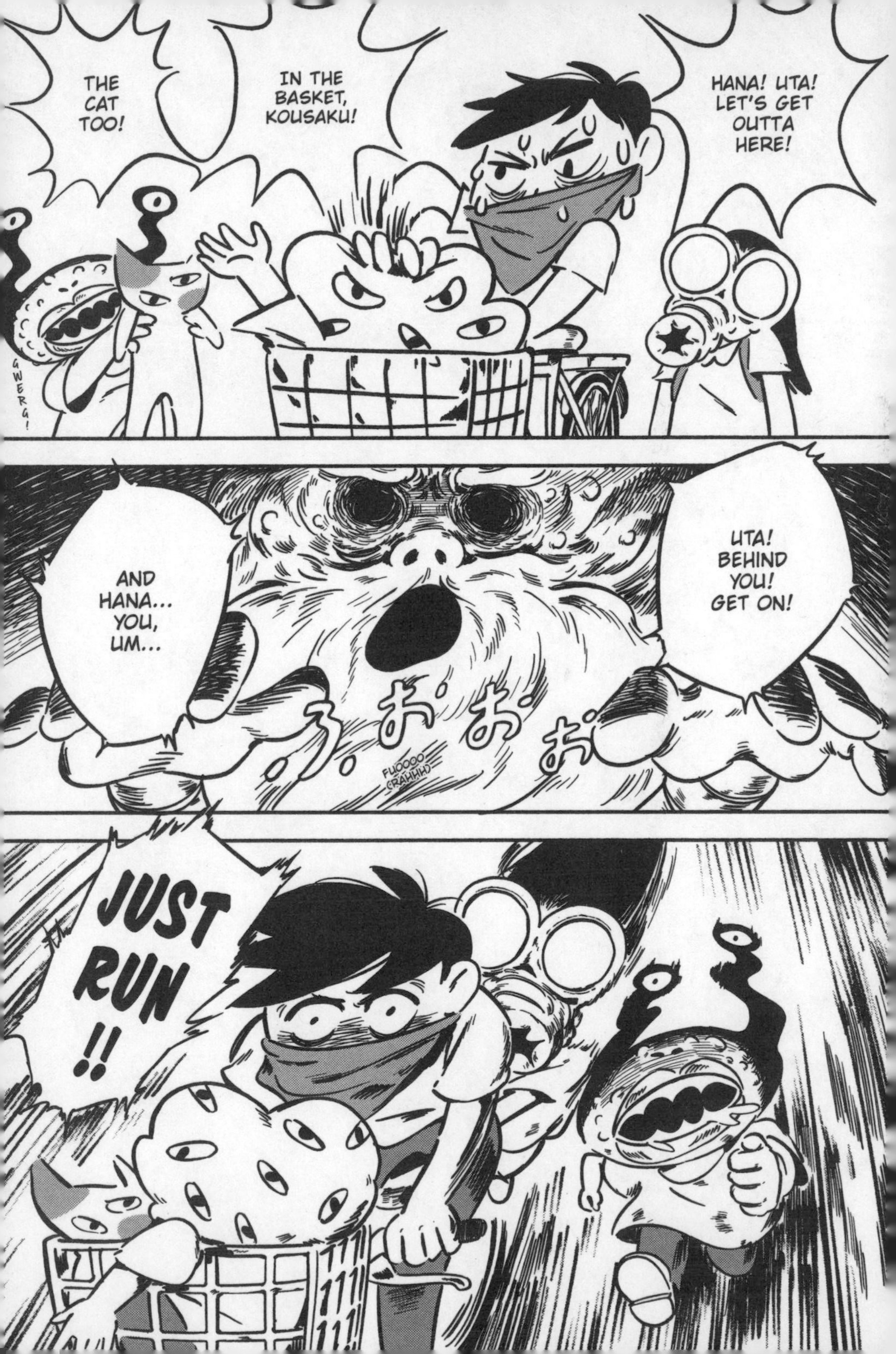

HANA! UTA! LET'S GET OUTTA HERE!
IN THE BASKET, KOUSAKU!
THE CAT TOO!
GWERG!
UTA! BEHIND YOU! GET ON!
FUOOOO (RAHHH)
AND HANA... YOU, UM...
JUST RUN!!

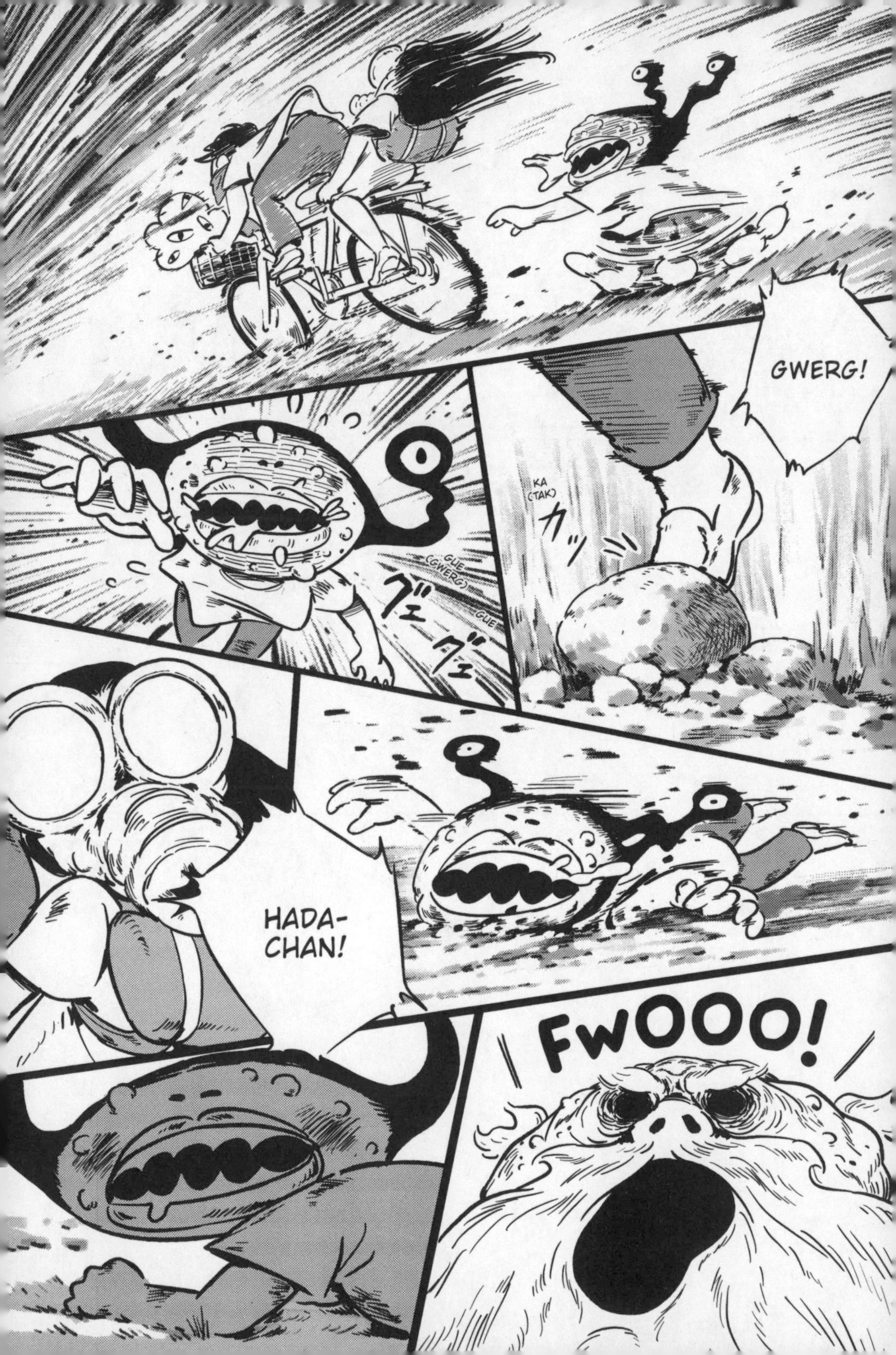
GWERG!
KA (TAK)
カッ
GUE (GWERG)
グェ
GUE
グェ
HADA-CHAN!
FwOOO!

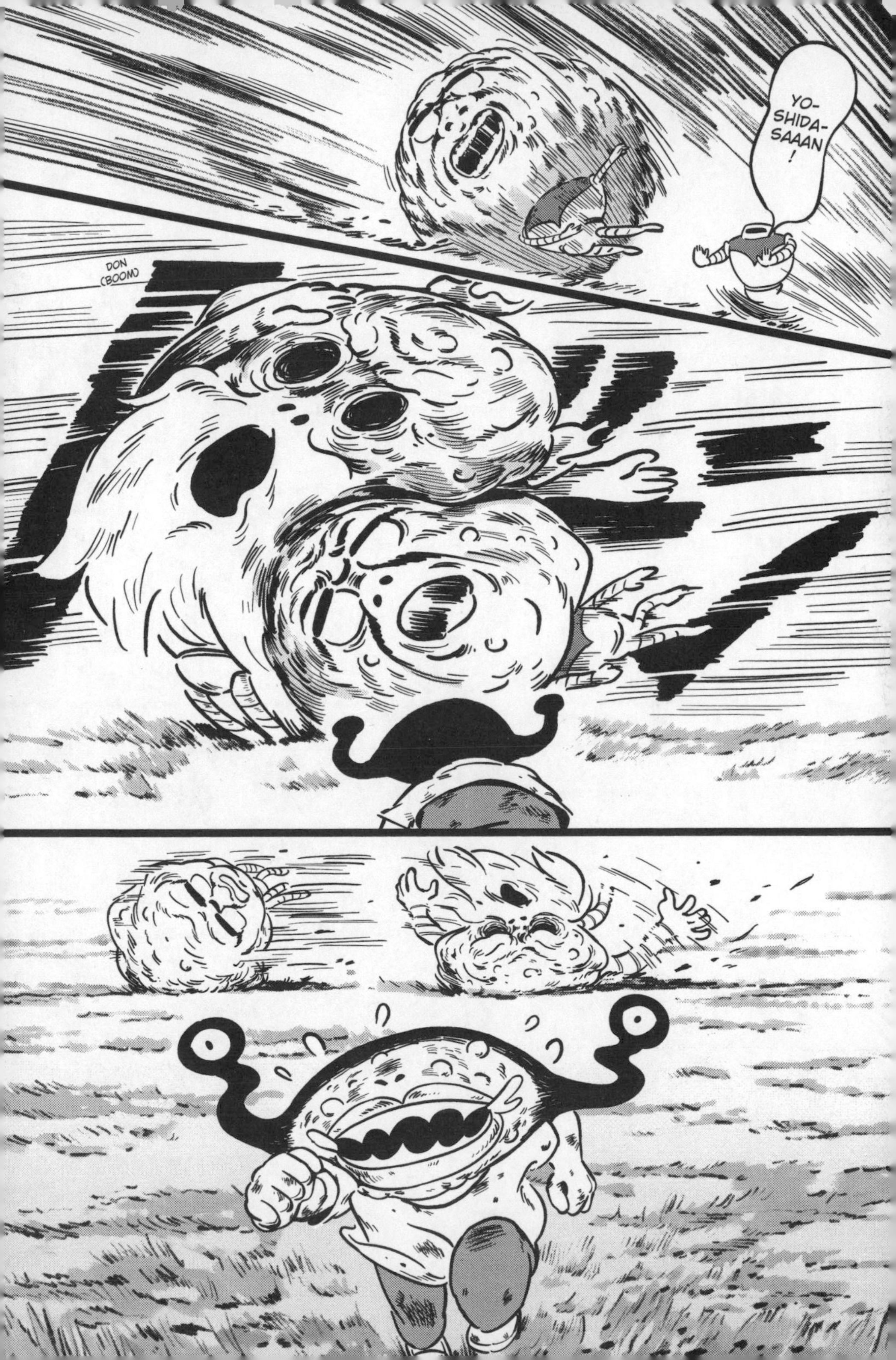
YO-
SHIDA-
SAAAN
!
DON
(BOOM)

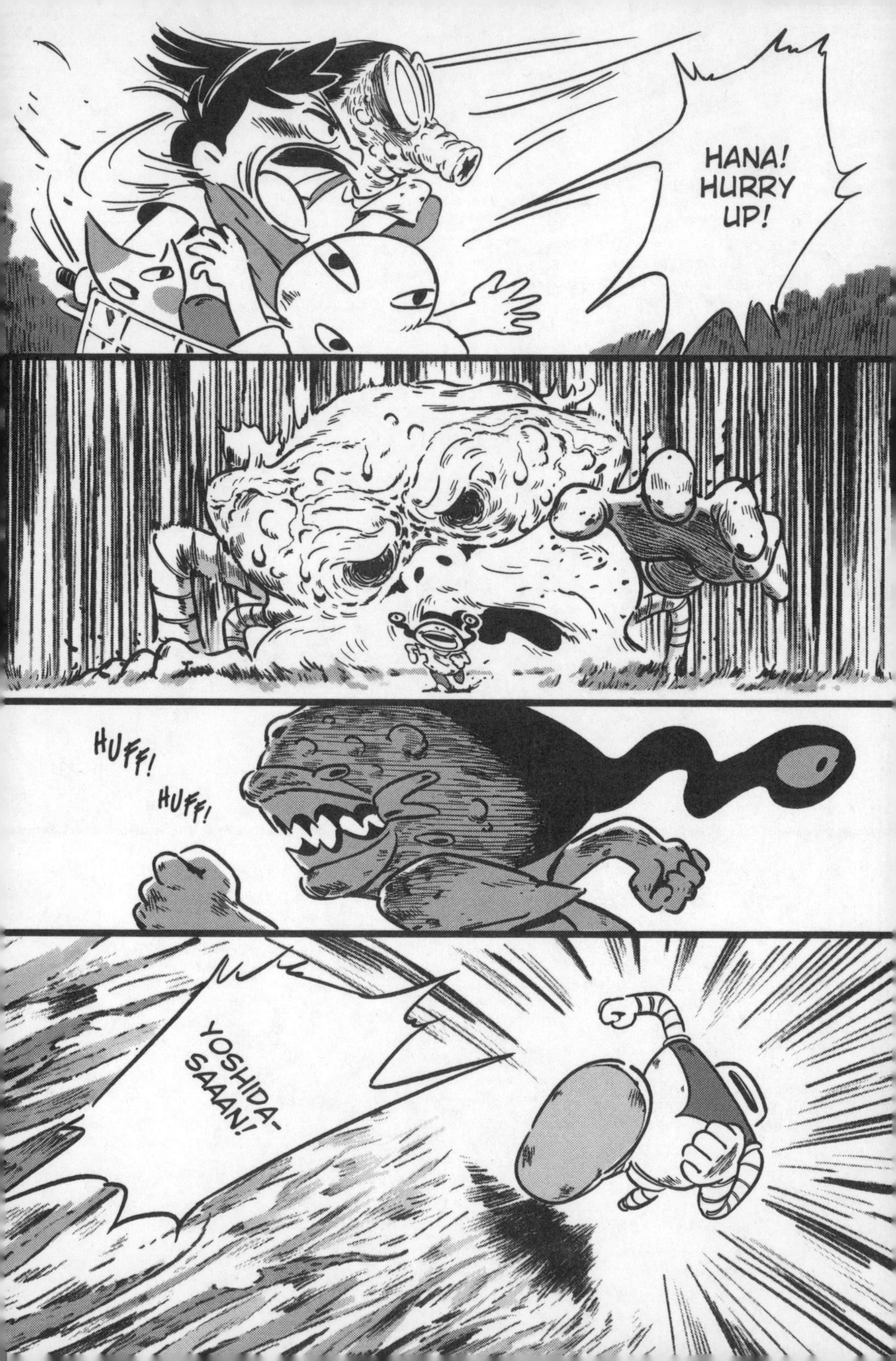
HANA! HURRY UP!
HUFF! HUFF!
YOSHIDA-SAAAN!

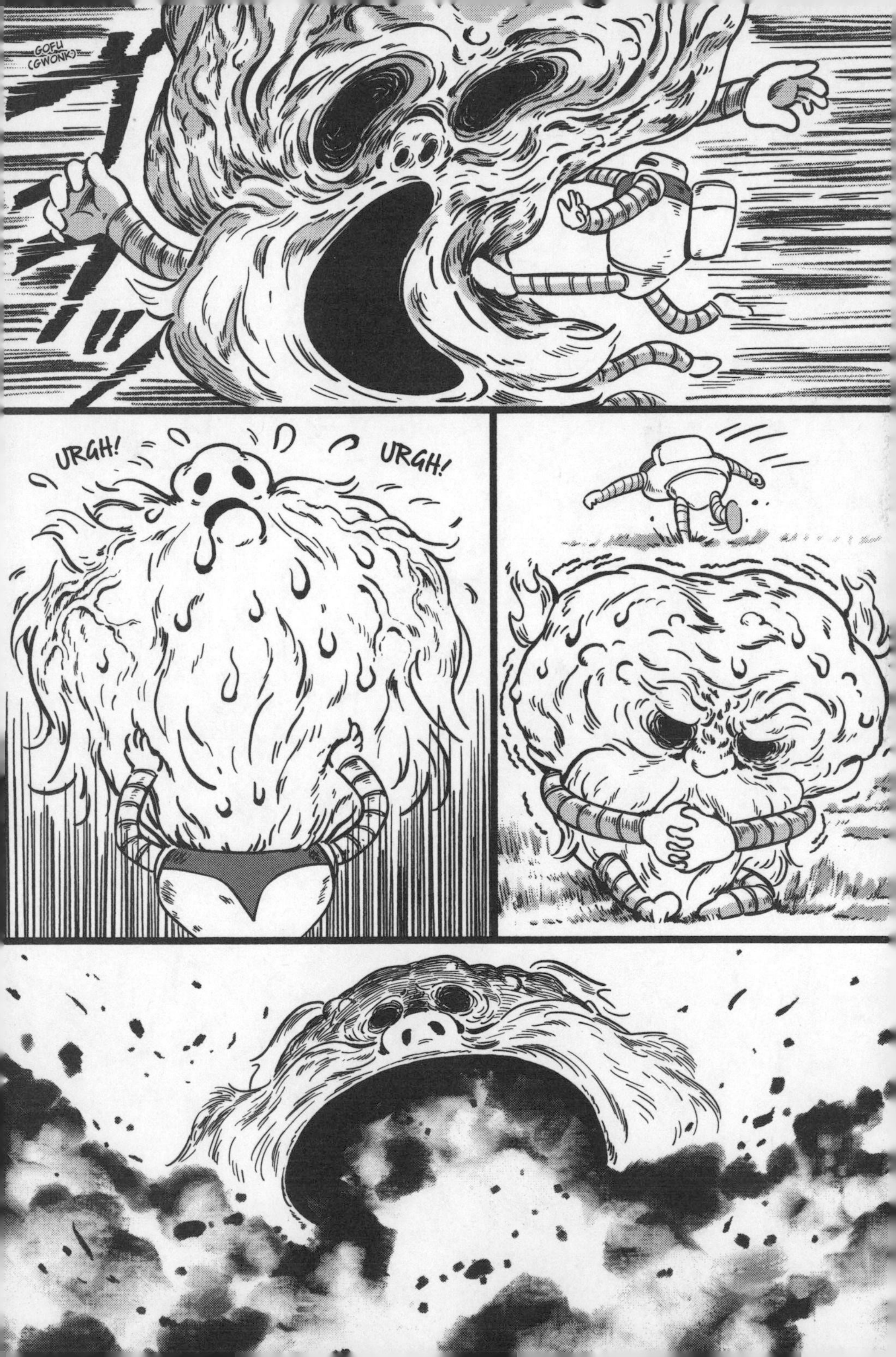
GOFU
(GWONK)
URGH!
URGH!

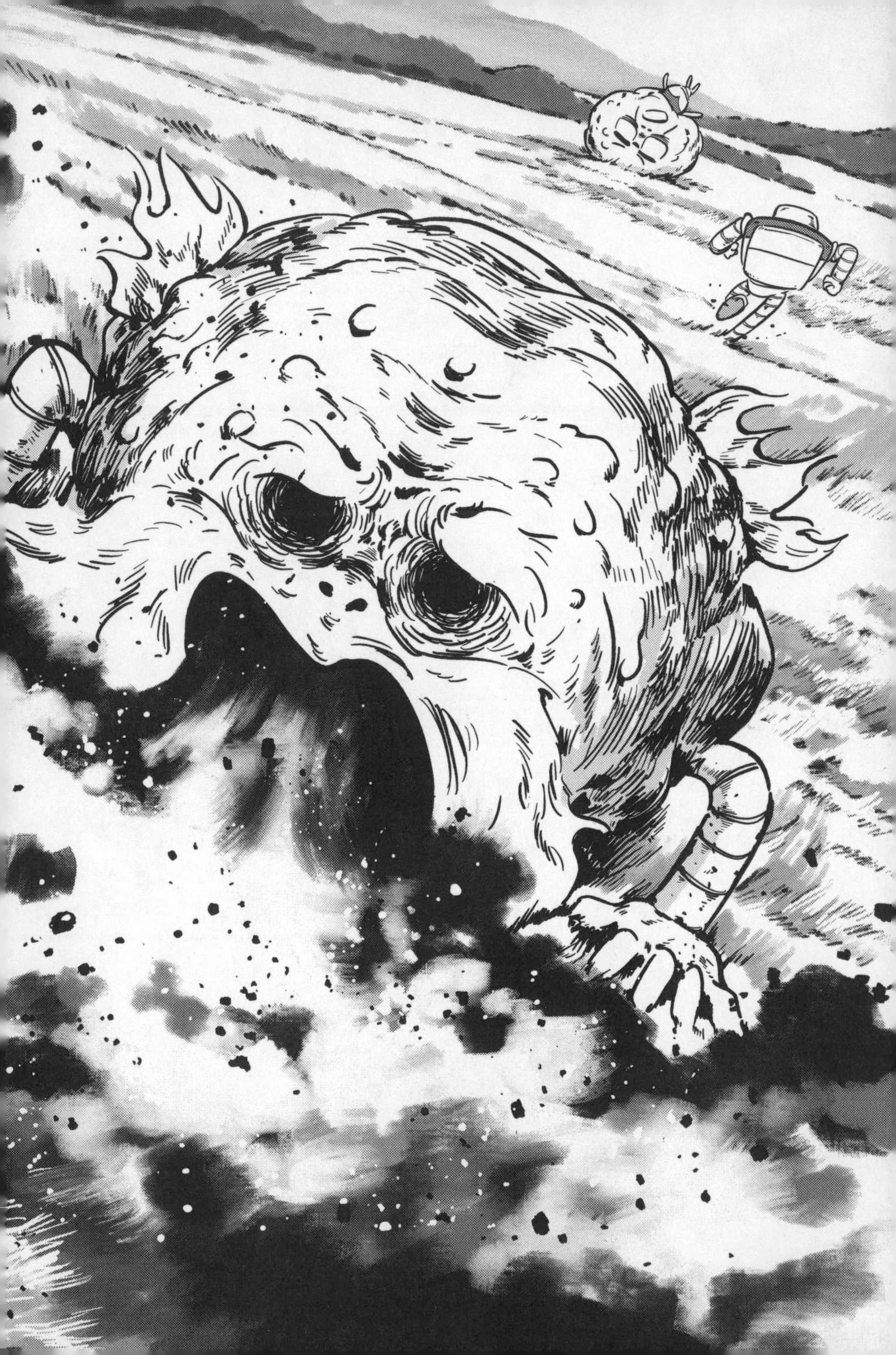

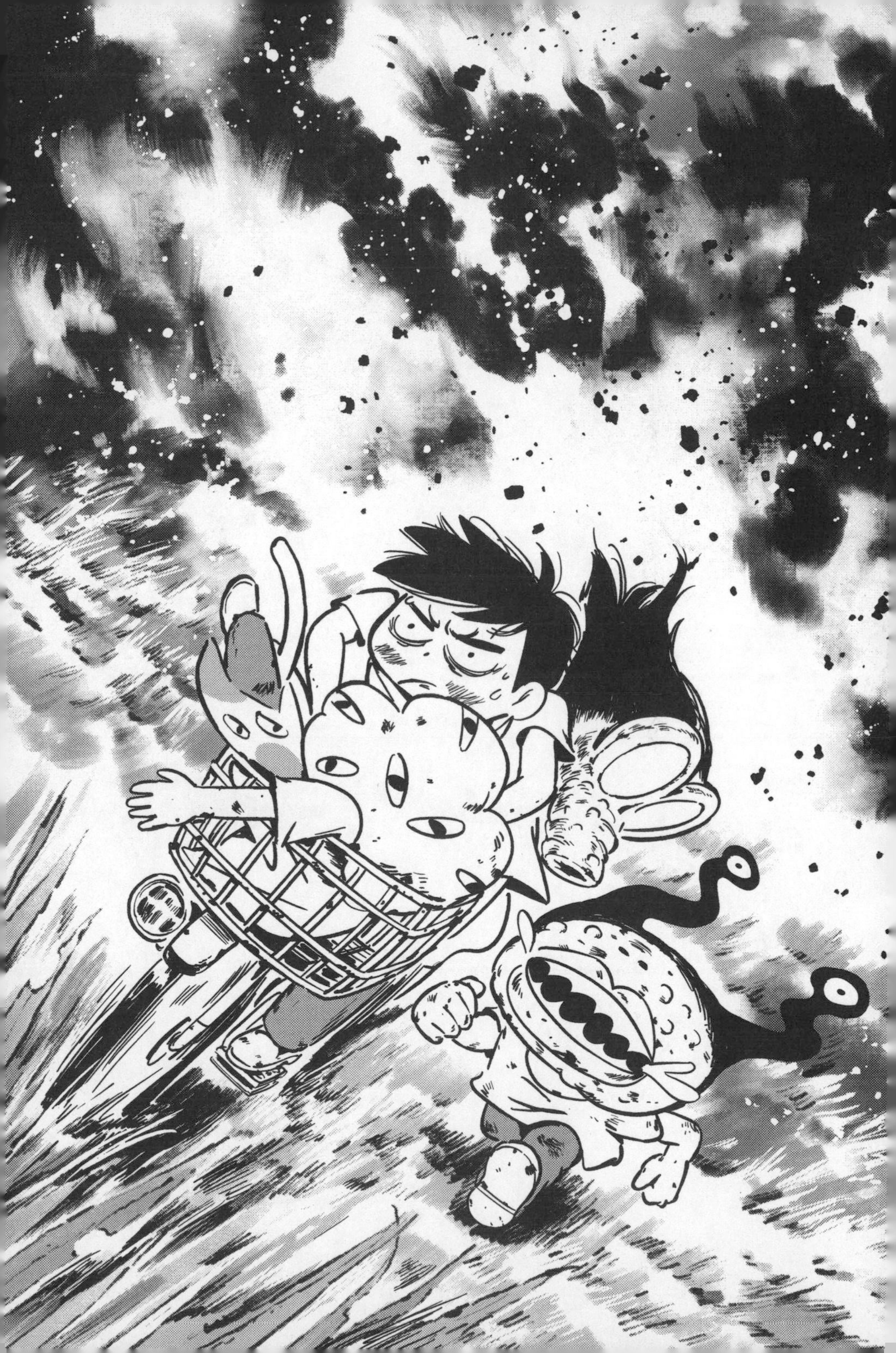

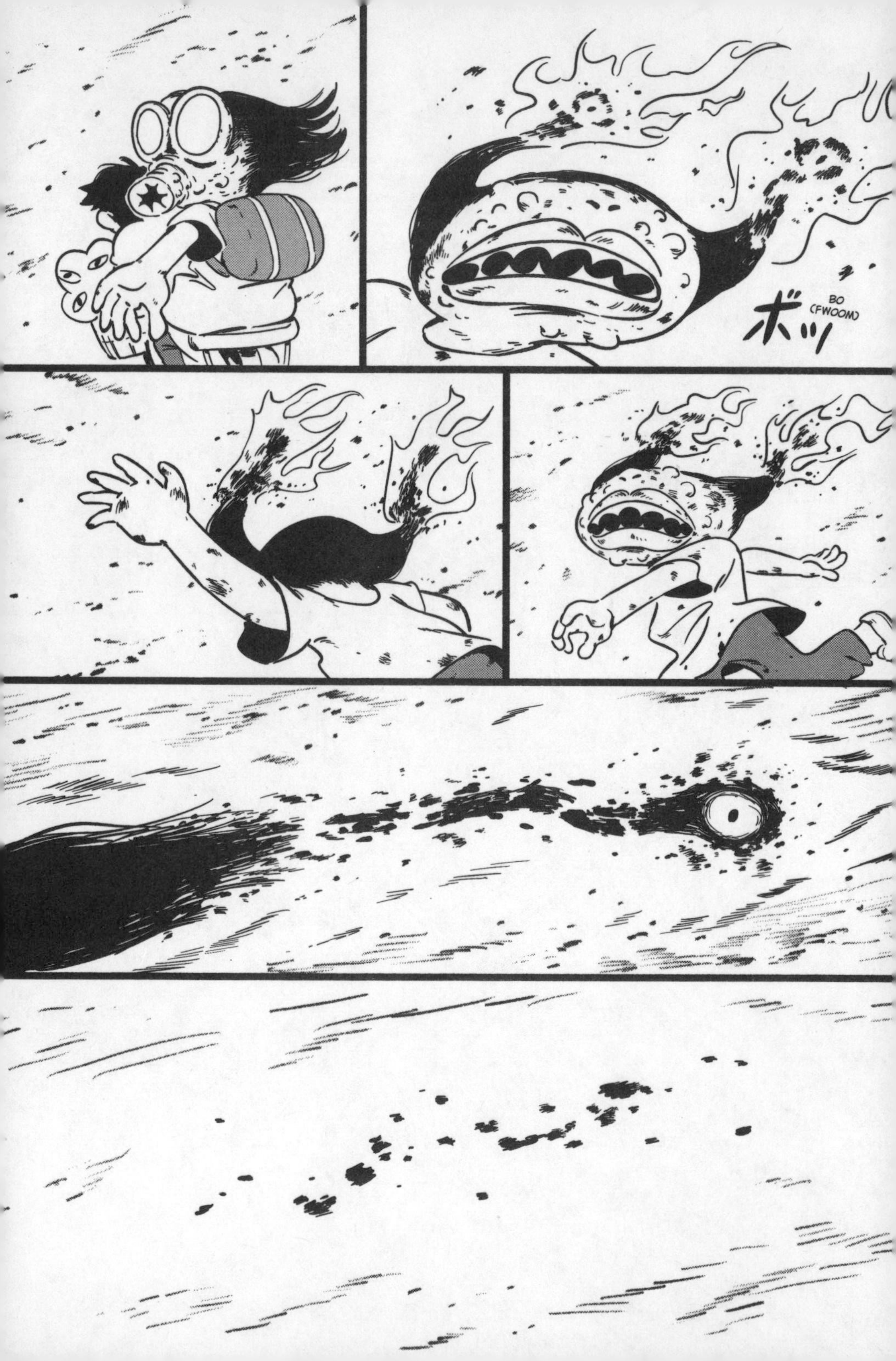
ボッ
BO
(FWOOM)

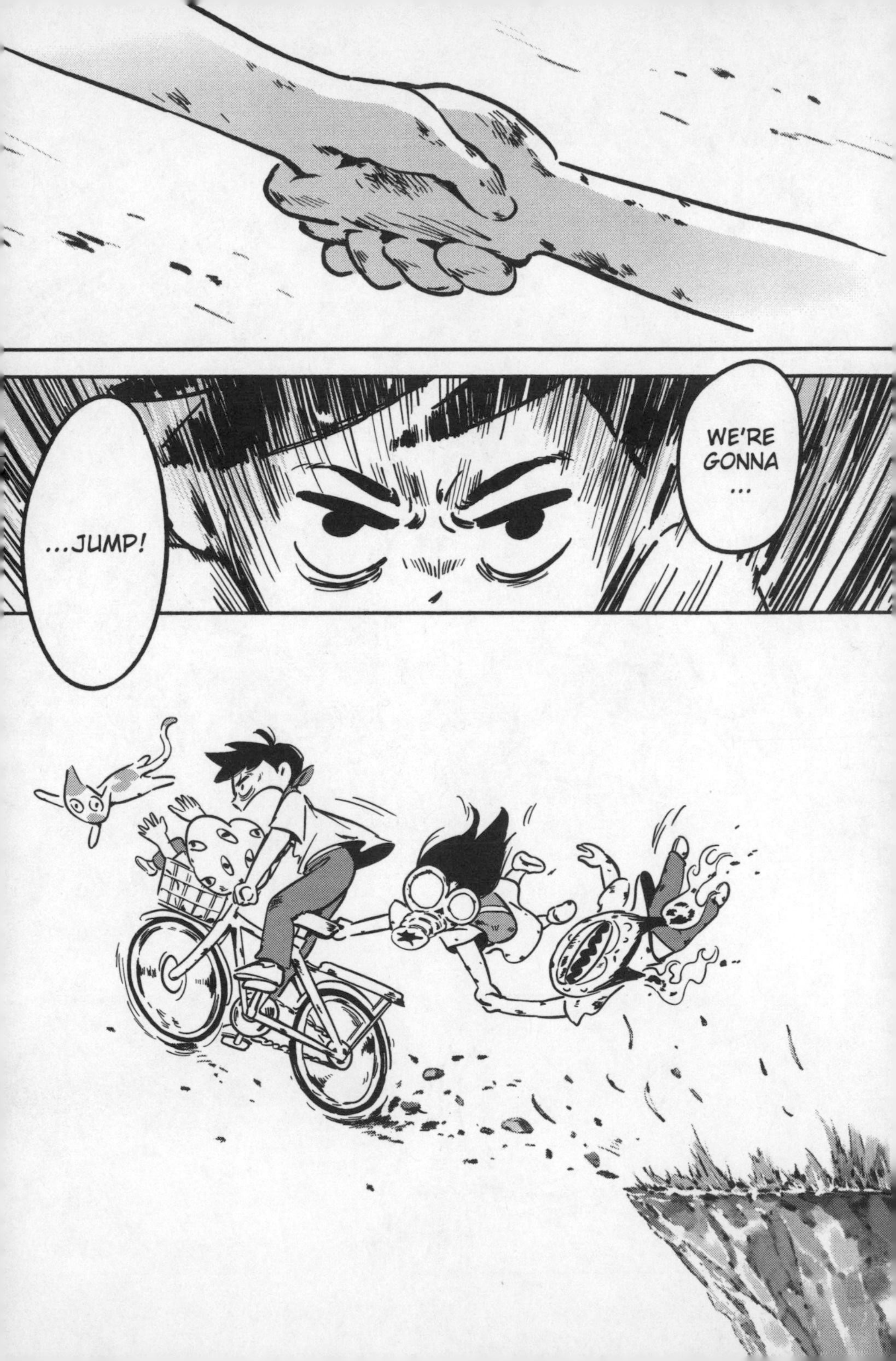
WE'RE GONNA ...
...JUMP!

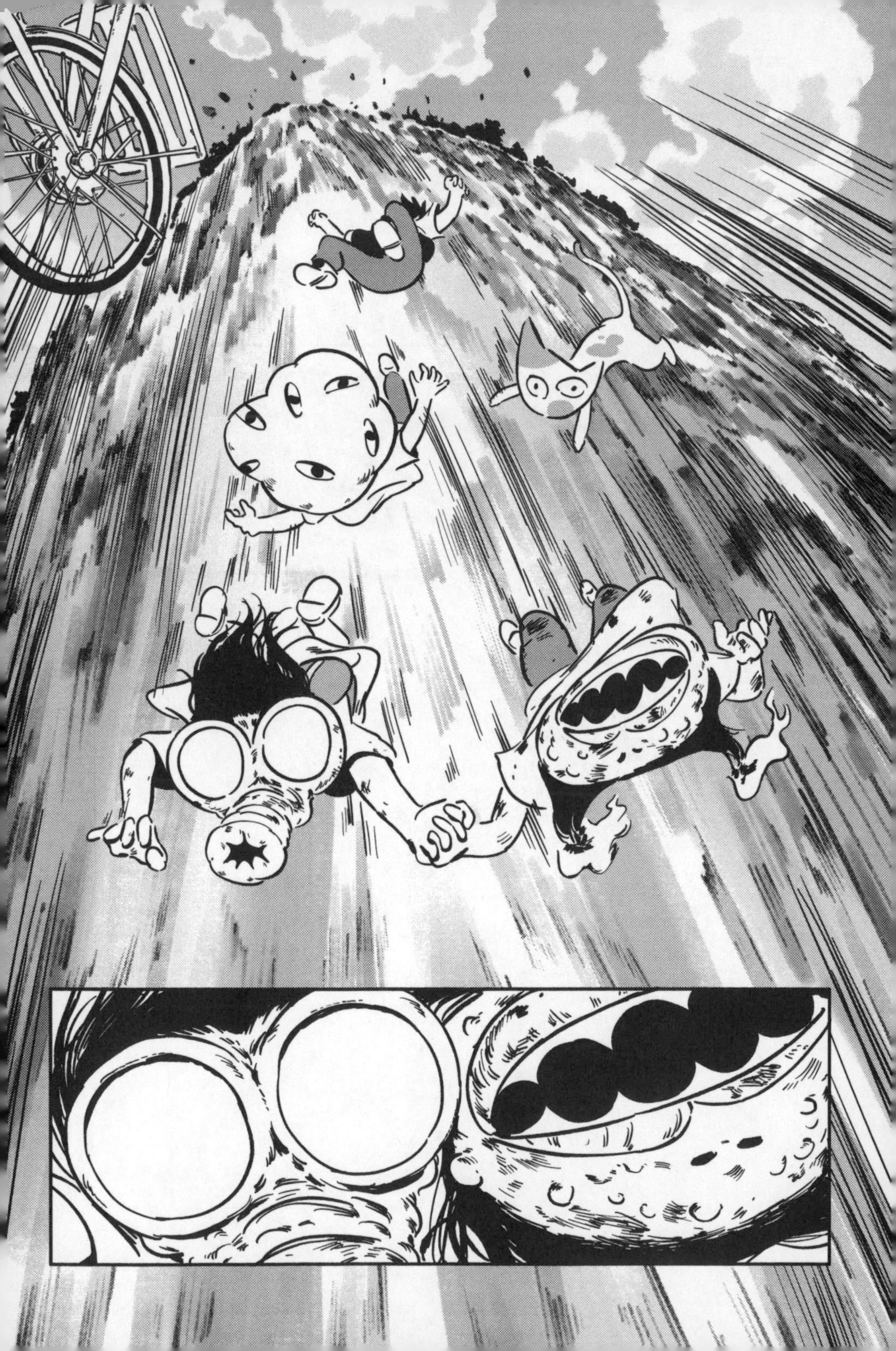

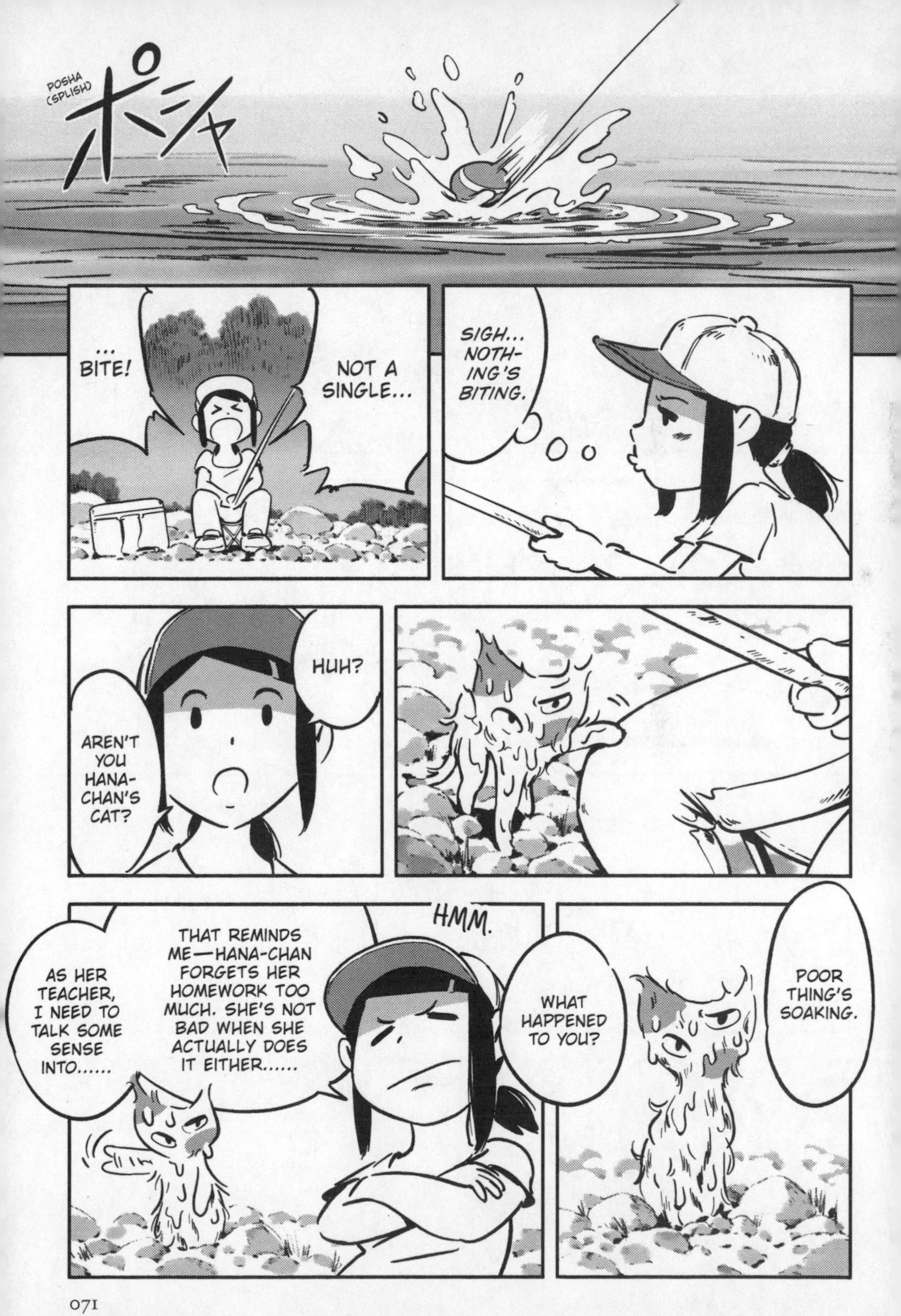

POSHA (SPLISH)
ポシャ
SIGH... NOTHING'S BITING.
NOT A SINGLE...
... BITE!
HUH?
AREN'T YOU HANA-CHAN'S CAT?
POOR THING'S SOAKING.
WHAT HAPPENED TO YOU?
HMM.
THAT REMINDS ME—HANA-CHAN FORGETS HER HOMEWORK TOO MUCH. SHE'S NOT BAD WHEN SHE ACTUALLY DOES IT EITHER......
AS HER TEACHER, I NEED TO TALK SOME SENSE INTO......

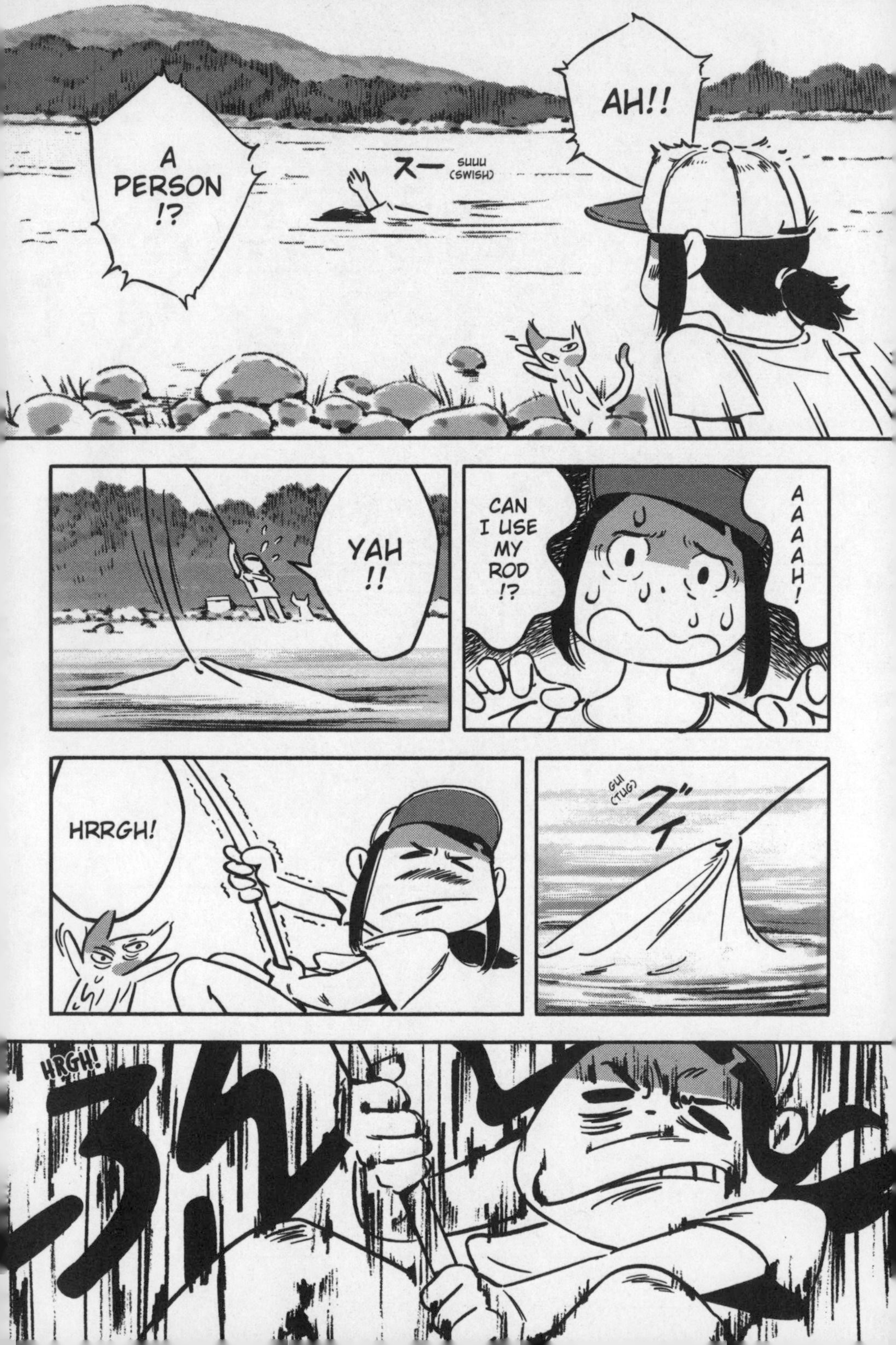
AH!!
A PERSON !?
スー
SUUU (SWISH)
AAAAAH!
CAN I USE MY ROD !?
YAH !!
グイ
GUI (TUG)
HRRGH!
ふん
HRGH!

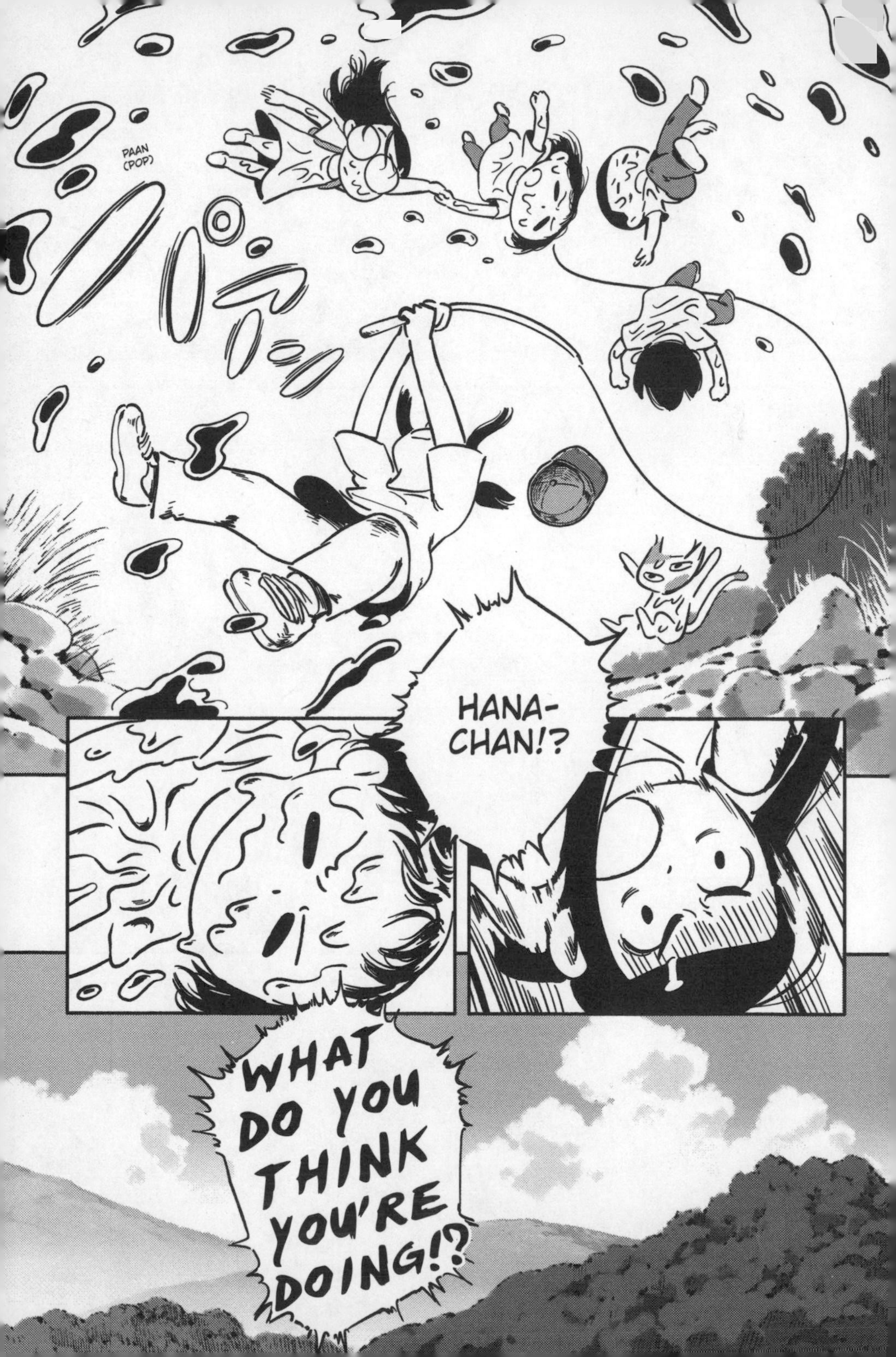
PAAN (POP)
HANA-CHAN!?
WHAT DO YOU THINK YOU'RE DOING!?

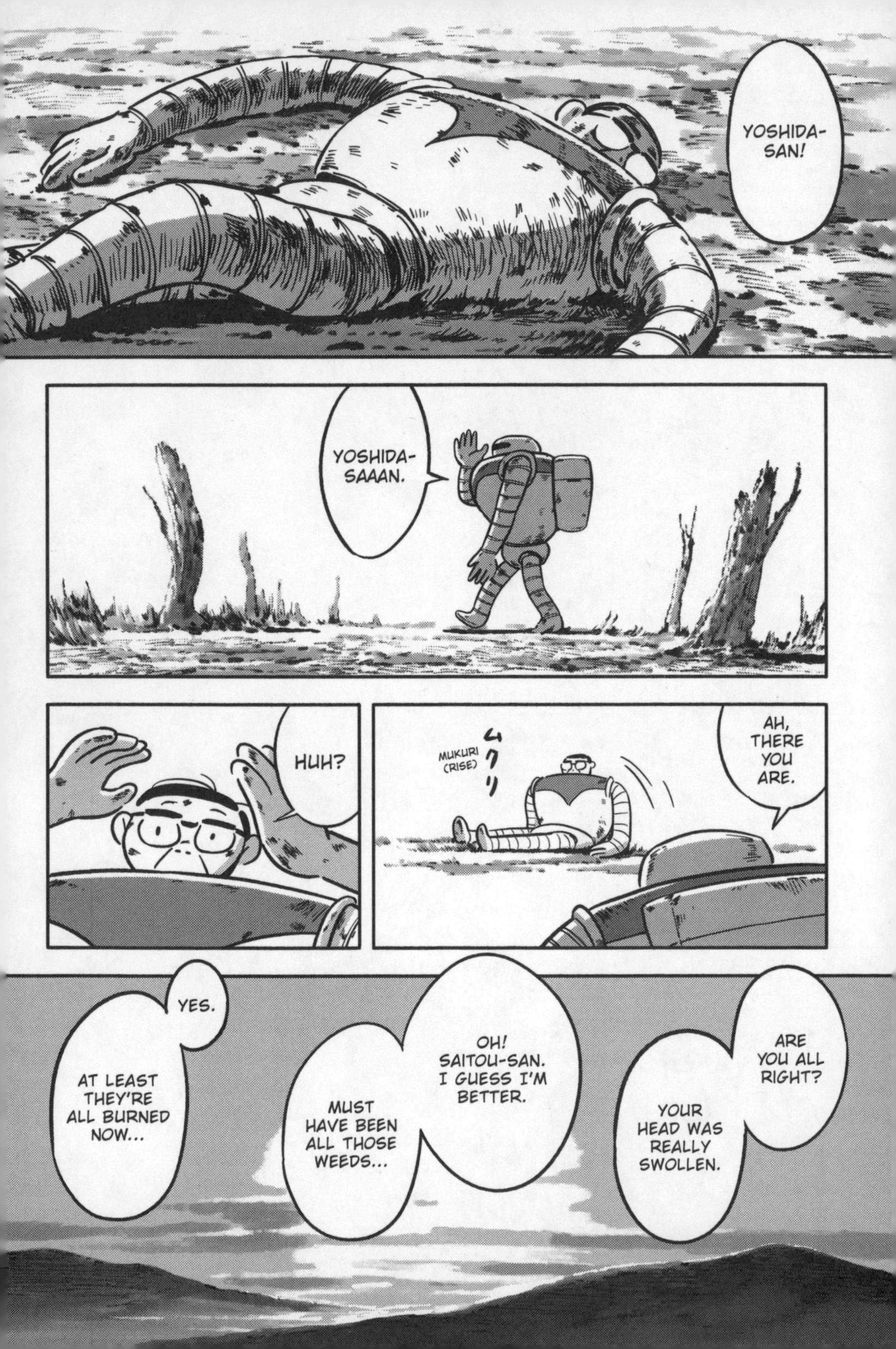
YOSHIDA-SAN!
YOSHIDA-SAAAN.
AH, THERE YOU ARE.
ムクリ
MUKURI (RISE)
HUH?
ARE YOU ALL RIGHT?
YOUR HEAD WAS REALLY SWOLLEN.
OH! SAITOU-SAN. I GUESS I'M BETTER.
MUST HAVE BEEN ALL THOSE WEEDS...
YES.
AT LEAST THEY'RE ALL BURNED NOW...

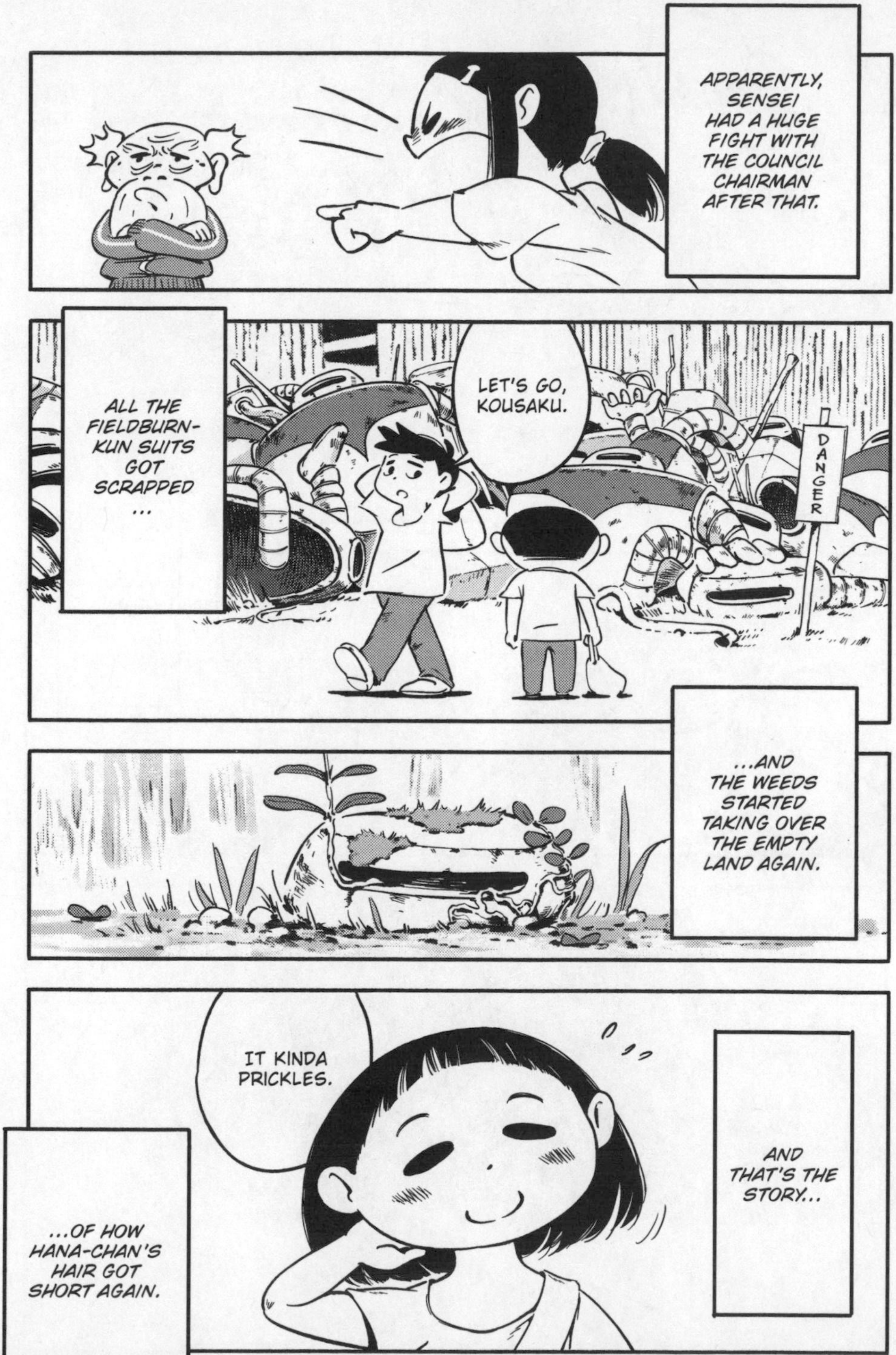
APPARENTLY, SENSEI HAD A HUGE FIGHT WITH THE COUNCIL CHAIRMAN AFTER THAT.
LET'S GO, KOUSAKU.
DANGER
ALL THE FIELDBURN-KUN SUITS GOT SCRAPPED ...
...AND THE WEEDS STARTED TAKING OVER THE EMPTY LAND AGAIN.
AND THAT'S THE STORY...
IT KINDA PRICKLES.
...OF HOW HANA-CHAN'S HAIR GOT SHORT AGAIN.

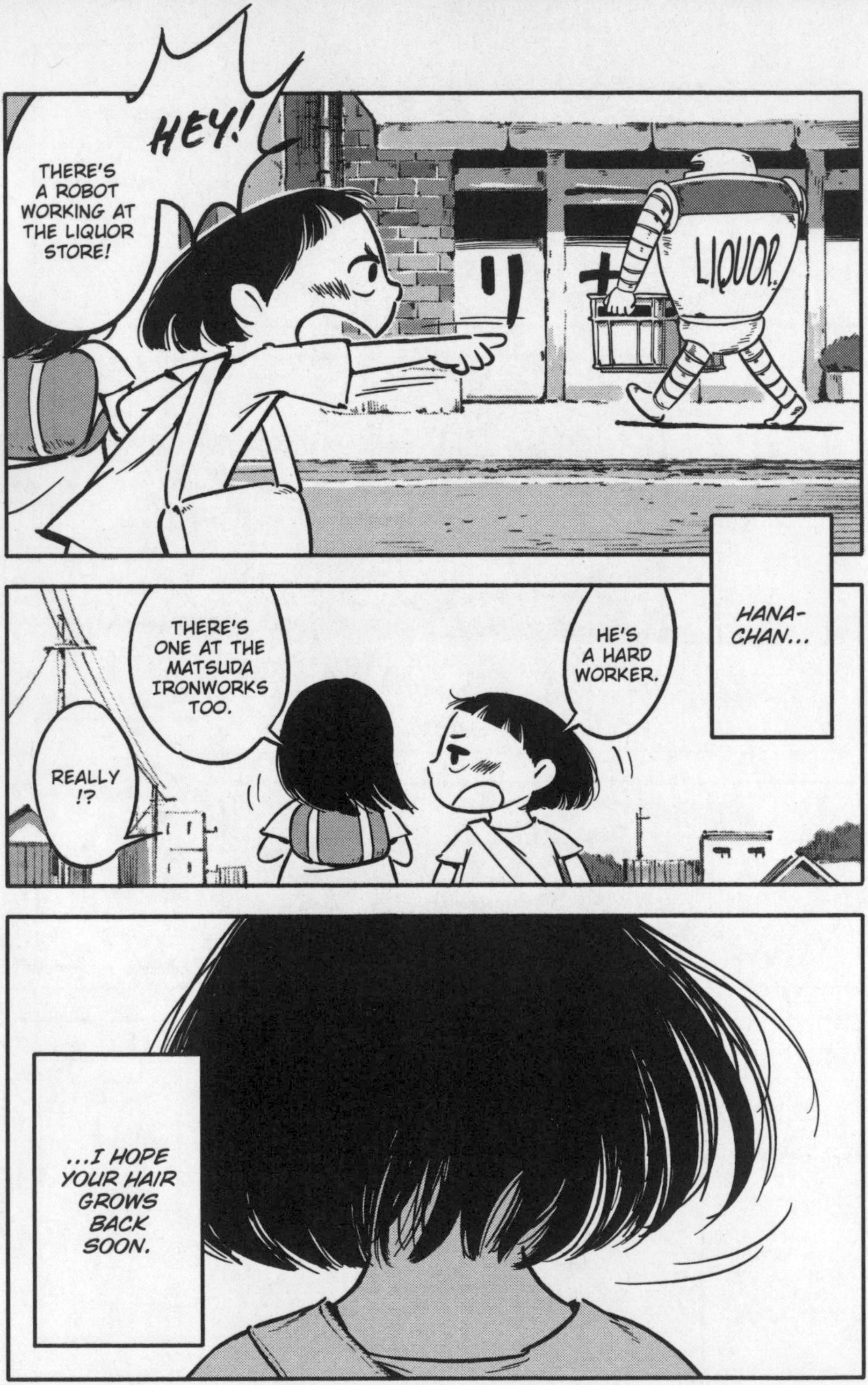
HEY!
THERE'S A ROBOT WORKING AT THE LIQUOR STORE!
LIQUOR
HANA-CHAN...
HE'S A HARD WORKER.
THERE'S ONE AT THE MATSUDA IRONWORKS TOO.
REALLY !?
...I HOPE YOUR HAIR GROWS BACK SOON.

Hana-chan
and the Shape of the World

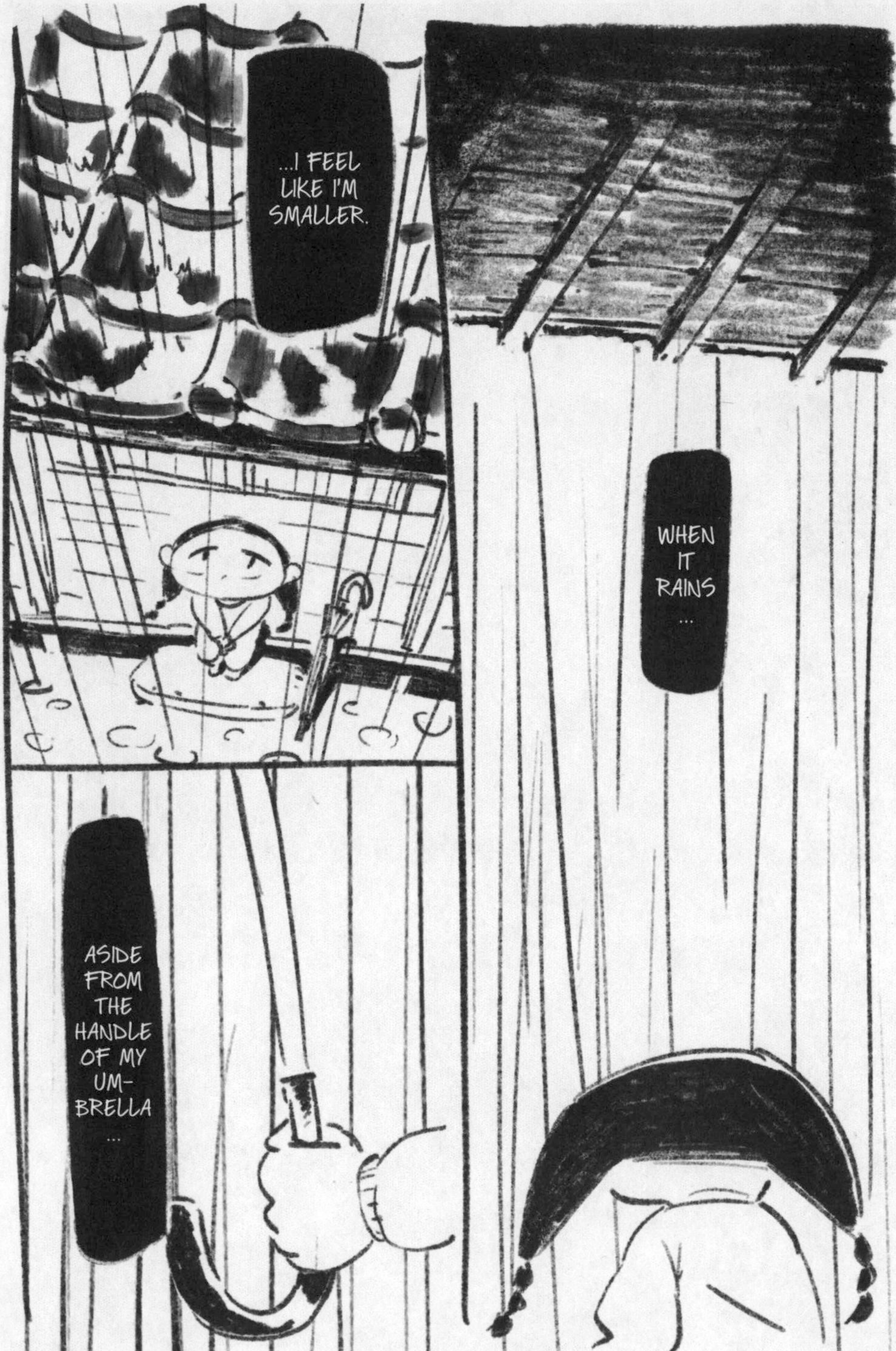
WHEN IT RAINS ...
...I FEEL LIKE I'M SMALLER.
ASIDE FROM THE HANDLE OF MY UM-BRELLA ...

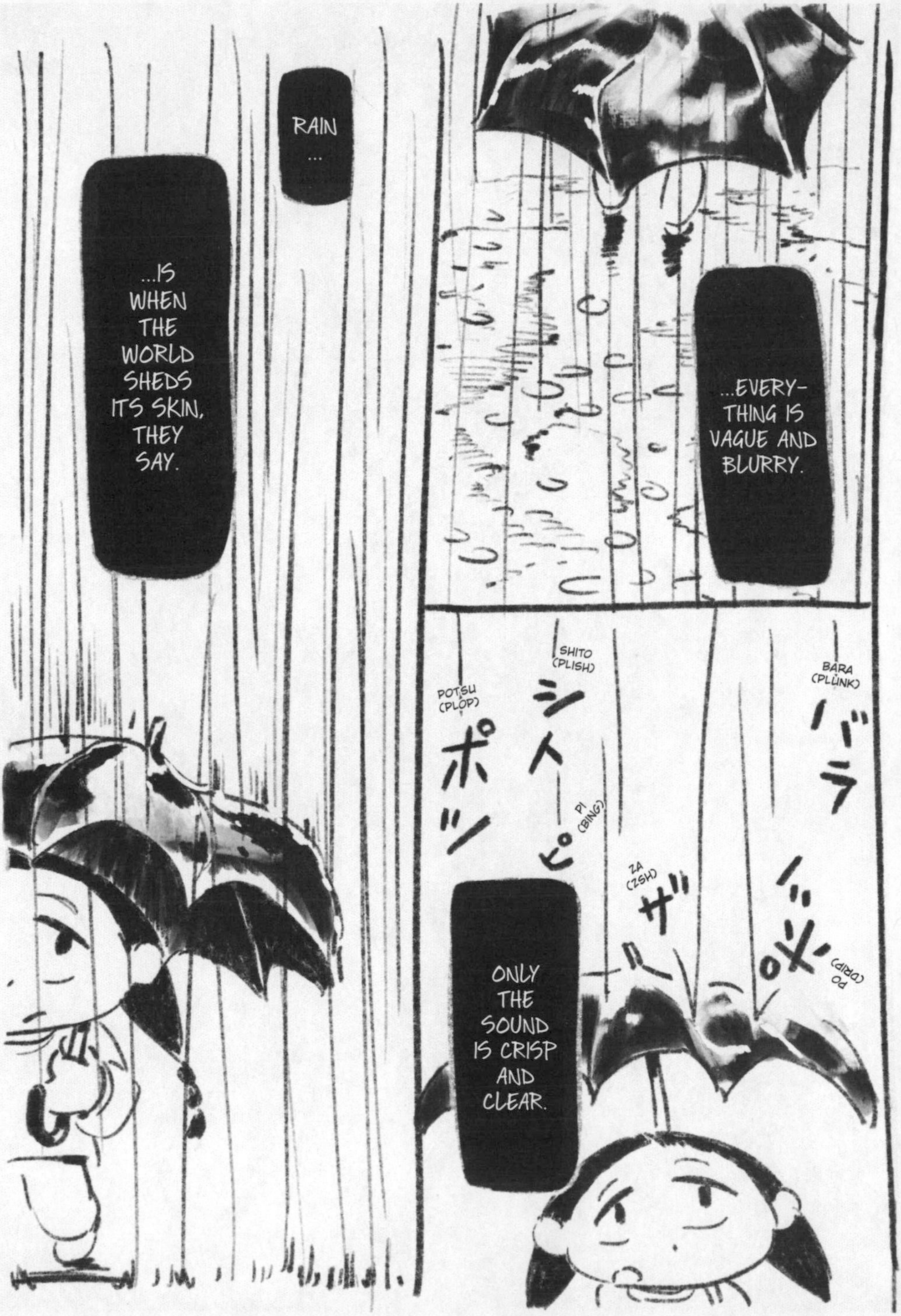

...EVERY-THING IS VAGUE AND BLURRY.
BARA (PLÜNK)
バラ
SHITO (PLISH)
シト
POTSU (PLOP)
ポツ
PI (BING)
ピ
ZA (ZSH)
ザ
PO (DRIP)
ONLY THE SOUND IS CRISP AND CLEAR.
RAIN ...
...IS WHEN THE WORLD SHEDS ITS SKIN, THEY SAY.

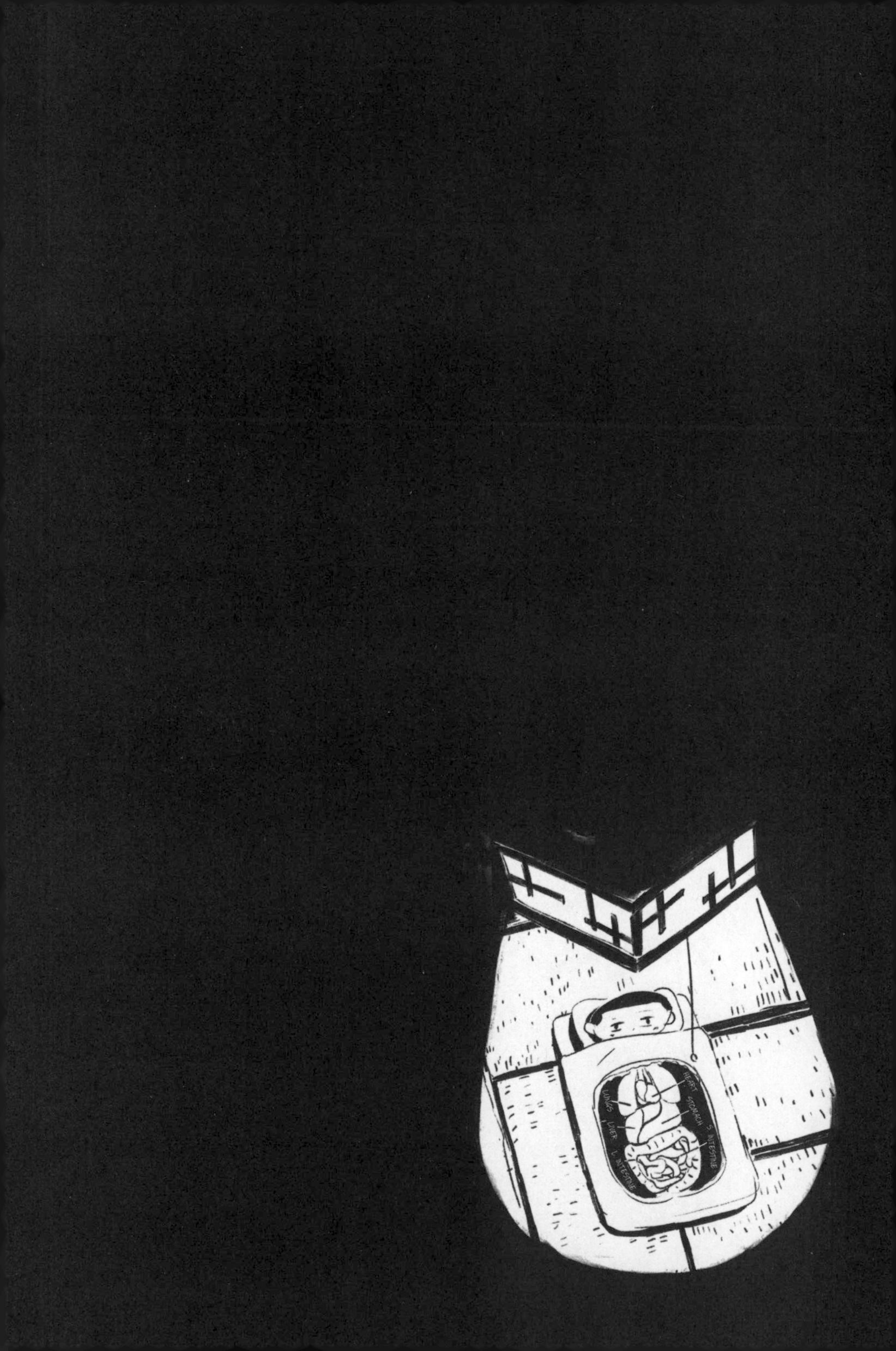
HEART
STOMACH
S INTESTINE
LUNGS
LIVER
L INTESTINE

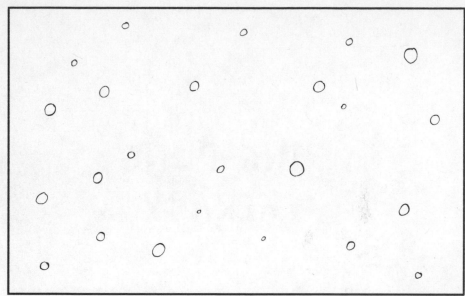

PING-PONG THERAPY

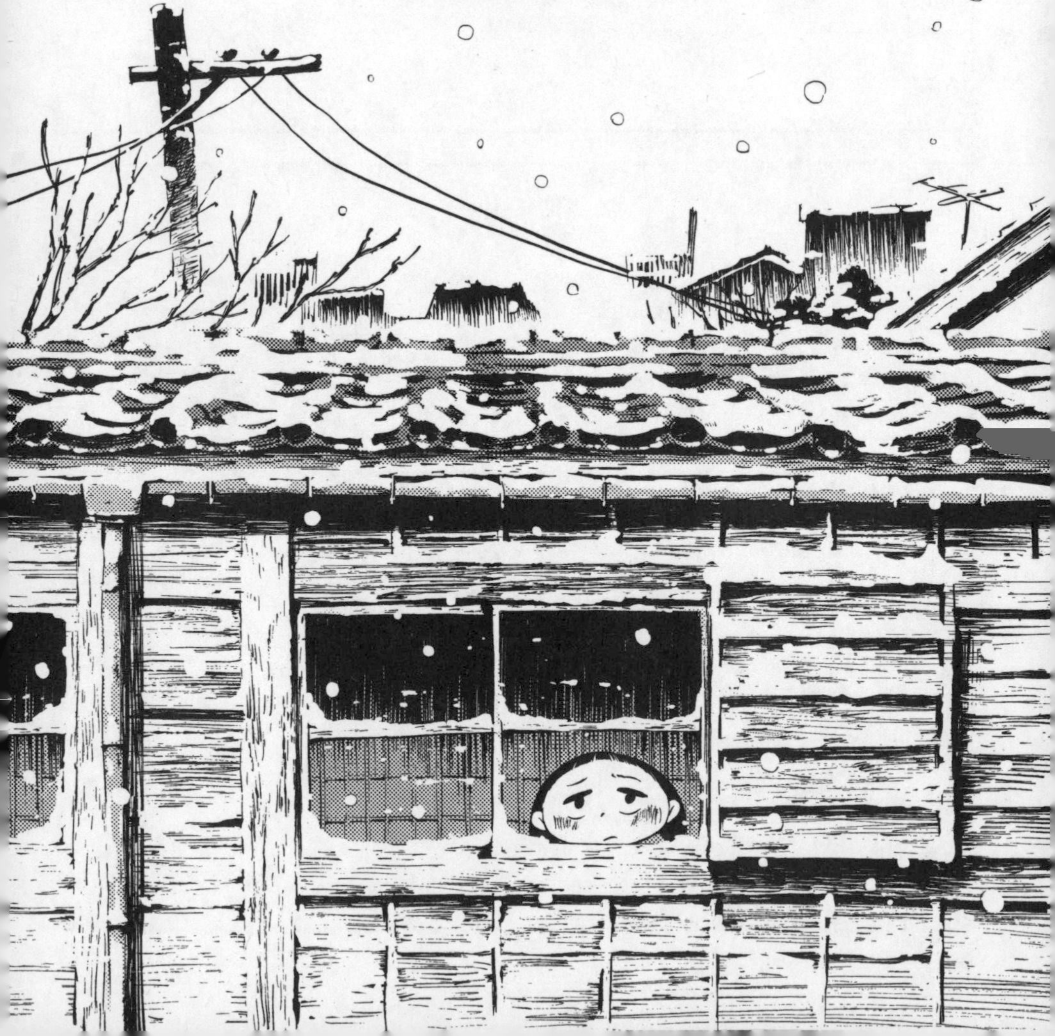

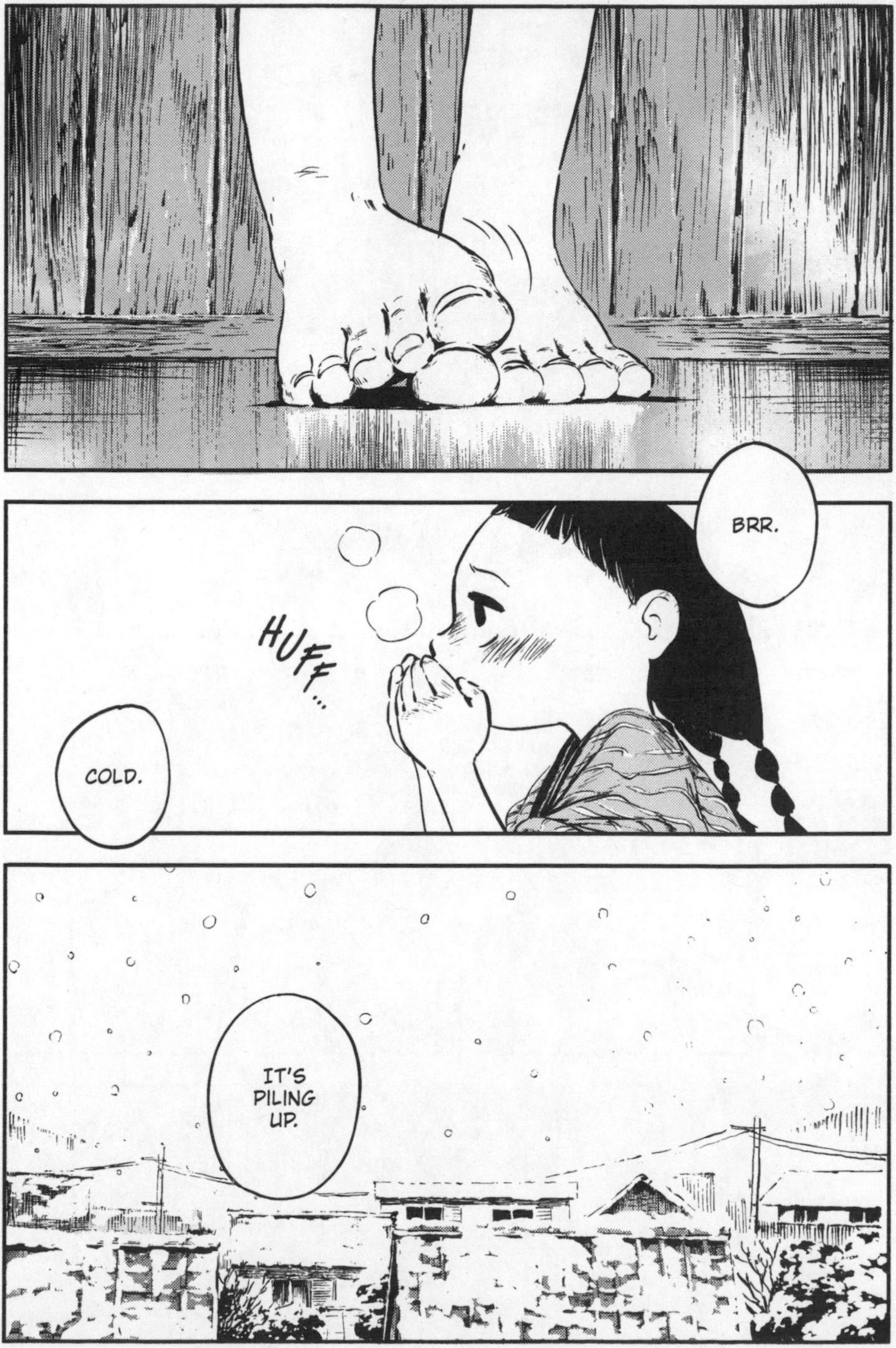
BRR.
HUFF...
COLD.
IT'S PILING UP.

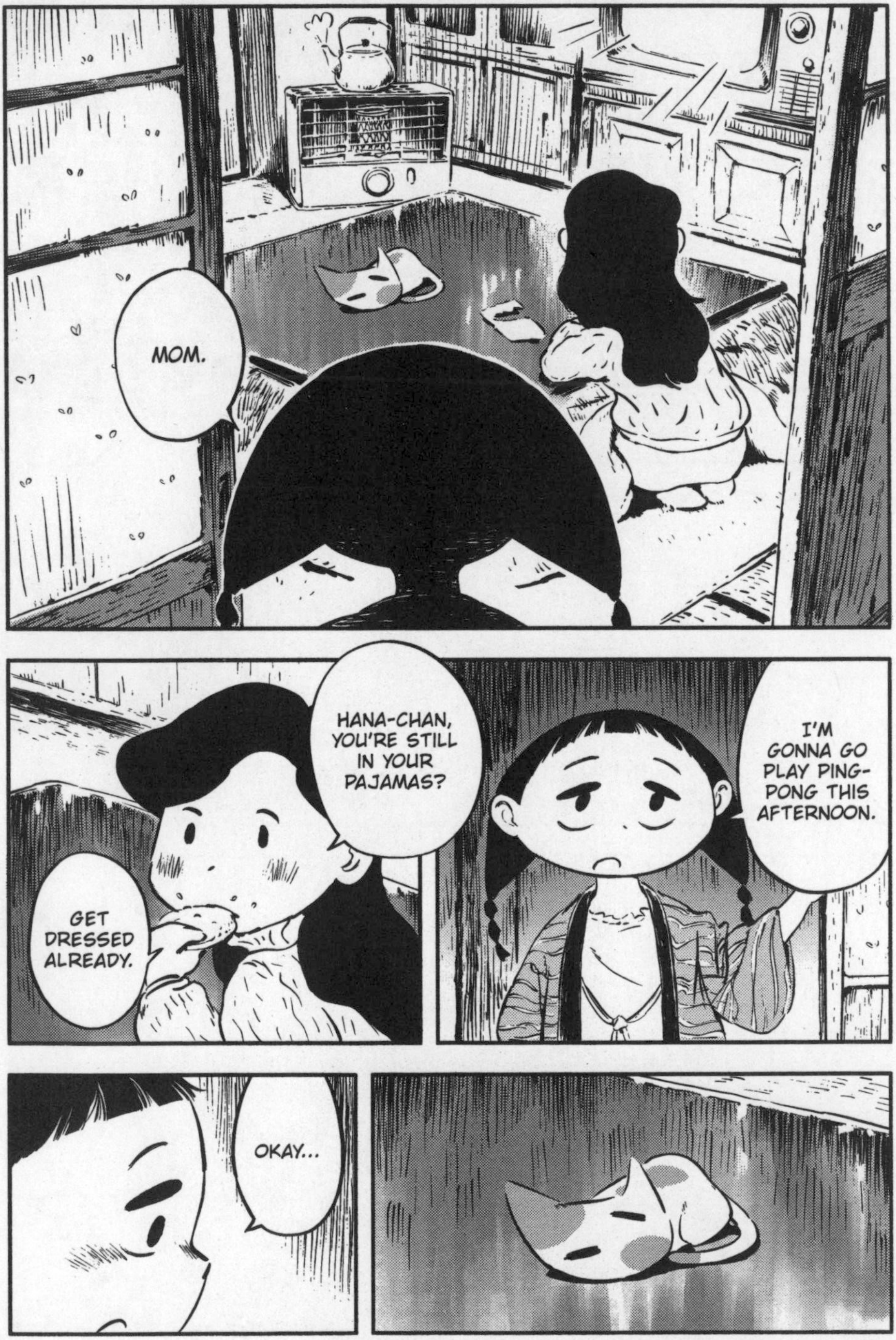
MOM.
I'M GONNA GO PLAY PING-PONG THIS AFTERNOON.
HANA-CHAN, YOU'RE STILL IN YOUR PAJAMAS?
GET DRESSED ALREADY.
OKAY...

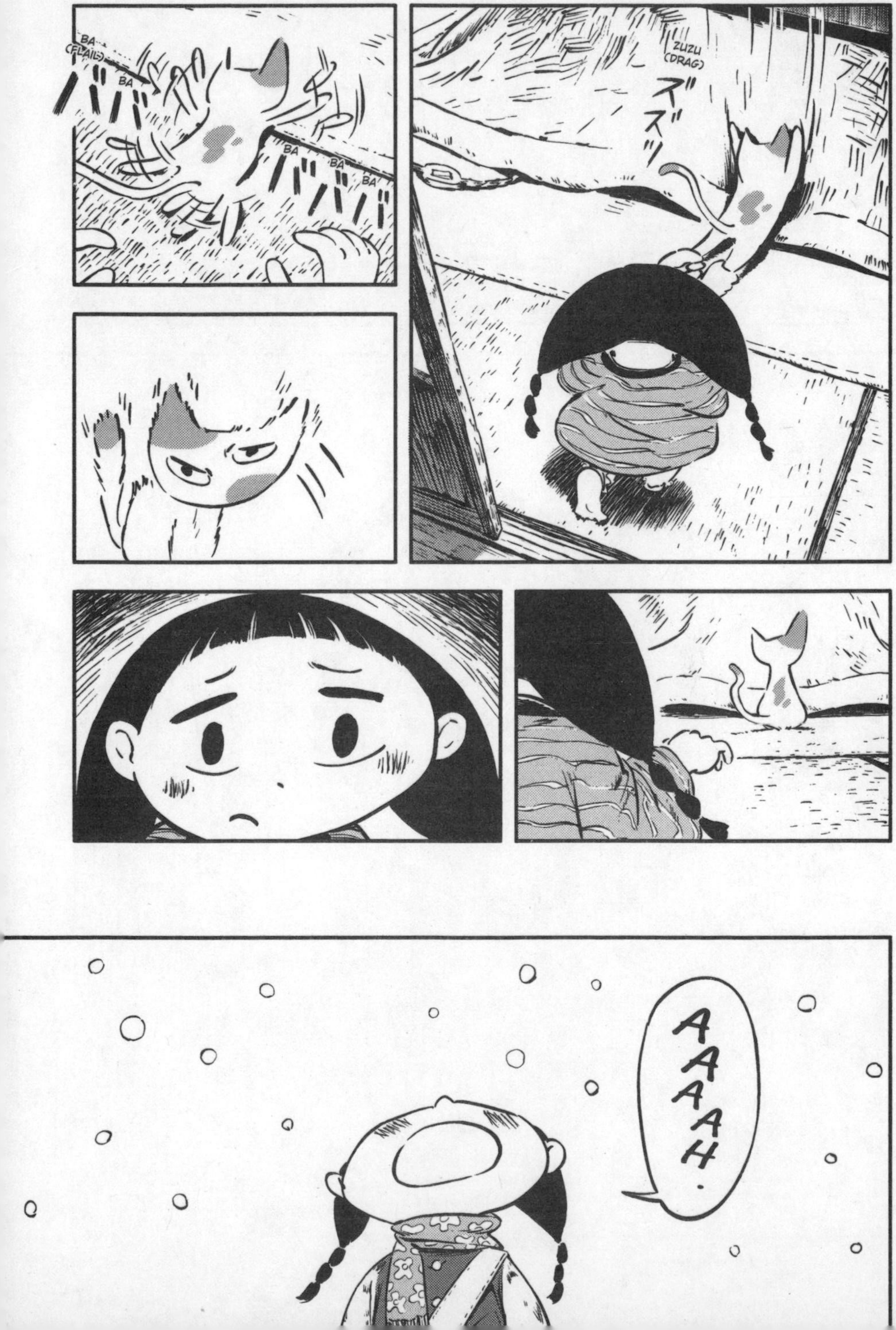
ZUZU (DRAG)
BA (FLAIL)
BA
BA
BA
BA
AAAAH.

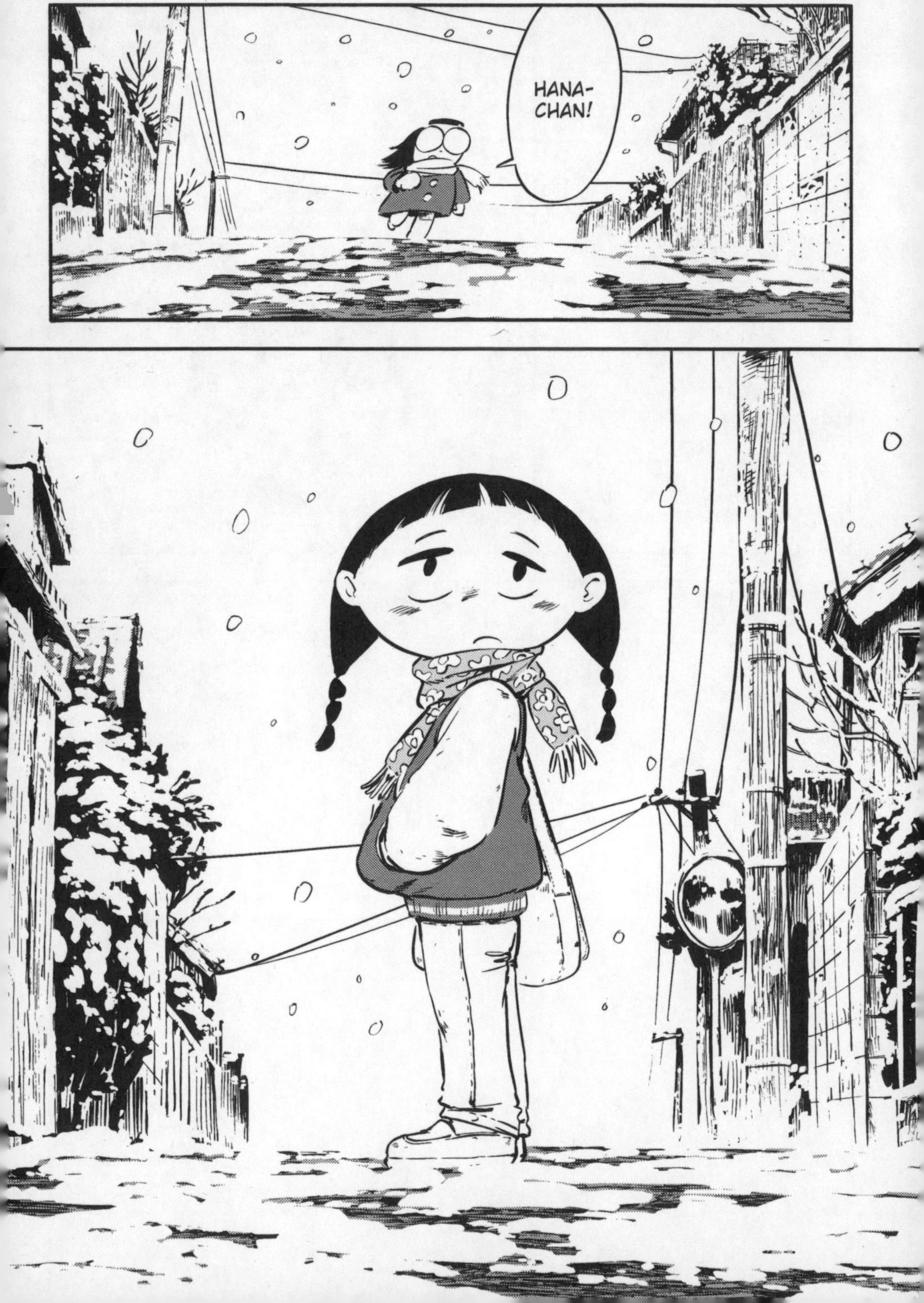
HANA-CHAN!

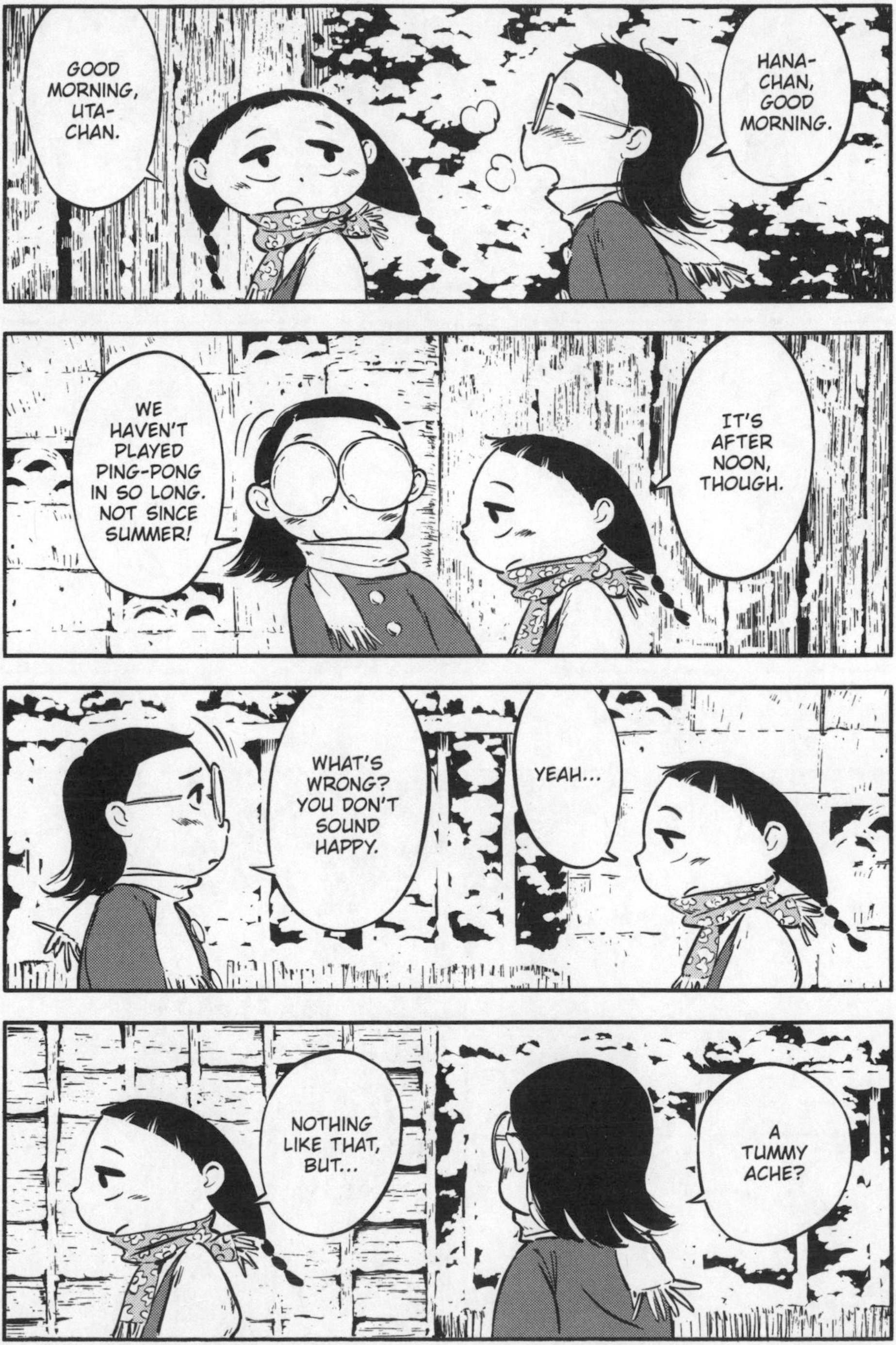
HANA-CHAN, GOOD MORNING.
GOOD MORNING, UTA-CHAN.
IT'S AFTER NOON, THOUGH.
WE HAVEN'T PLAYED PING-PONG IN SO LONG. NOT SINCE SUMMER!
YEAH...
WHAT'S WRONG? YOU DON'T SOUND HAPPY.
A TUMMY ACHE?
NOTHING LIKE THAT, BUT...

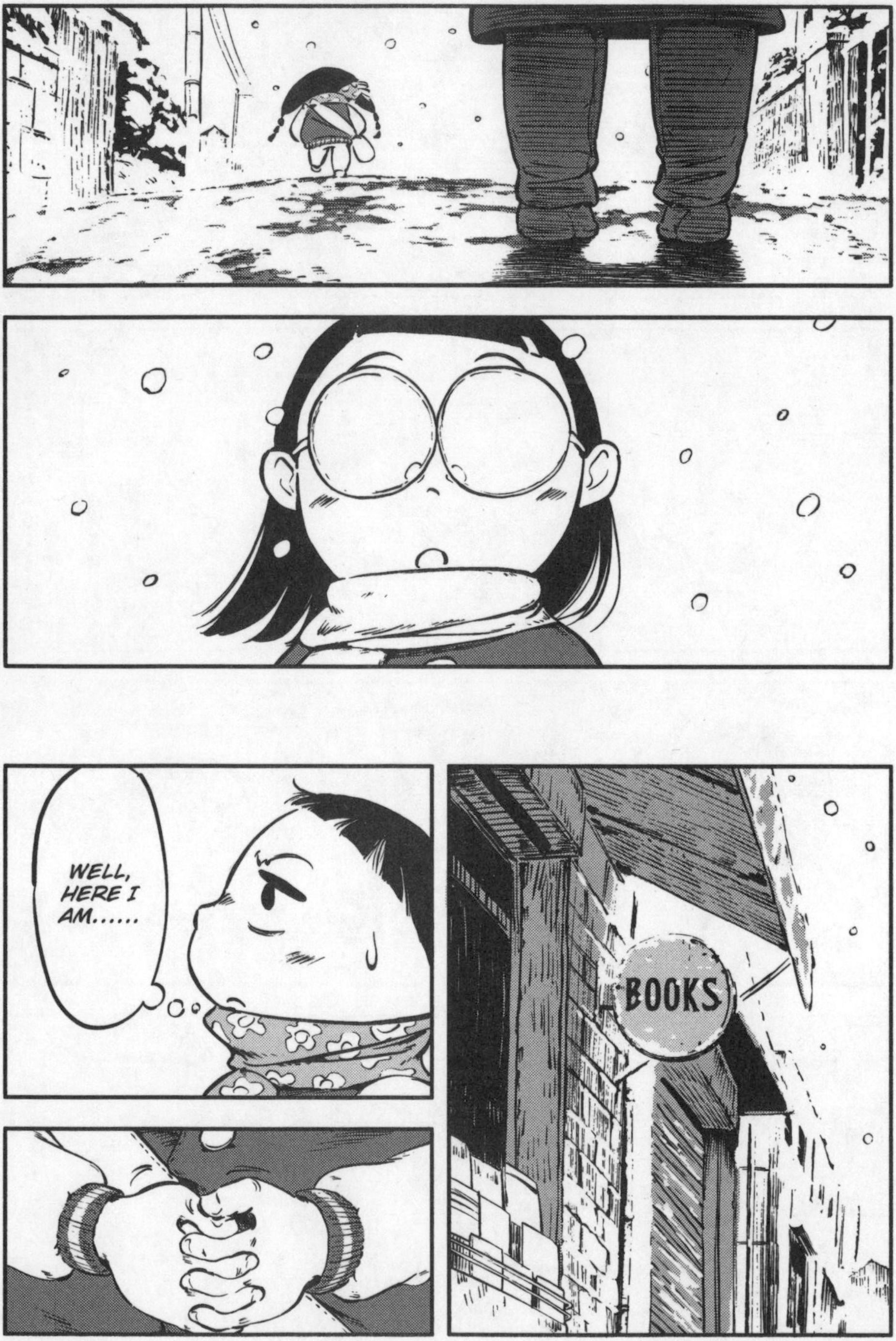
BOOKS
WELL, HERE I AM......

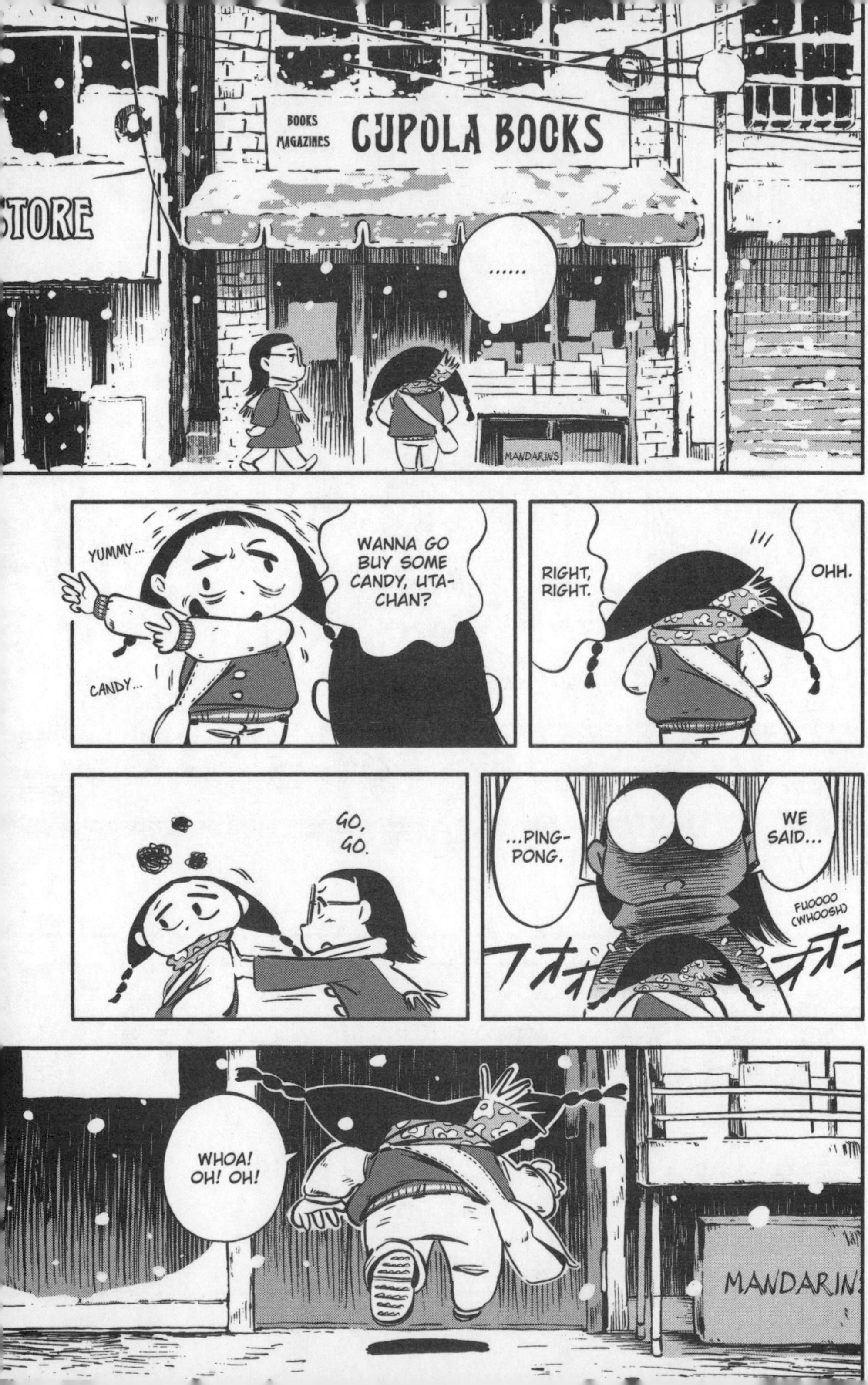
BOOKS
MAGAZINES
CUPOLA BOOKS
STORE
......
MANDARINS
OHH.
RIGHT, RIGHT.
WANNA GO BUY SOME CANDY, UTA-CHAN?
YUMMY...
CANDY...
WE SAID...
...PING-PONG.
FUOOOO (WHOOSH)
GO, GO.
WHOA! OH! OH!
MANDARIN

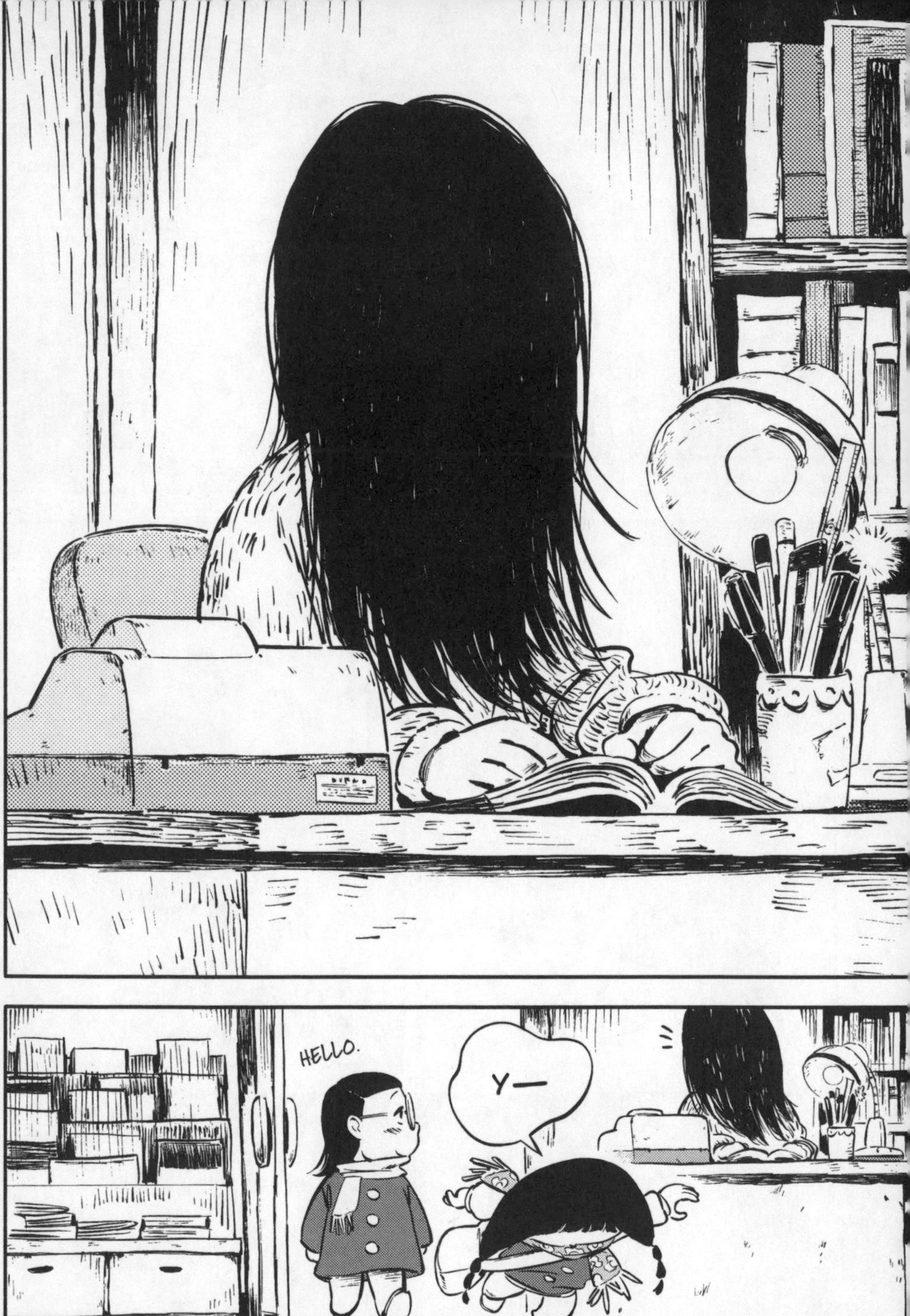
Y—
HELLO.

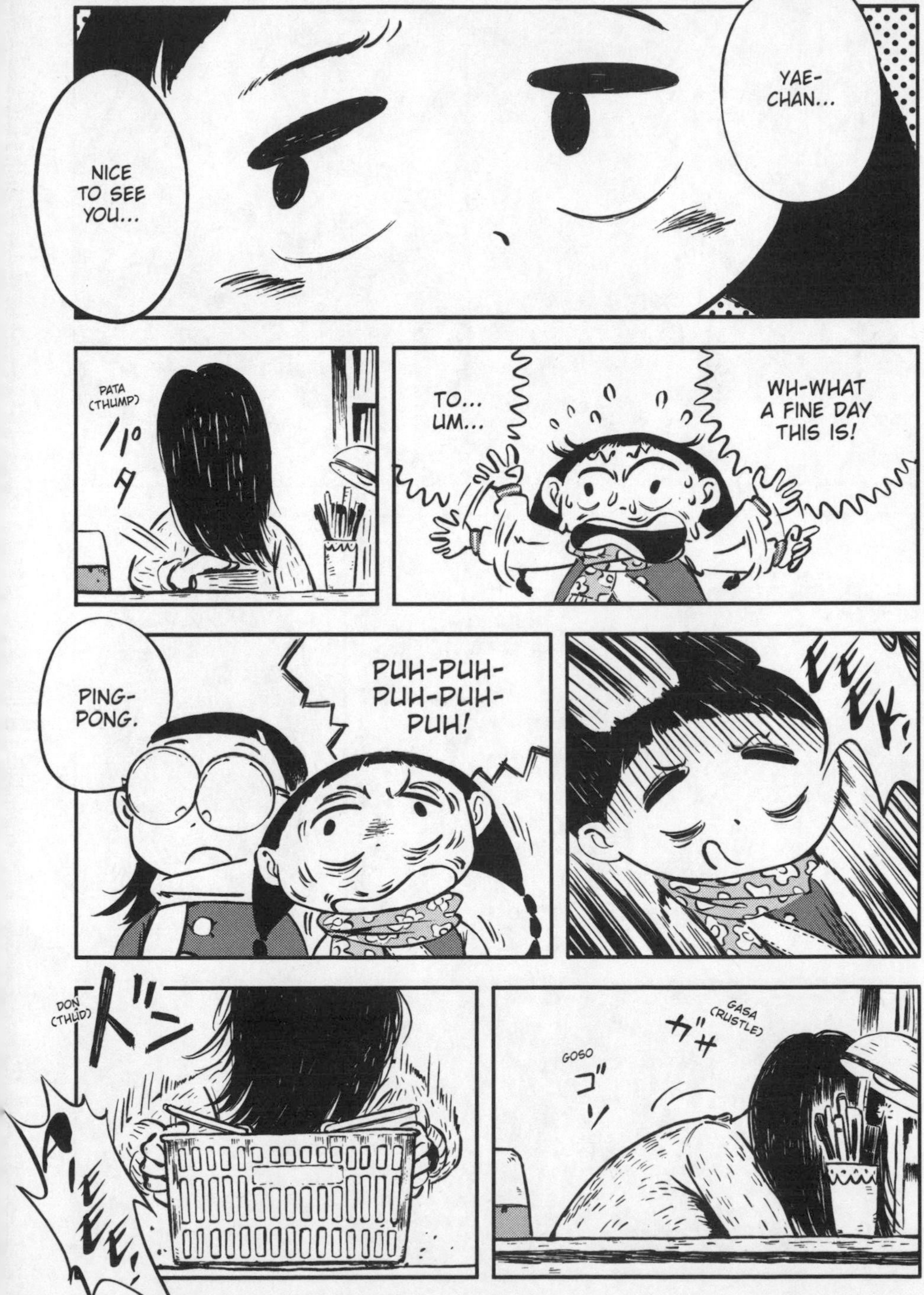
YAE-CHAN...
NICE TO SEE YOU...
WH-WHAT A FINE DAY THIS IS!
TO... UM...
PATA (THUMP)
パタ
EEEK!
PUH-PUH-PUH-PUH-PUH!
PING-PONG.
GASA (RUSTLE)
ガサ
GOSO
ゴソ
DON (THUD)
ドン
AIEEE!

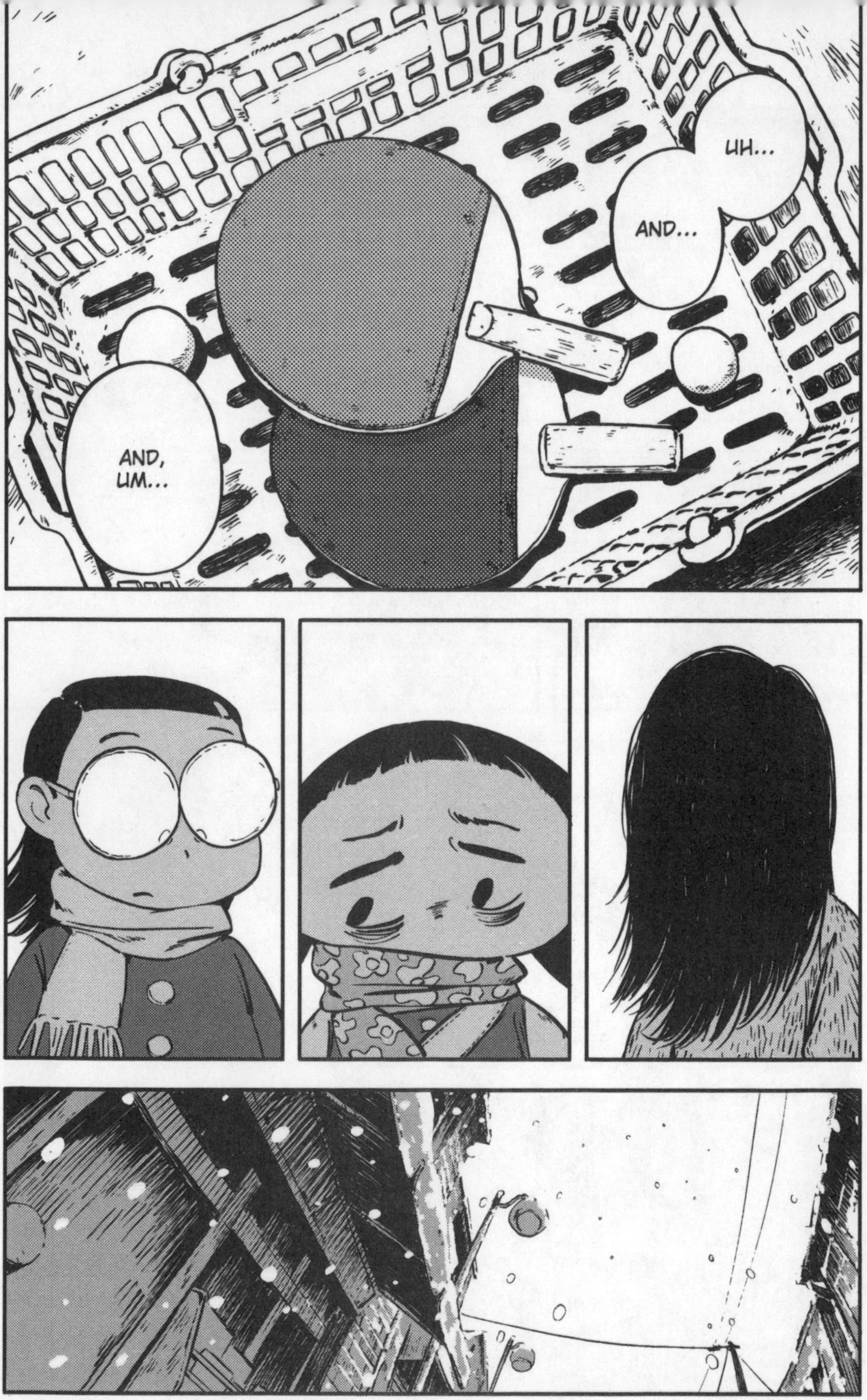
UH...
AND...
AND, UM...

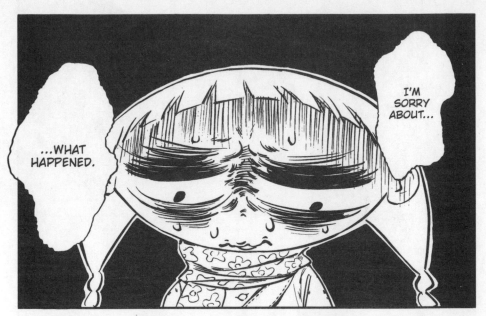

I'M SORRY ABOUT...

...WHAT HAPPENED.

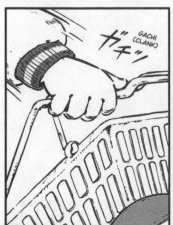

GACHI
(CLANK)

DA

DA

DA
(DASH)

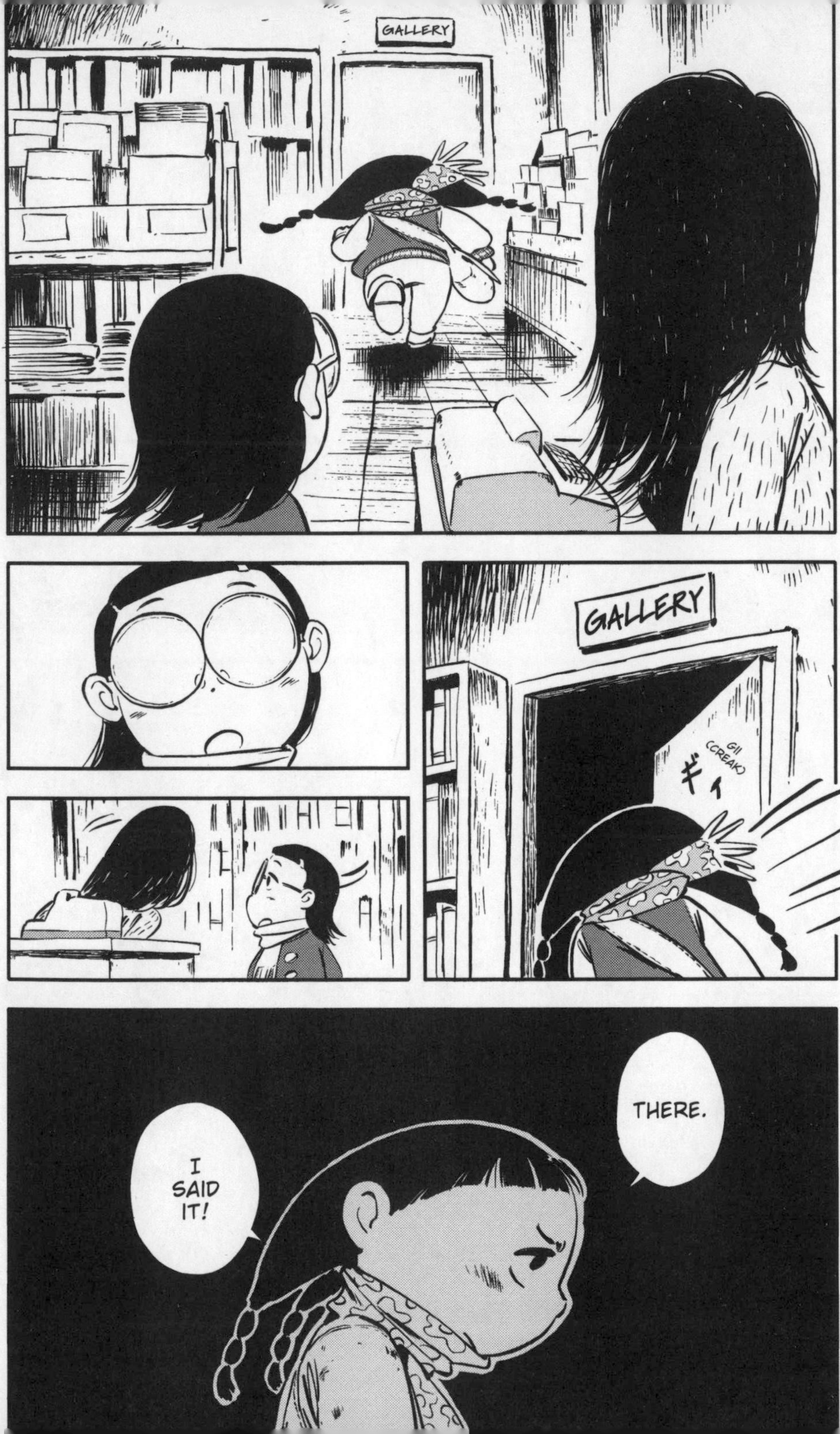
GALLERY
GALLERY
GII (CREAK)
ギィ
THERE.
I SAID IT!

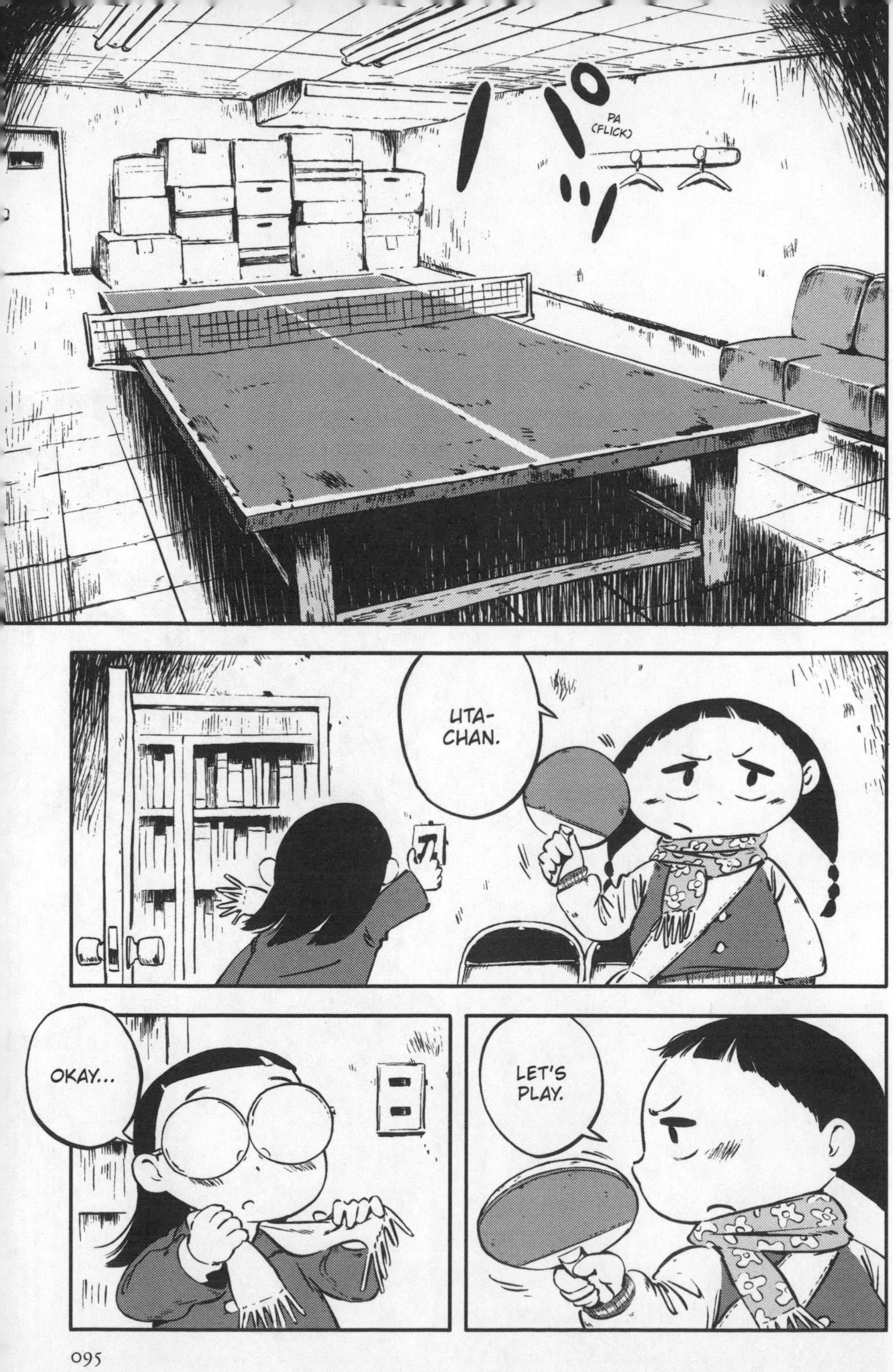
パッ
PA
(FLICK)
UTA-
CHAN.
LET'S
PLAY.
OKAY...

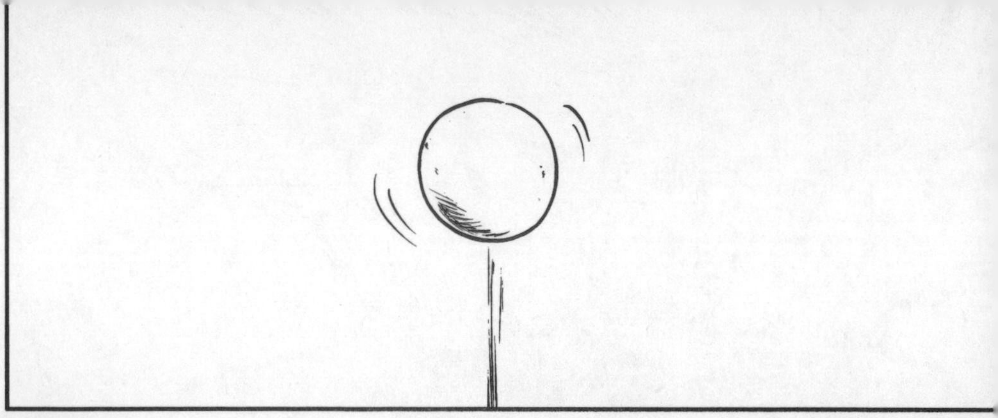

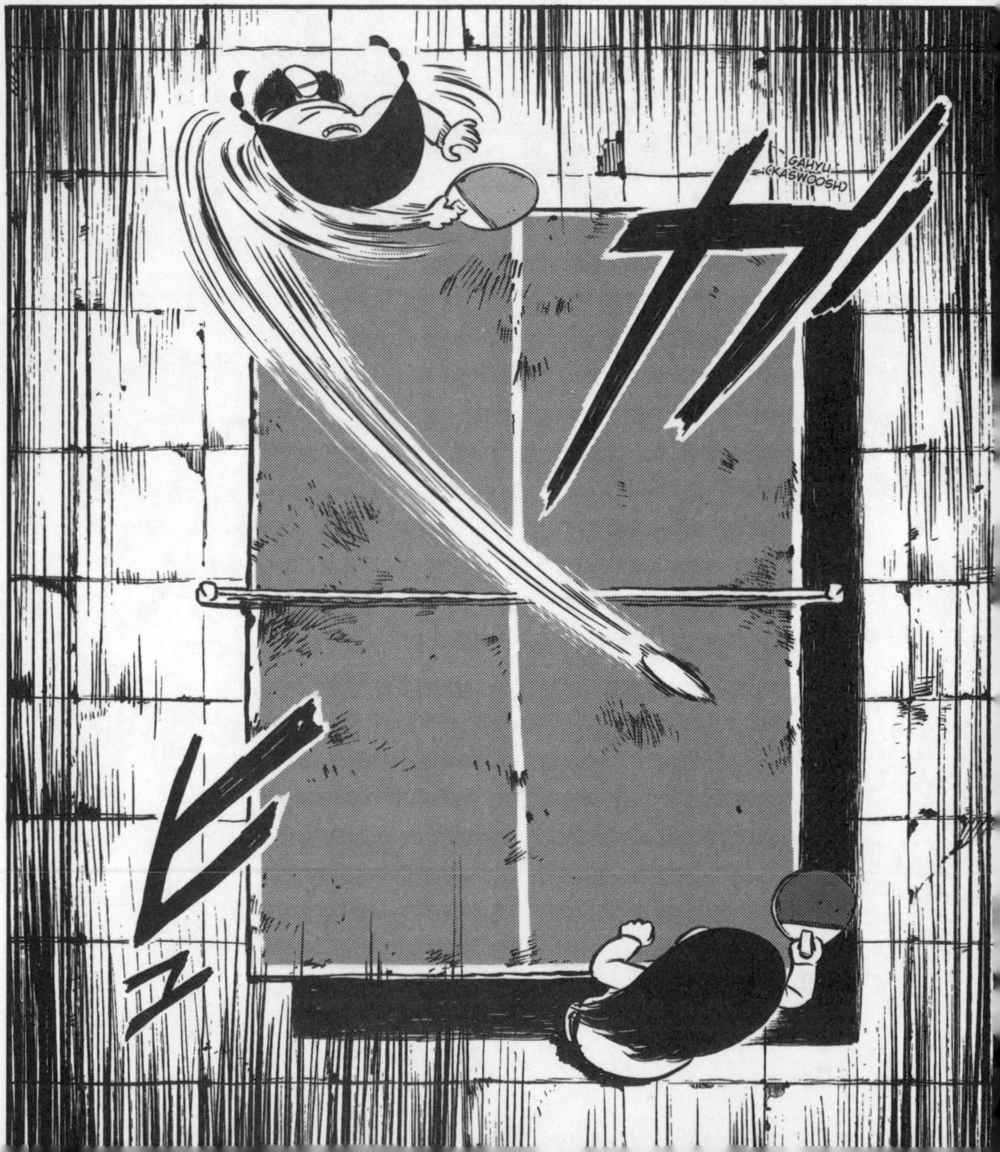
GAHYU
(KASWOOSH)

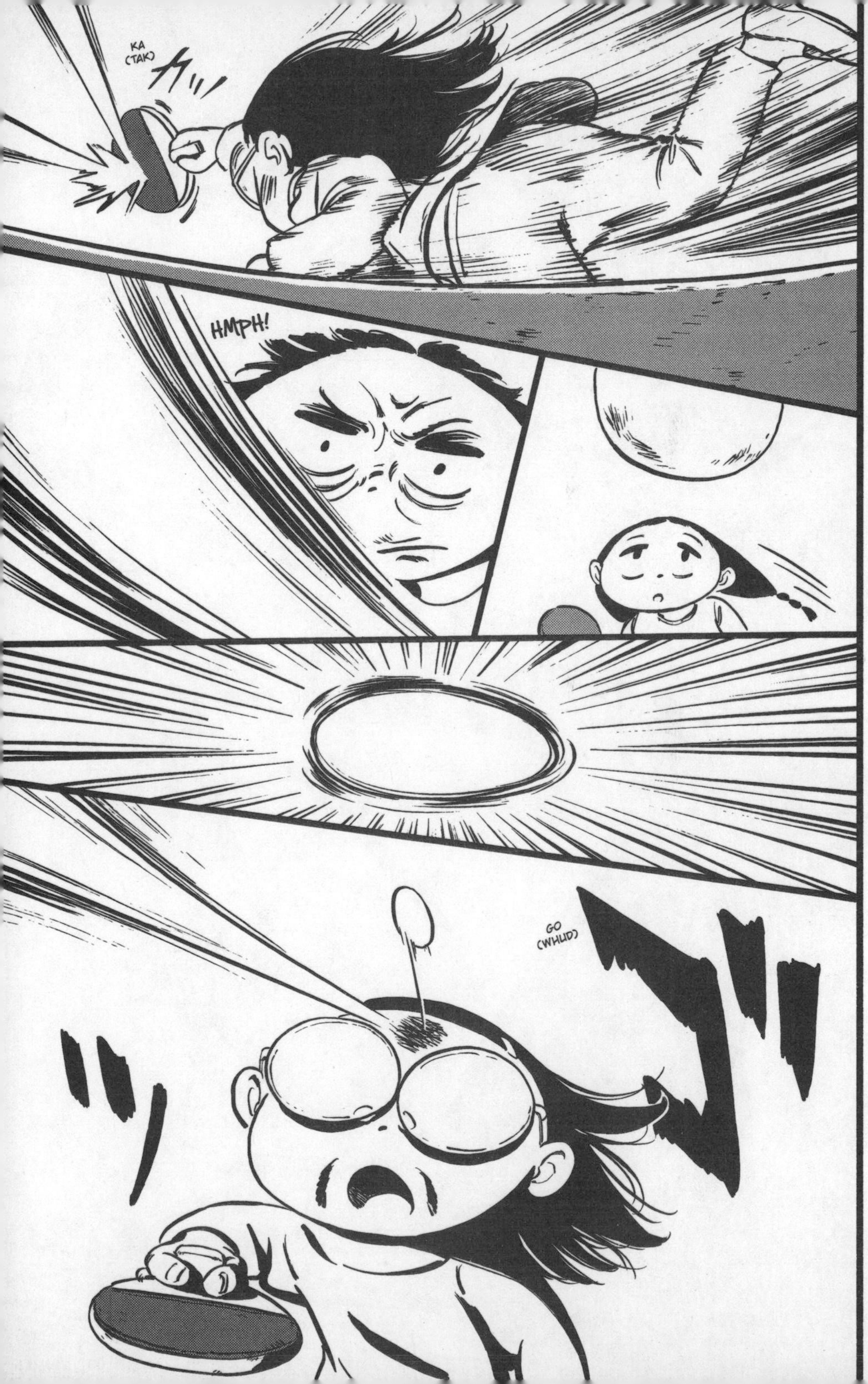
KA
(TAK)
HMPH!
GO
(WHUD)

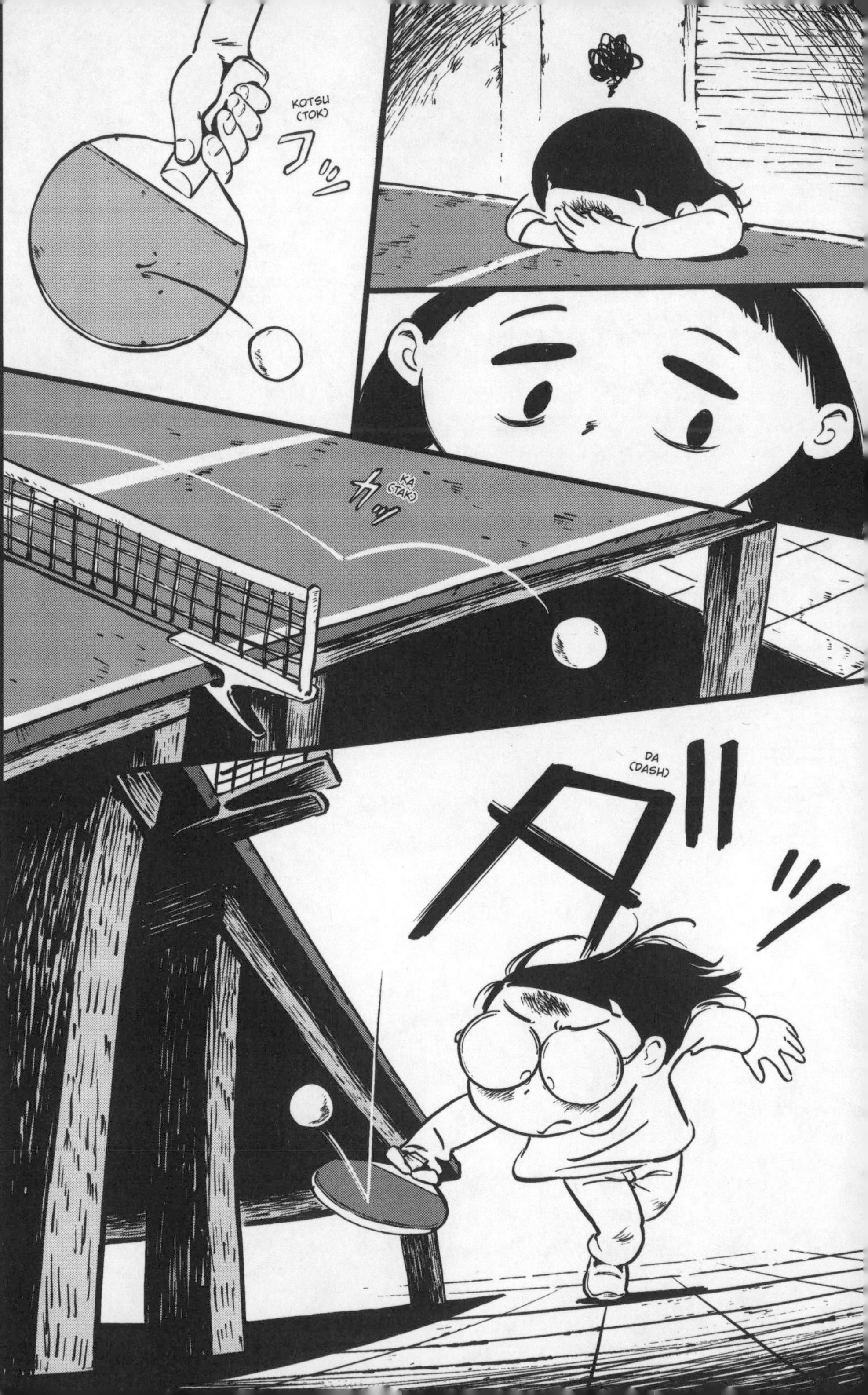
KOTSU (TOK)
KA (TAK)
DA (DASH)

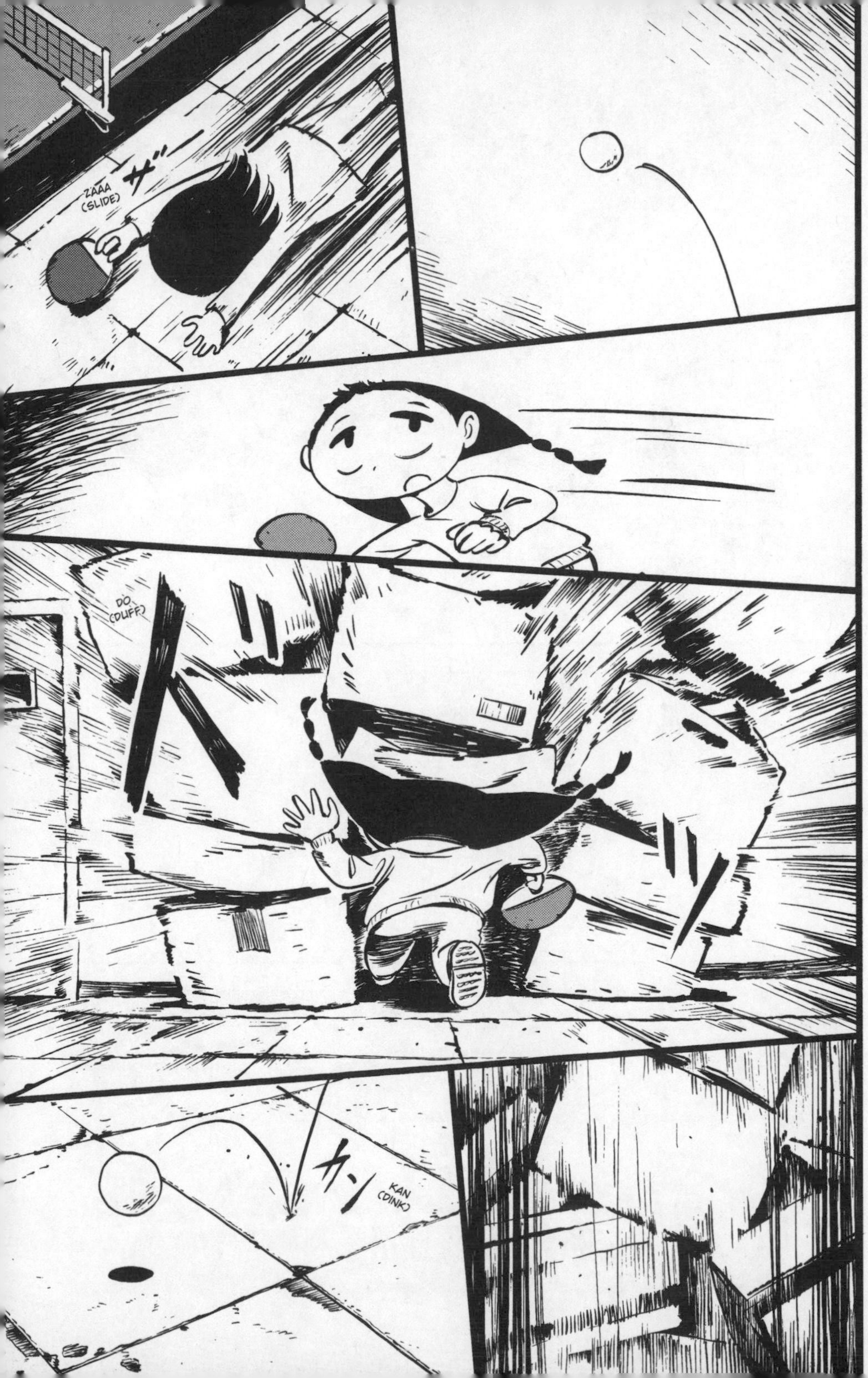
ZAAA (SLIDE)
DO (DUFF)
KAN (DINK)

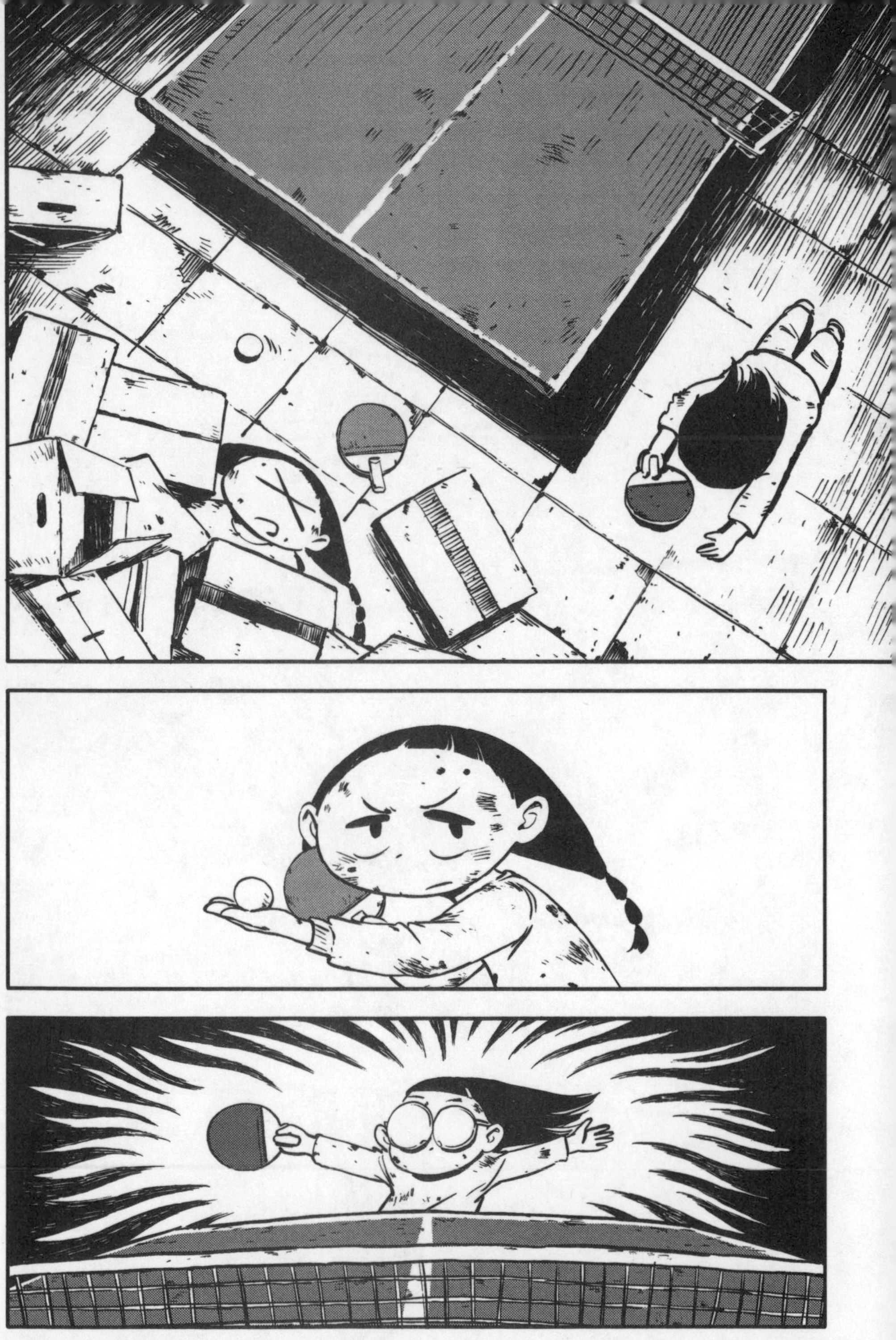

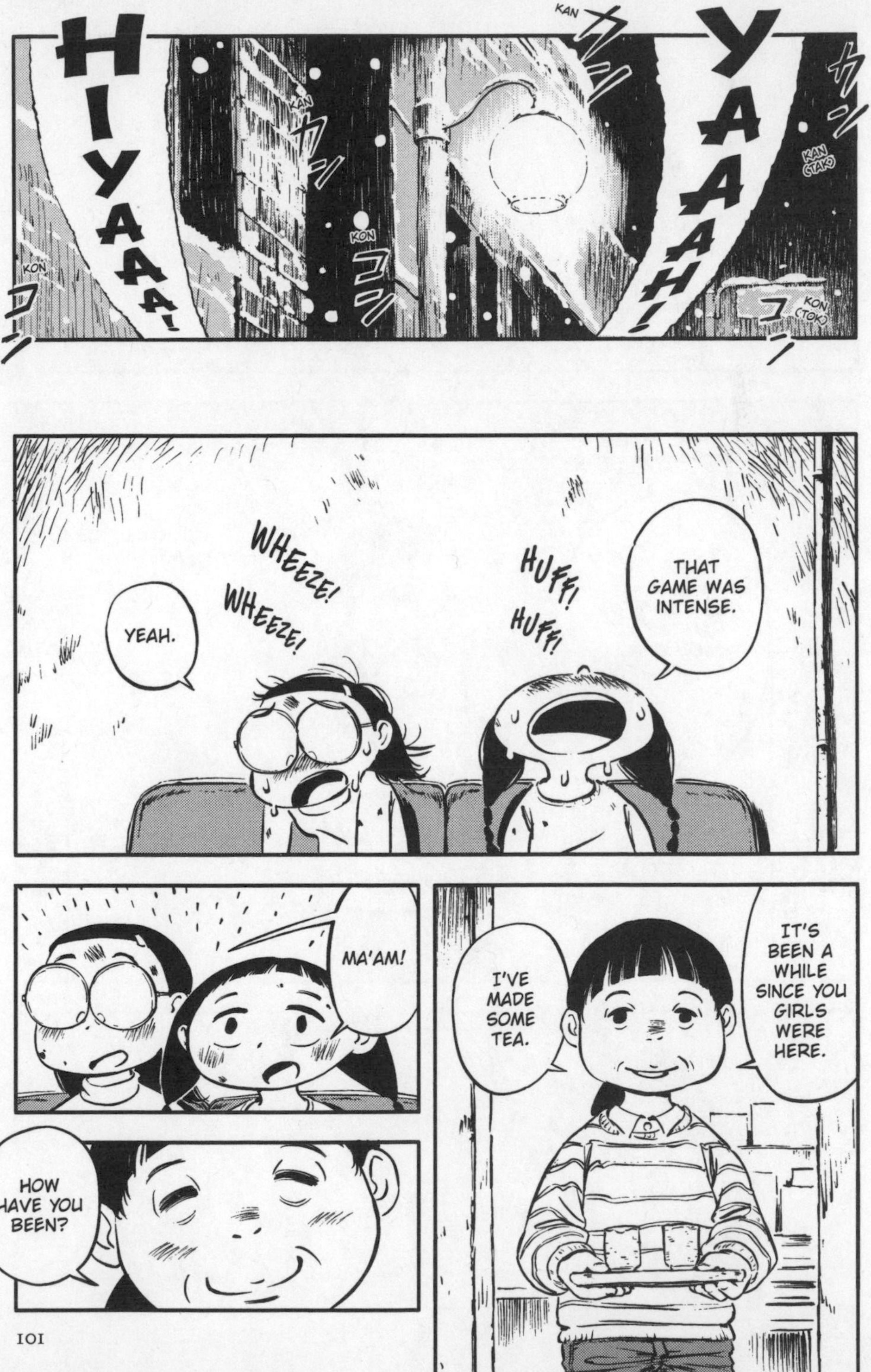
KAN
YAAAAH!
KAN (TAK)
KON (TOK)
KAN
HIYAAAA!
KON
KON
THAT GAME WAS INTENSE.
HUFF! HUFF!
WHEEZE! WHEEZE!
YEAH.
IT'S BEEN A WHILE SINCE YOU GIRLS WERE HERE.
I'VE MADE SOME TEA.
MA'AM!
HOW HAVE YOU BEEN?

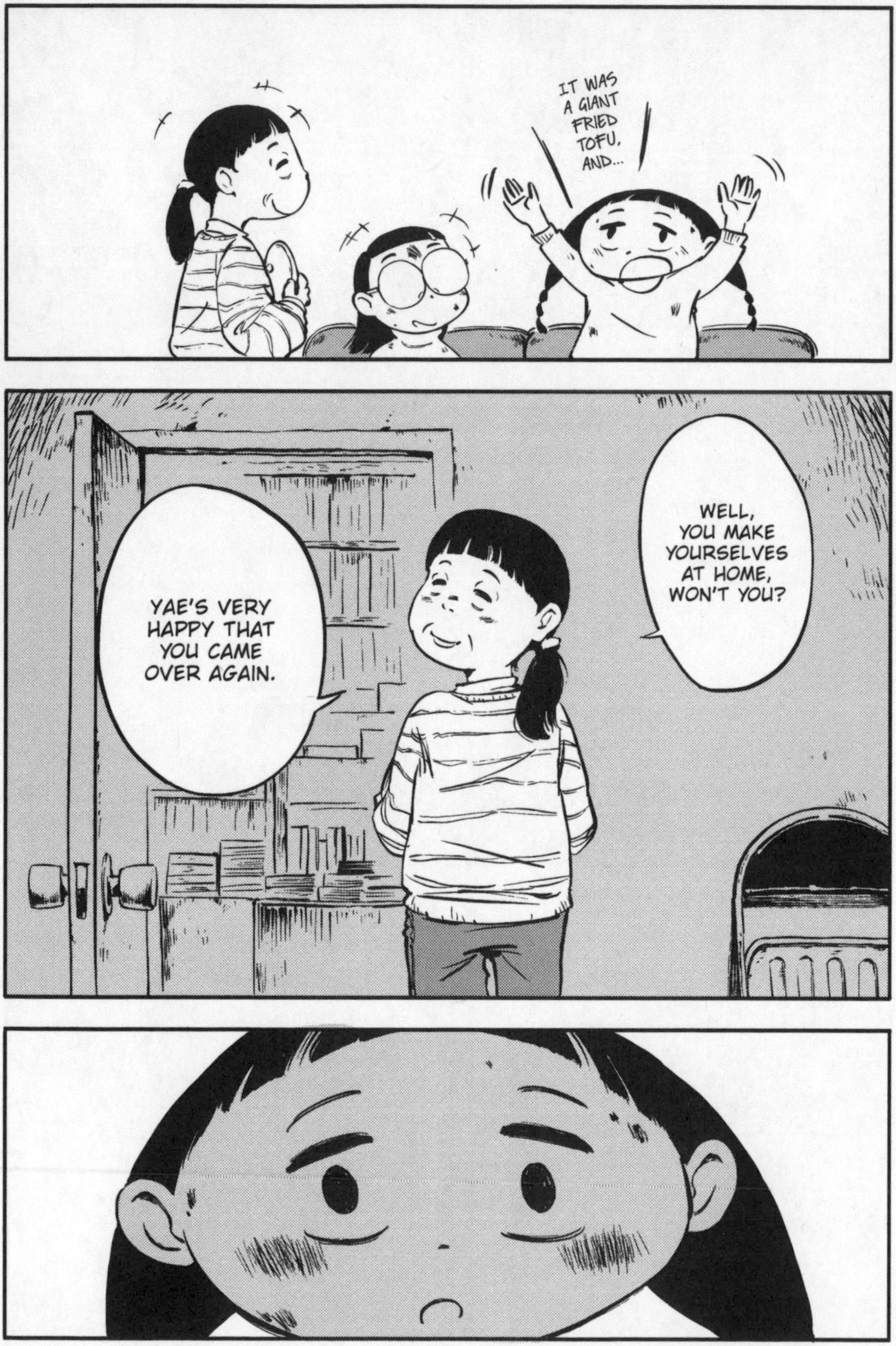
IT WAS A GIANT FRIED TOFU, AND...
WELL, YOU MAKE YOURSELVES AT HOME, WON'T YOU?
YAE'S VERY HAPPY THAT YOU CAME OVER AGAIN.

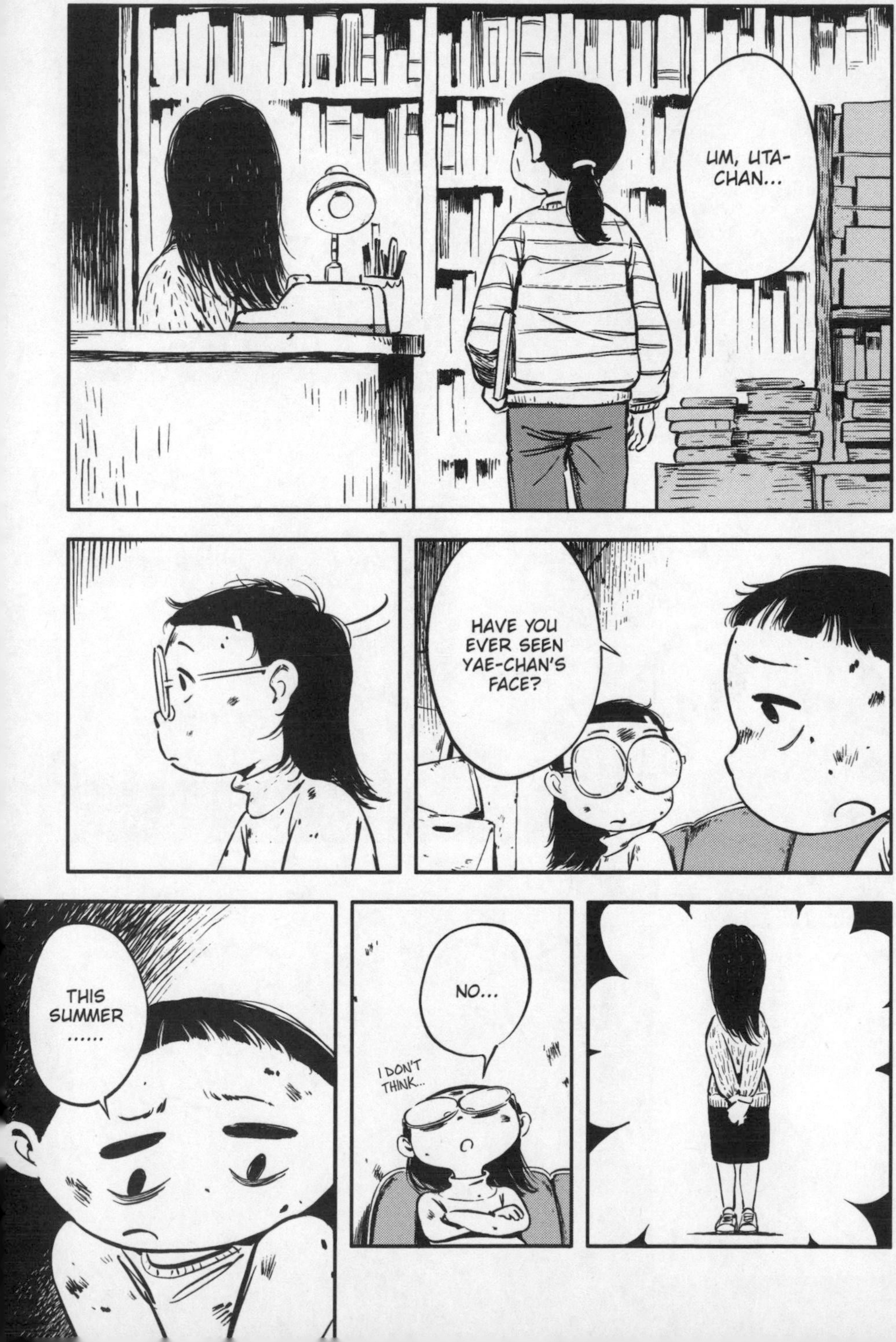
UM, UTA-CHAN...
HAVE YOU EVER SEEN YAE-CHAN'S FACE?
NO...
I DON'T THINK...
THIS SUMMER ......

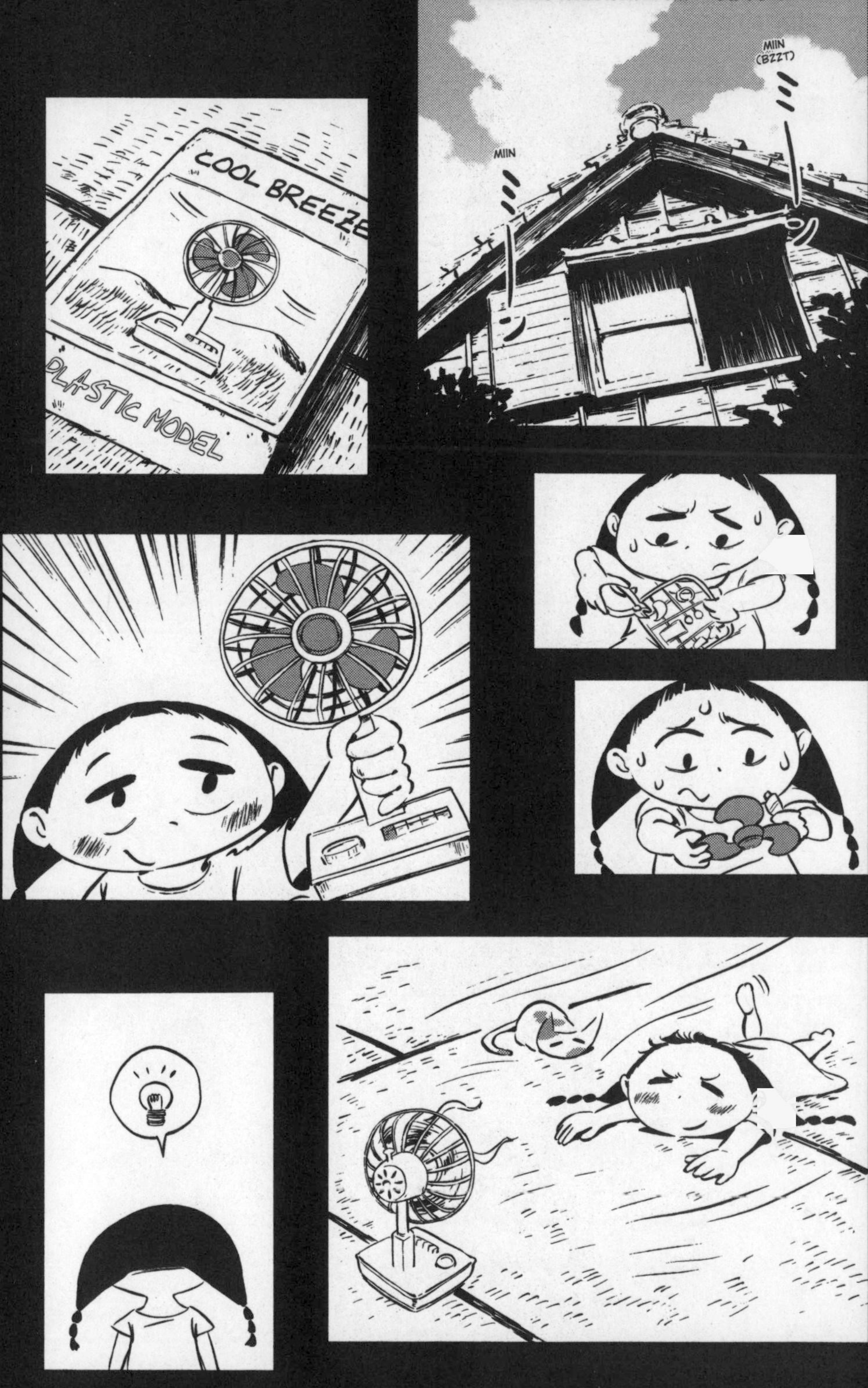
MIIN (BZZT)
MIIN
COOL BREEZE
PLASTIC MODEL

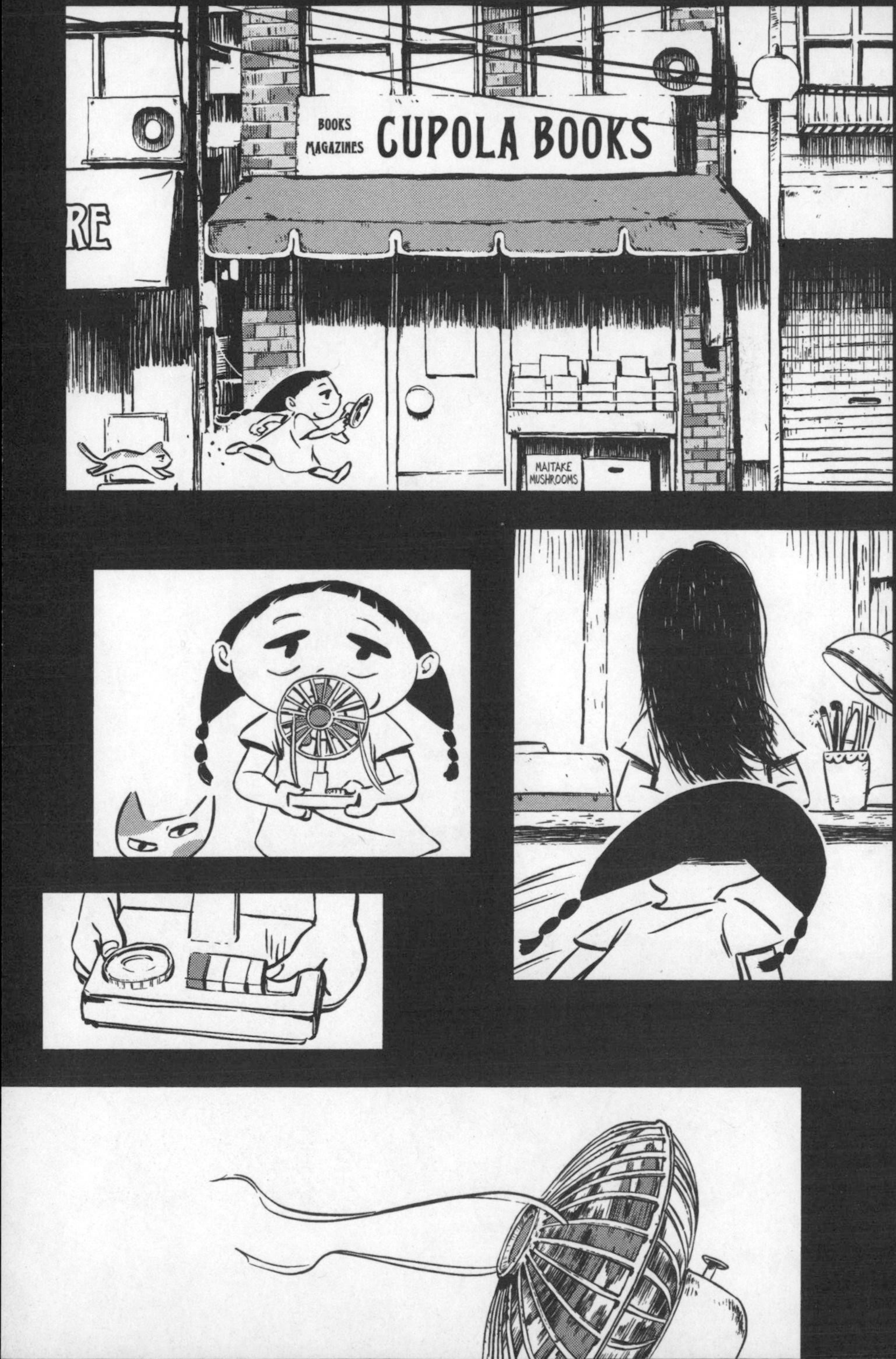
BOOKS
MAGAZINES
CUPOLA BOOKS
RE
MAITAKE
MUSHROOMS

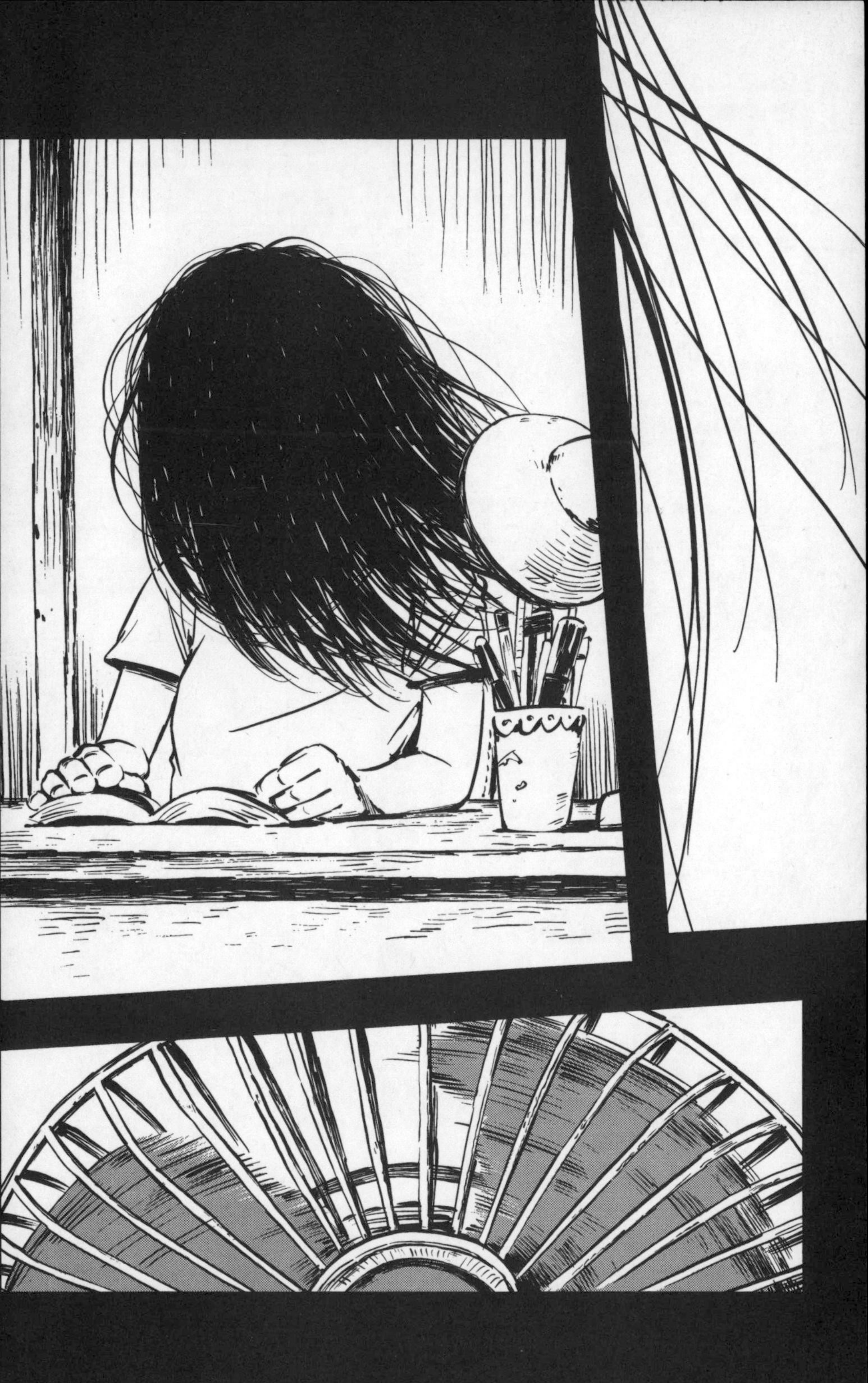

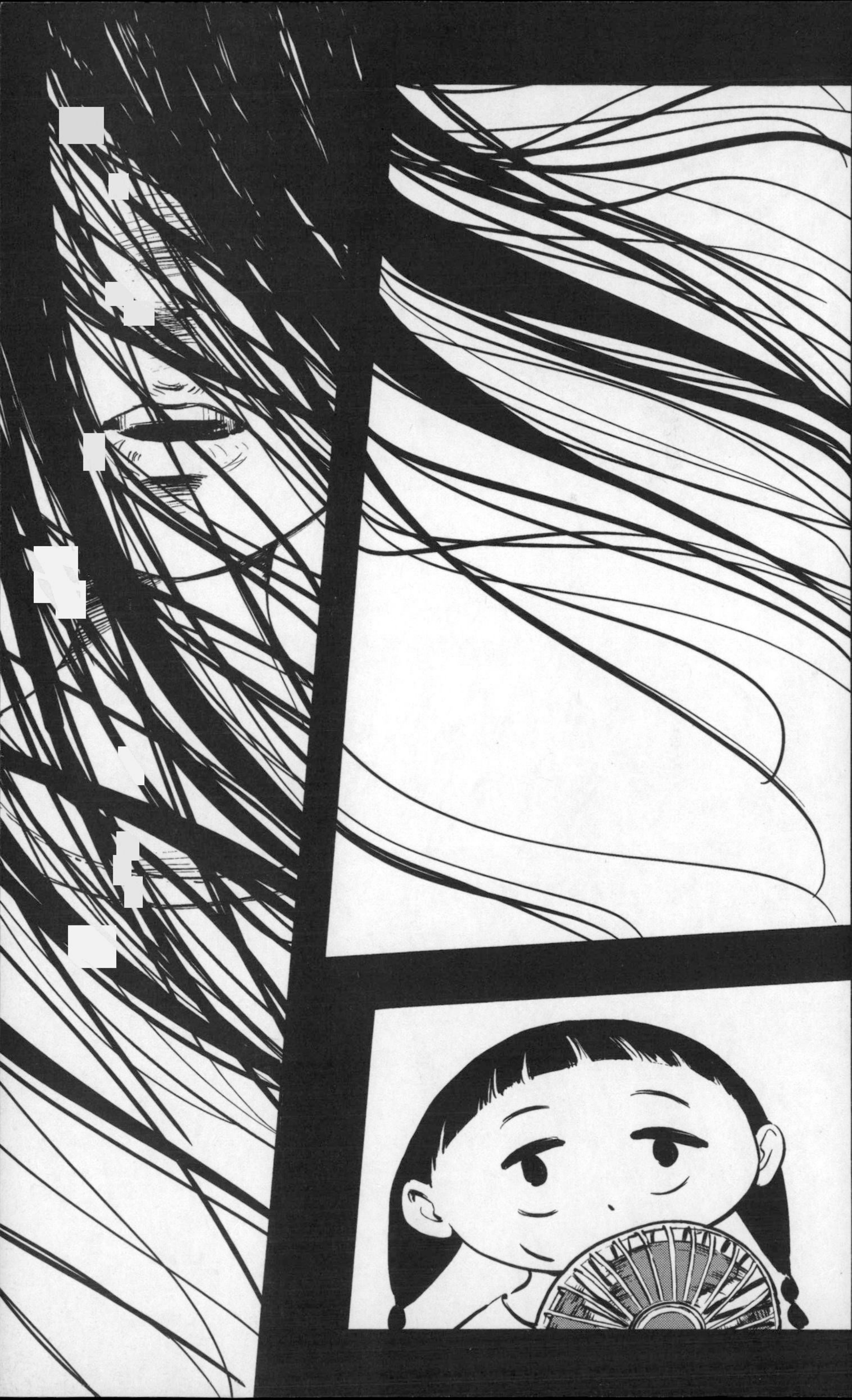

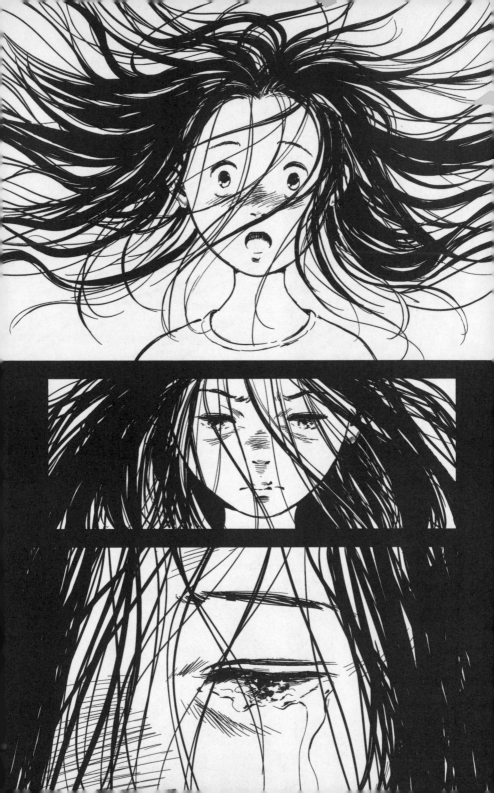

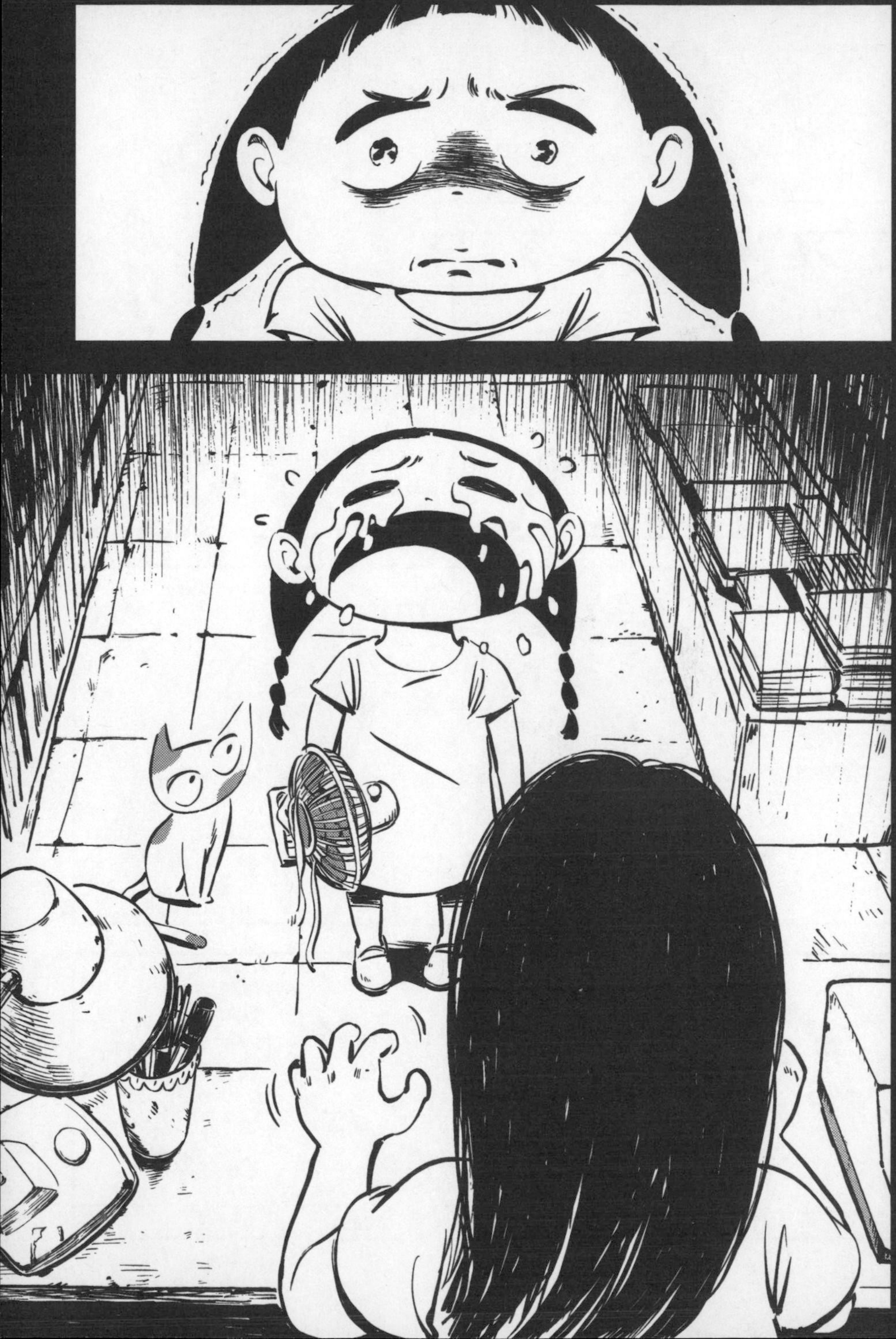

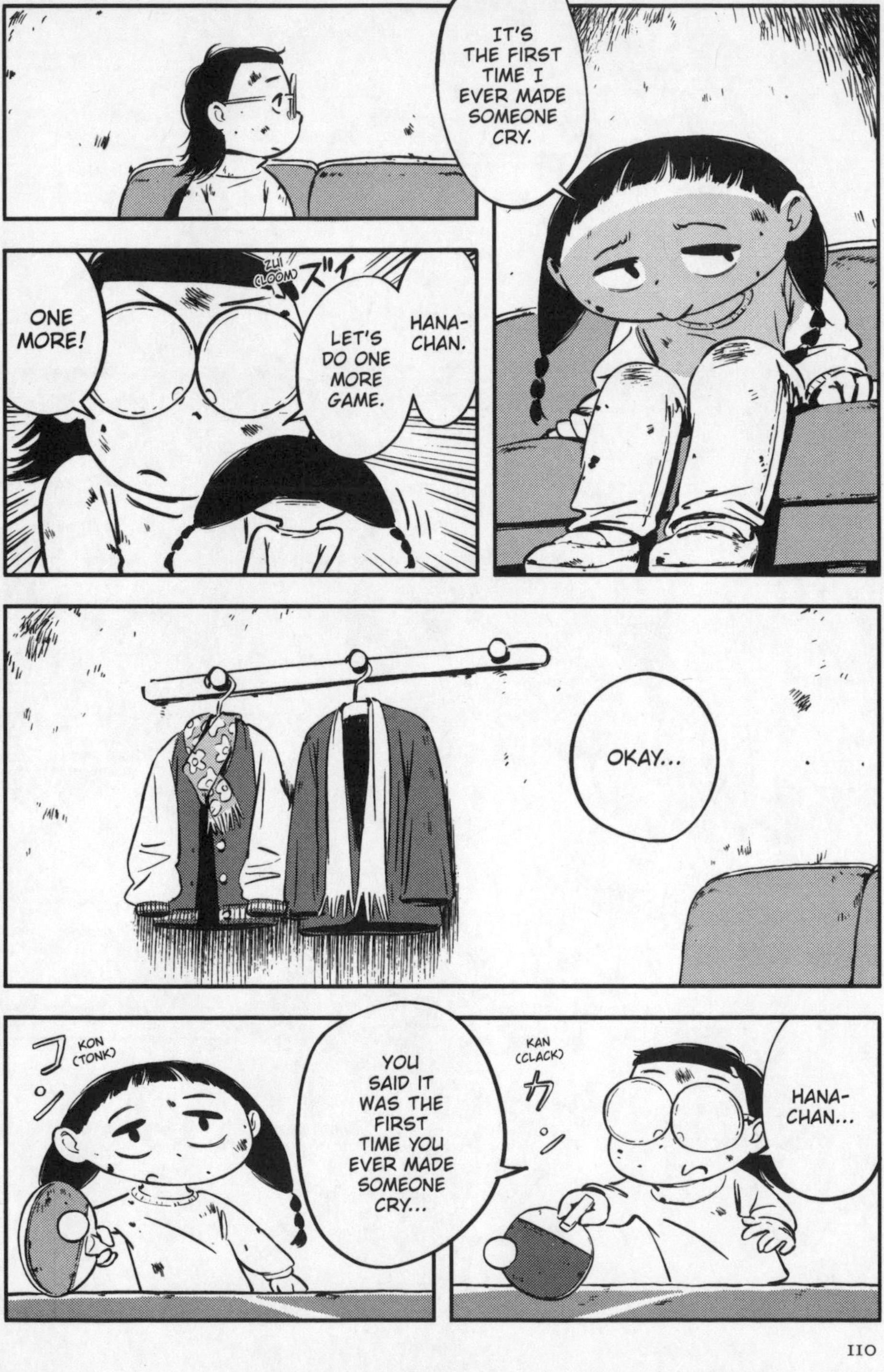
IT'S THE FIRST TIME I EVER MADE SOMEONE CRY.
ズイ
ZUI (LOOM)
HANA-CHAN.
LET'S DO ONE MORE GAME.
ONE MORE!
OKAY...
HANA-CHAN...
カン
KAN (CLACK)
YOU SAID IT WAS THE FIRST TIME YOU EVER MADE SOMEONE CRY...
コン
KON (TONK)

BUT WHEN WE WERE LITTLE...
...YOU MADE ME CRY ALL THE TIME.
N...
NO WAY!
KAN
YES WAY.
NO WAY.
KON
YES WAY.

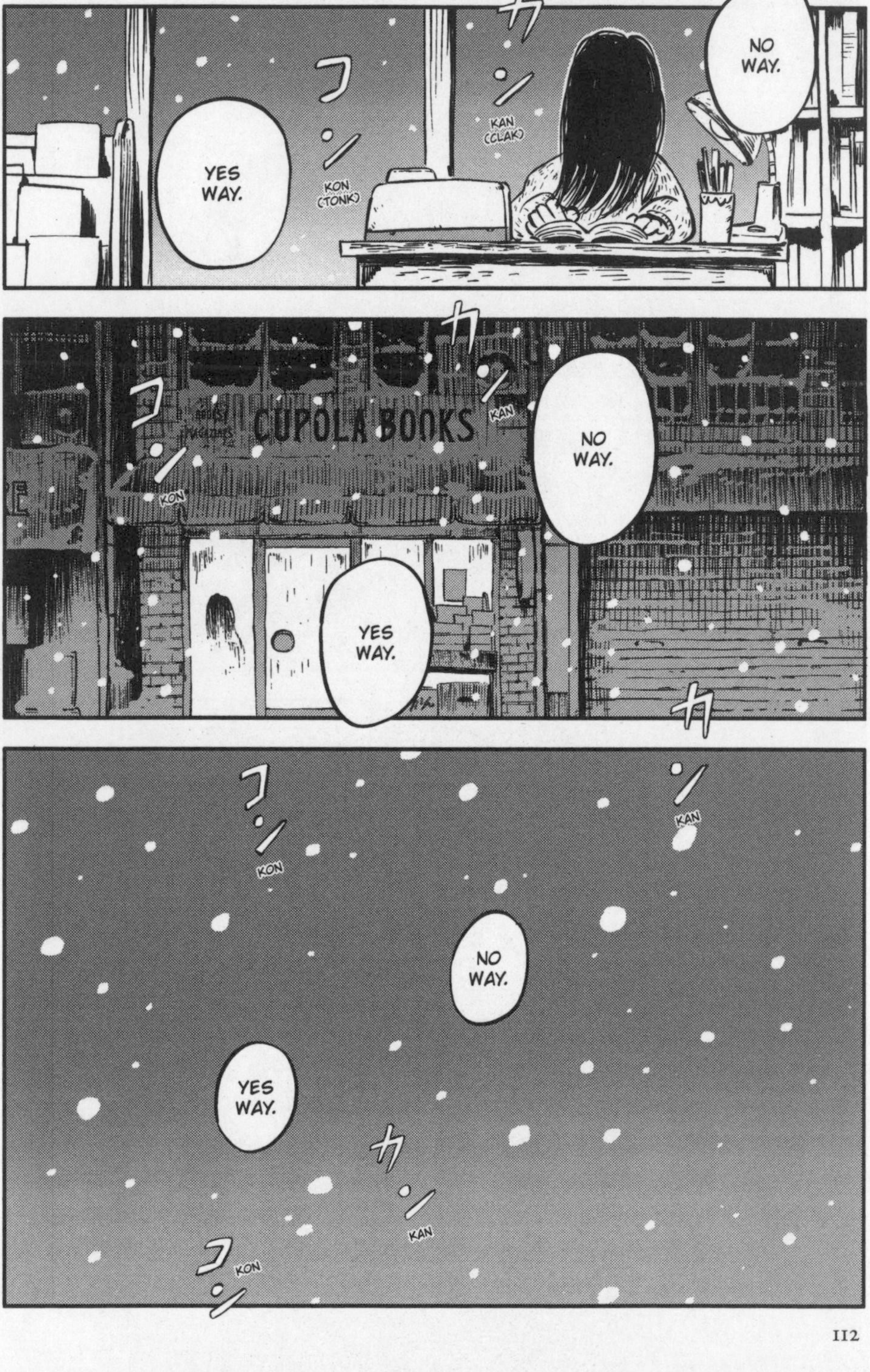
NO WAY.
カン
KAN (CLAK)
コン
KON (TONK)
YES WAY.
NO WAY.
カン
KAN
CUPOLA BOOKS
コン
KON
YES WAY.
カン
KAN
コン
KON
NO WAY.
YES WAY.
カン
KAN
コン
KON

Hana-chan
and the Shape of the World

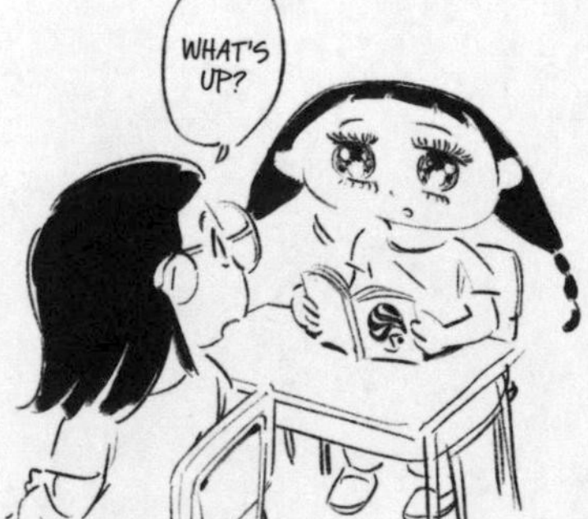
WHAT'S UP?

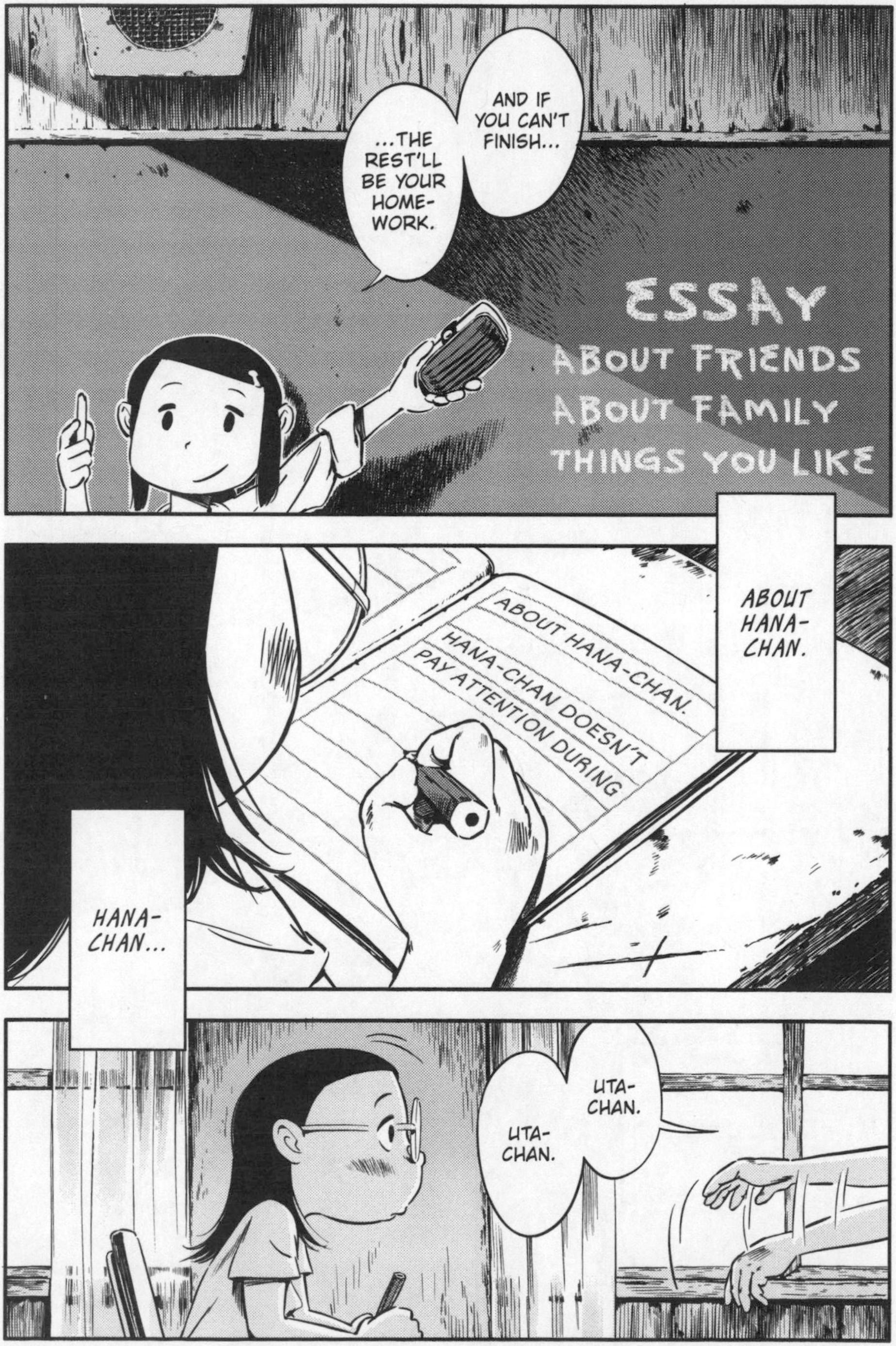
AND IF YOU CAN'T FINISH...
...THE REST'LL BE YOUR HOME-WORK.
ESSAY
ABOUT FRIENDS
ABOUT FAMILY
THINGS YOU LIKE
ABOUT HANA-CHAN.
ABOUT HANA-CHAN.
HANA-CHAN DOESN'T
PAY ATTENTION DURING
HANA-CHAN...
UTA-CHAN.
UTA-CHAN.

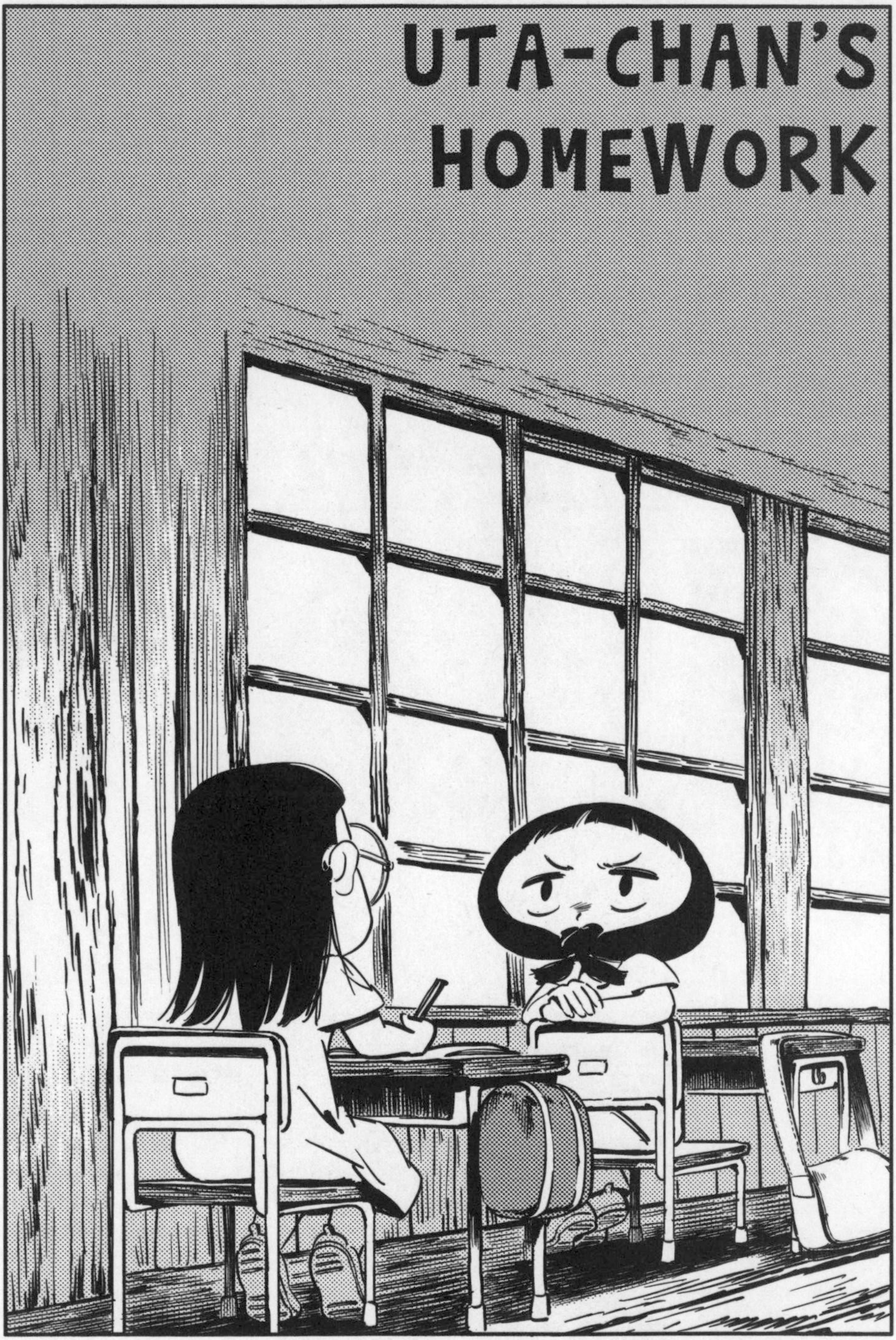
UTA-CHAN'S
HOMEWORK

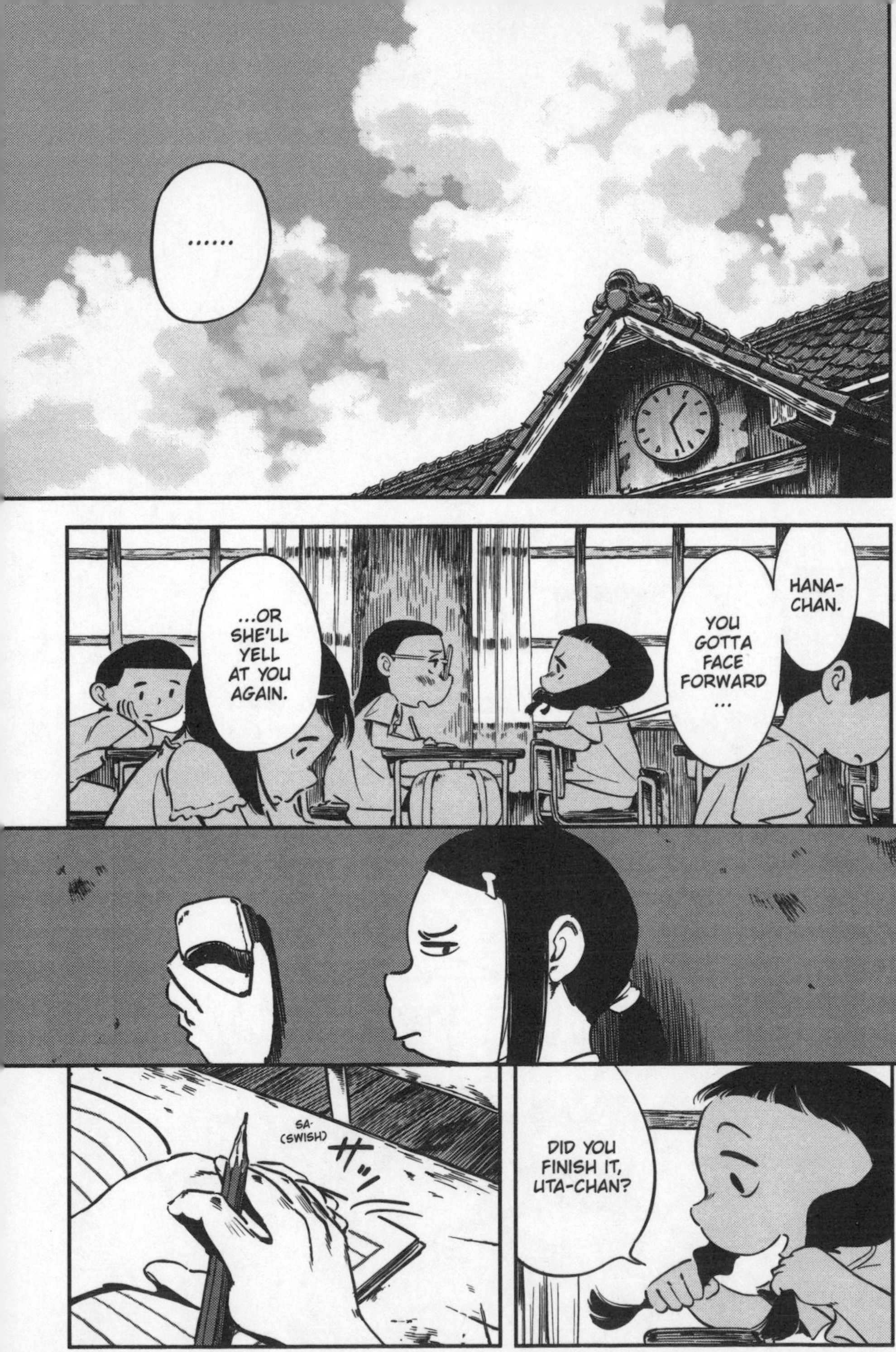

......
HANA-CHAN.
YOU GOTTA FACE FORWARD ...
...OR SHE'LL YELL AT YOU AGAIN.
DID YOU FINISH IT, UTA-CHAN?
SA- (SWISH)

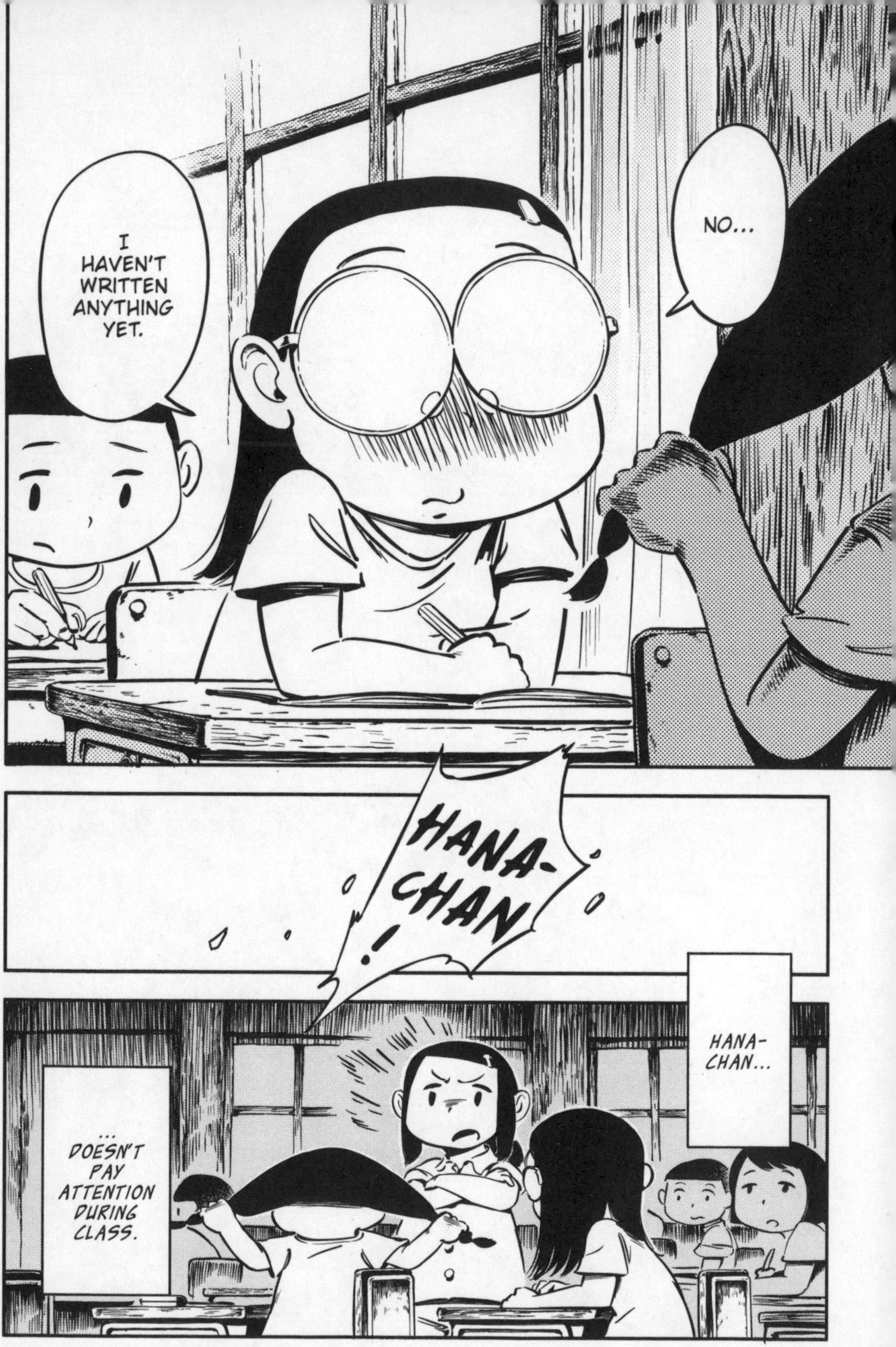
NO...
I HAVEN'T WRITTEN ANYTHING YET.
HANA-CHAN!
HANA-CHAN...
...DOESN'T PAY ATTENTION DURING CLASS.

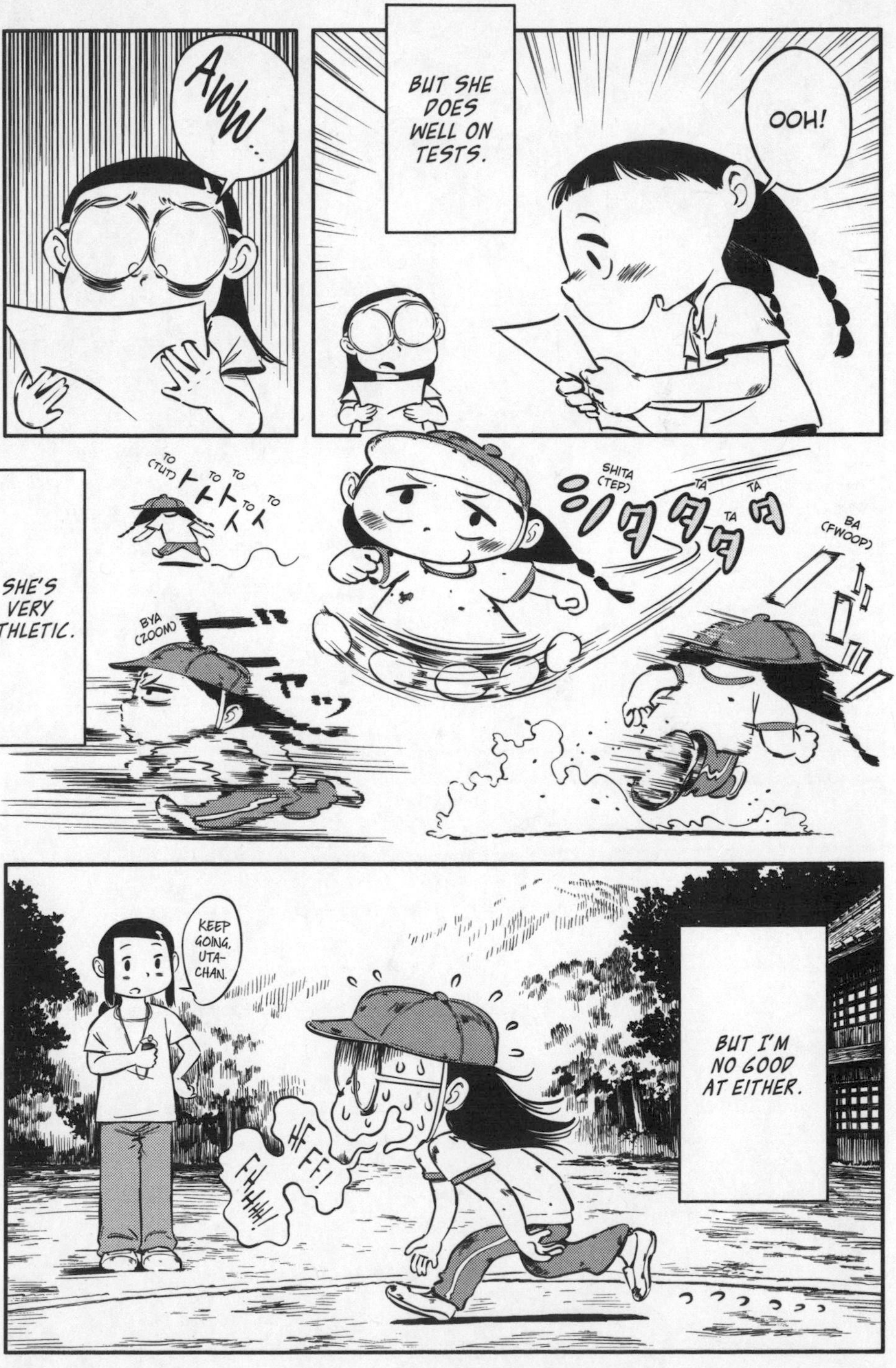
BUT SHE DOES WELL ON TESTS.
OOH!
AWW...
BA (FWOOP)
SHITA (TEP)
TA TA TA
TO (TUT) TO TO TO TO
SHE'S VERY ATHLETIC.
BYA (ZOOM)
BUT I'M NO GOOD AT EITHER.
HFF!
FHHH!
KEEP GOING, UTA-CHAN.

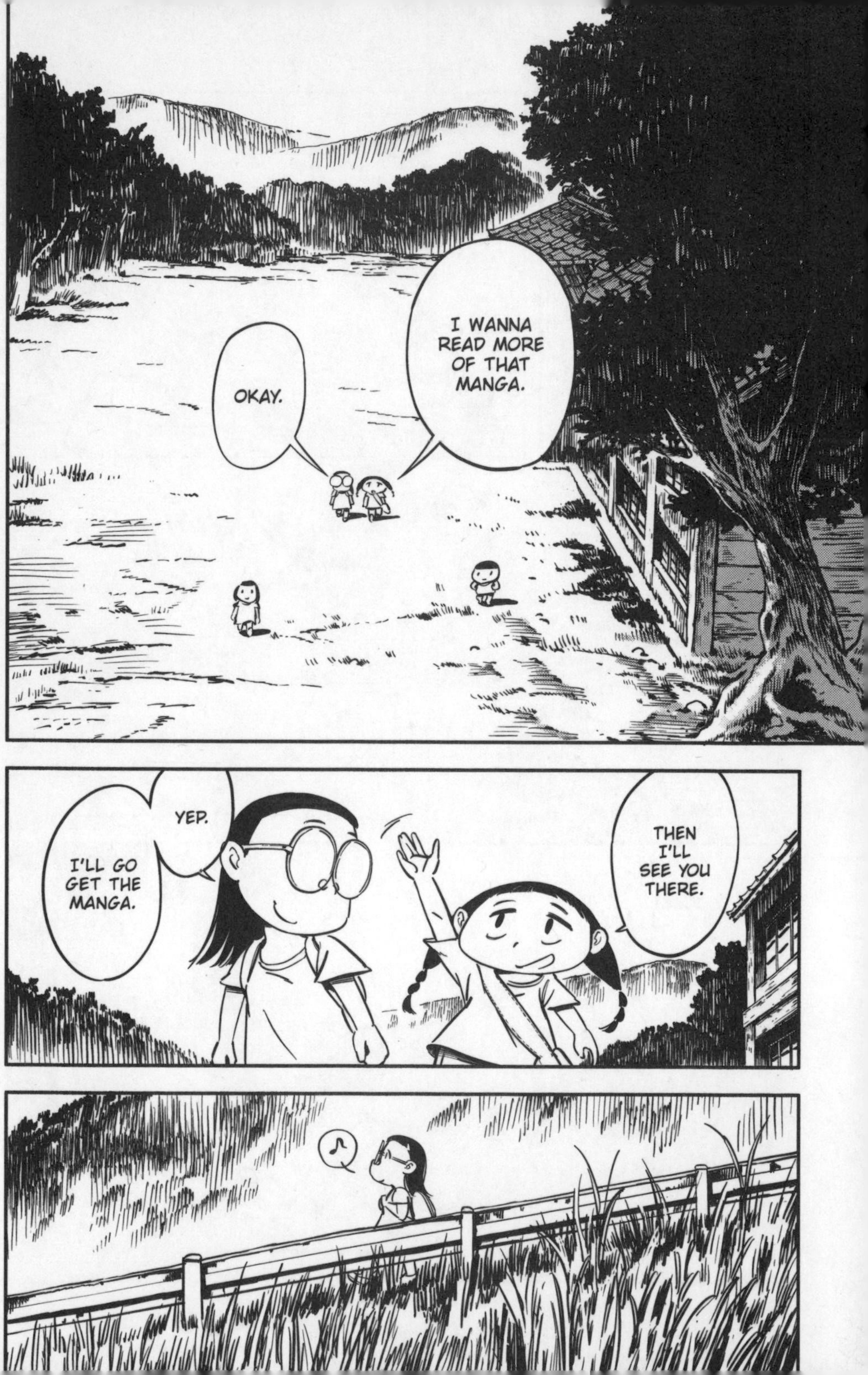
I WANNA READ MORE OF THAT MANGA.
OKAY.
THEN I'LL SEE YOU THERE.
YEP.
I'LL GO GET THE MANGA.
♪

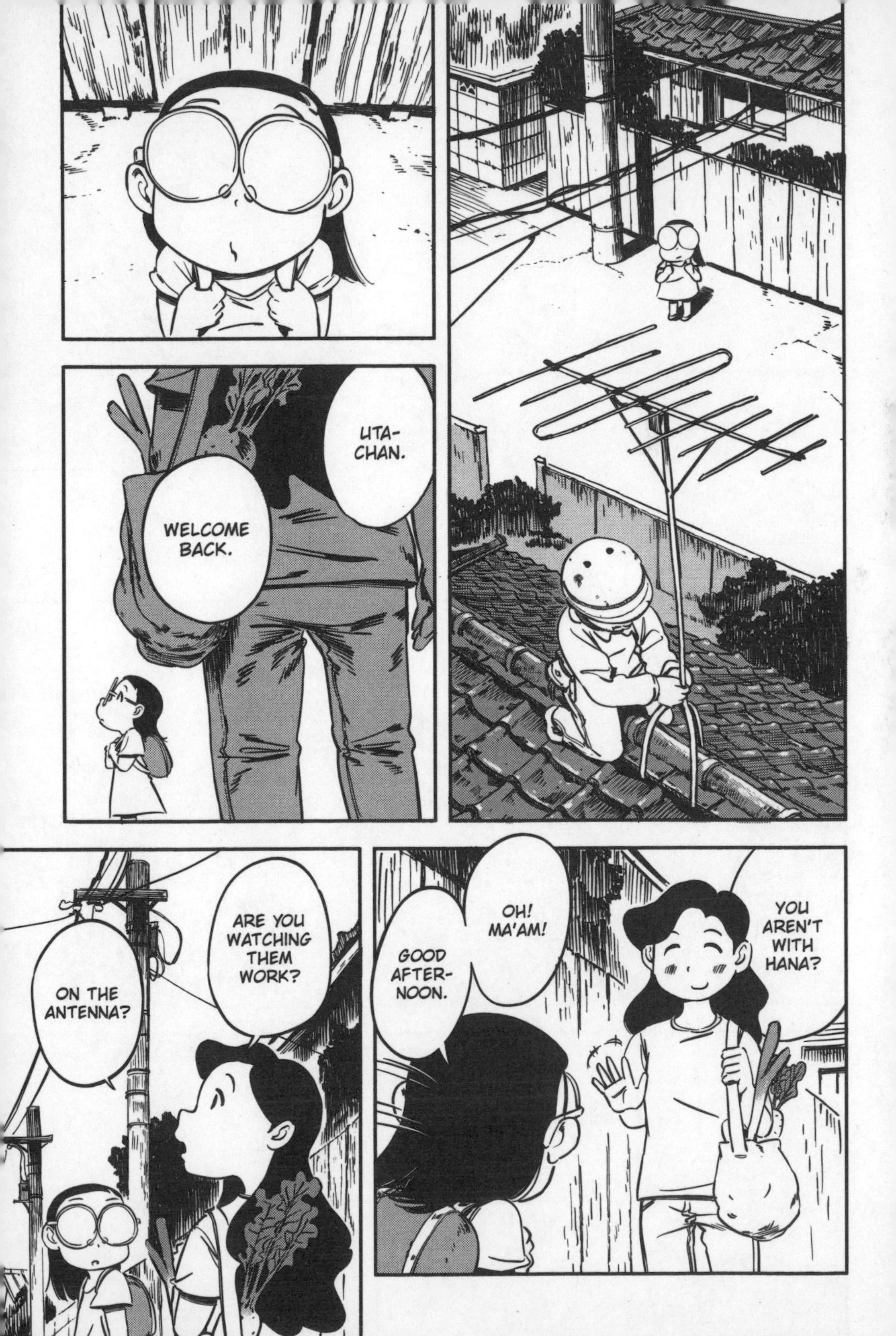

UTA-CHAN.
WELCOME BACK.
YOU AREN'T WITH HANA?
OH! MA'AM!
GOOD AFTER-NOON.
ARE YOU WATCHING THEM WORK?
ON THE ANTENNA?

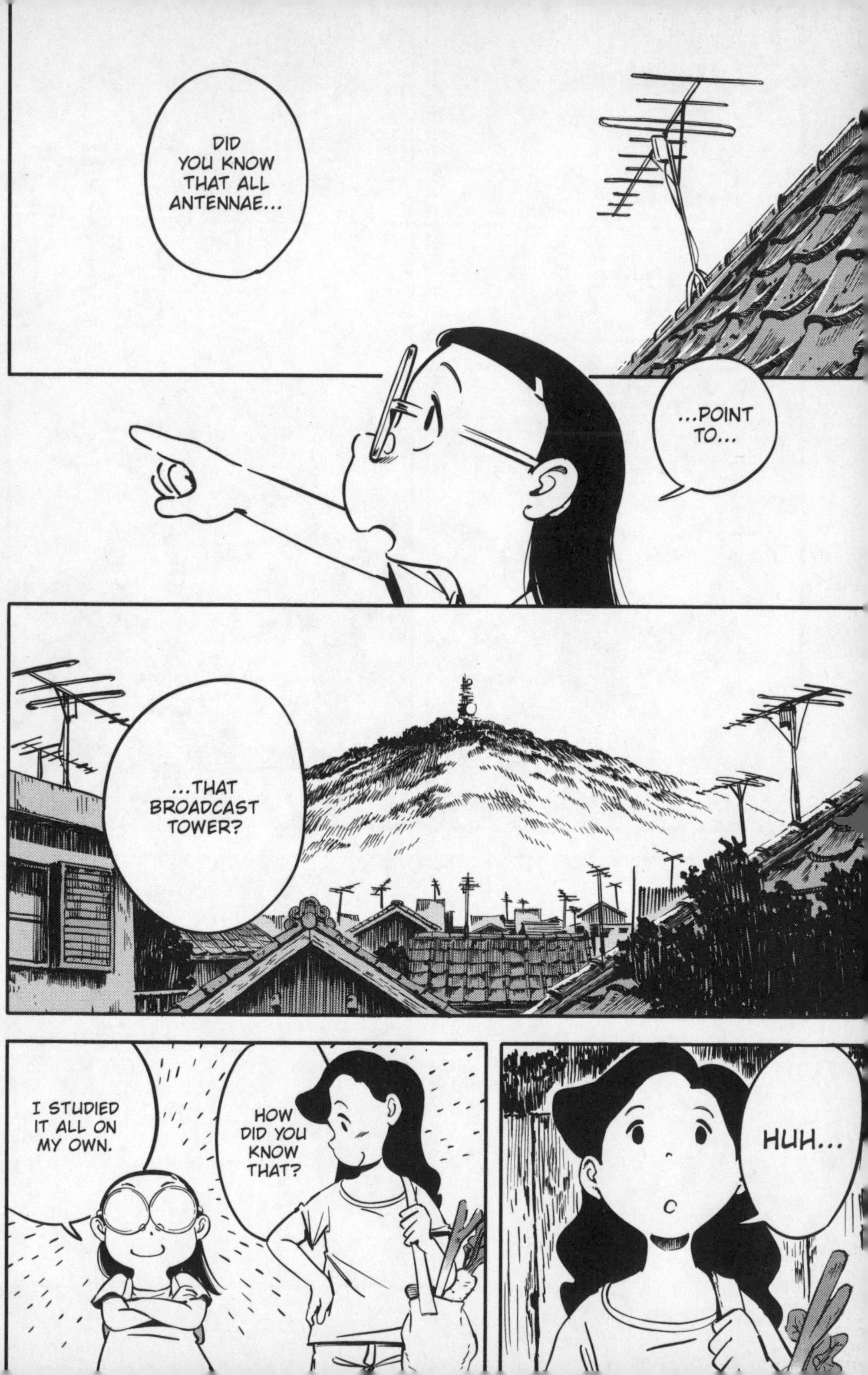
DID YOU KNOW THAT ALL ANTENNAE...
...POINT TO...
...THAT BROADCAST TOWER?
HUH...
HOW DID YOU KNOW THAT?
I STUDIED IT ALL ON MY OWN.

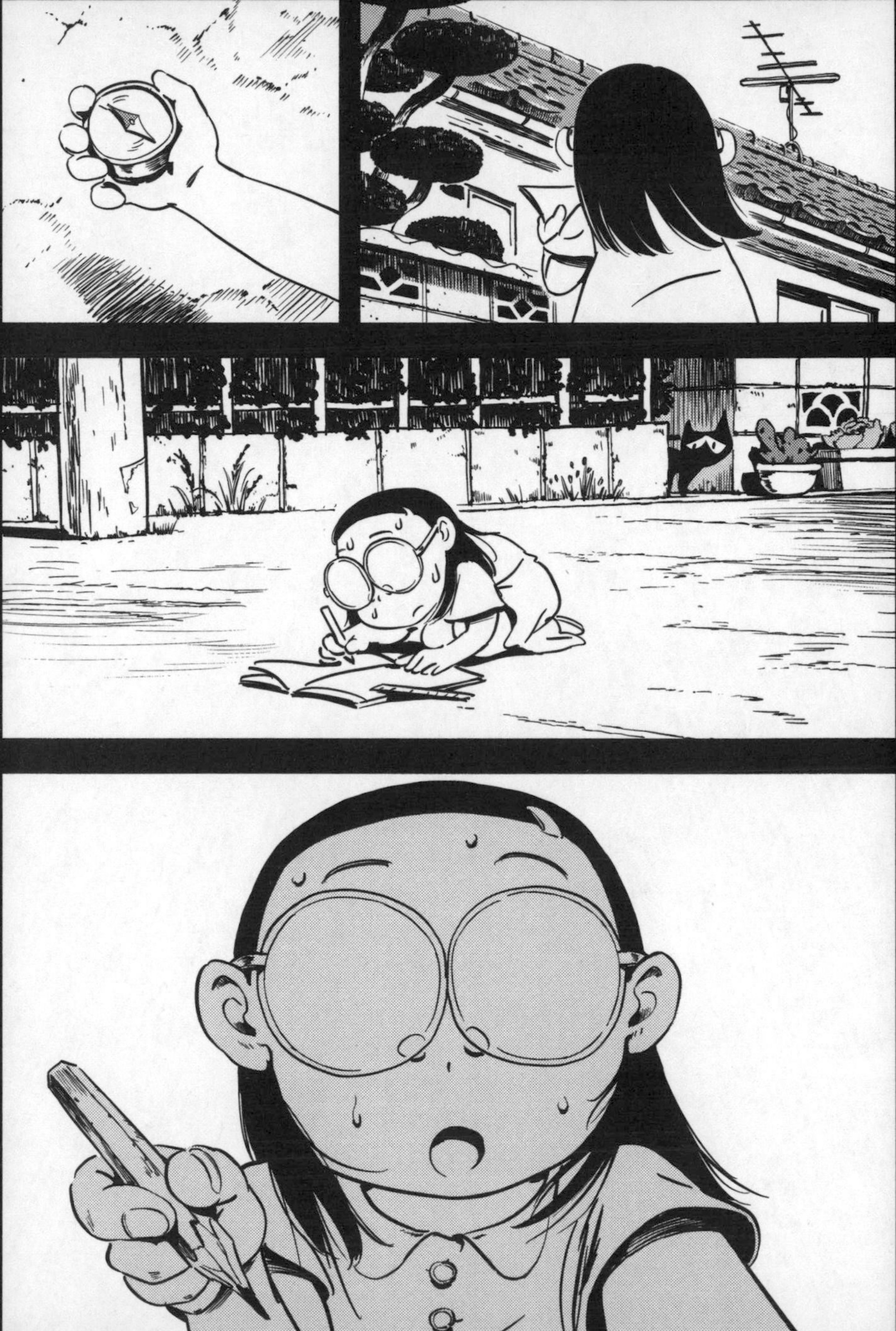

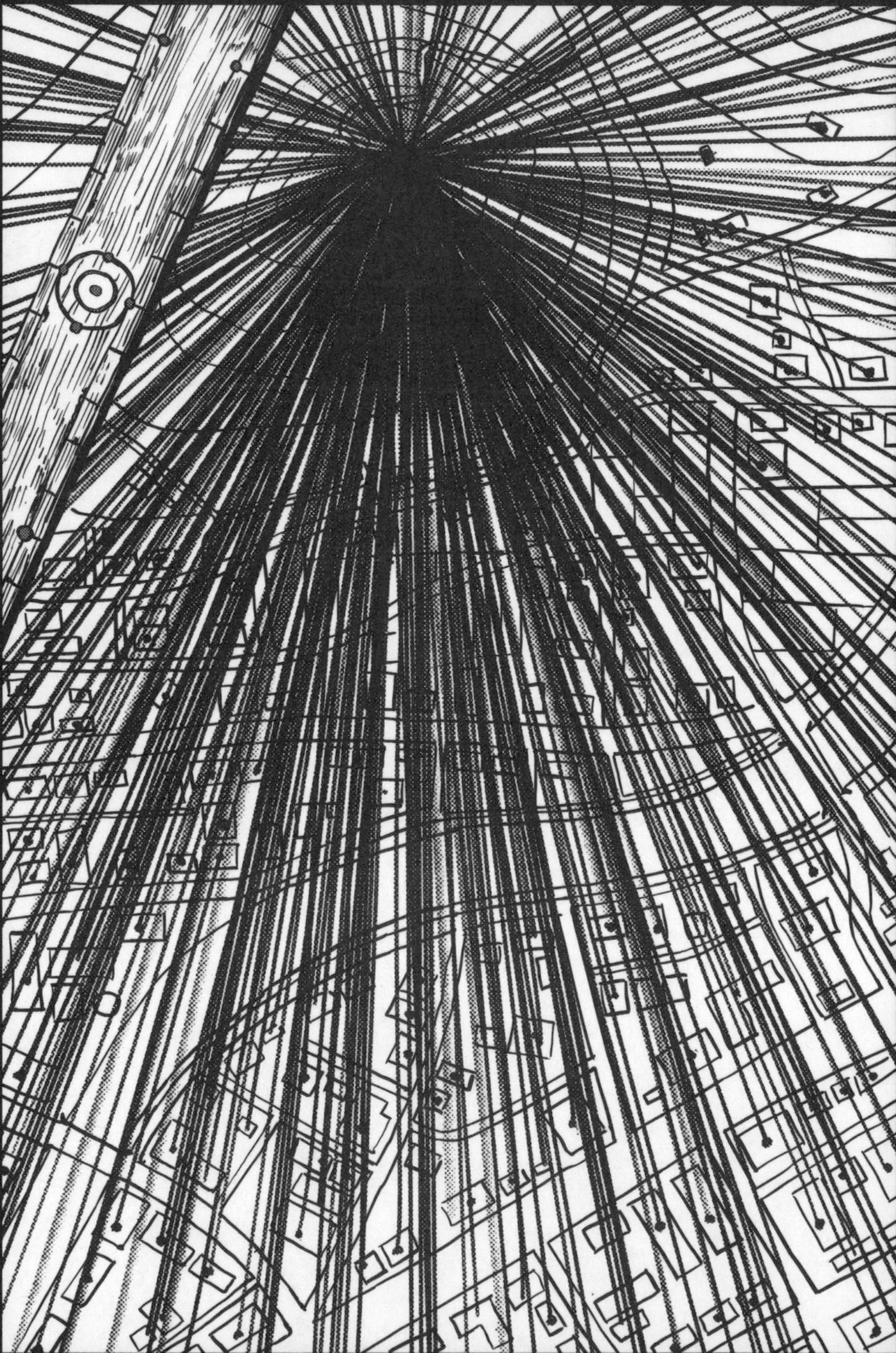

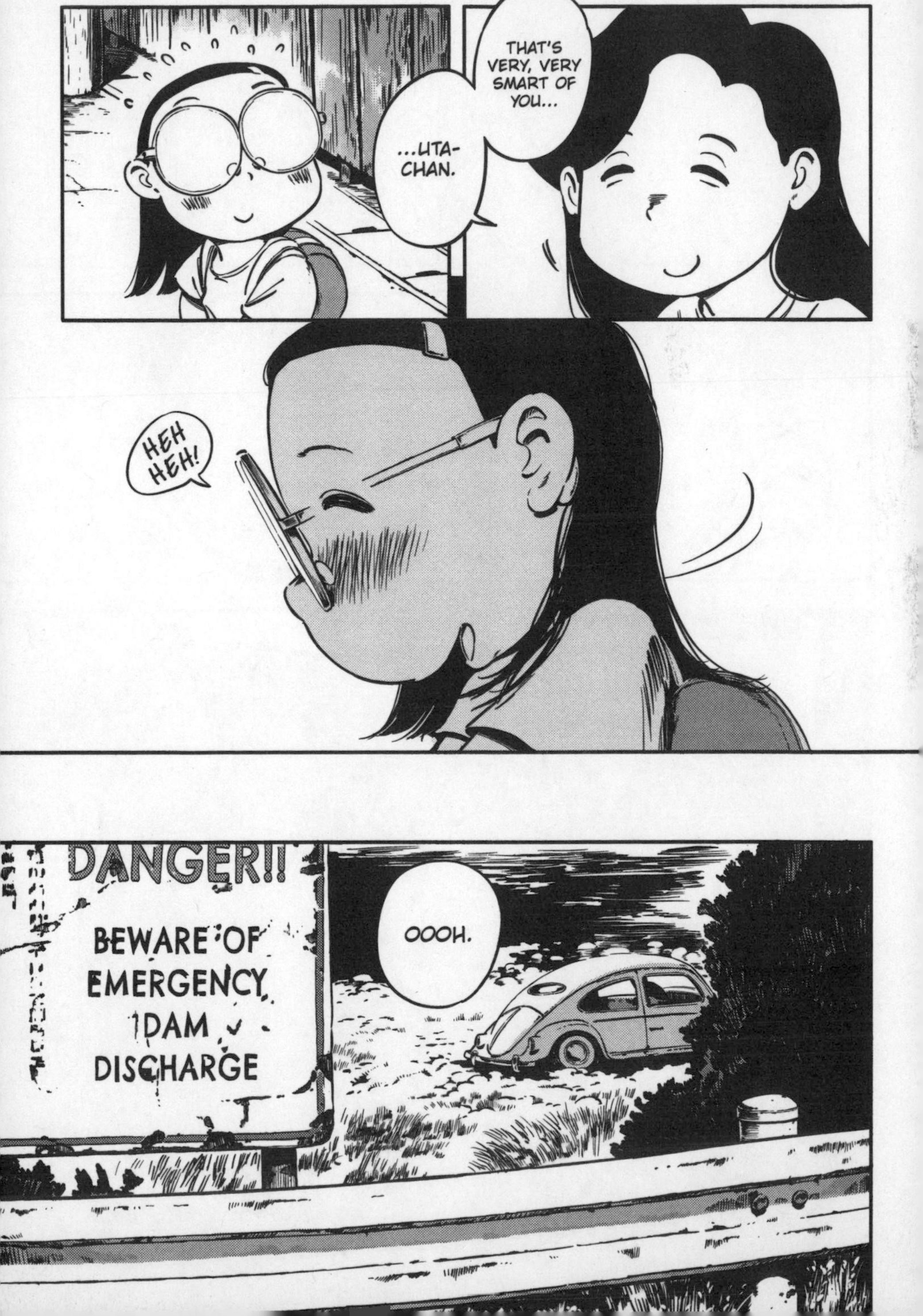
THAT'S VERY, VERY SMART OF YOU...
...UTA-CHAN.
HEH HEH!
OOOH.
DANGER!!
BEWARE OF EMERGENCY DAM DISCHARGE

WHEN YOU WATCH THE CLOUDS...
THEY'RE MOVING...
...SO MUCH.
... FLOAT BY...
THE EARTH'S MOVING FAST TODAY.
...IT FEELS LIKE YOU'RE THE ONE MOVING...

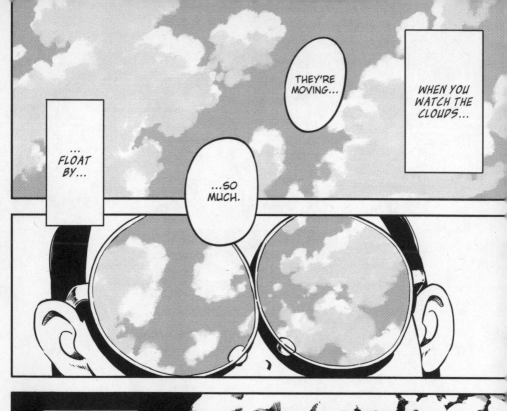

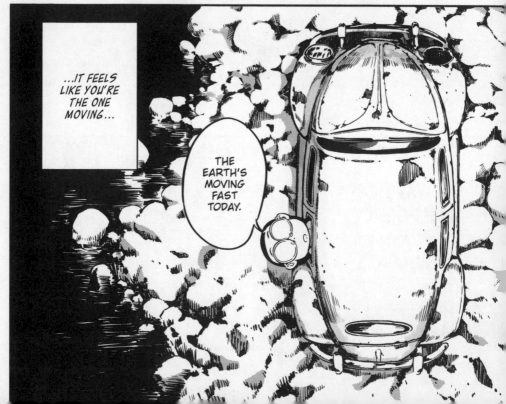

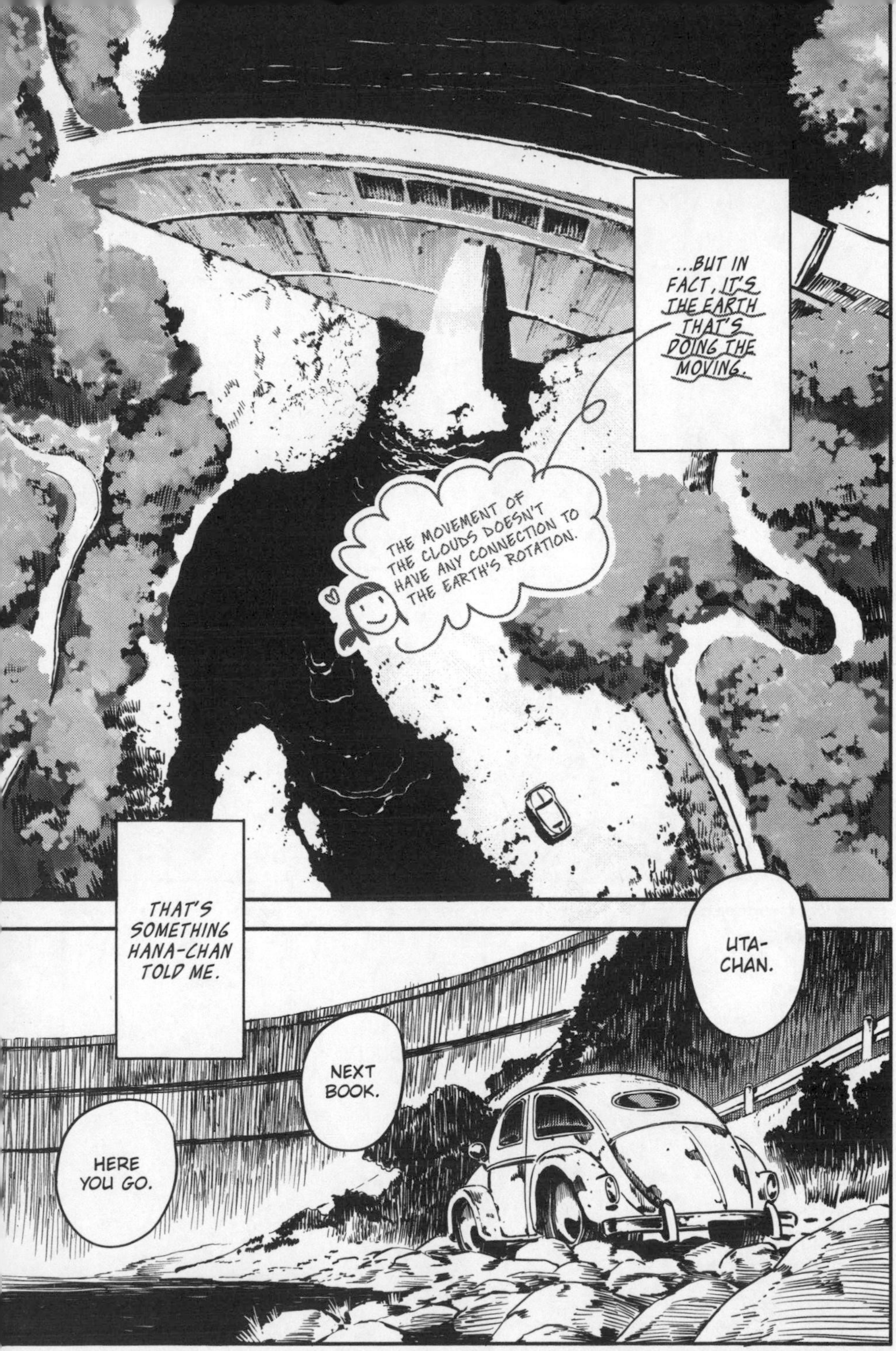
...BUT IN FACT, IT'S THE EARTH THAT'S DOING THE MOVING.
THE MOVEMENT OF THE CLOUDS DOESN'T HAVE ANY CONNECTION TO THE EARTH'S ROTATION.
THAT'S SOMETHING HANA-CHAN TOLD ME.
UTA-CHAN.
NEXT BOOK.
HERE YOU GO.

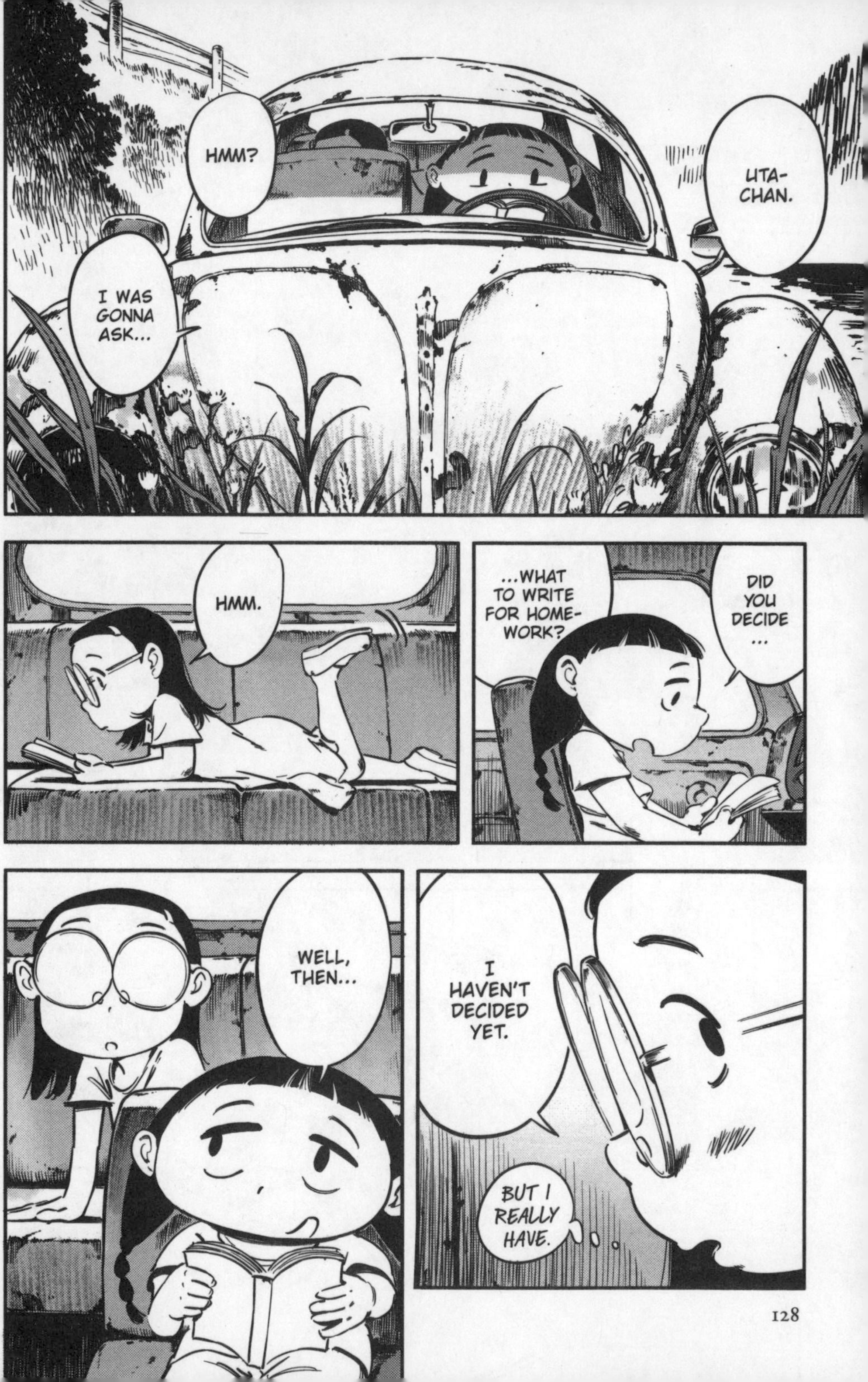
UTA-CHAN.
HMM?
I WAS GONNA ASK...
DID YOU DECIDE ...
...WHAT TO WRITE FOR HOME-WORK?
HMM.
I HAVEN'T DECIDED YET.
BUT I REALLY HAVE.
WELL, THEN...

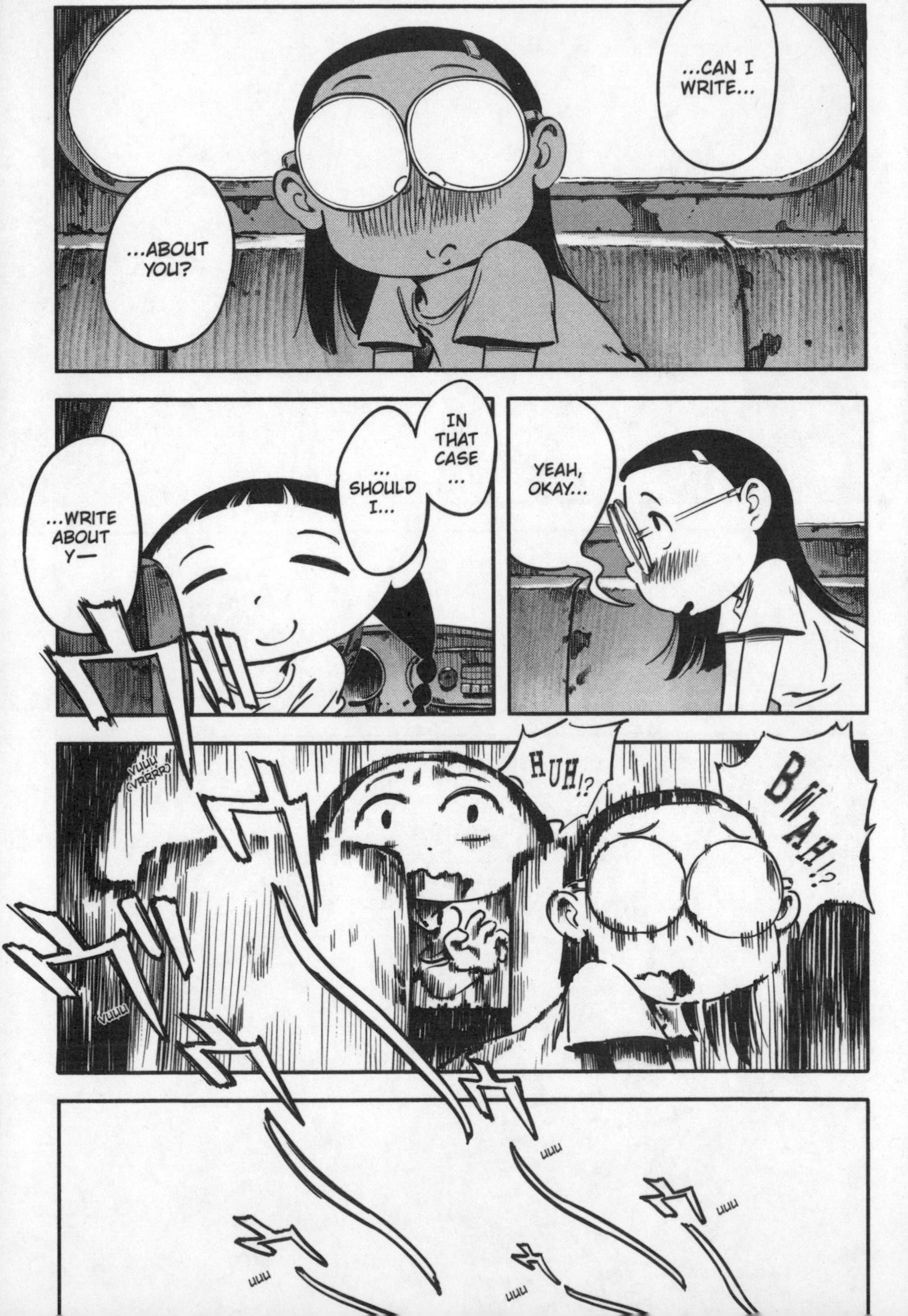
...CAN I WRITE...
...ABOUT YOU?
YEAH, OKAY...
IN THAT CASE...
...SHOULD I...
...WRITE ABOUT Y—
BWAH!?
HUH!?
VUUU (VRRRR)
VUUU
UUU
UUU
UUU
UUU

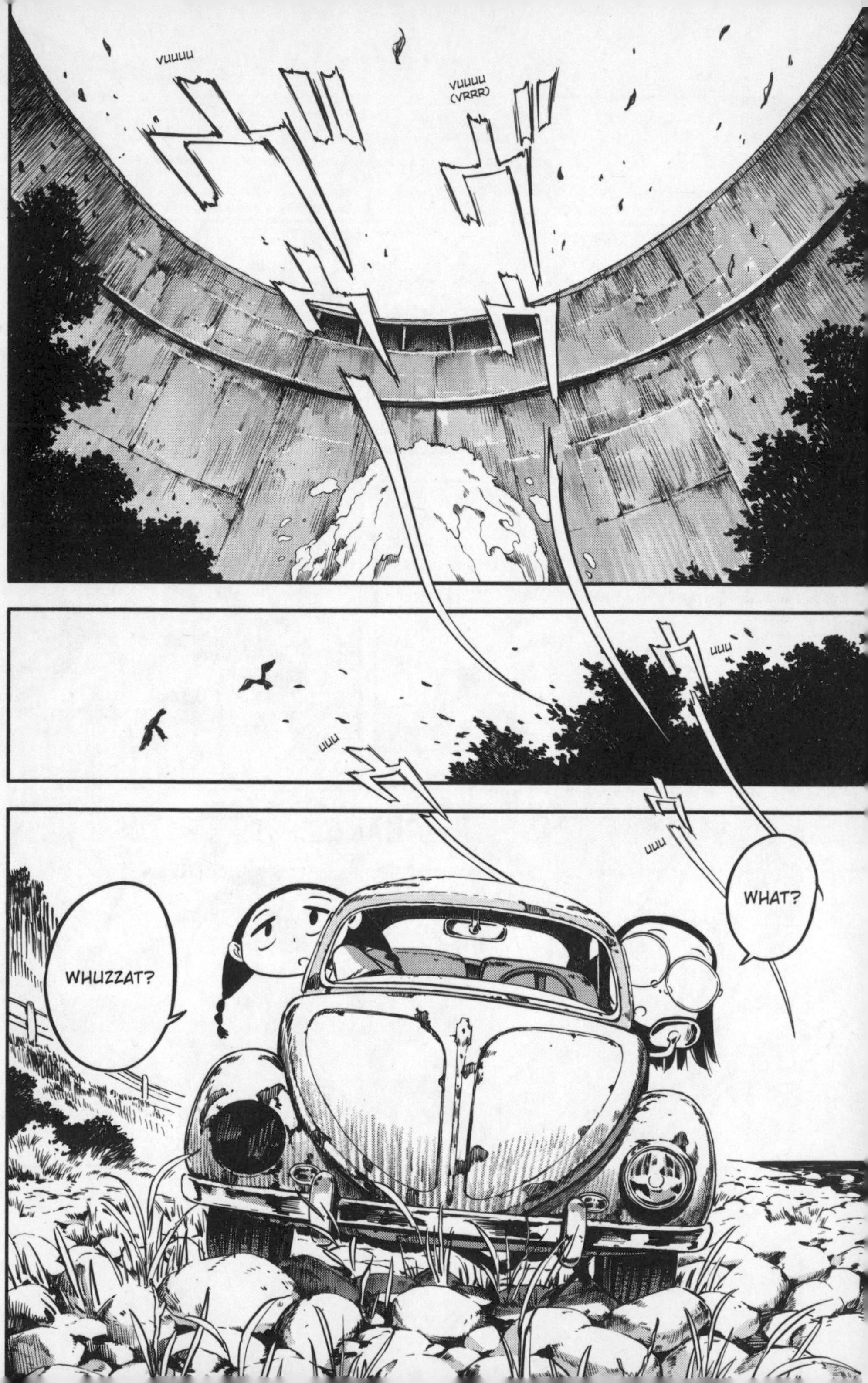
vuuuu
(VRRR)
vuuuu
uuu
uuu
WHAT?
uuu
WHUZZAT?

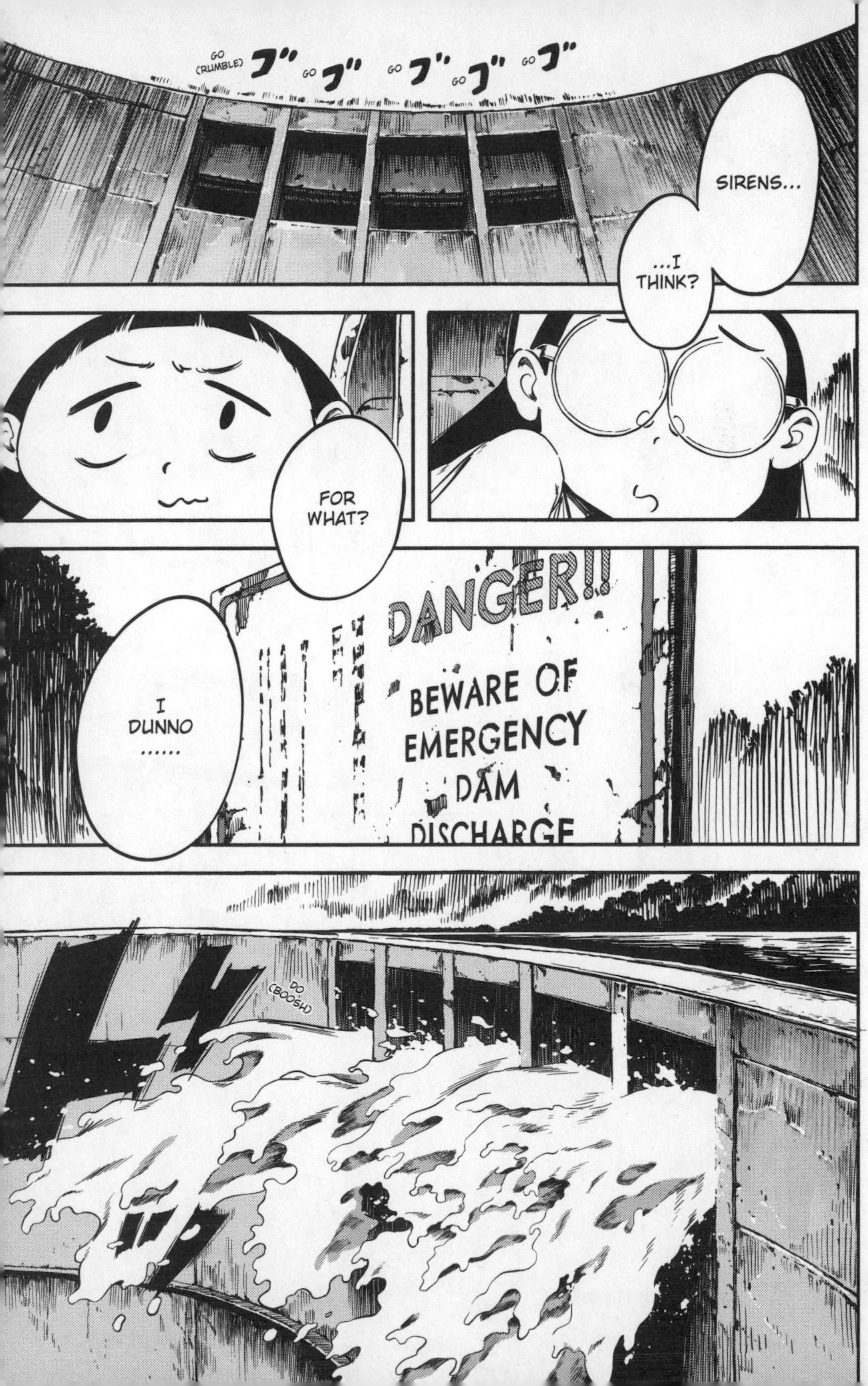
GO (RUMBLE) ゴ GO ゴ GO ゴ GO ゴ GO ゴ
SIRENS...
...I THINK?
FOR WHAT?
DANGER!!
BEWARE OF EMERGENCY DAM DISCHARGE
I DUNNO ......
DO (BOOSH)

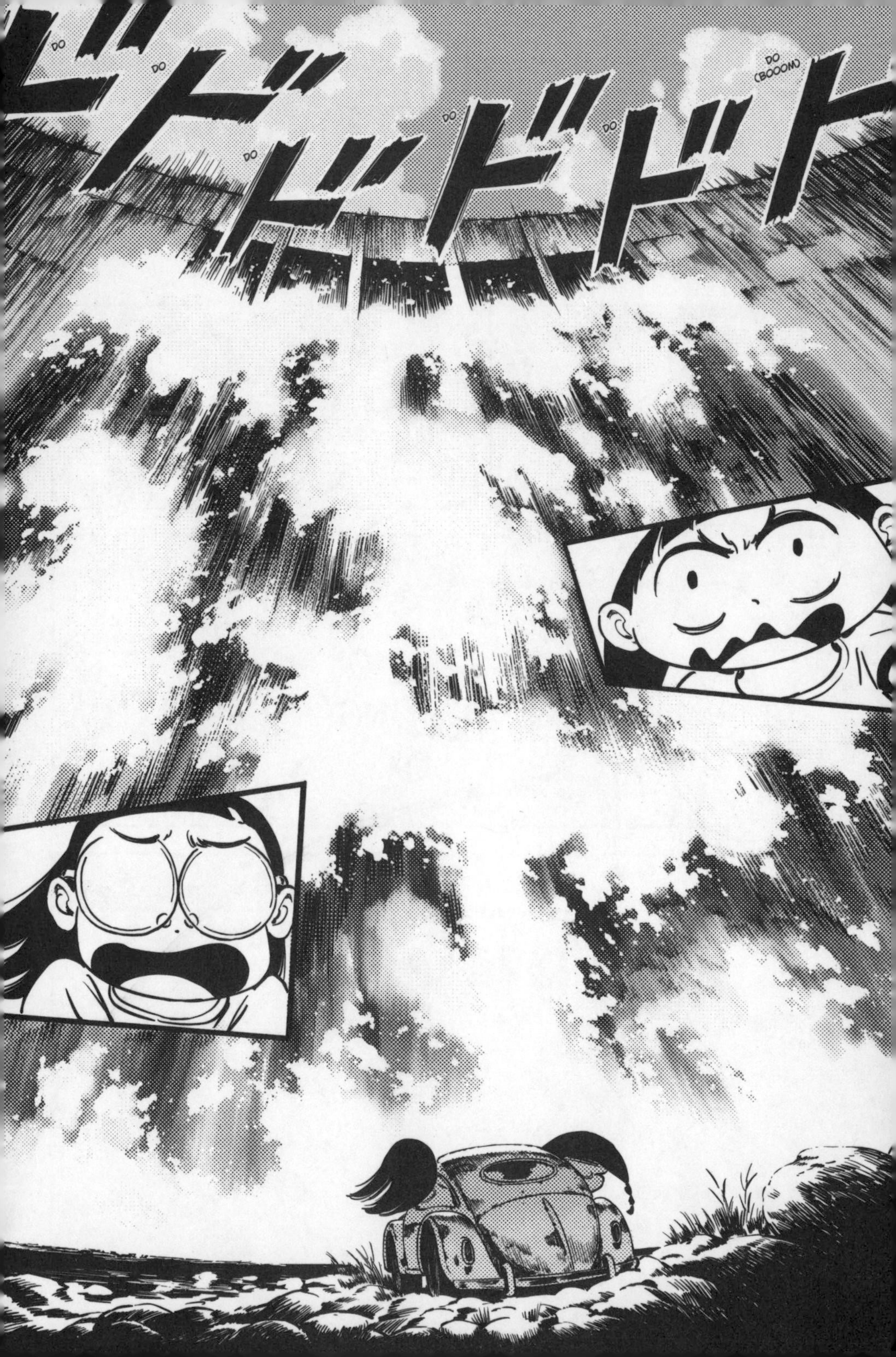

DO DO DO DO DO DO (BOOOM)

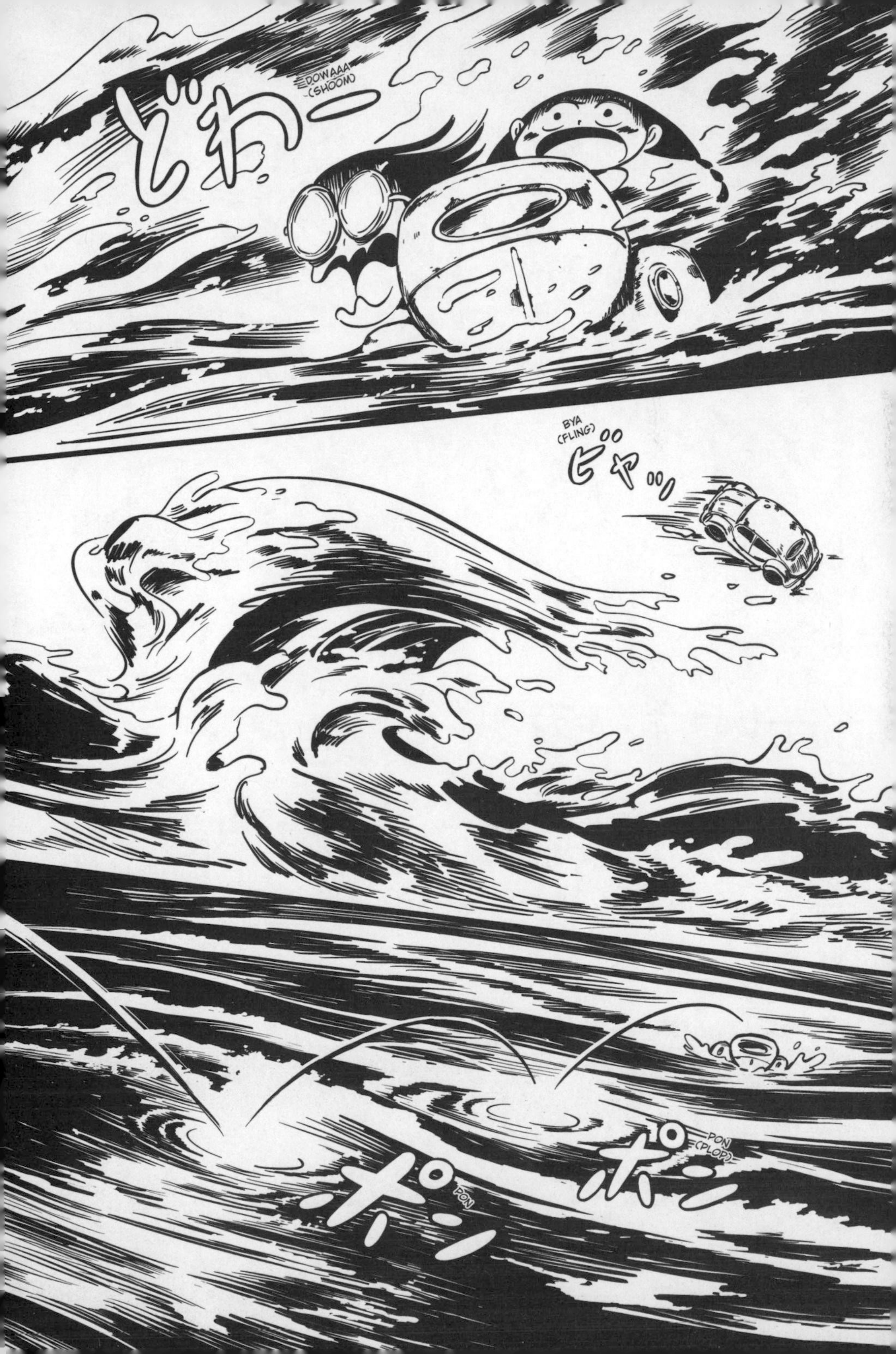
どわー
DOWAAA (SHOOM)
BYA (FLING)
PON (PLOP)
PON

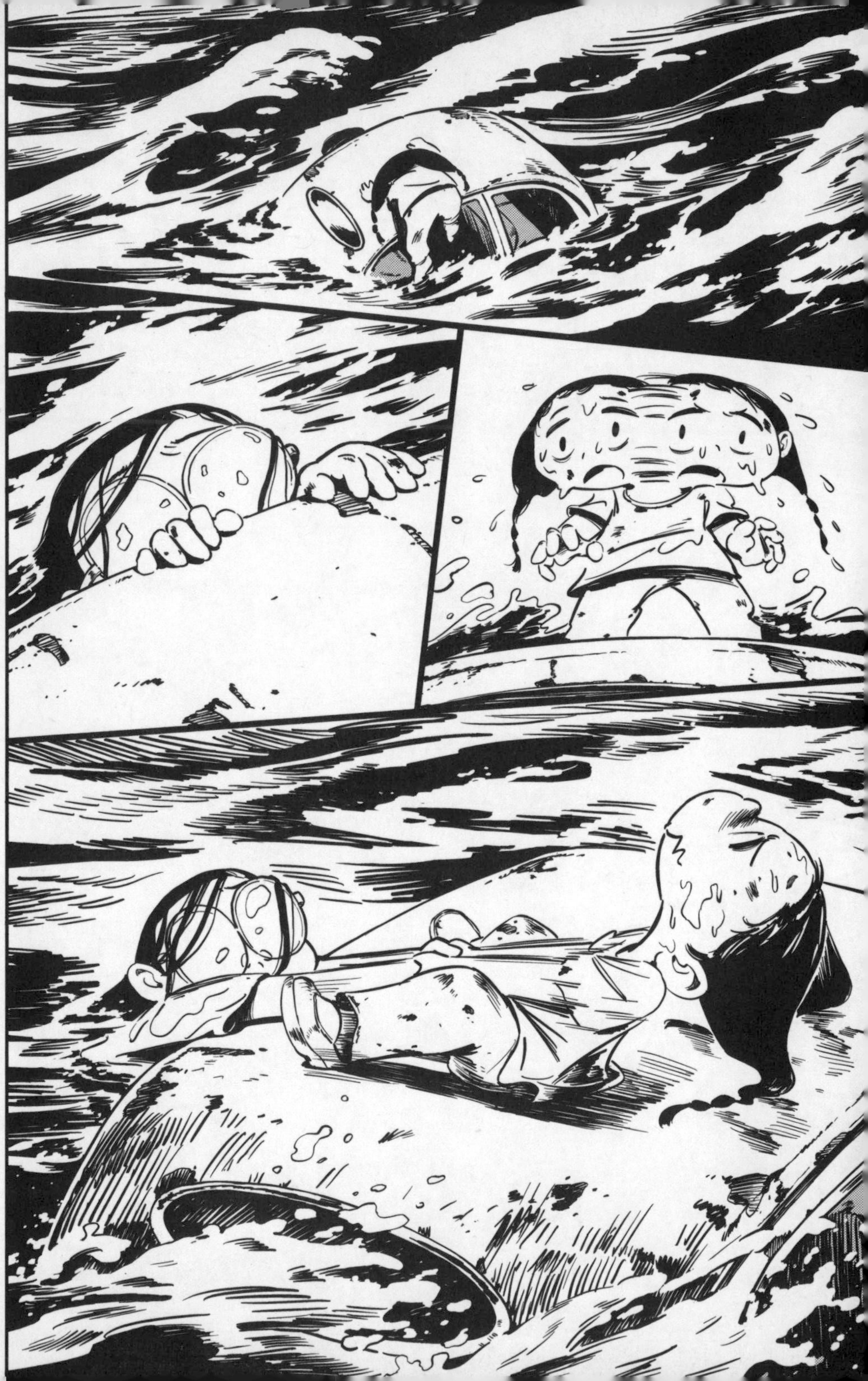

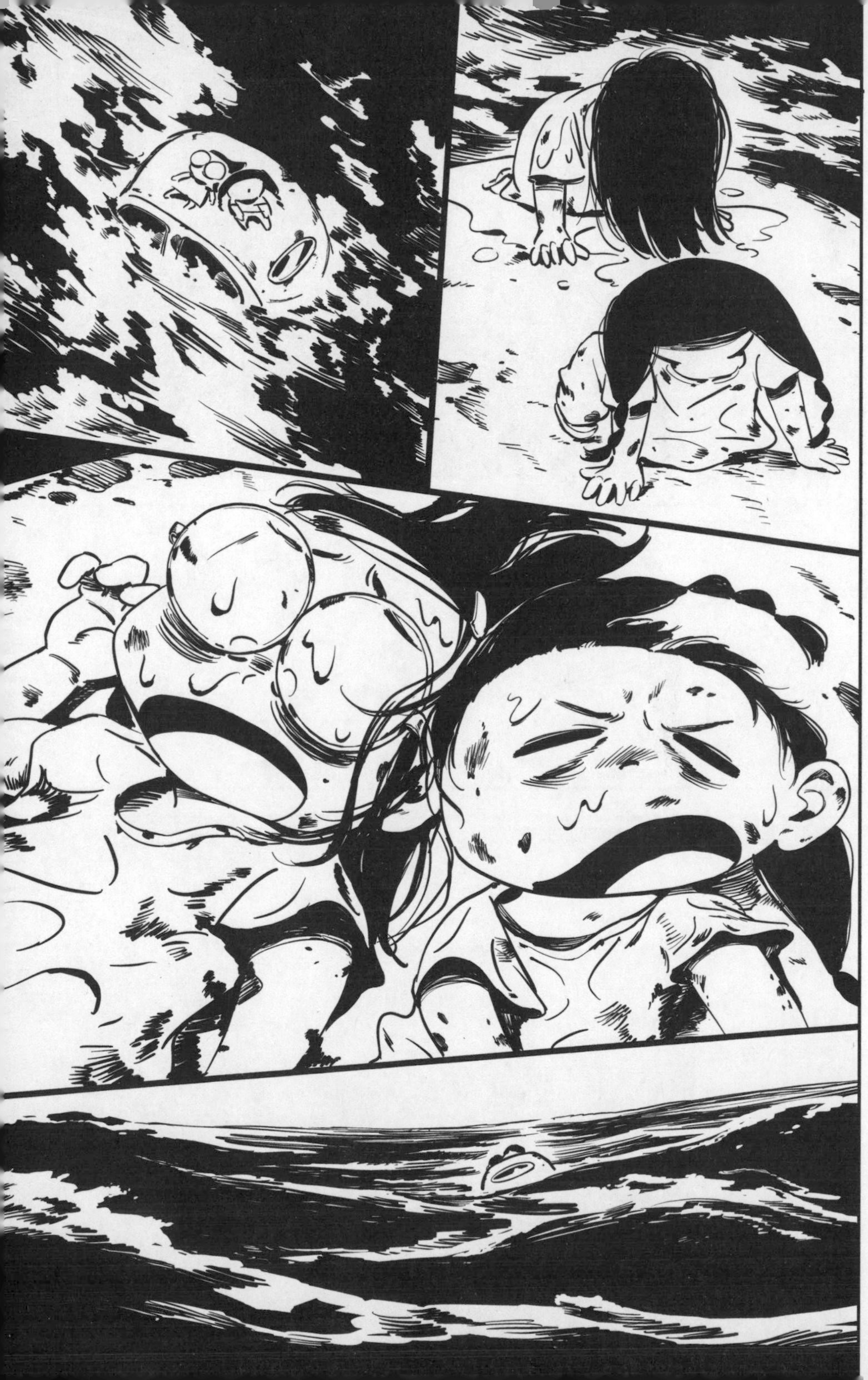

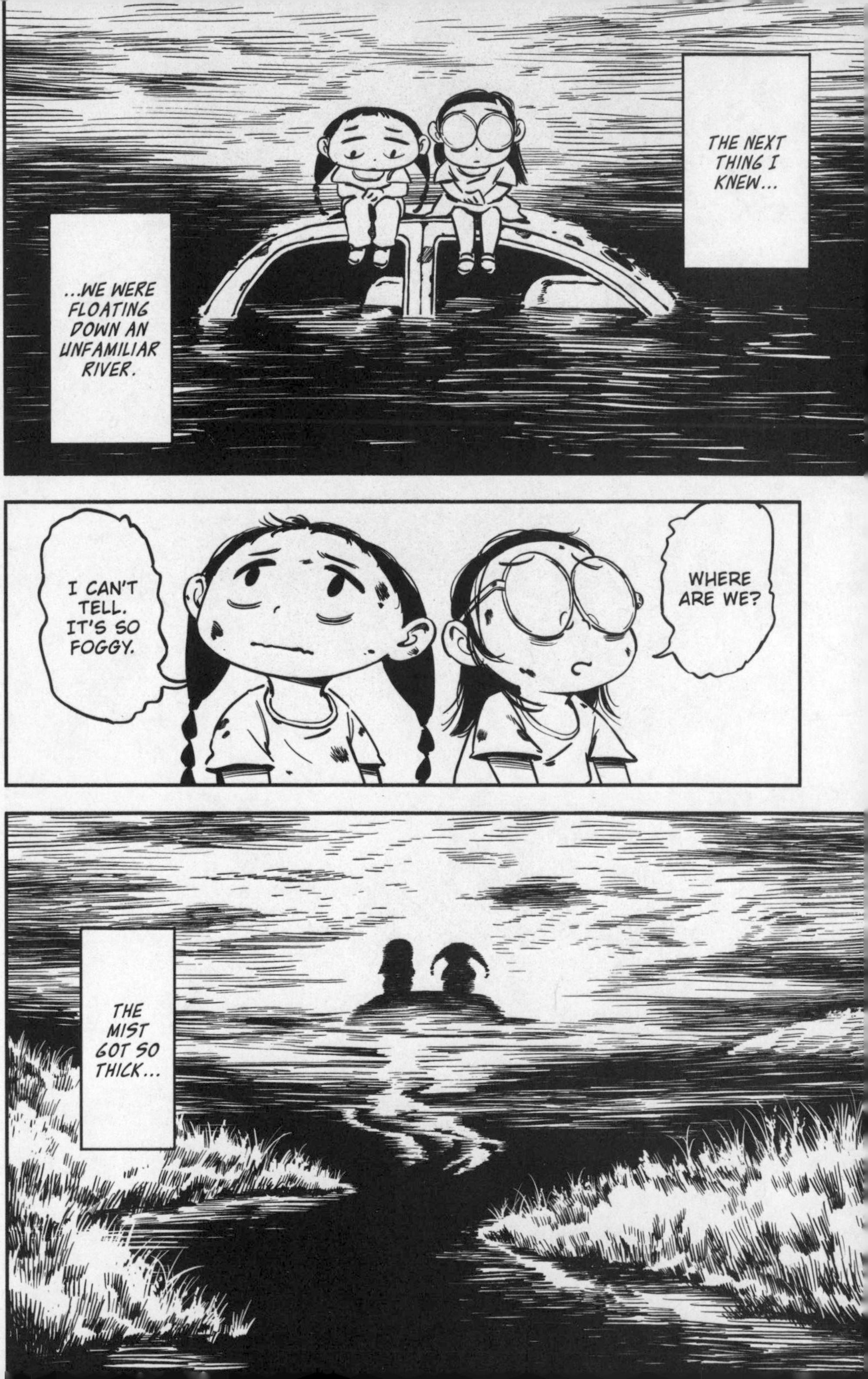
THE NEXT THING I KNEW...
...WE WERE FLOATING DOWN AN UNFAMILIAR RIVER.
WHERE ARE WE?
I CAN'T TELL. IT'S SO FOGGY.
THE MIST GOT SO THICK...

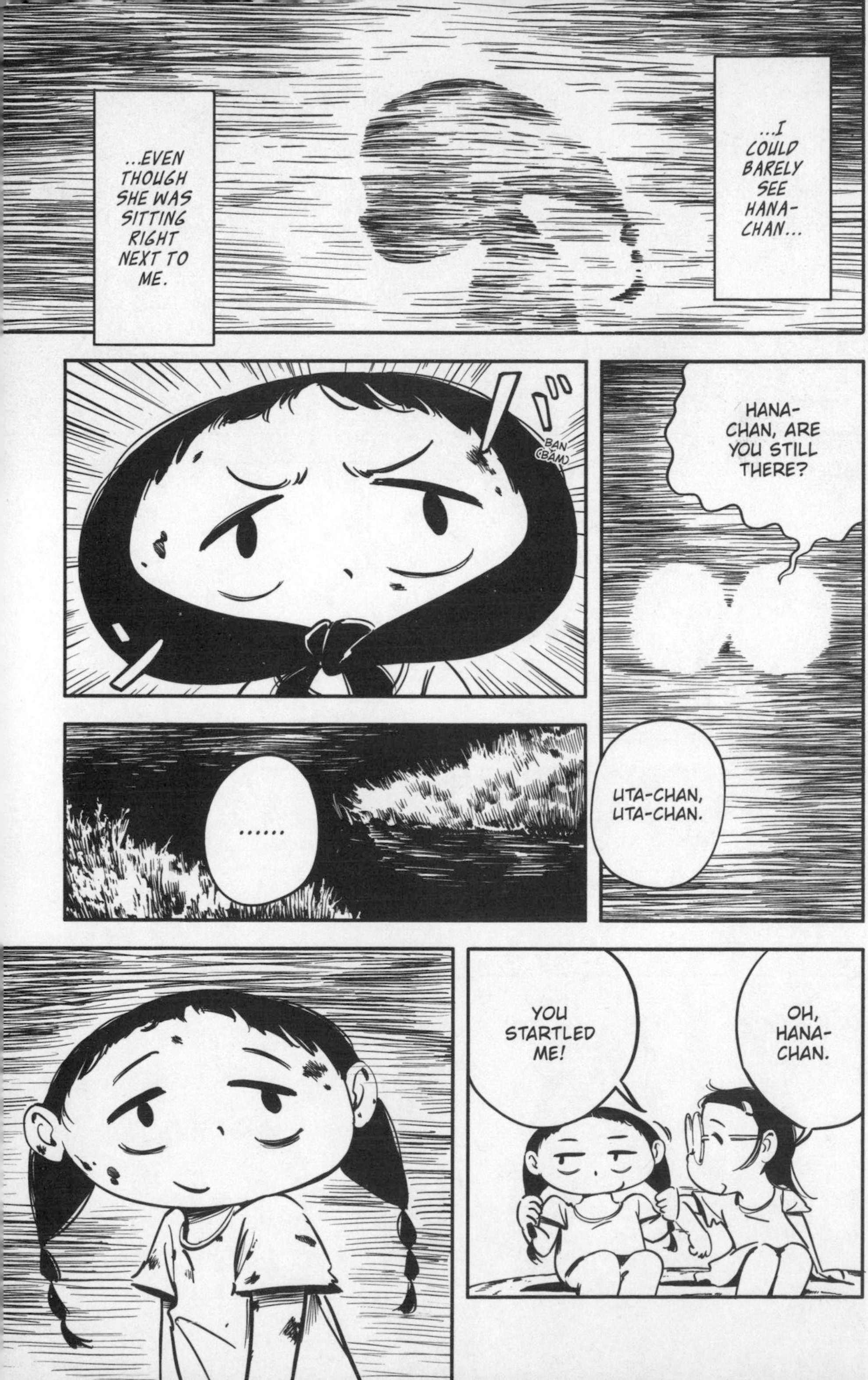
...I COULD BARELY SEE HANA-CHAN...
...EVEN THOUGH SHE WAS SITTING RIGHT NEXT TO ME.
HANA-CHAN, ARE YOU STILL THERE?
UTA-CHAN, UTA-CHAN.
BAN (BAM)
......
OH, HANA-CHAN.
YOU STARTLED ME!

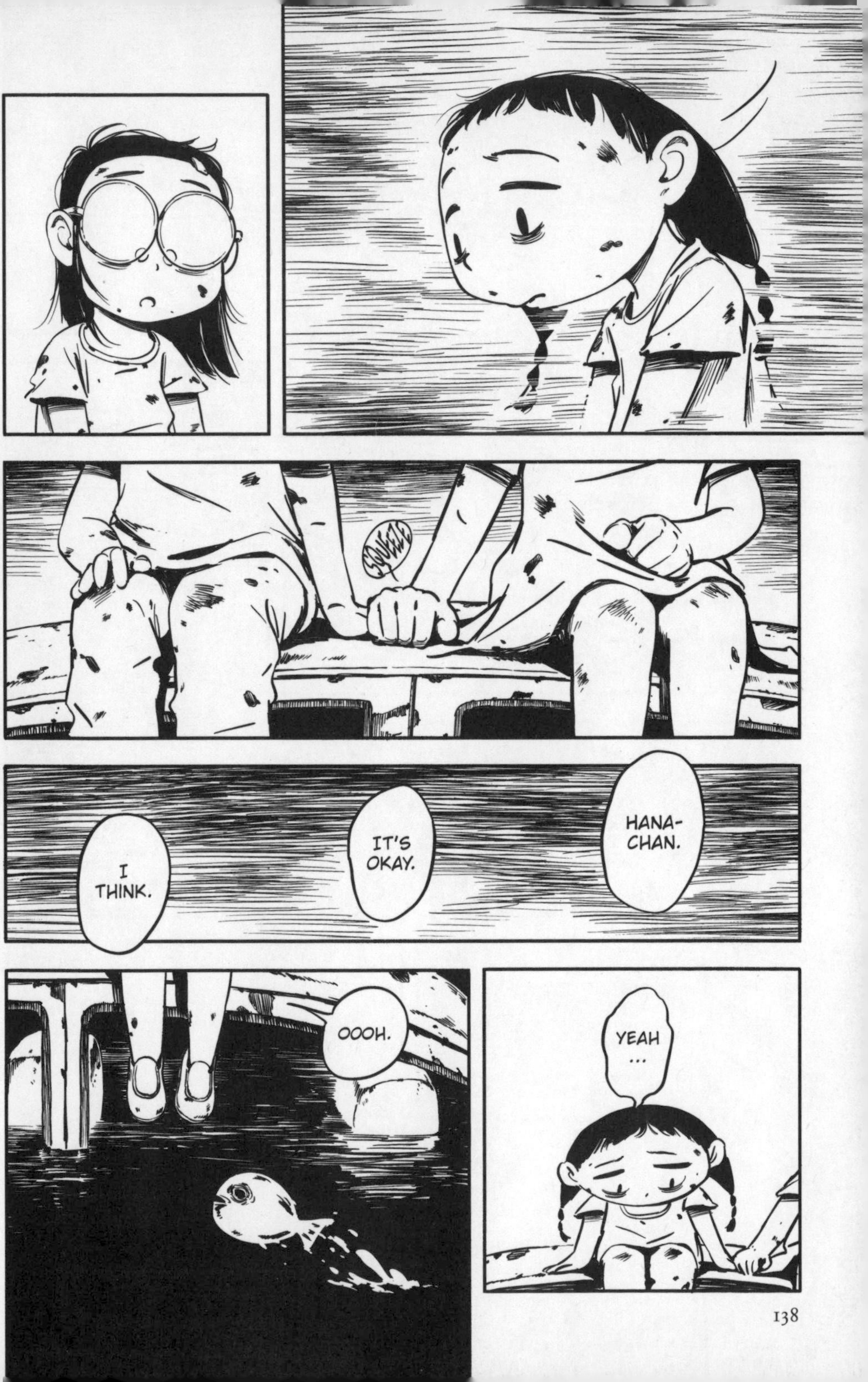
SQUEEZE
HANA-CHAN.
IT'S OKAY.
I THINK.
YEAH ...
OOOH.

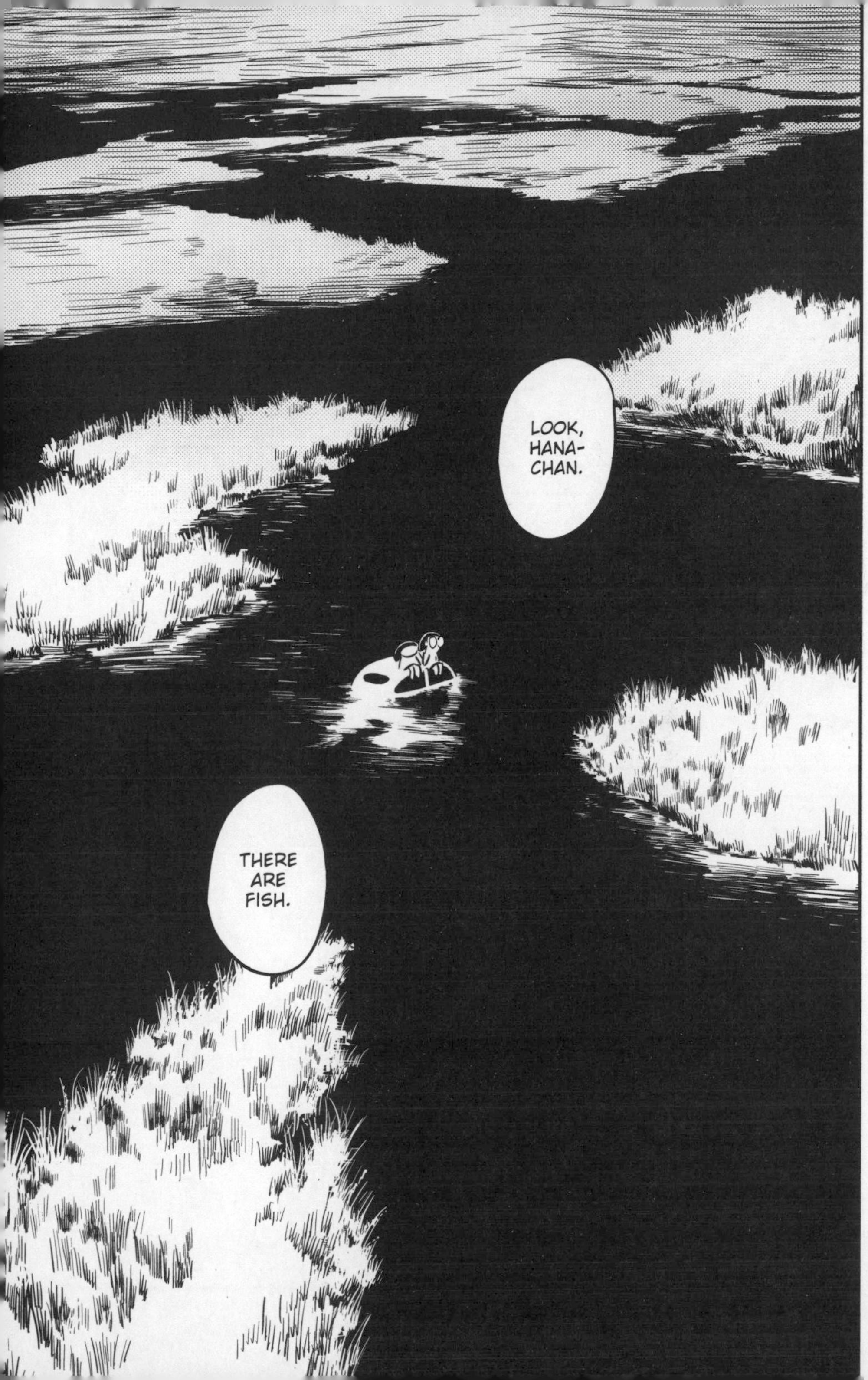
LOOK, HANA-CHAN.
THERE ARE FISH.

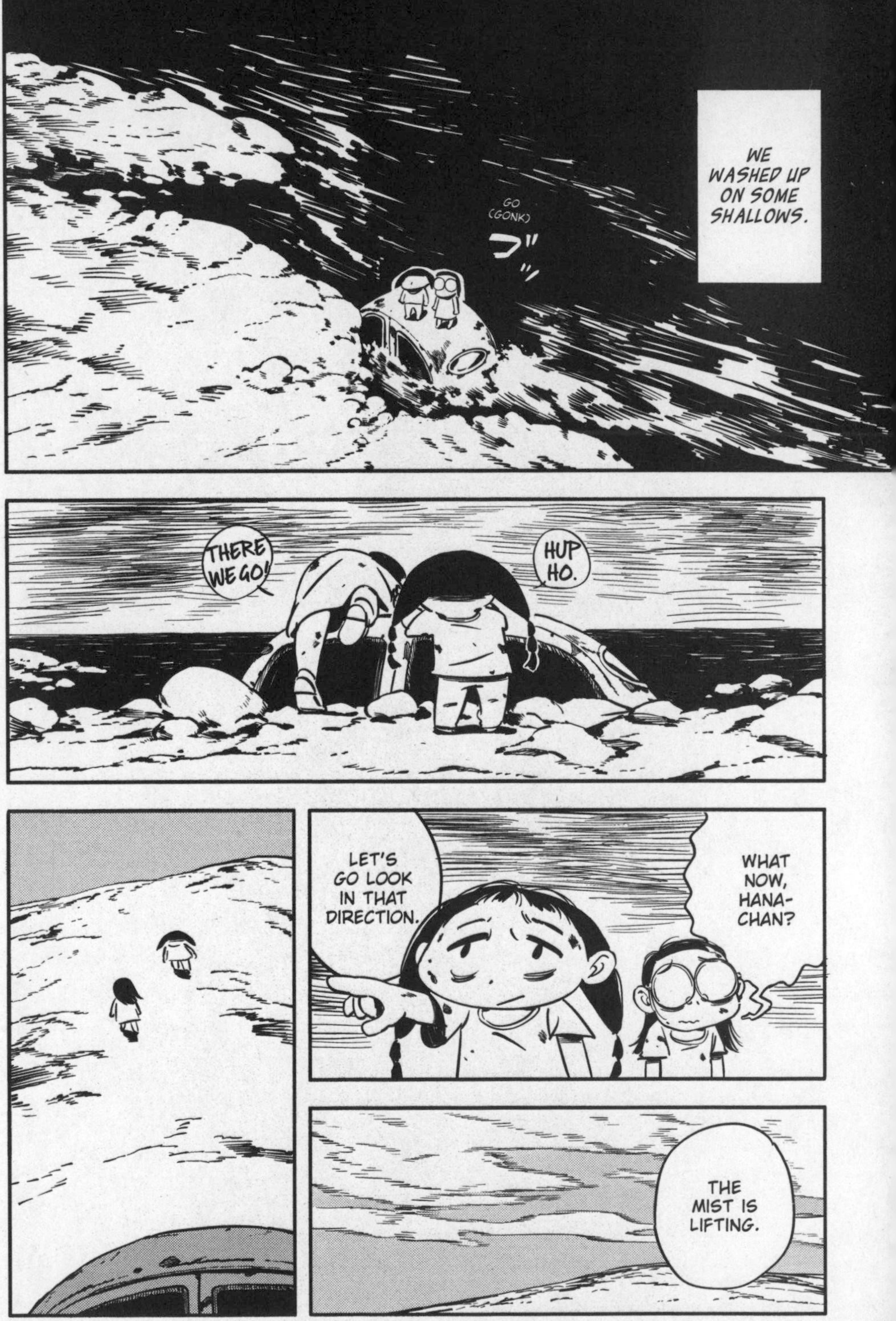
WE WASHED UP ON SOME SHALLOWS.
GO (GONK)
ゴ
HUP HO.
THERE WE GO!
WHAT NOW, HANA-CHAN?
LET'S GO LOOK IN THAT DIRECTION.
THE MIST IS LIFTING.

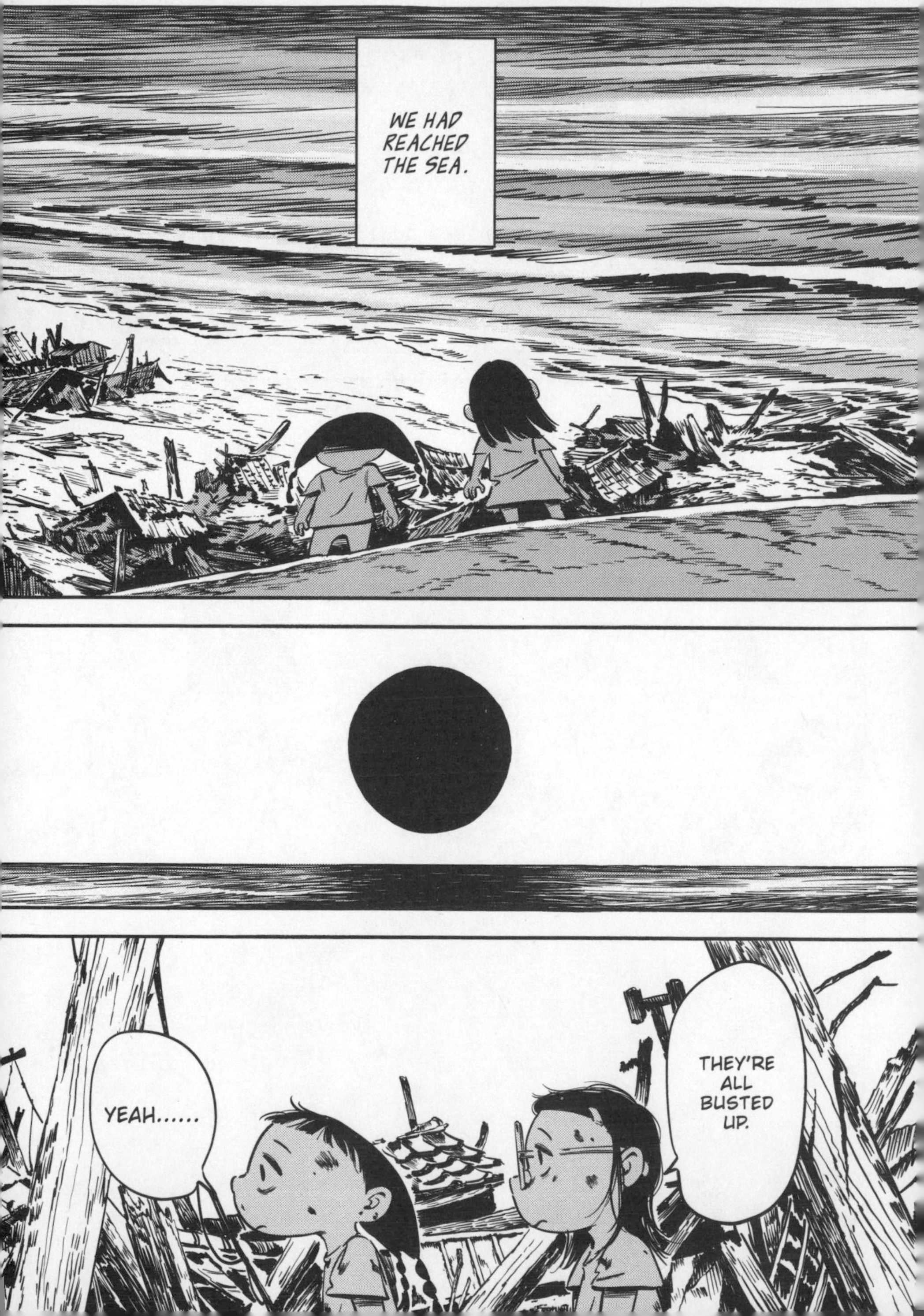
WE HAD REACHED THE SEA.
THEY'RE ALL BUSTED UP.
YEAH......

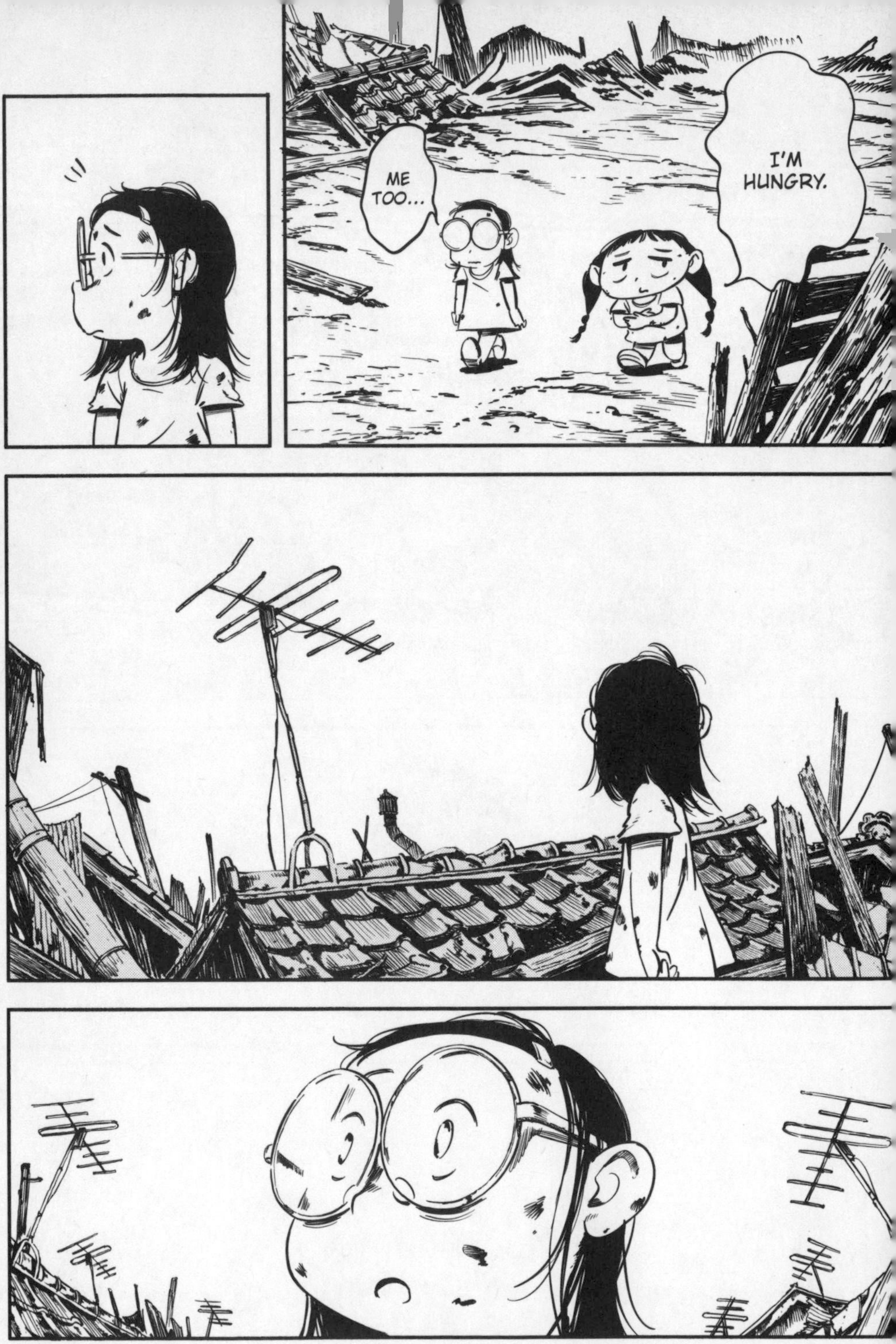
I'M HUNGRY.
ME TOO…

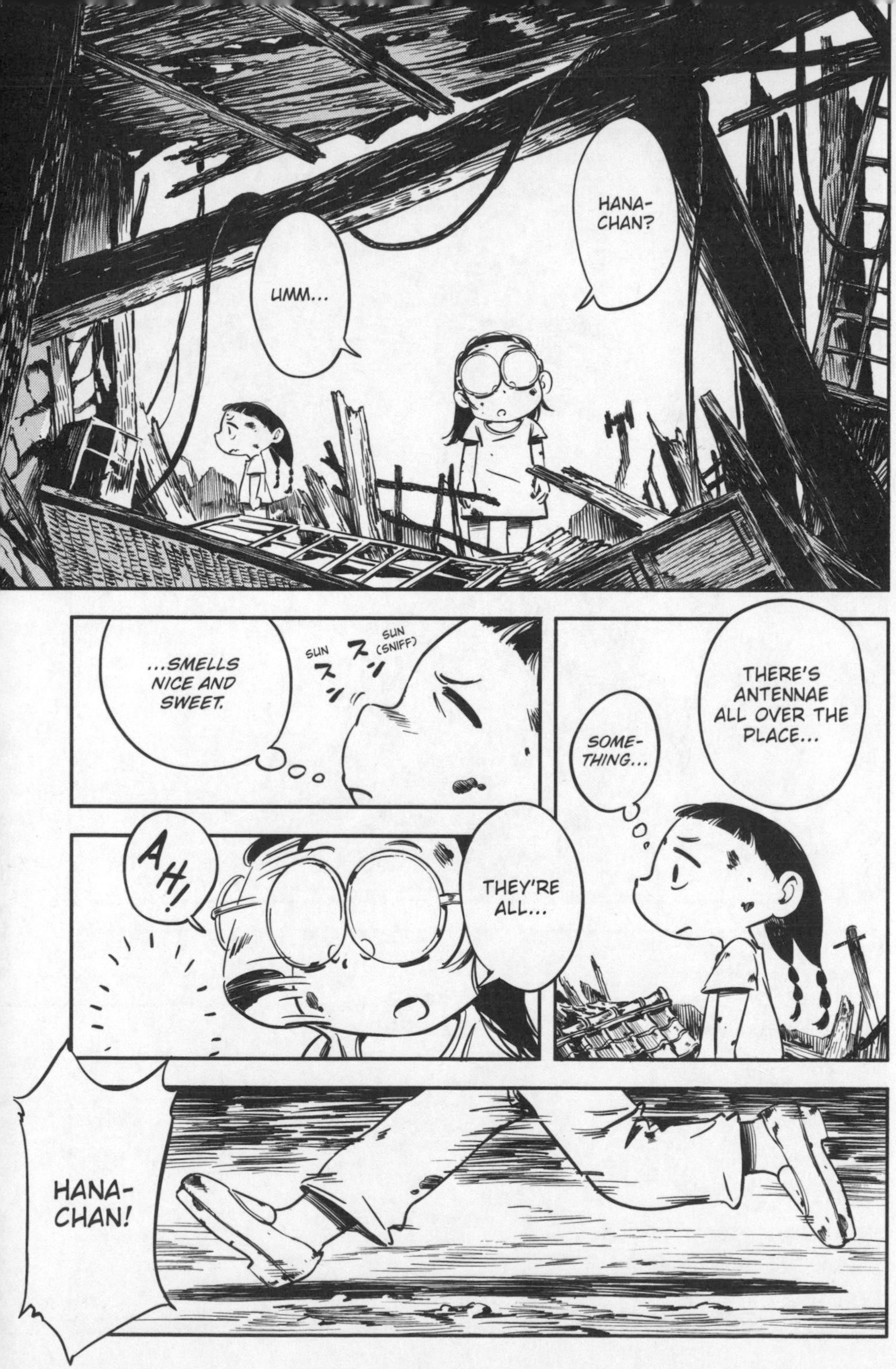
HANA-CHAN?
UMM...
THERE'S ANTENNAE ALL OVER THE PLACE...
SOME-THING...
SUN SUN (SNIFF)
...SMELLS NICE AND SWEET.
THEY'RE ALL...
AH!
HANA-CHAN!

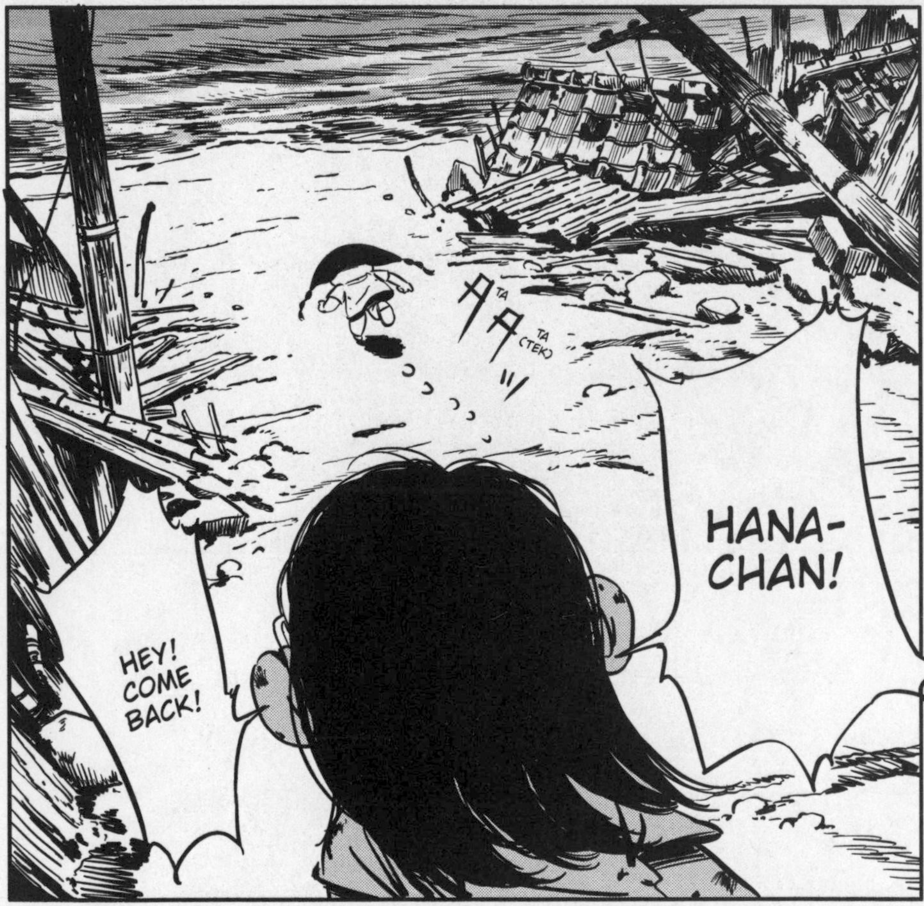

タタッ
TA
TA (TEK)
HANA-CHAN!
HEY! COME BACK!

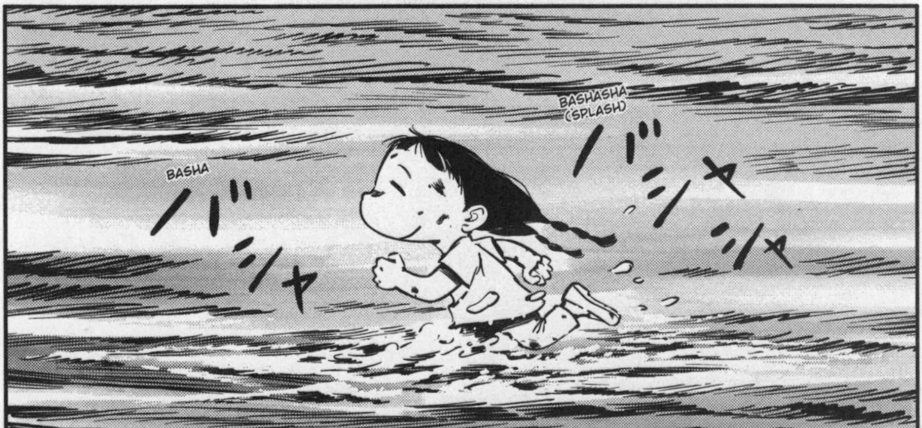

BASHASHA (SPLASH)
バシャシャ
BASHA
バシャ

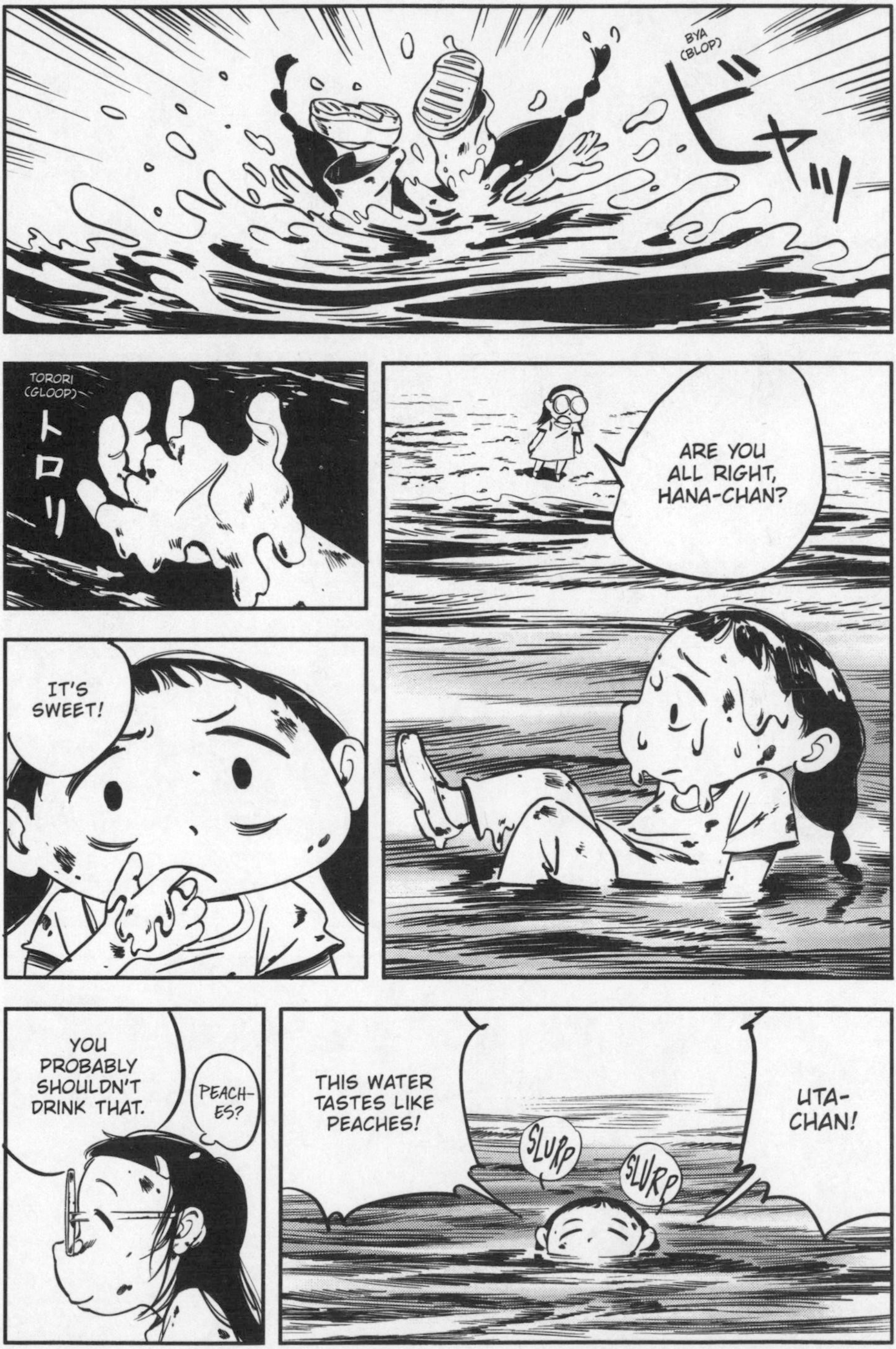
BYA (BLOP)
ビャッ
ARE YOU ALL RIGHT, HANA-CHAN?
TORORI (GLOOP)
トロリ
IT'S SWEET!
UTA-CHAN!
THIS WATER TASTES LIKE PEACHES!
SLURP
SLURP
PEACH-ES?
YOU PROBABLY SHOULDN'T DRINK THAT.

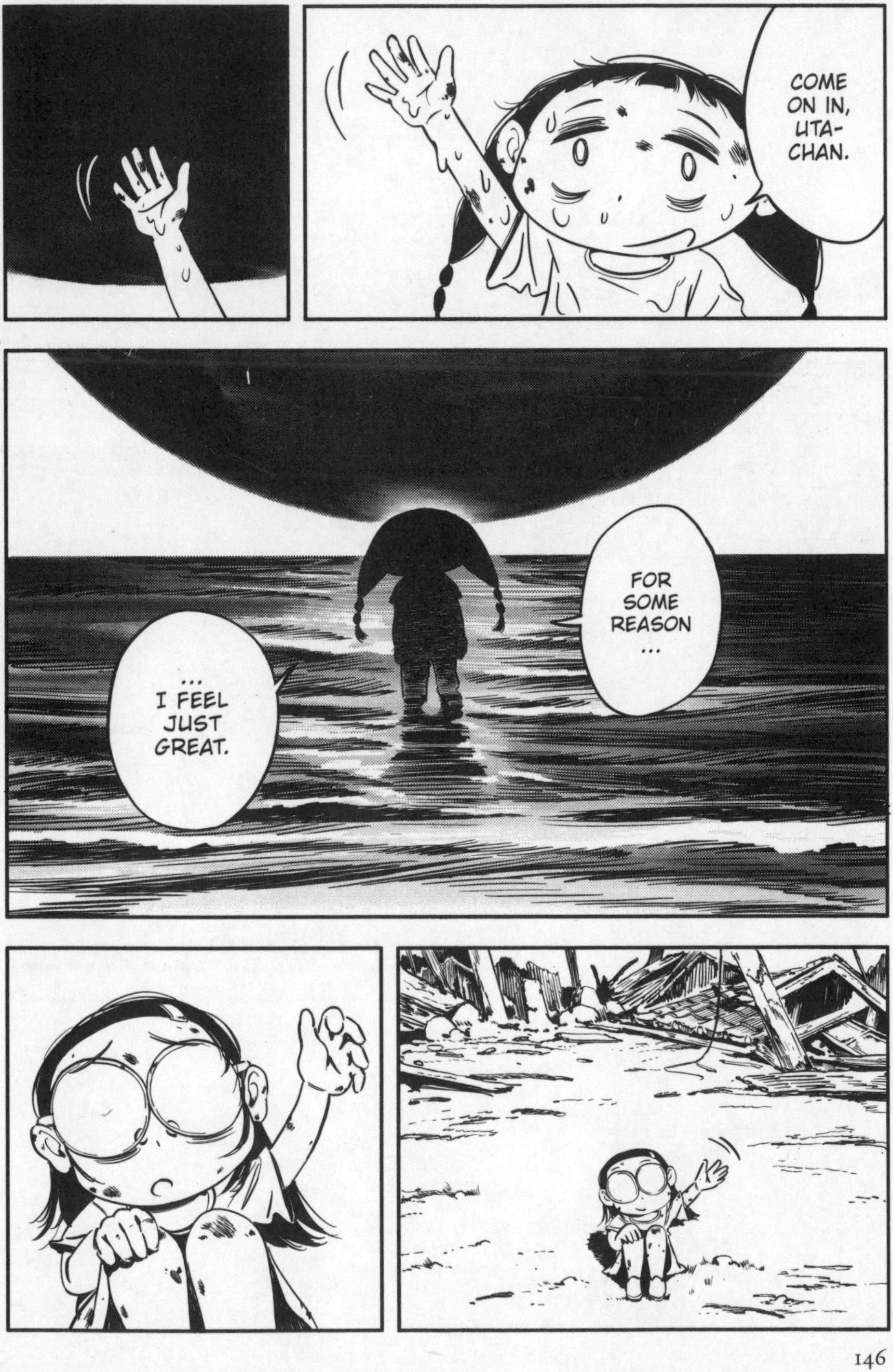
COME ON IN, UTA-CHAN.
FOR SOME REASON ...
... I FEEL JUST GREAT.

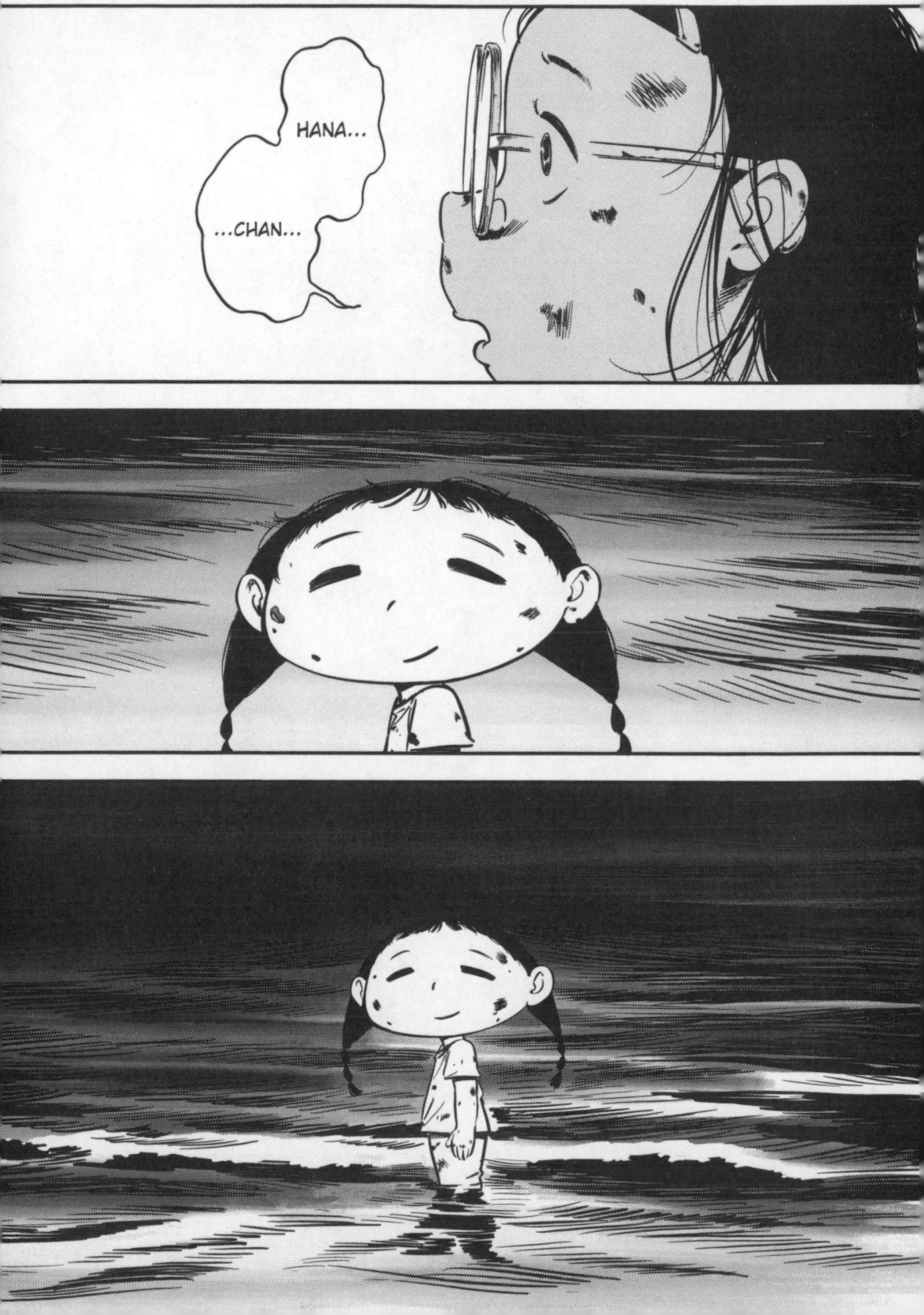
HANA...
...CHAN...

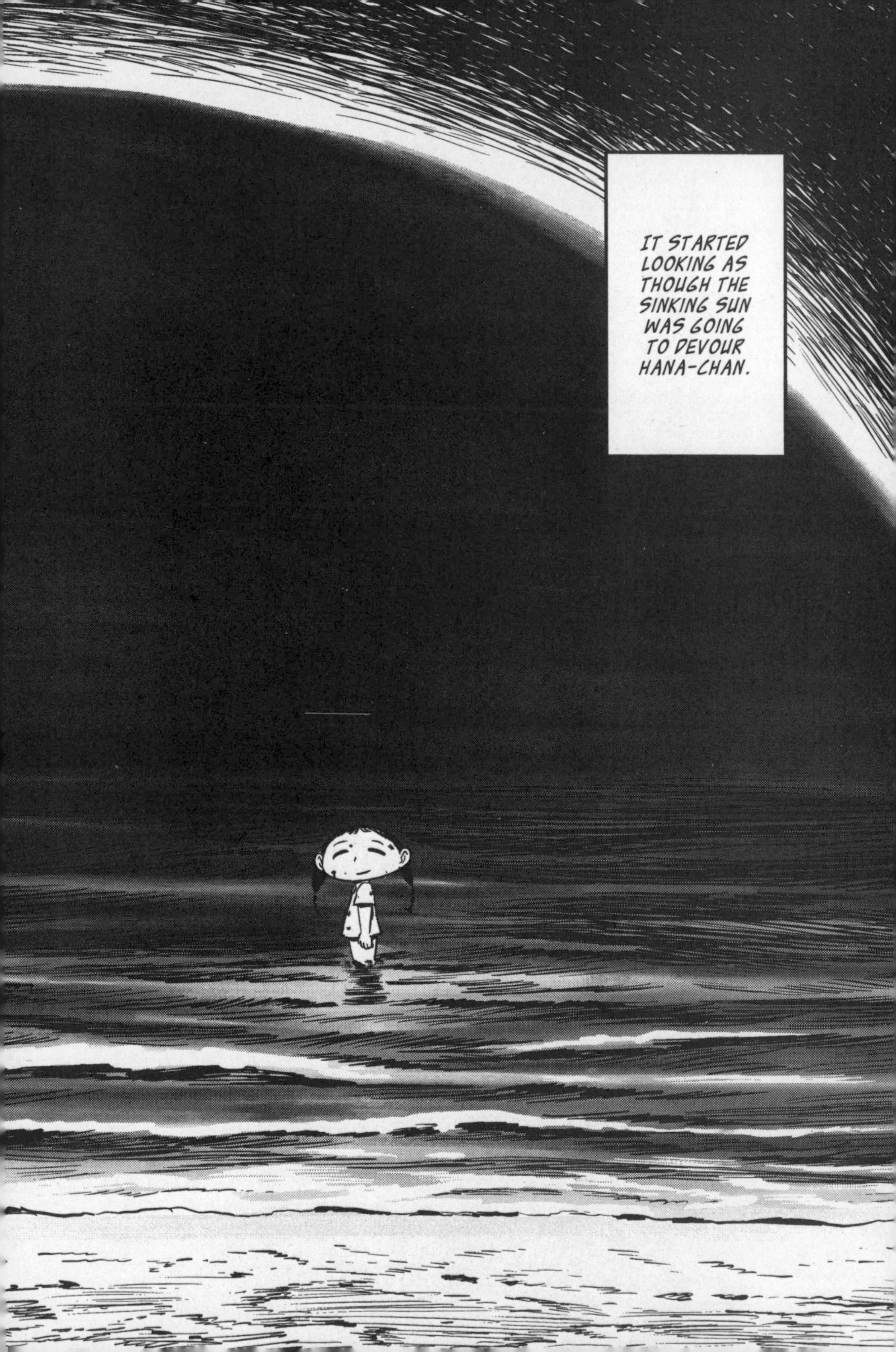
IT STARTED LOOKING AS THOUGH THE SINKING SUN WAS GOING TO DEVOUR HANA-CHAN.

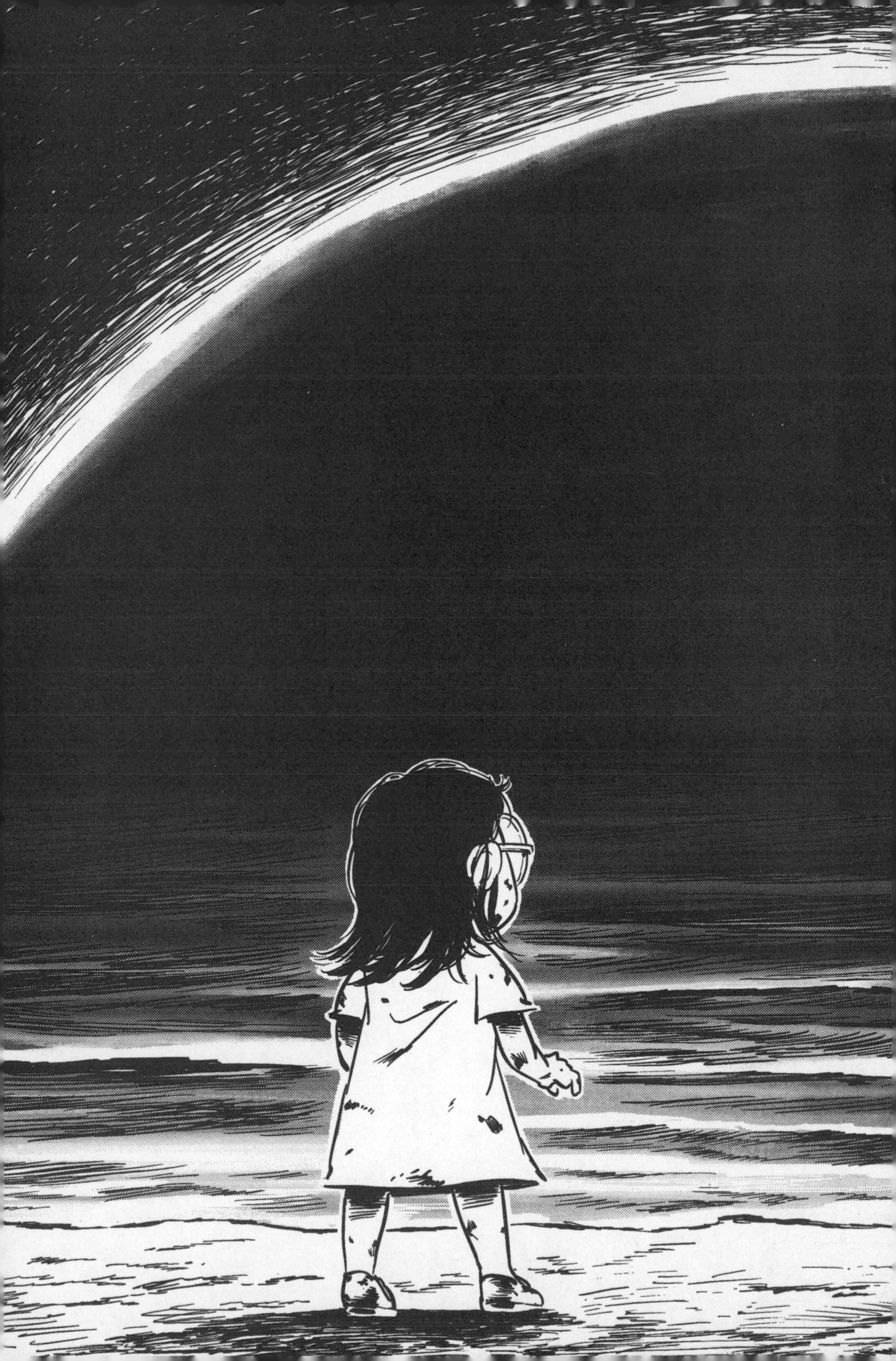

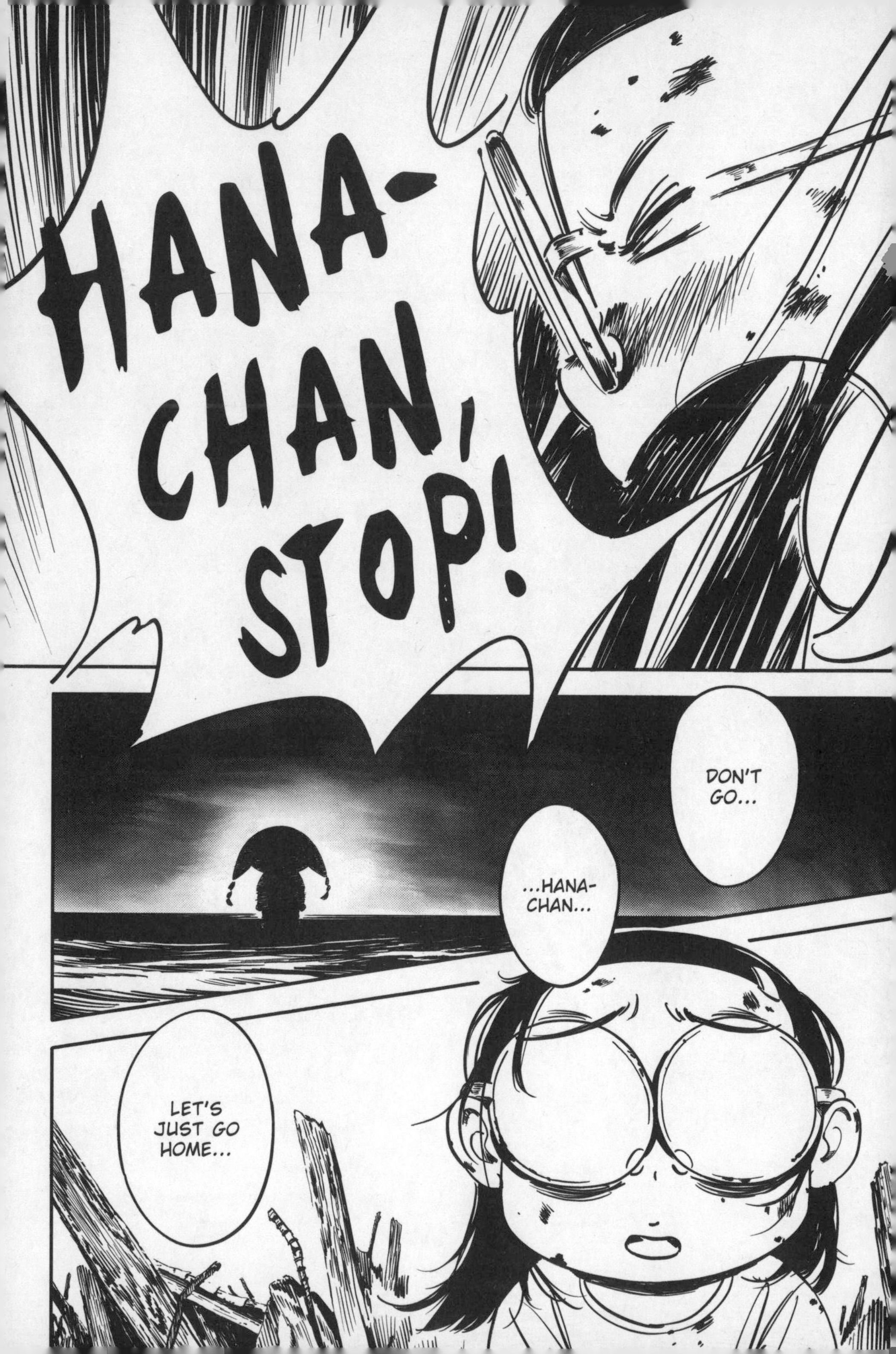
HANA-CHAN, STOP!
DON'T GO...
...HANA-CHAN...
LET'S JUST GO HOME...

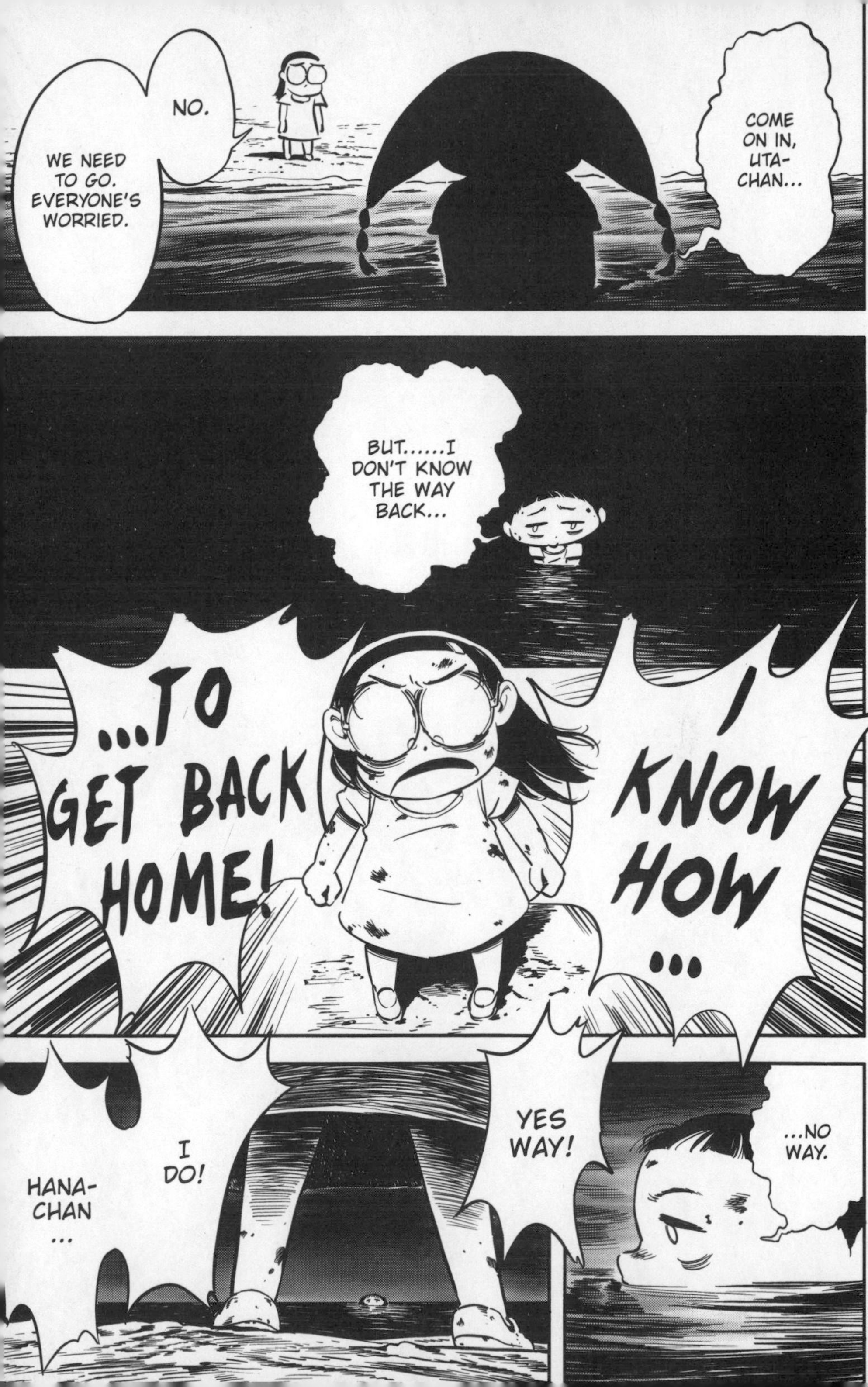
COME ON IN, UTA-CHAN...
NO.
WE NEED TO GO. EVERYONE'S WORRIED.
BUT......I DON'T KNOW THE WAY BACK...
I KNOW HOW...
...TO GET BACK HOME!
...NO WAY.
YES WAY!
I DO!
HANA-CHAN...

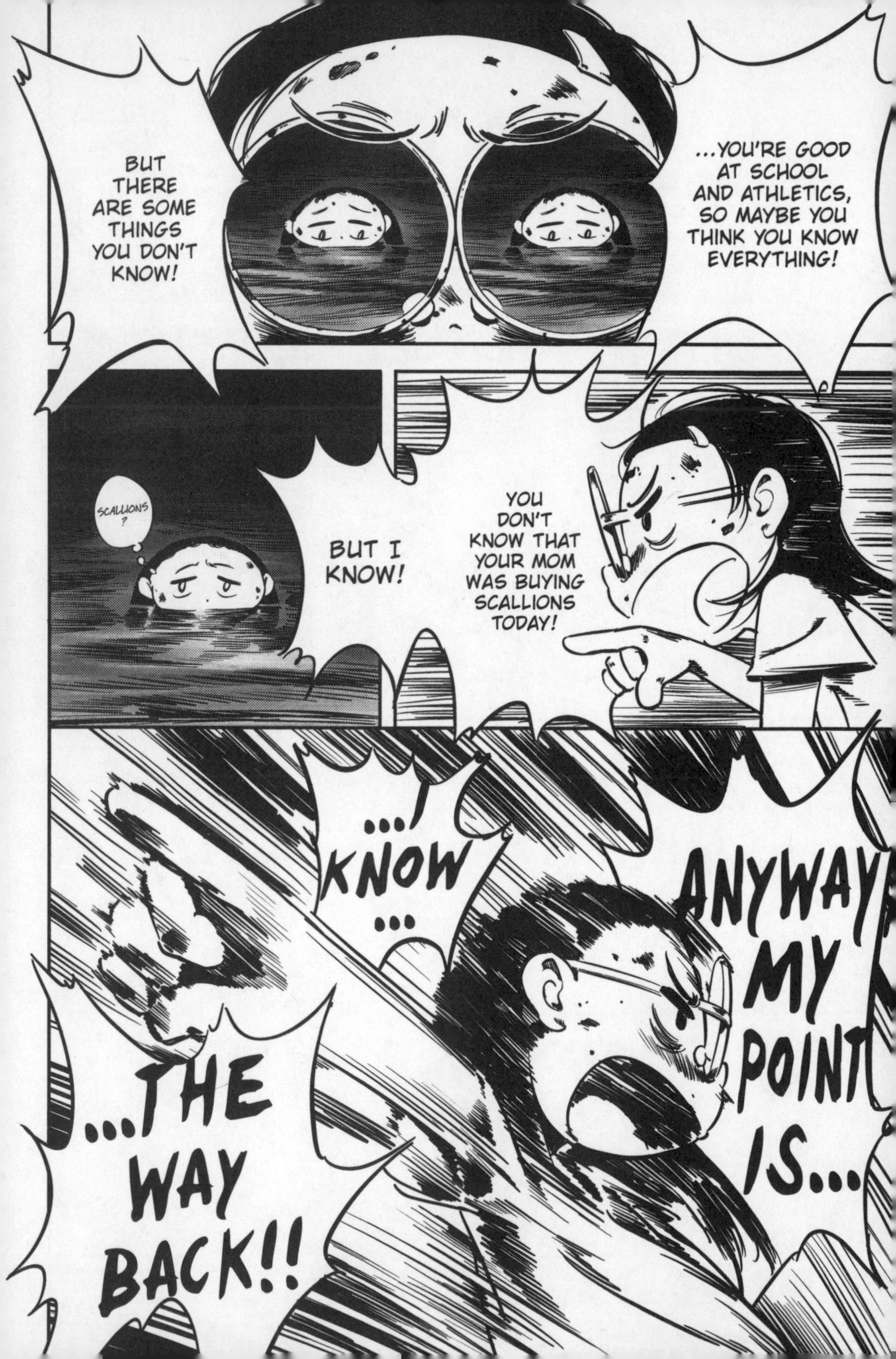
...YOU'RE GOOD AT SCHOOL AND ATHLETICS, SO MAYBE YOU THINK YOU KNOW EVERYTHING!
BUT THERE ARE SOME THINGS YOU DON'T KNOW!
YOU DON'T KNOW THAT YOUR MOM WAS BUYING SCALLIONS TODAY!
BUT I KNOW!
SCALLIONS ?
ANYWAY MY POINT IS...
...KNOW...
...THE WAY BACK!!

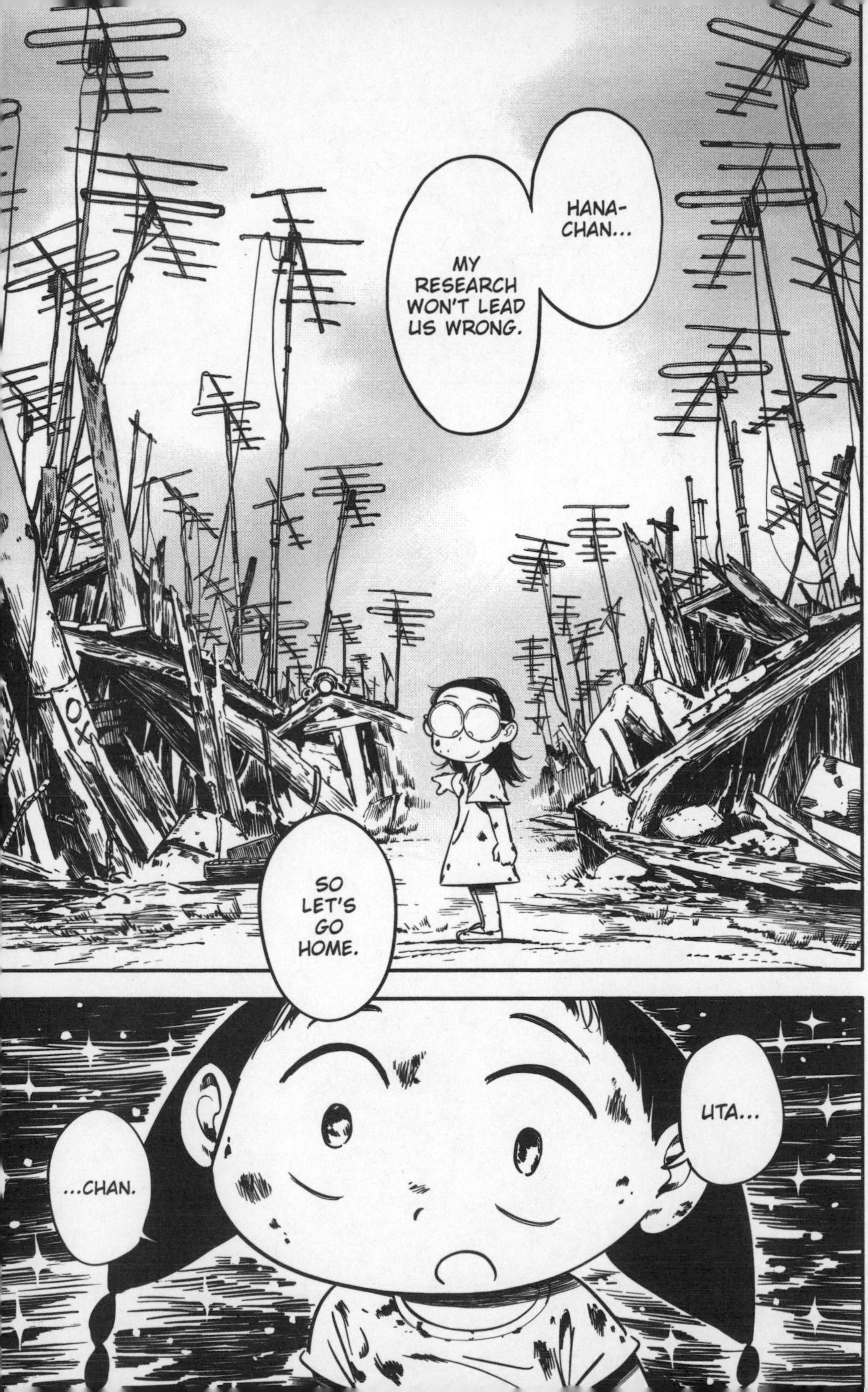
HANA-CHAN...
MY RESEARCH WON'T LEAD US WRONG.
SO LET'S GO HOME.
UTA...
...CHAN.

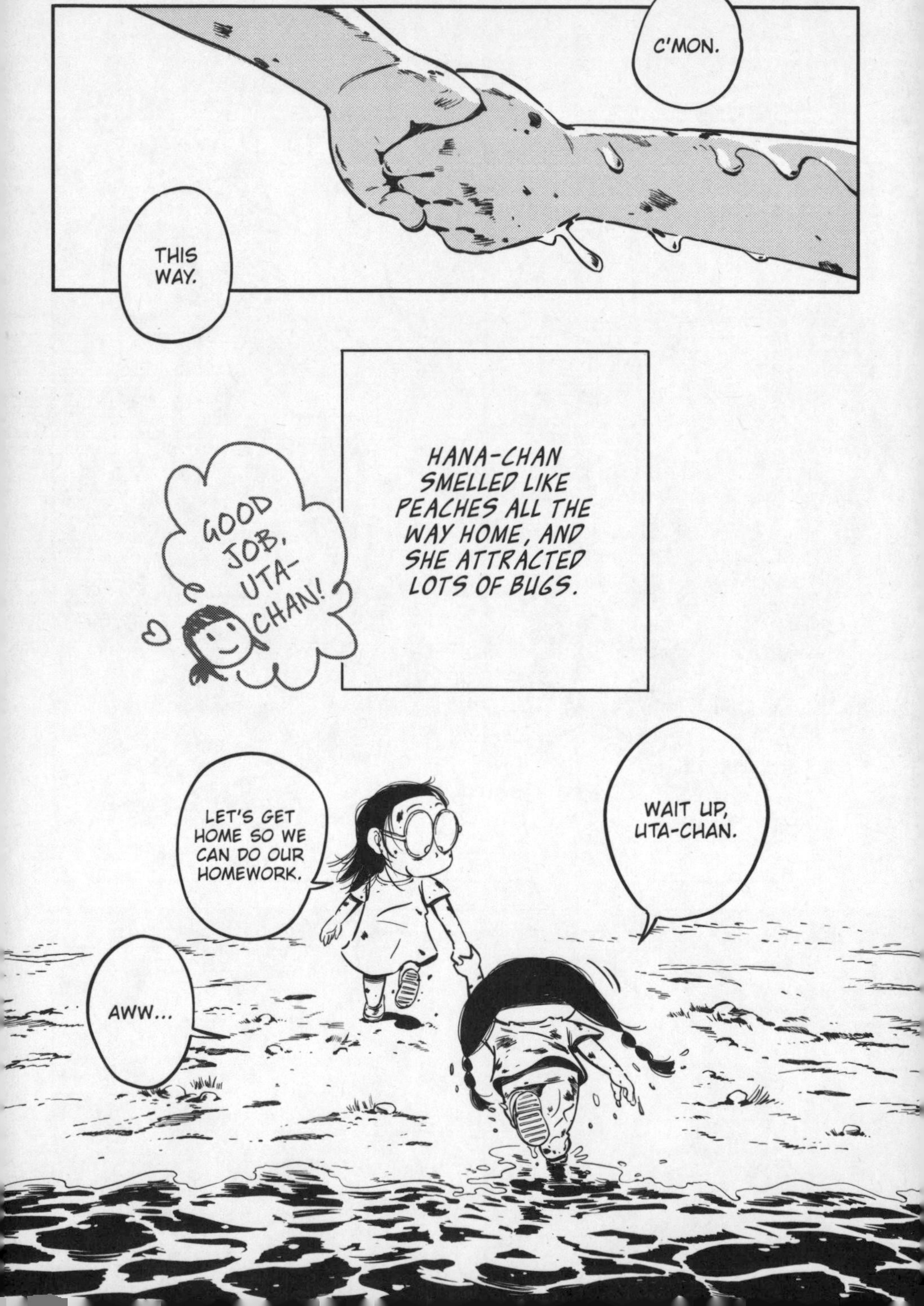
C'MON.
THIS WAY.
HANA-CHAN SMELLED LIKE PEACHES ALL THE WAY HOME, AND SHE ATTRACTED LOTS OF BUGS.
GOOD JOB, UTA-CHAN!
WAIT UP, UTA-CHAN.
LET'S GET HOME SO WE CAN DO OUR HOMEWORK.
AWW...

Hana-chan
and the Shape of the World

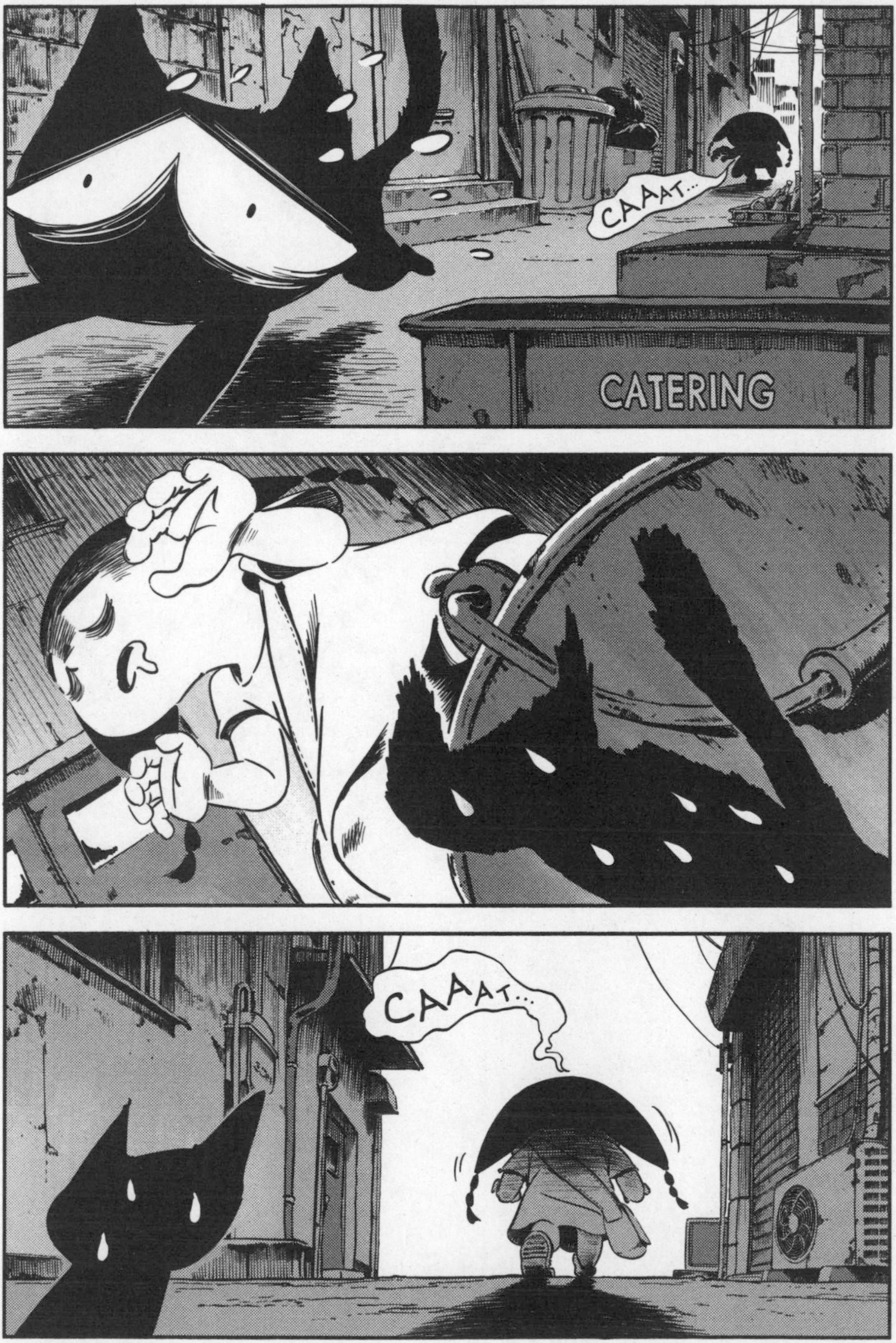
CAAAT...
CATERING
CAAAT...

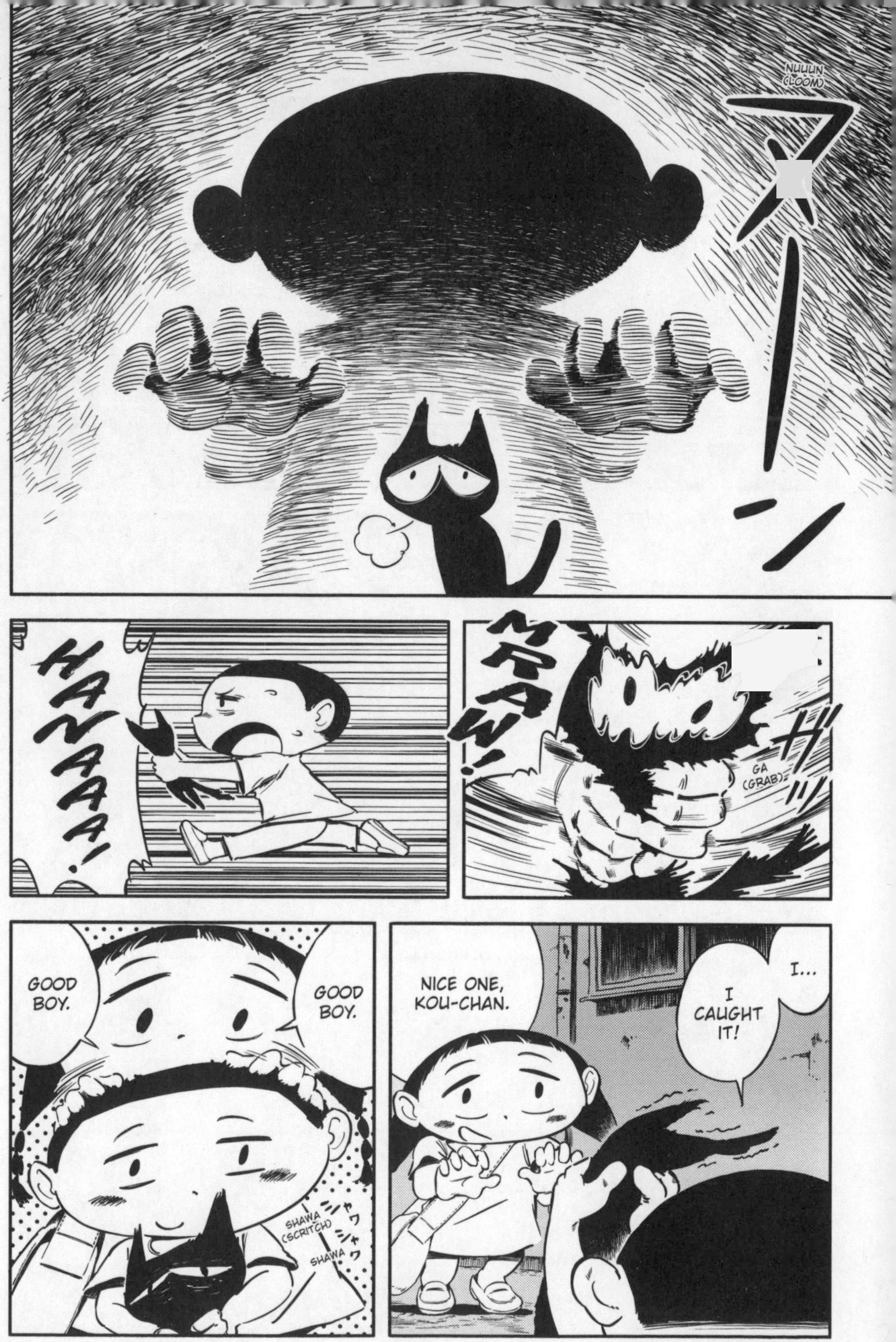
NUUUN (LOOM)
MRAW!!
GA (GRAB)
HANAAAAA!
I...
I CAUGHT IT!
NICE ONE, KOU-CHAN.
GOOD BOY.
GOOD BOY.
SHAWA (SCRITCH) SHAWA

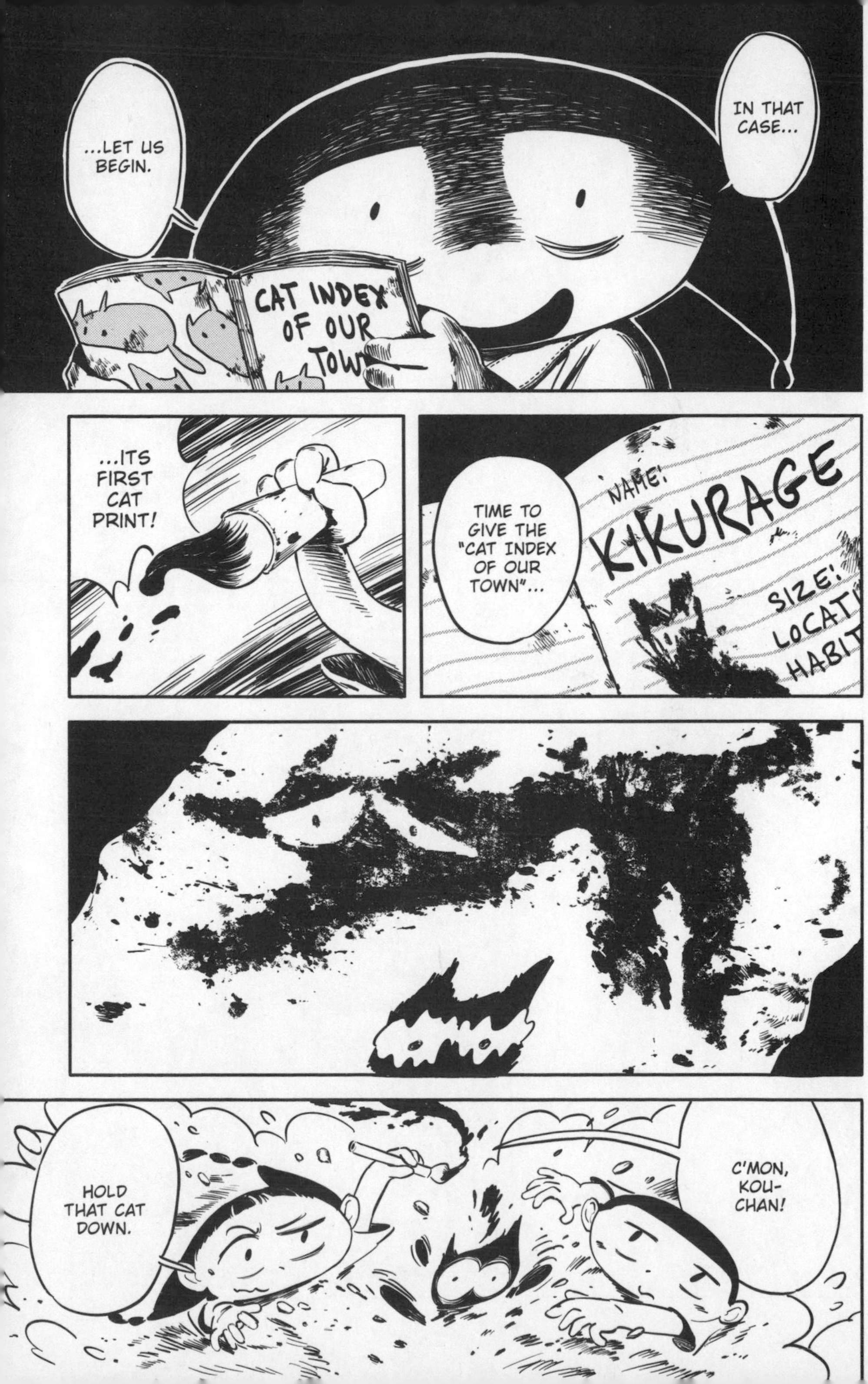
IN THAT CASE...
...LET US BEGIN.
CAT INDEX OF OUR
TIME TO GIVE THE "CAT INDEX OF OUR TOWN"...
NAME!
KIKURAGE
SIZE!
...ITS FIRST CAT PRINT!
C'MON, KOU-CHAN!
HOLD THAT CAT DOWN.

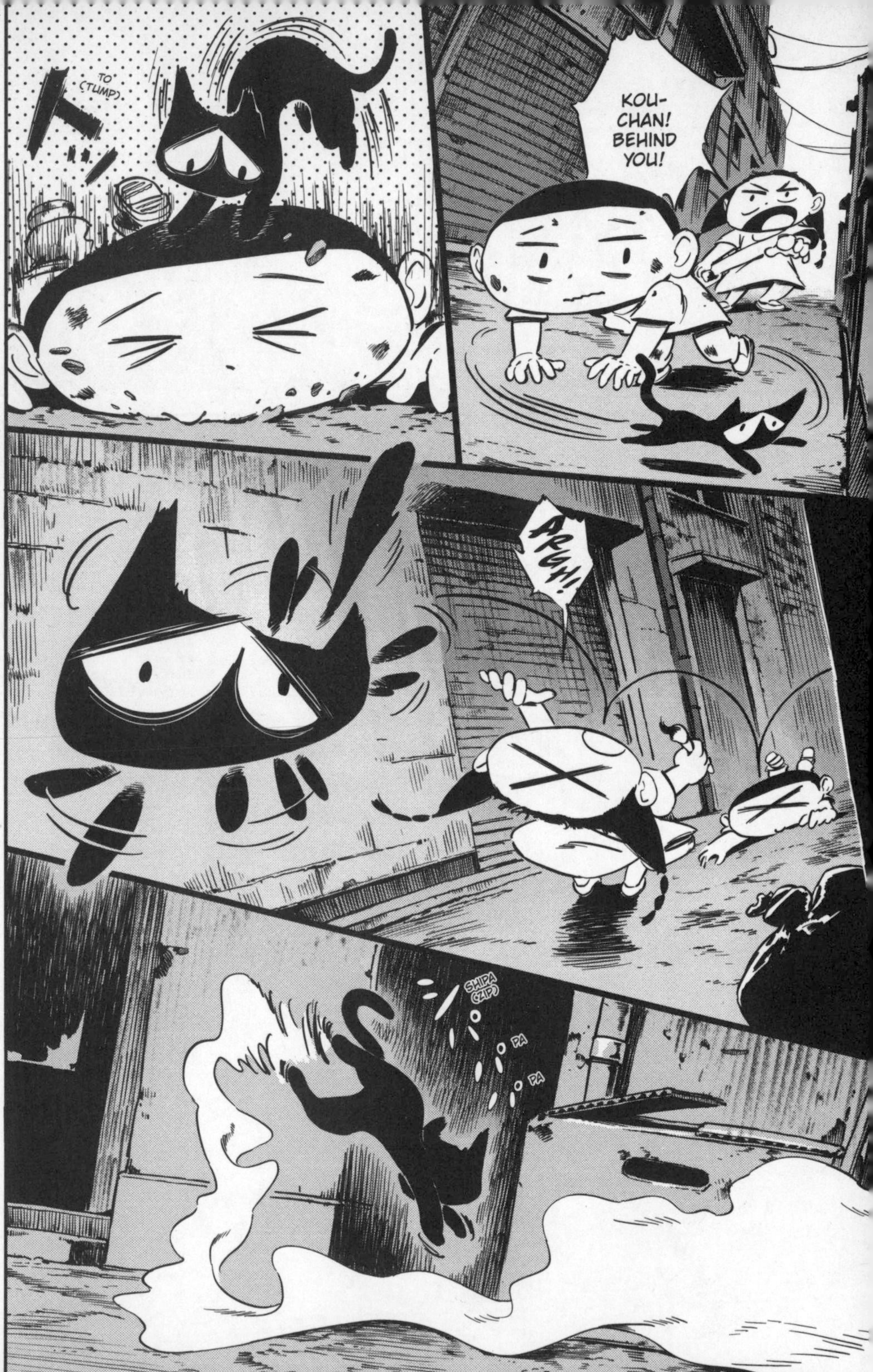
KOU-CHAN! BEHIND YOU!
TO (TUMP)
ARGH!!
SHIPA (ZIP)
PA
PA

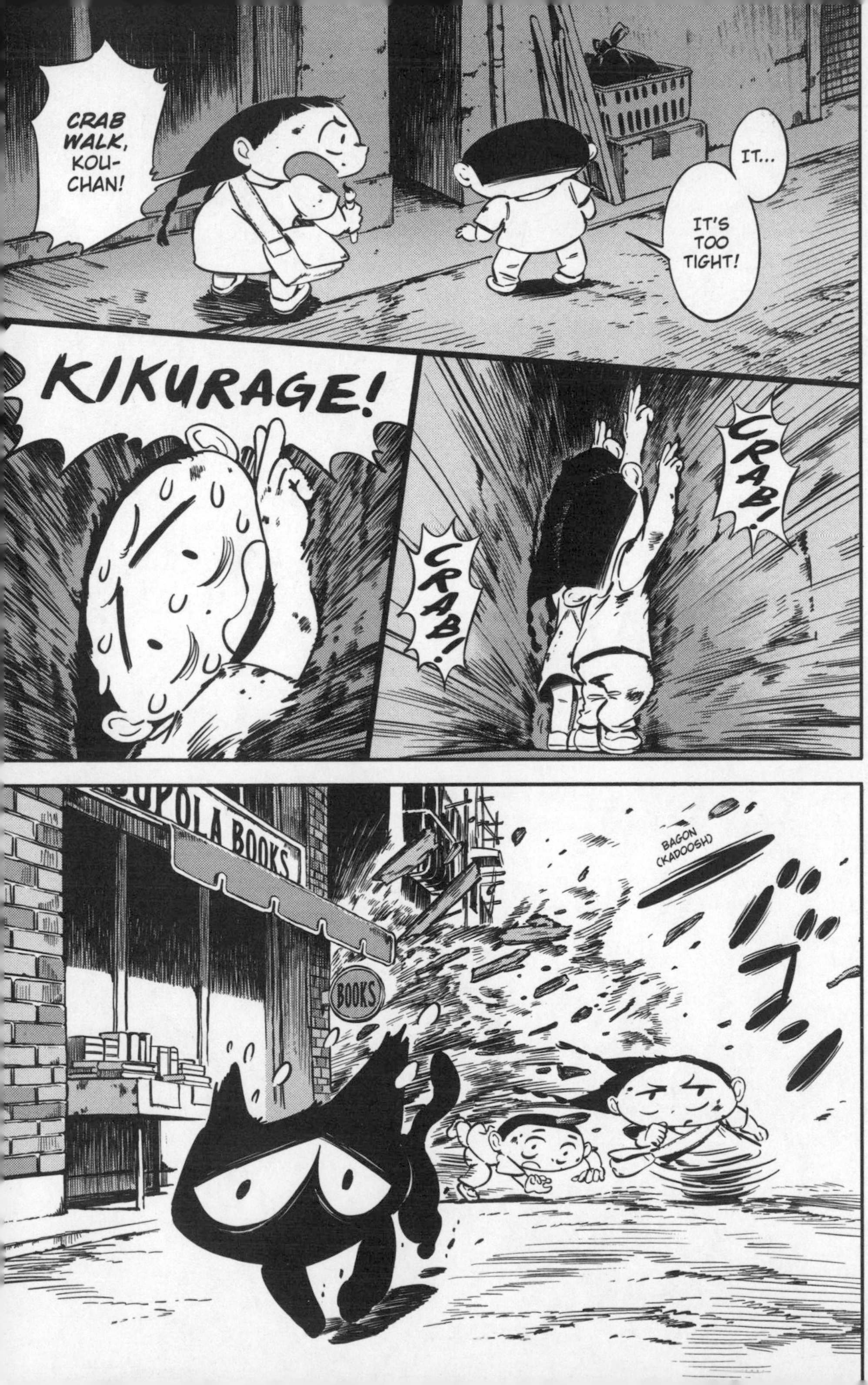
IT...
IT'S TOO TIGHT!
CRAB WALK, KOU-CHAN!
CRAB!
CRAB!
KIKURAGE!
BAGON (KADOOSH)
BOOKS
BOOKS

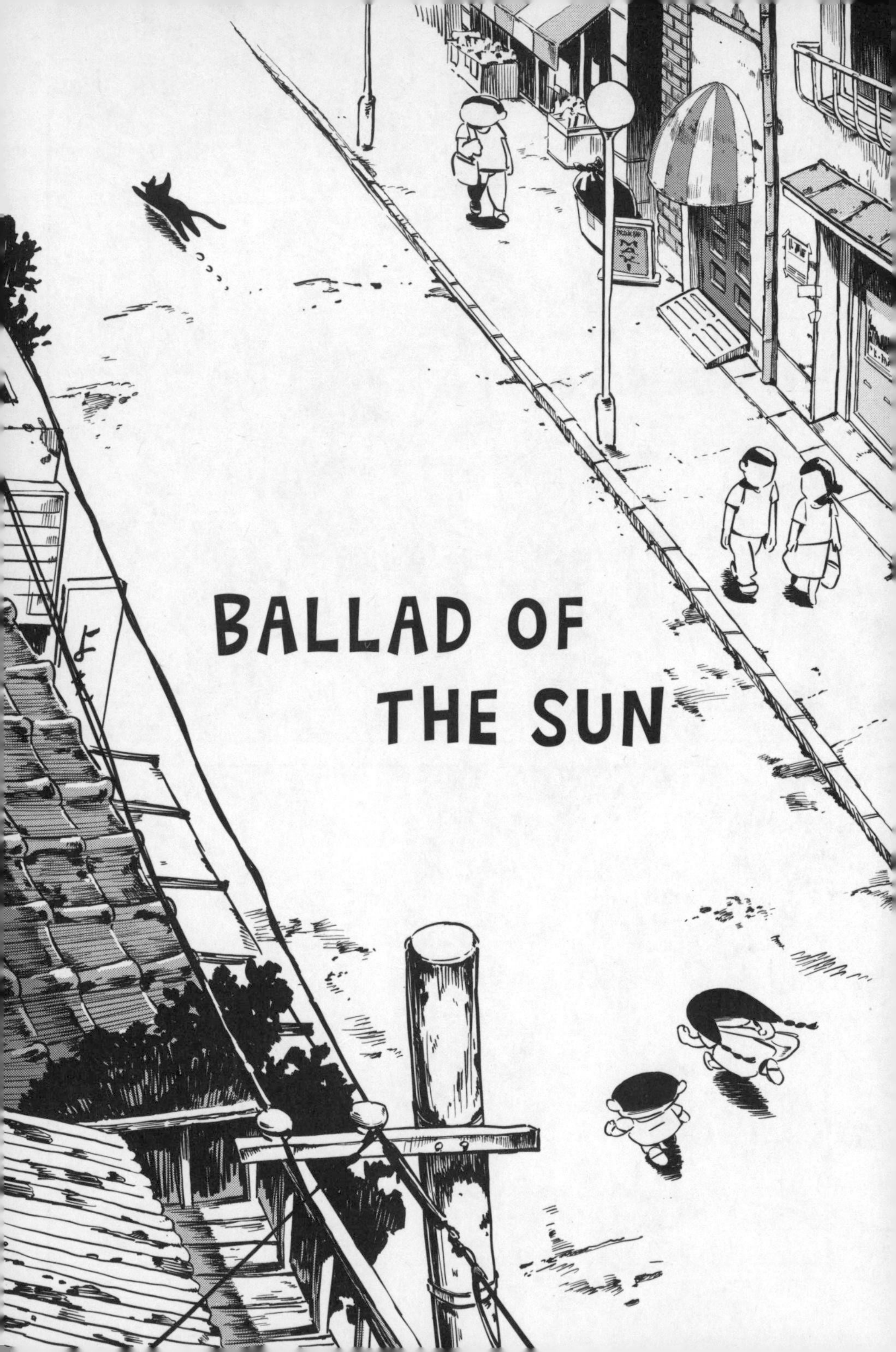
BALLAD OF THE SUN

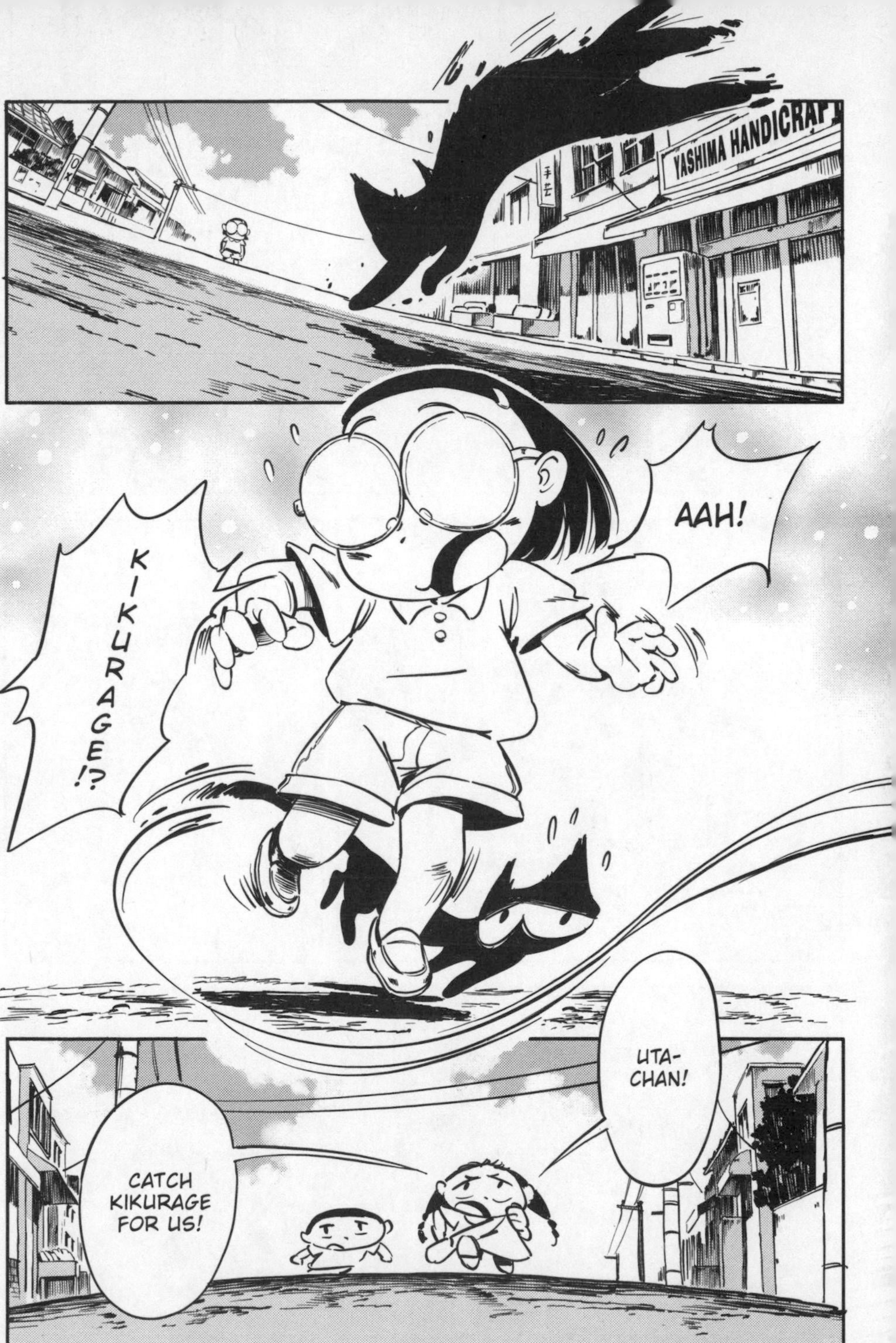
YASHIMA HANDICRAF
手芸
AAH!
KIKURAGE!?
UTA-CHAN!
CATCH KIKURAGE FOR US!

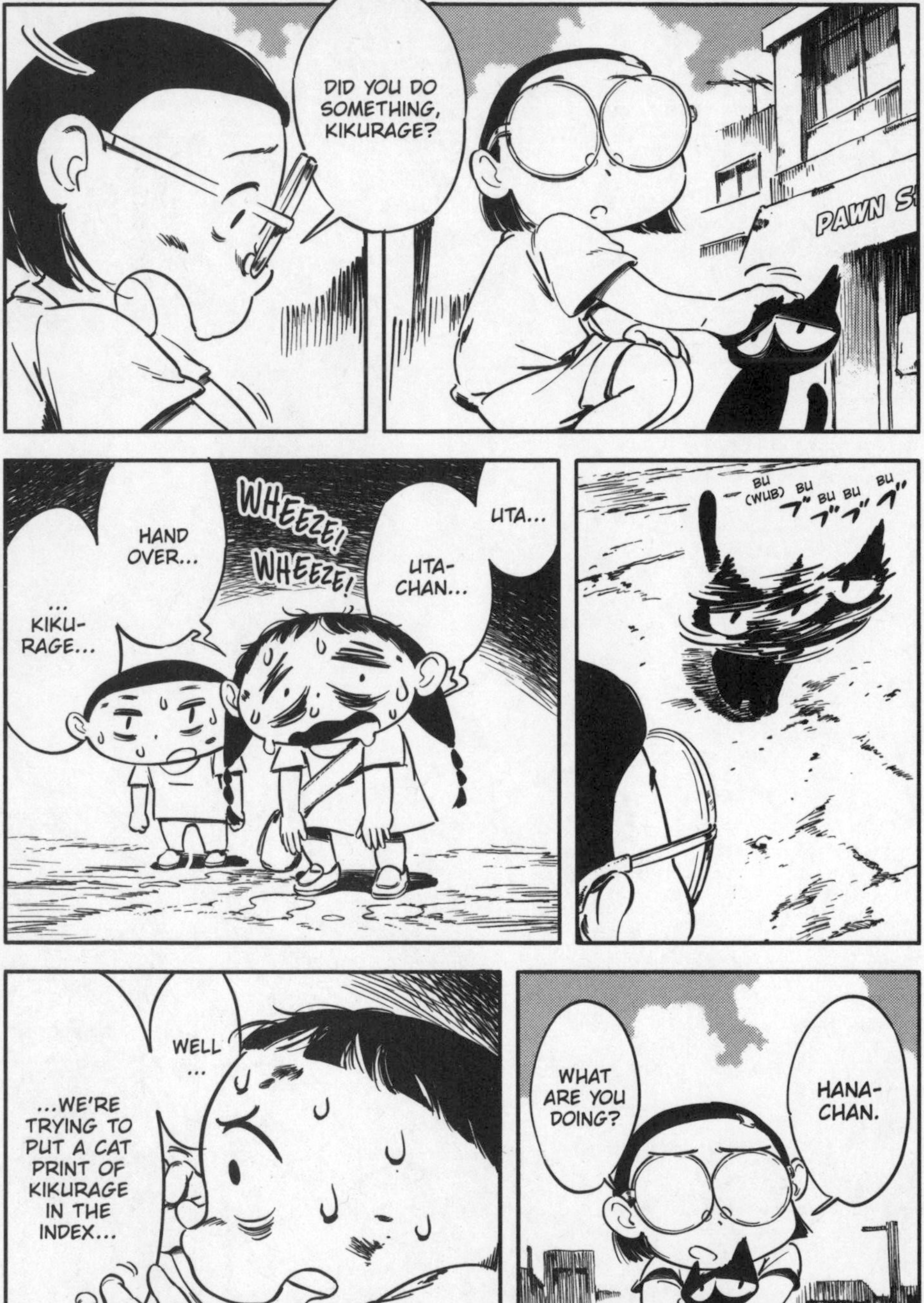
PAWN S
DID YOU DO SOMETHING, KIKURAGE?
BU (WUB) BU BU BU BU
ブブブブ
UTA...
UTA-CHAN...
WHEEZE! WHEEZE!
HAND OVER...
... KIKU-RAGE...
HANA-CHAN.
WHAT ARE YOU DOING?
WELL ...
...WE'RE TRYING TO PUT A CAT PRINT OF KIKURAGE IN THE INDEX...

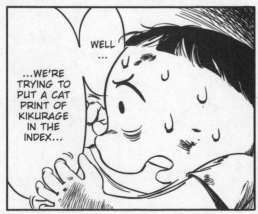

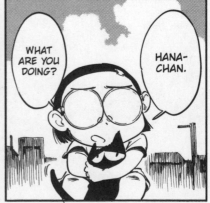

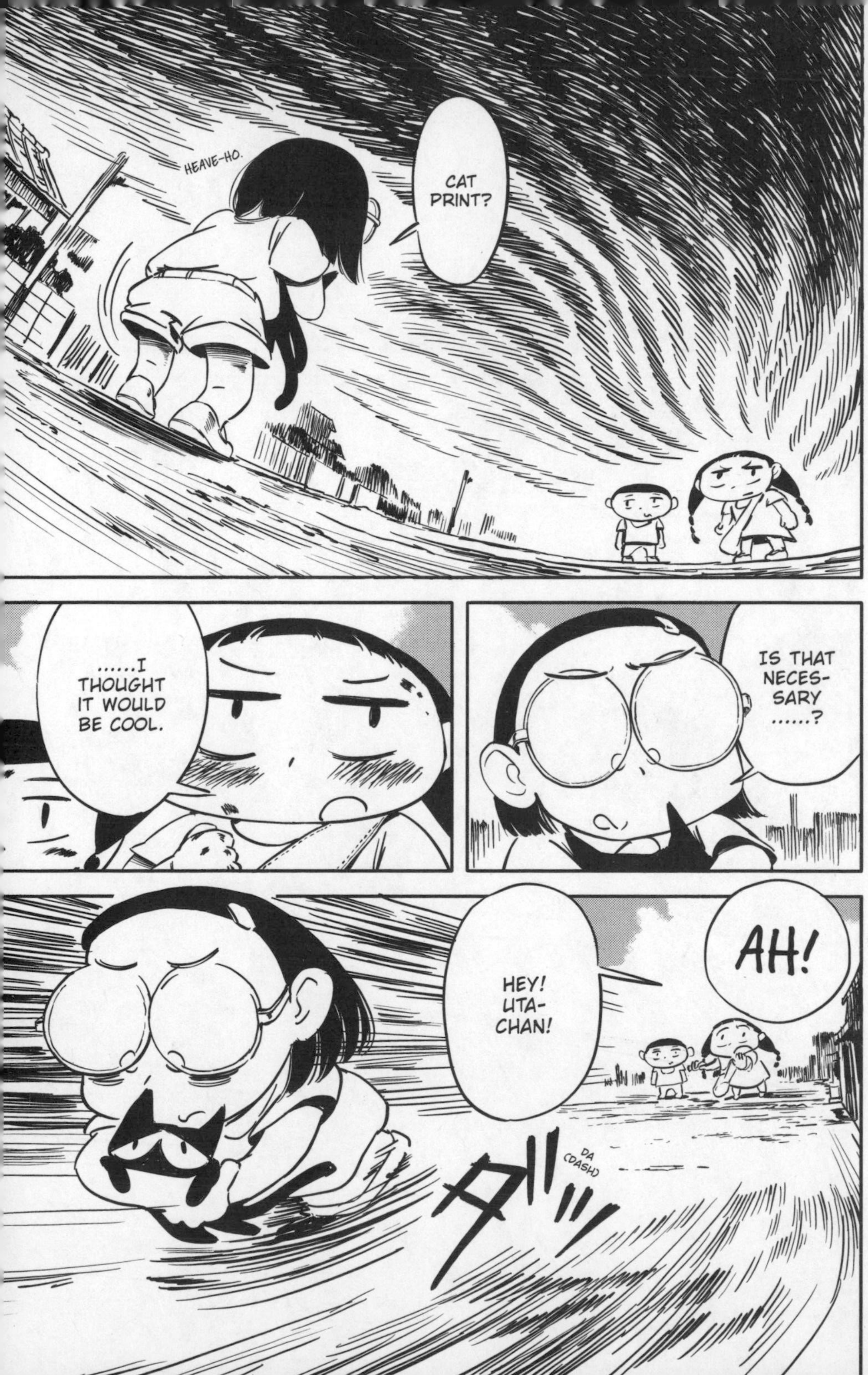
CAT PRINT?
HEAVE-HO.
IS THAT NECES-SARY ......?
......I THOUGHT IT WOULD BE COOL.
AH!
HEY! UTA-CHAN!
DA (DASH)

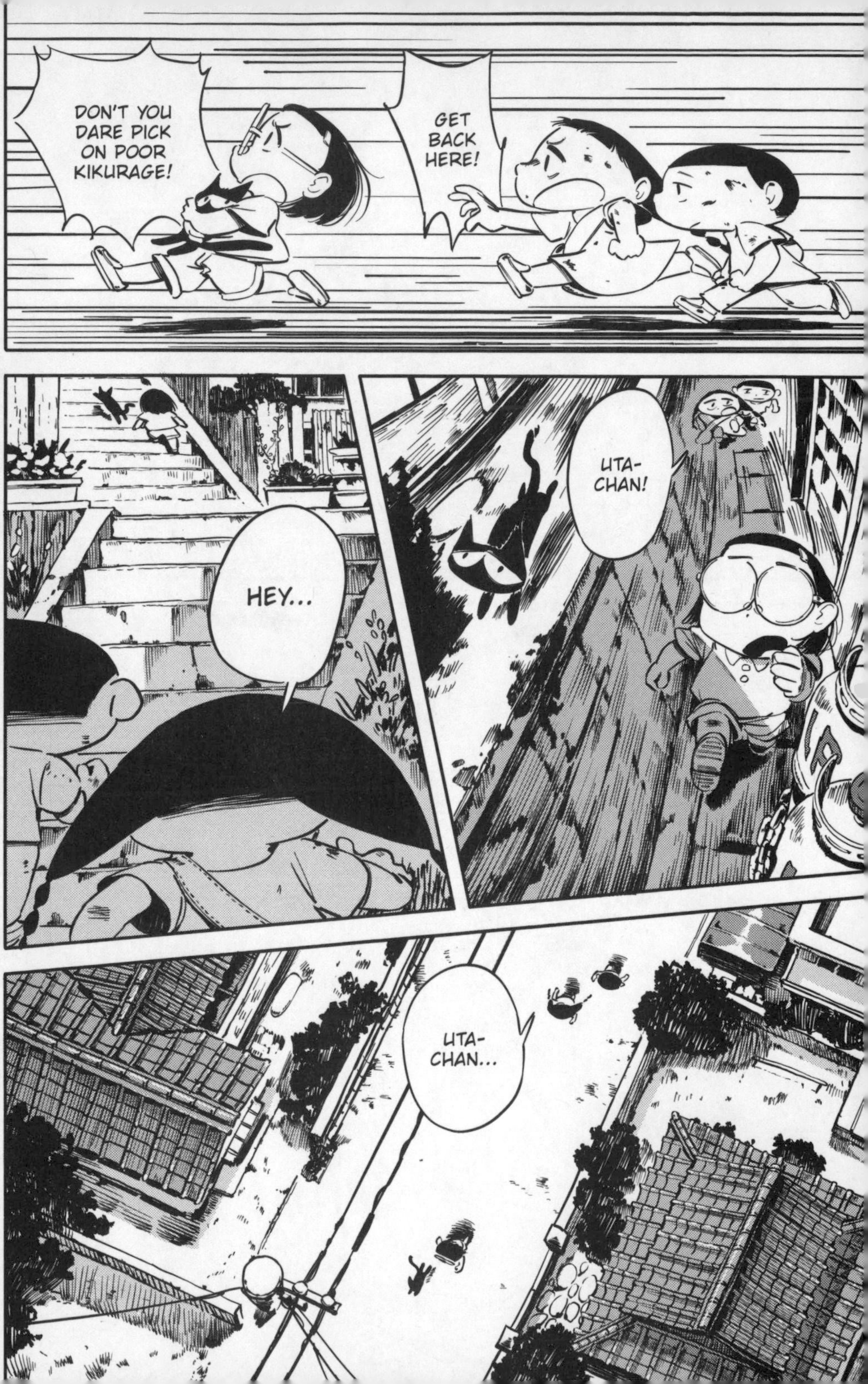
GET BACK HERE!
DON'T YOU DARE PICK ON POOR KIKURAGE!
UTA-CHAN!
HEY...
UTA-CHAN...

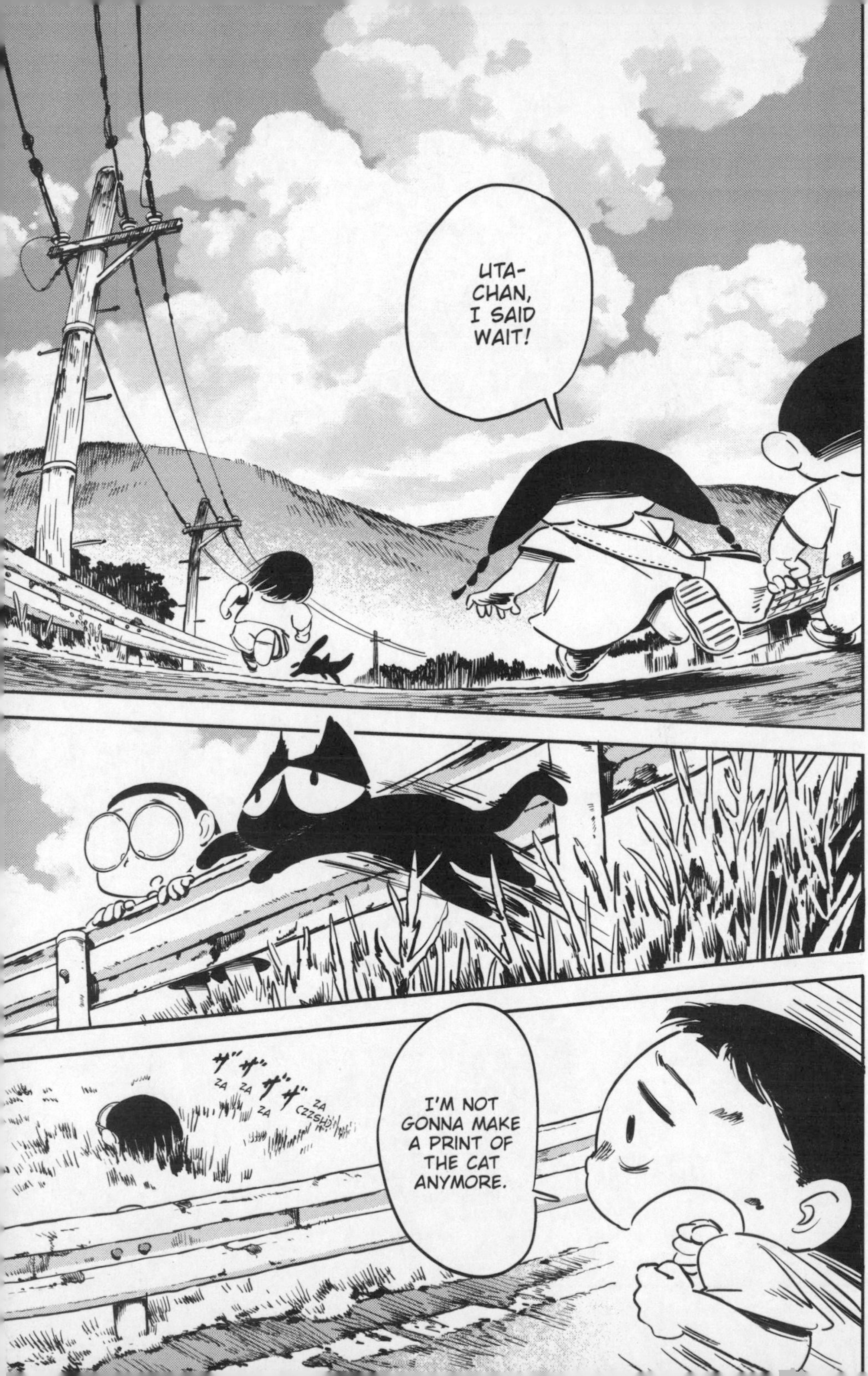
UTA-CHAN, I SAID WAIT!
ザザ
ZA ZA
ザザ
ZA ZA
(ZZSH)
I'M NOT GONNA MAKE A PRINT OF THE CAT ANYMORE.

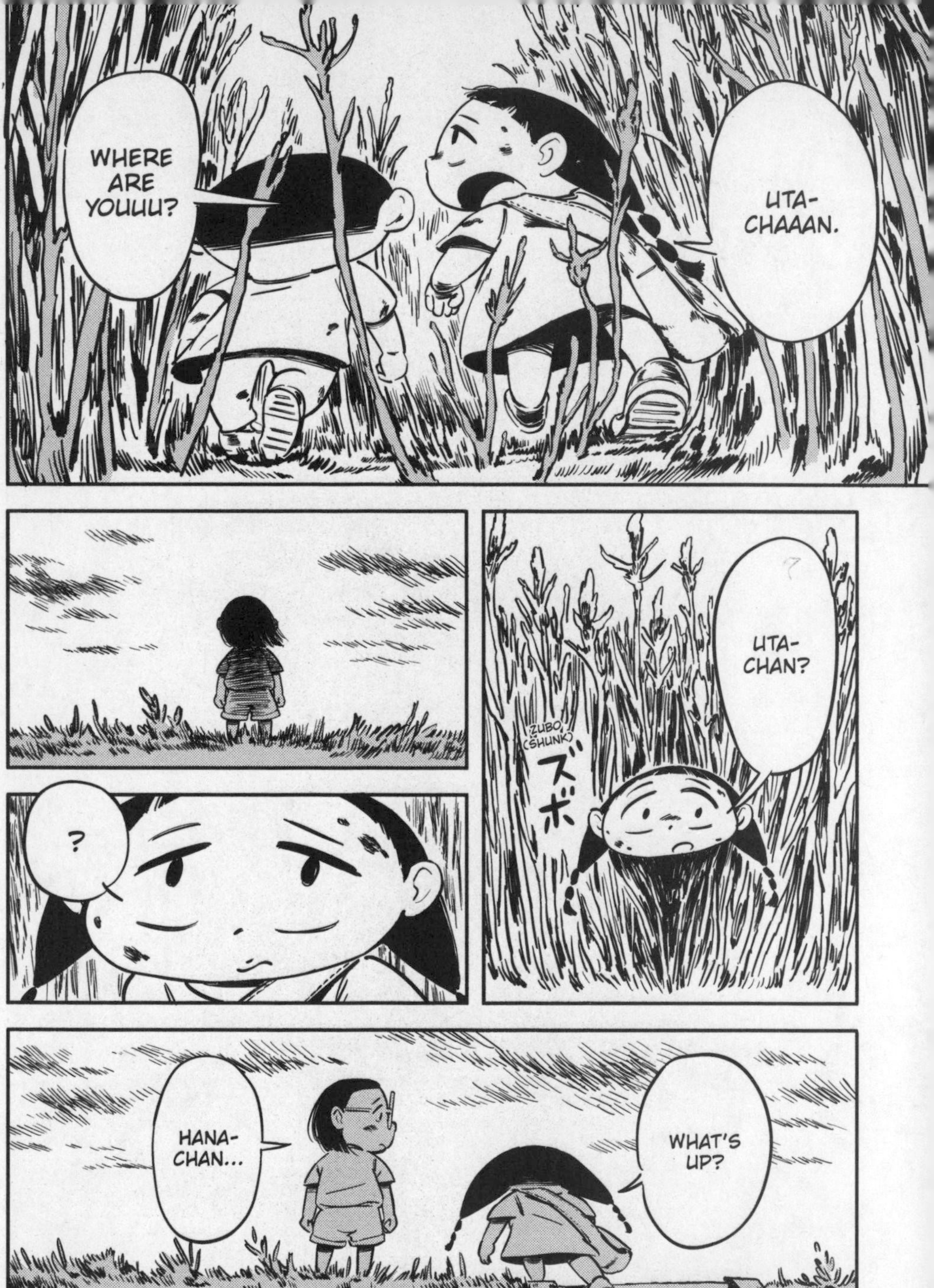
UTA-CHAAAN.
WHERE ARE YOUUU?
UTA-CHAN?
ズボ
ZUBO (SHUNK)
?
WHAT'S UP?
HANA-CHAN...

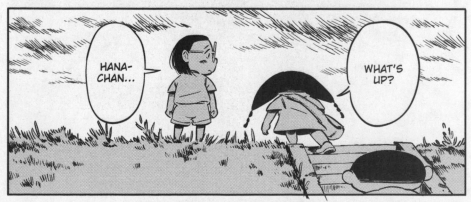

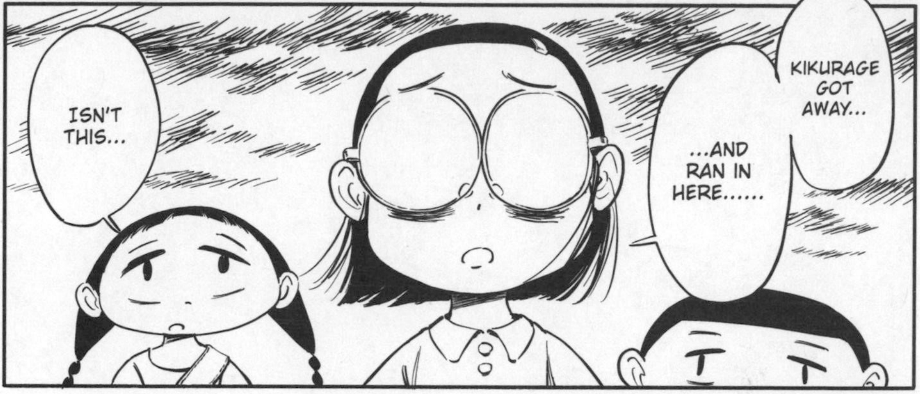
KIKURAGE GOT AWAY...
...AND RAN IN HERE......
ISN'T THIS...

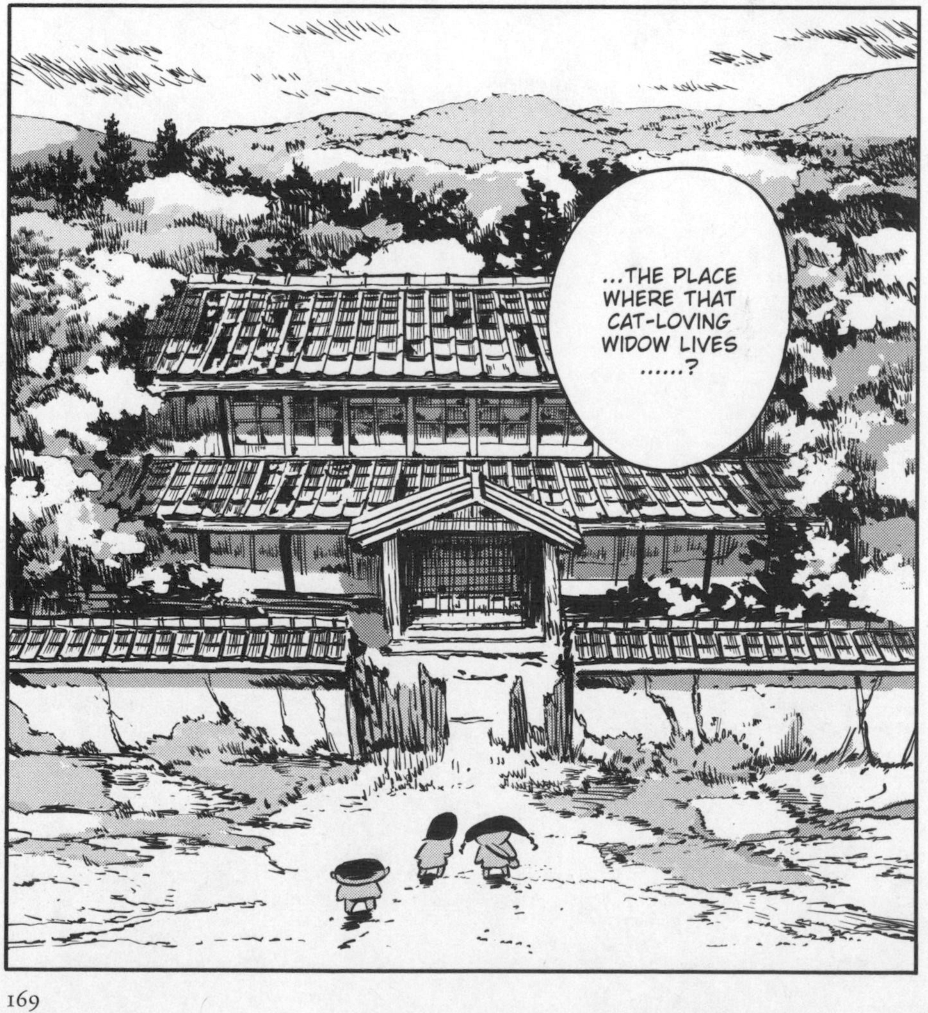
...THE PLACE WHERE THAT CAT-LOVING WIDOW LIVES ......?

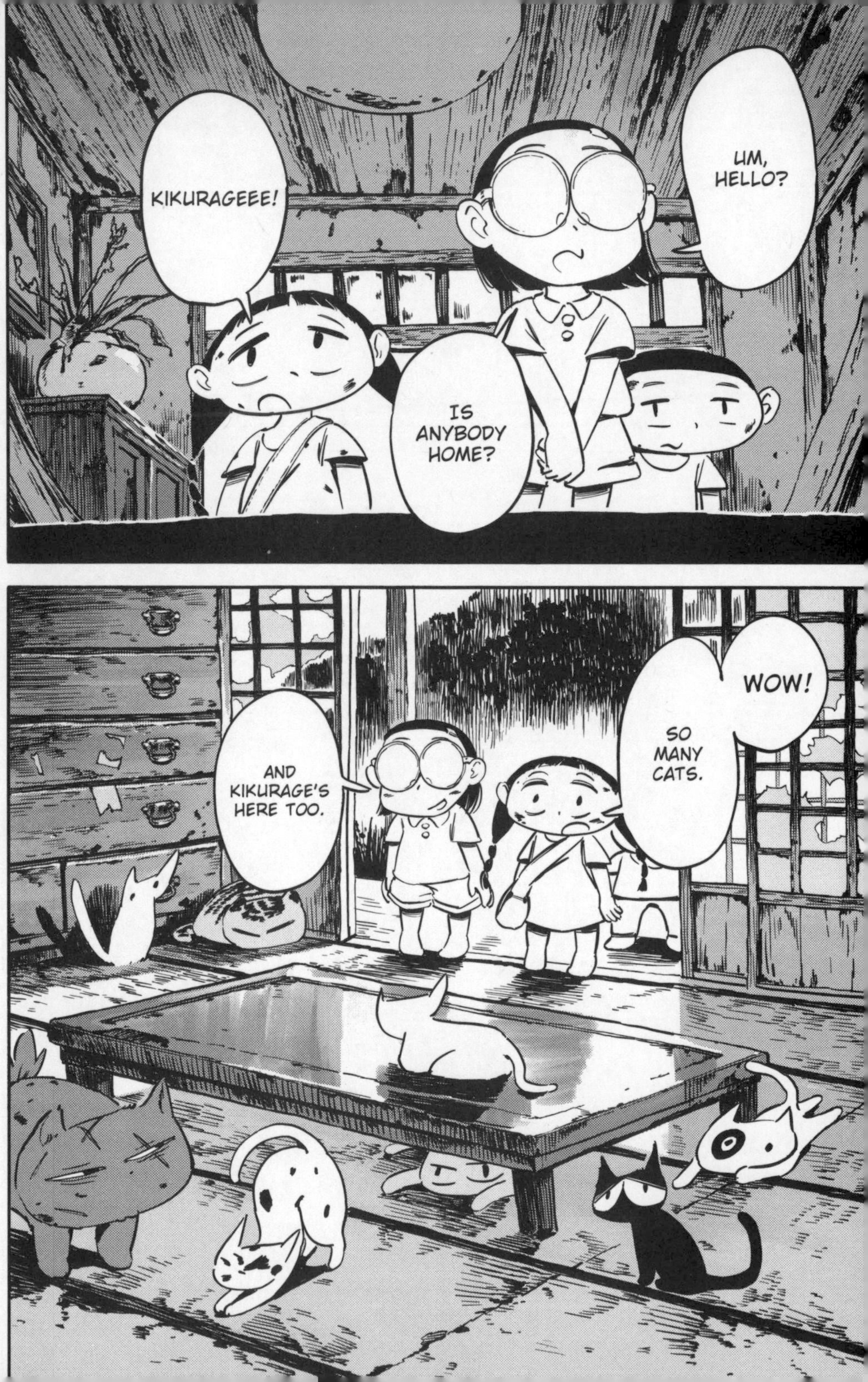
UM, HELLO?
KIKURAGEEE!
IS ANYBODY HOME?
WOW! SO MANY CATS.
AND KIKURAGE'S HERE TOO.

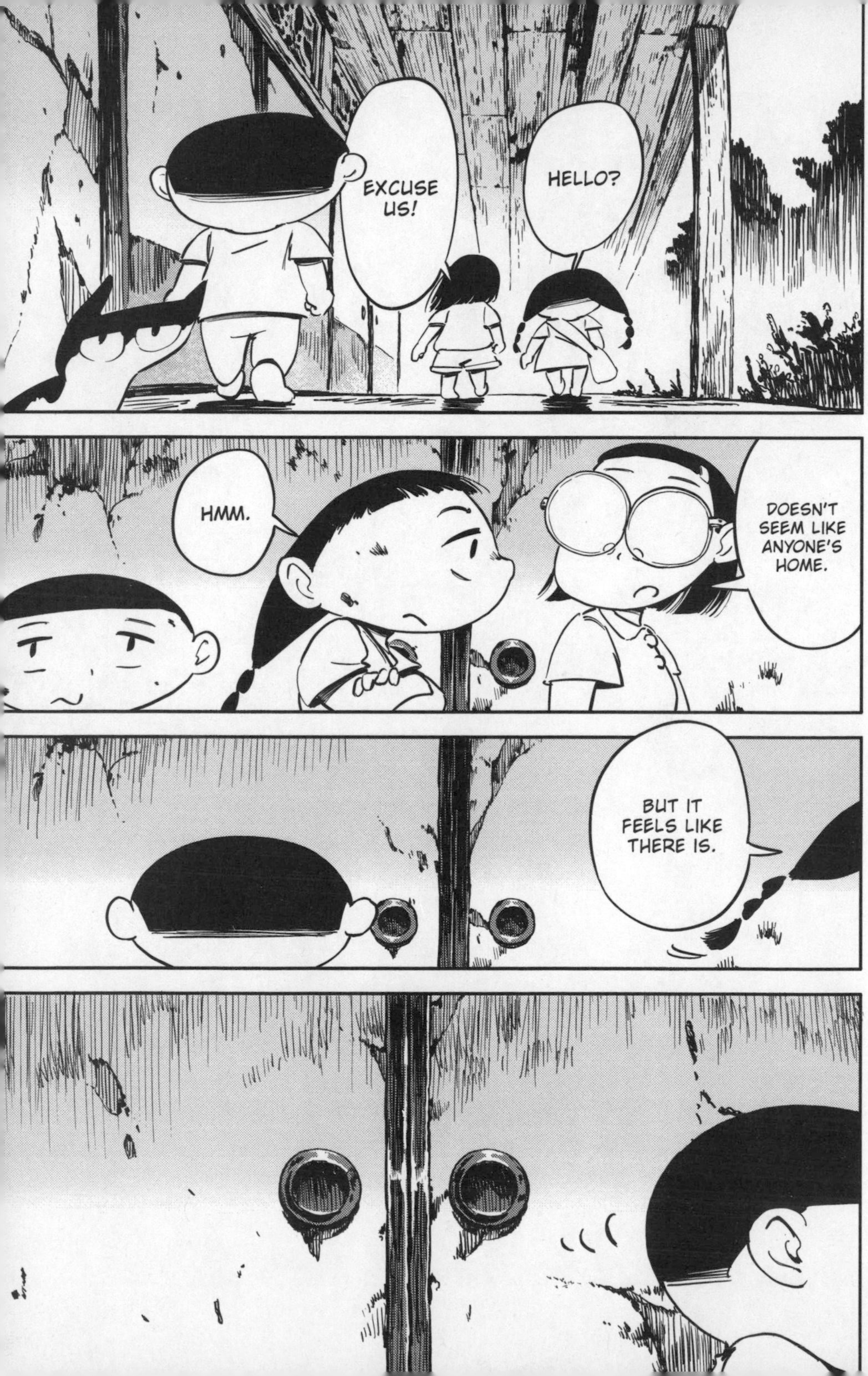
HELLO?
EXCUSE US!
DOESN'T SEEM LIKE ANYONE'S HOME.
HMM.
BUT IT FEELS LIKE THERE IS.

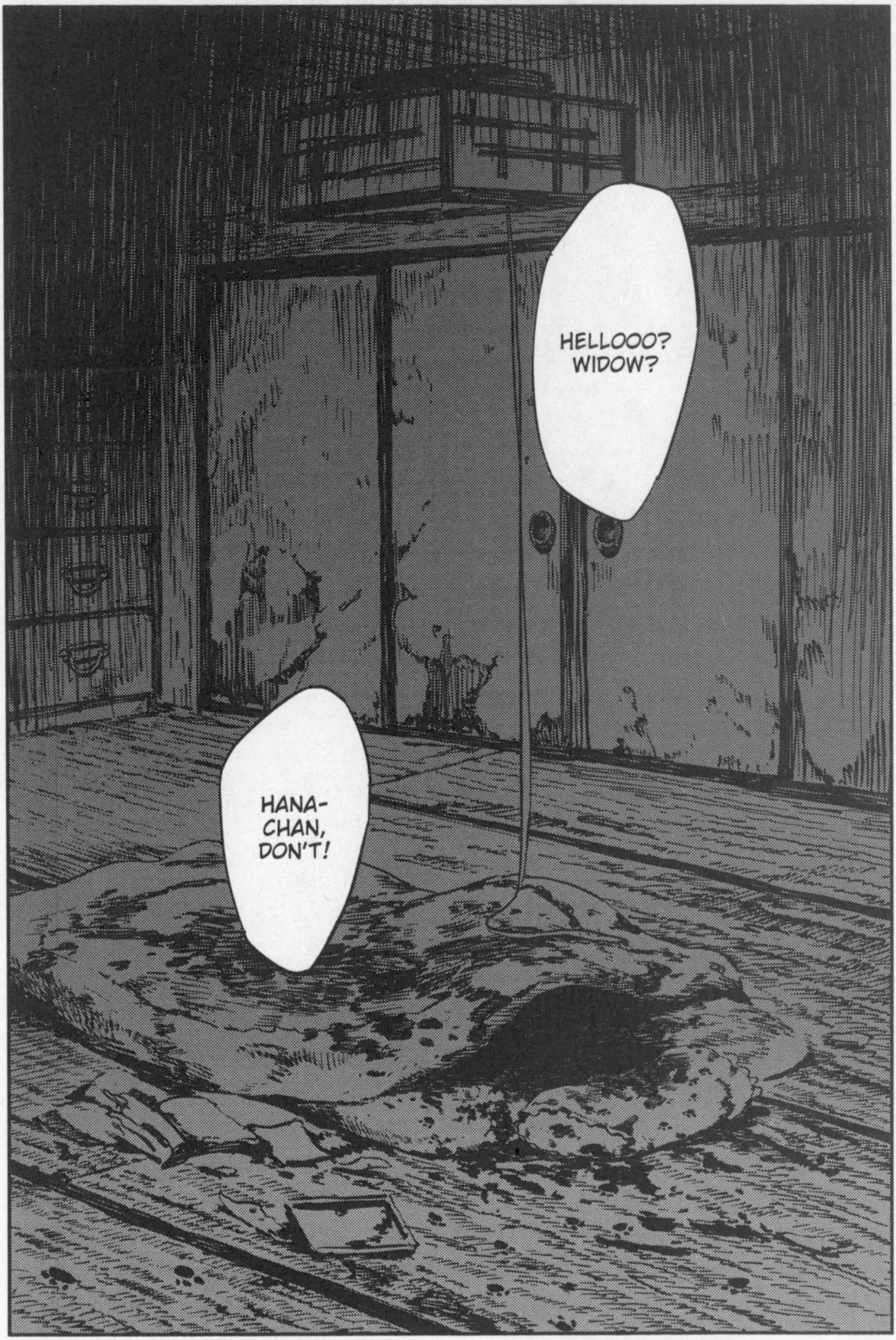
HELLOOO? WIDOW?
HANA-CHAN, DON'T!

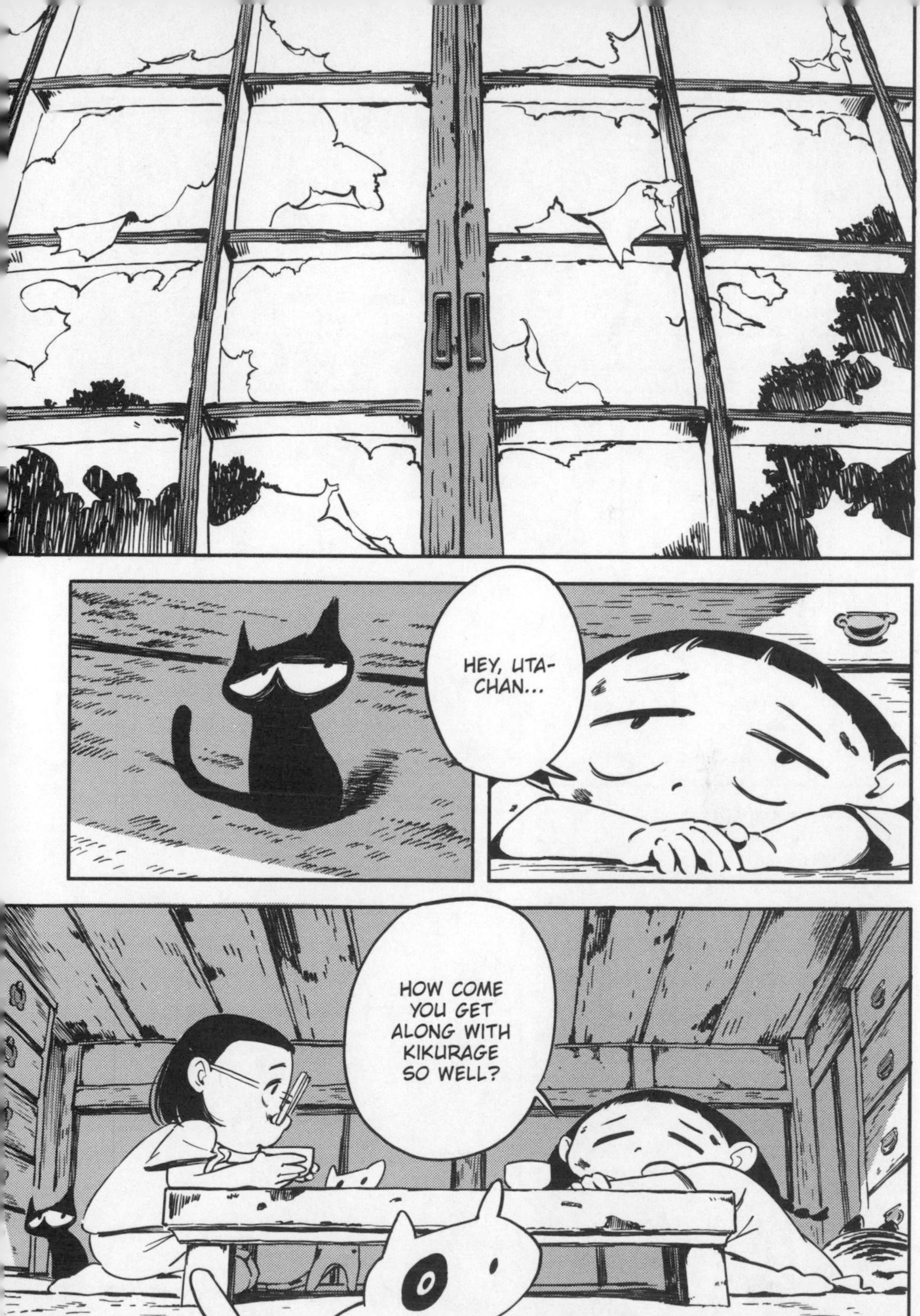
HEY, UTA-CHAN...
HOW COME YOU GET ALONG WITH KIKURAGE SO WELL?

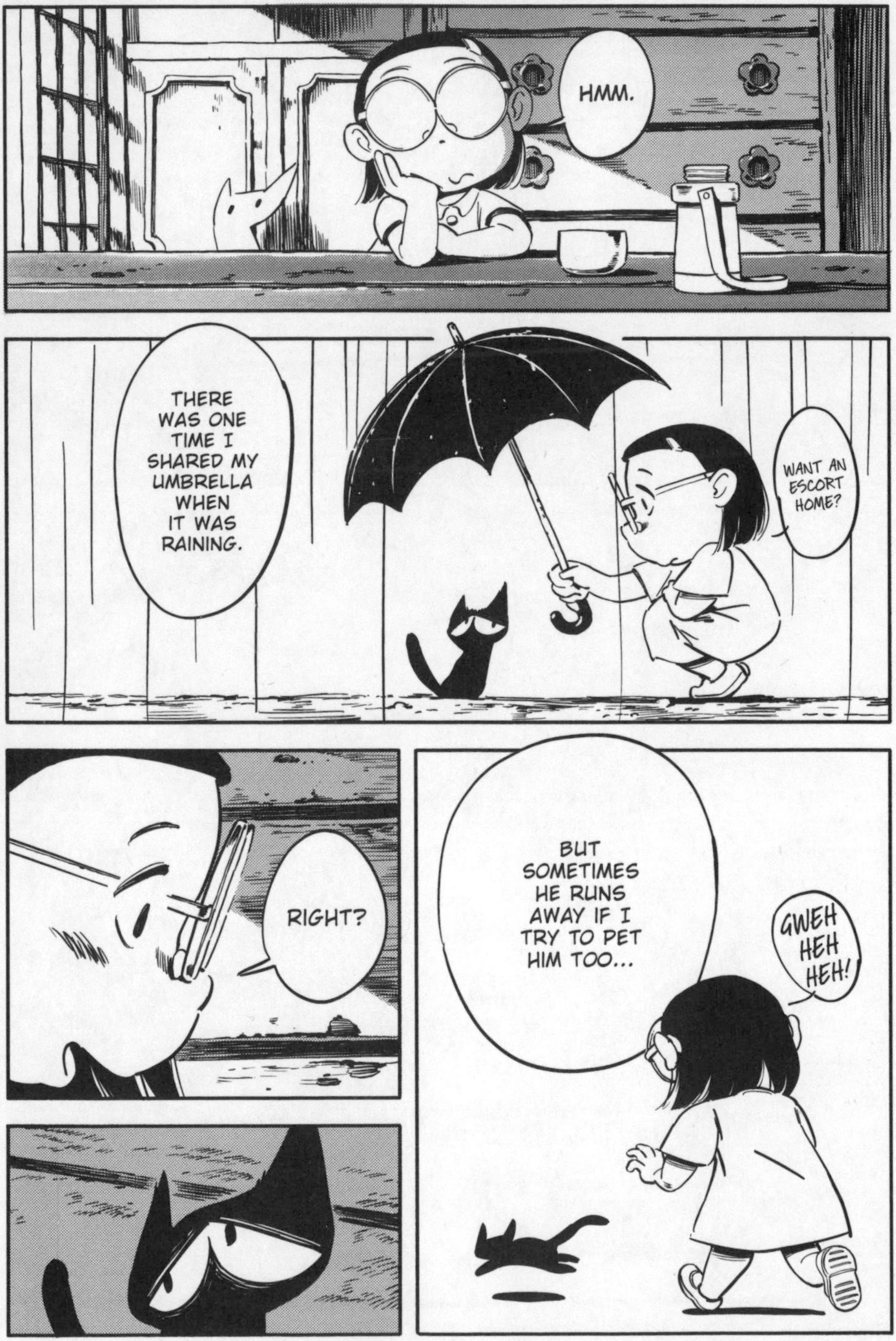
HMM.
WANT AN ESCORT HOME?
THERE WAS ONE TIME I SHARED MY UMBRELLA WHEN IT WAS RAINING.
BUT SOMETIMES HE RUNS AWAY IF I TRY TO PET HIM TOO...
GWEH HEH HEH!
RIGHT?

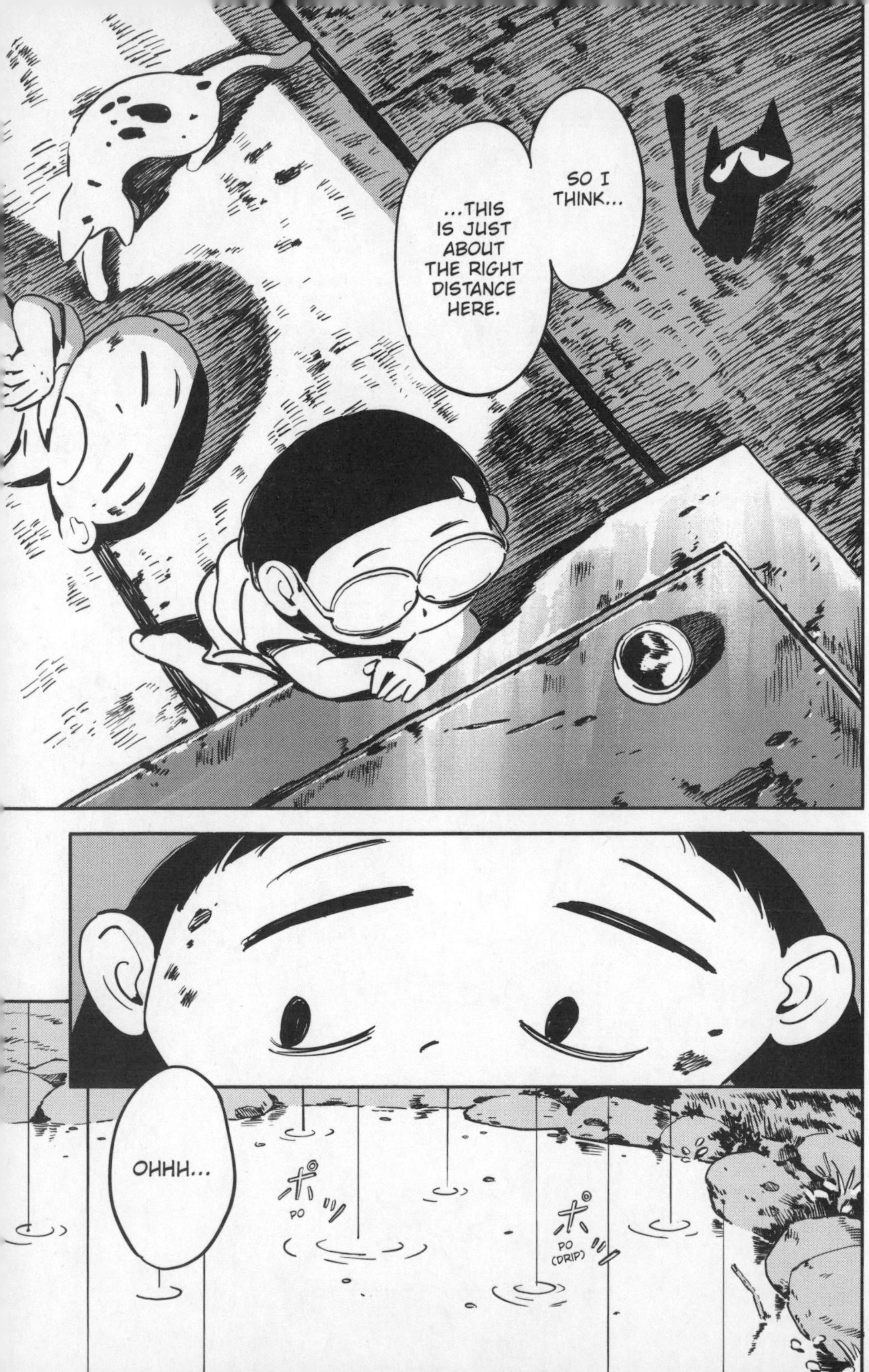
SO I THINK...
...THIS IS JUST ABOUT THE RIGHT DISTANCE HERE.
ポ
PO (DRIP)
ポ
PO
OHHH...

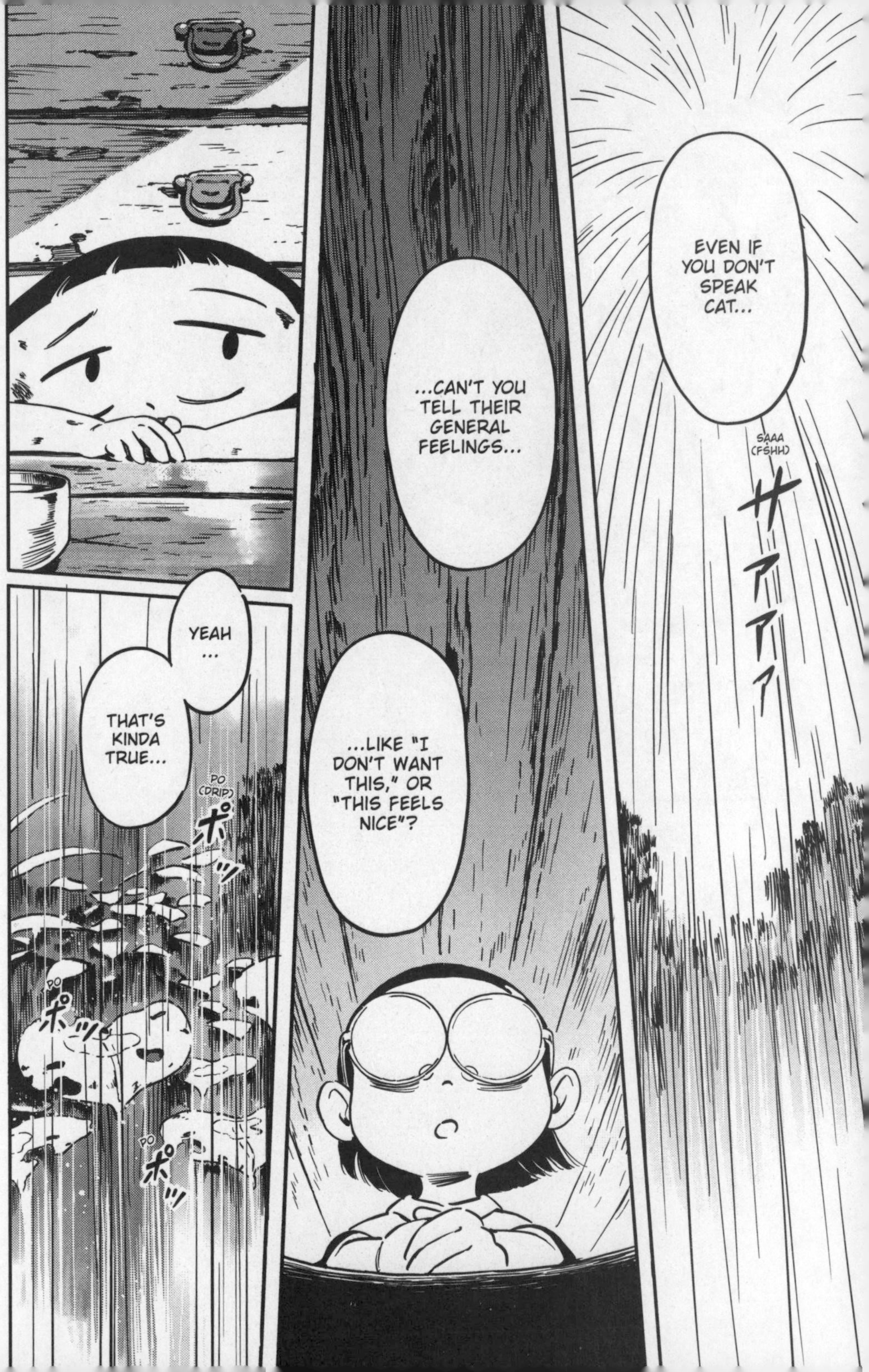
EVEN IF YOU DON'T SPEAK CAT...
SAAA (FSHH)
サァァァ
...CAN'T YOU TELL THEIR GENERAL FEELINGS...
...LIKE "I DON'T WANT THIS," OR "THIS FEELS NICE"?
YEAH ...
THAT'S KINDA TRUE...
PO (DRIP)
ポッ
PO
ポッ
PO
ポッ

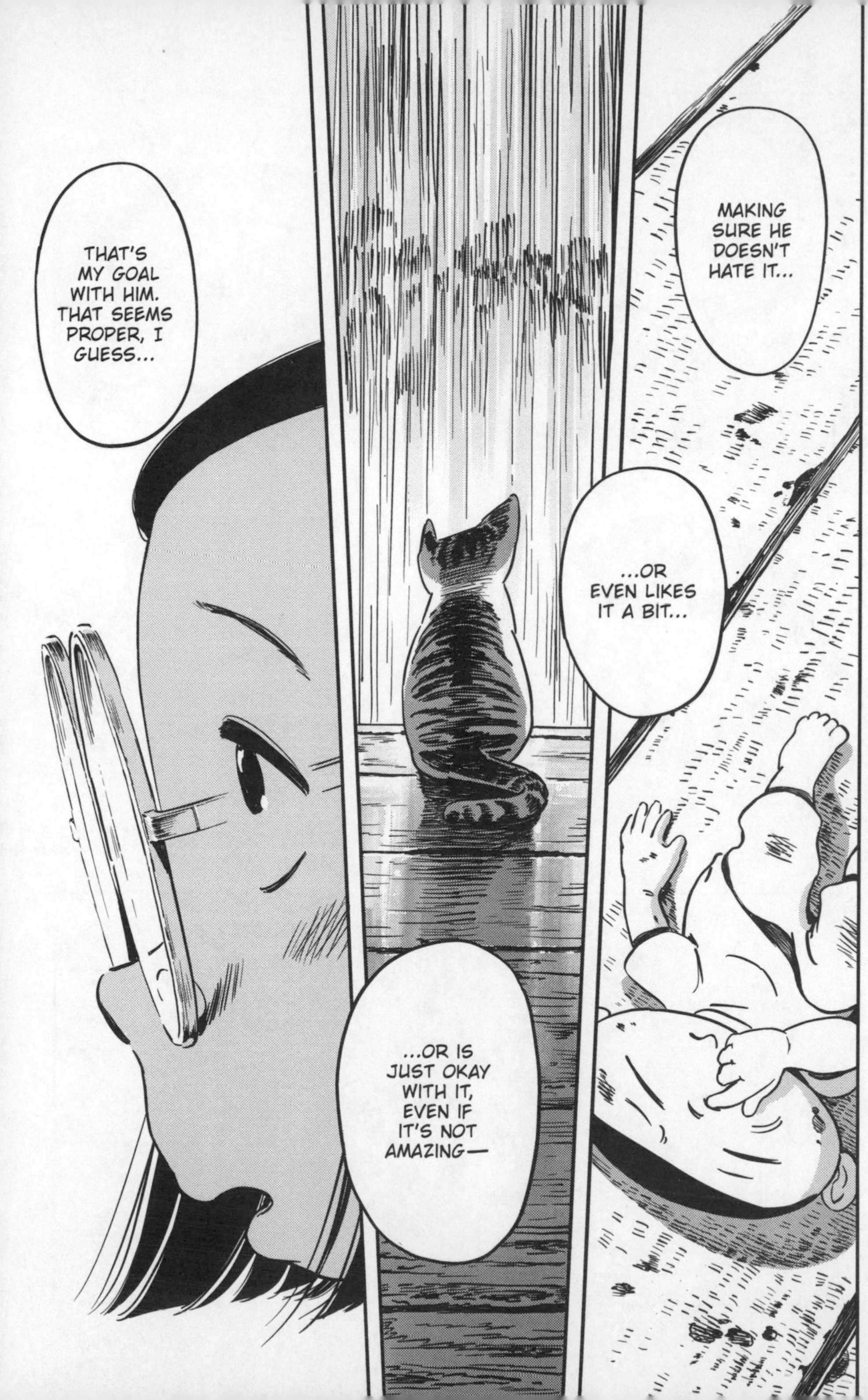
MAKING SURE HE DOESN'T HATE IT...
...OR EVEN LIKES IT A BIT...
...OR IS JUST OKAY WITH IT, EVEN IF IT'S NOT AMAZING—
THAT'S MY GOAL WITH HIM. THAT SEEMS PROPER, I GUESS...

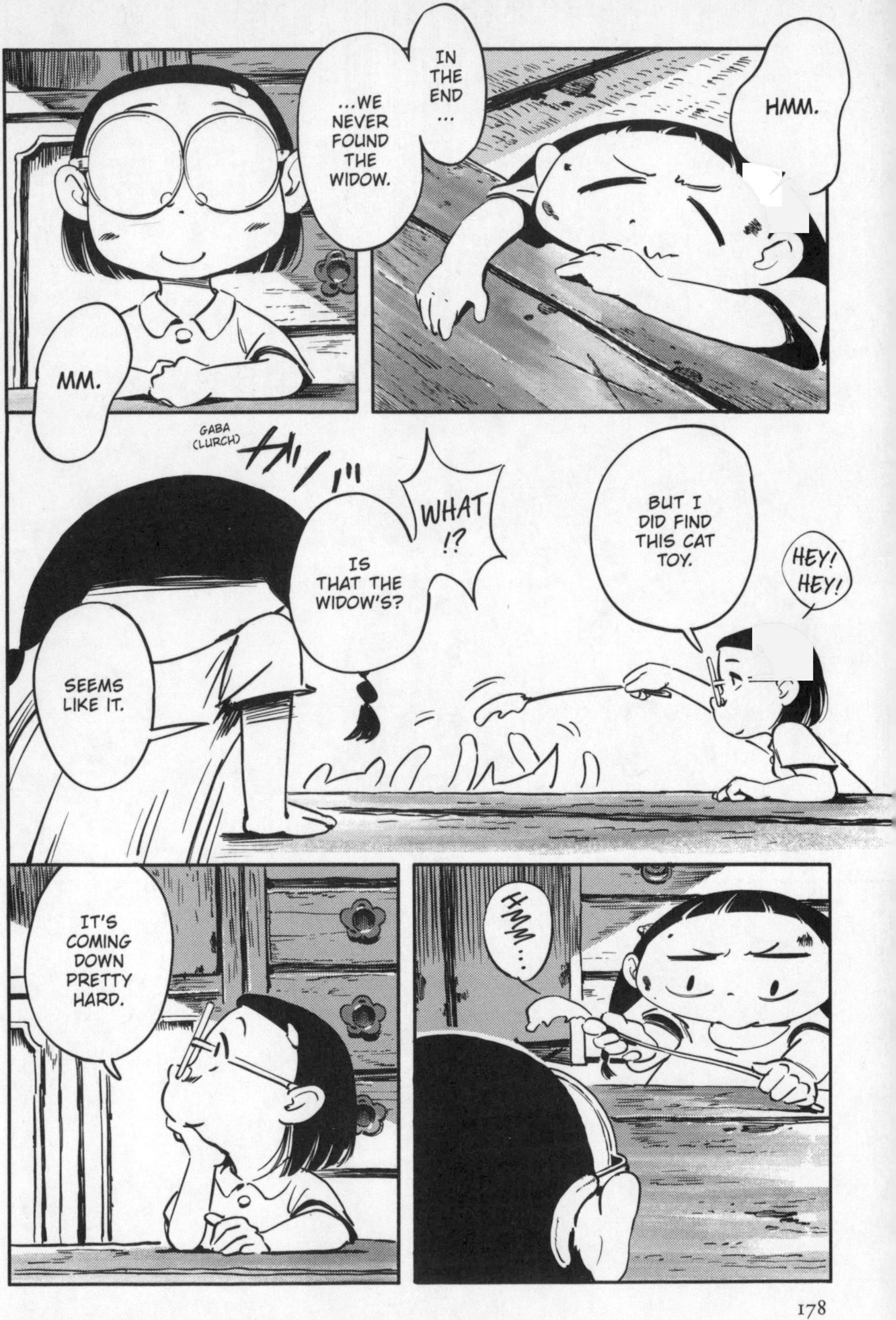
HMM.
IN THE END...
...WE NEVER FOUND THE WIDOW.
MM.
BUT I DID FIND THIS CAT TOY.
HEY! HEY!
GABA (LURCH)
WHAT!?
IS THAT THE WIDOW'S?
SEEMS LIKE IT.
HMM...
IT'S COMING DOWN PRETTY HARD.

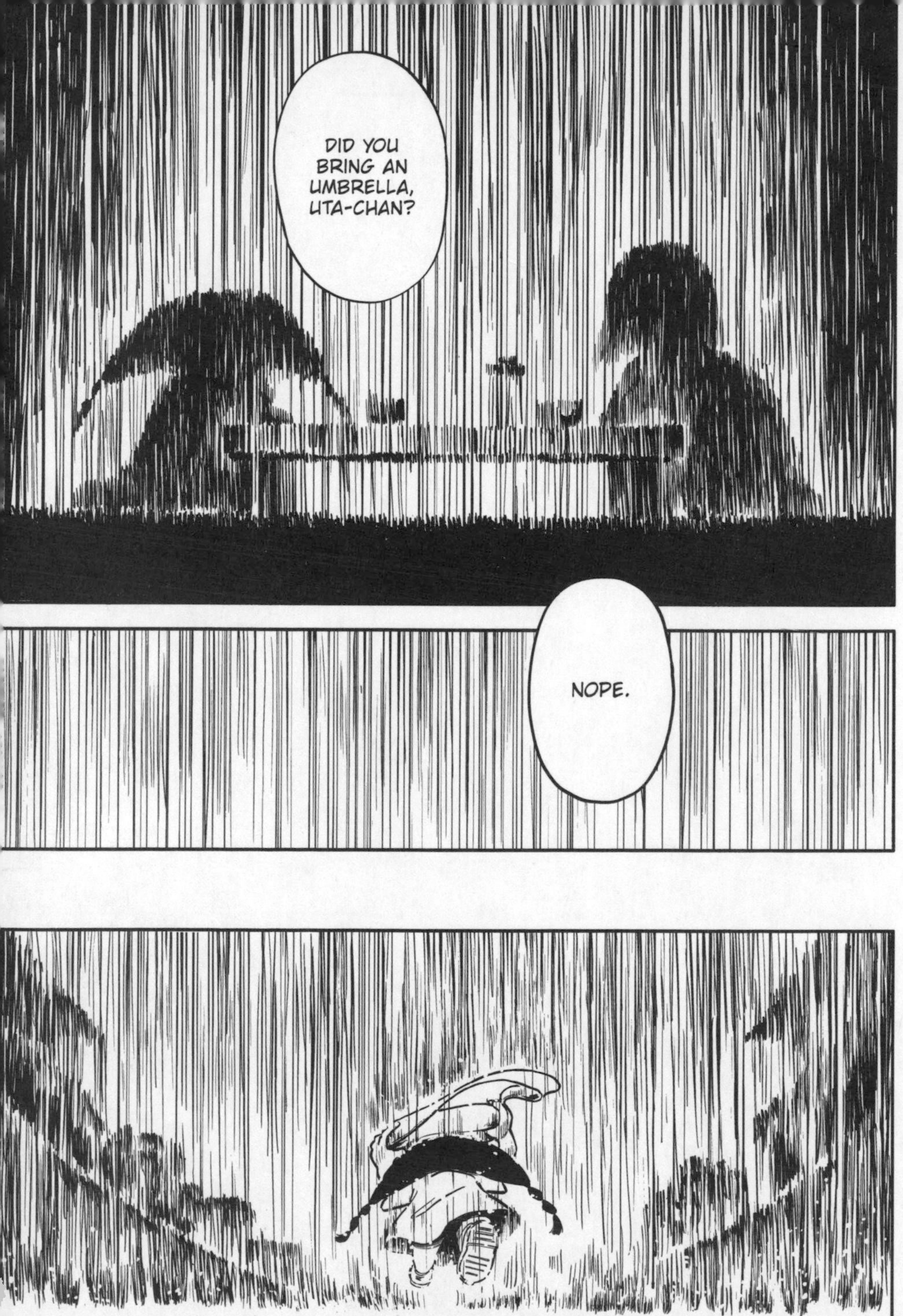
DID YOU BRING AN UMBRELLA, UTA-CHAN?
NOPE.

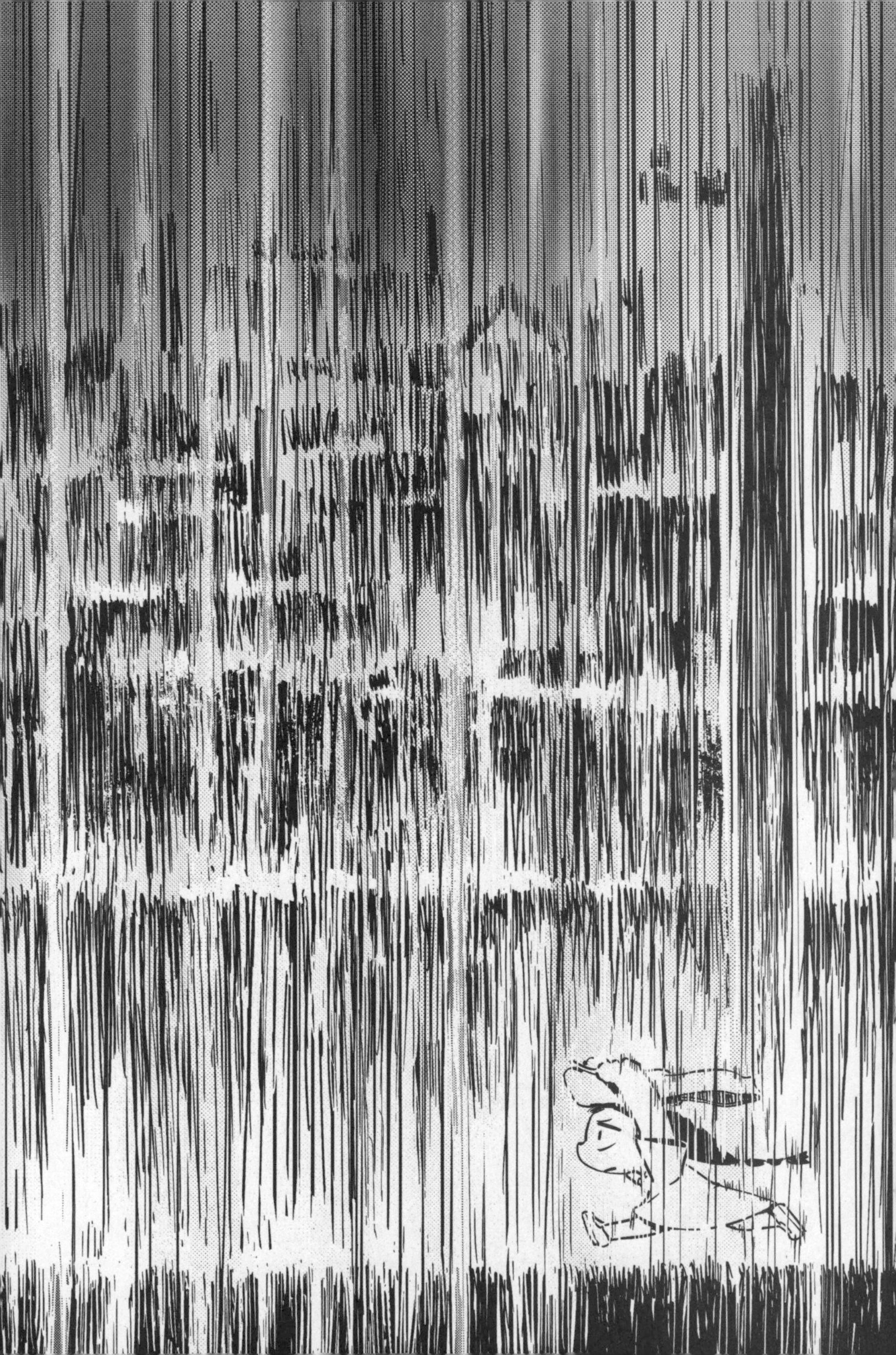

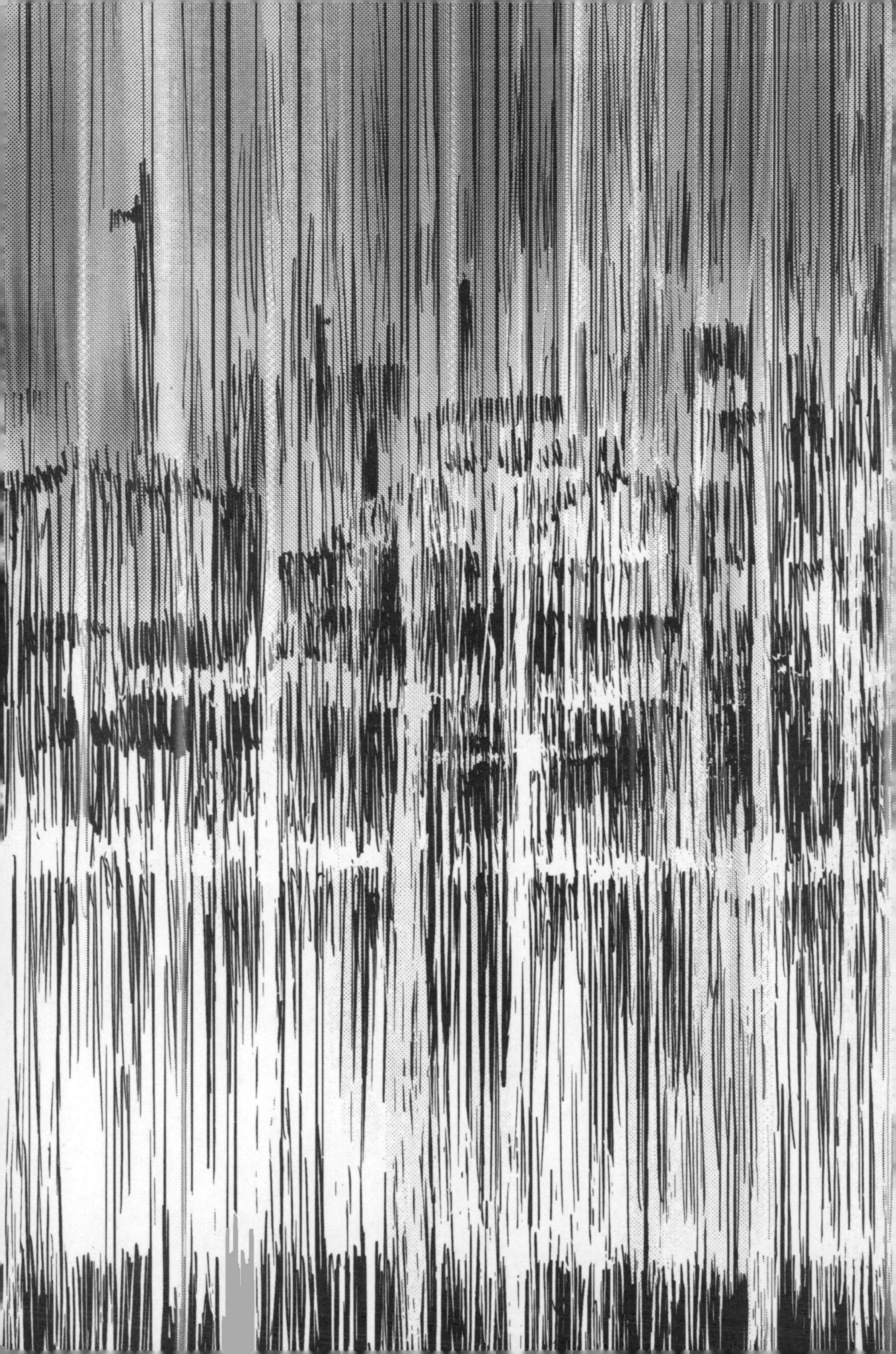

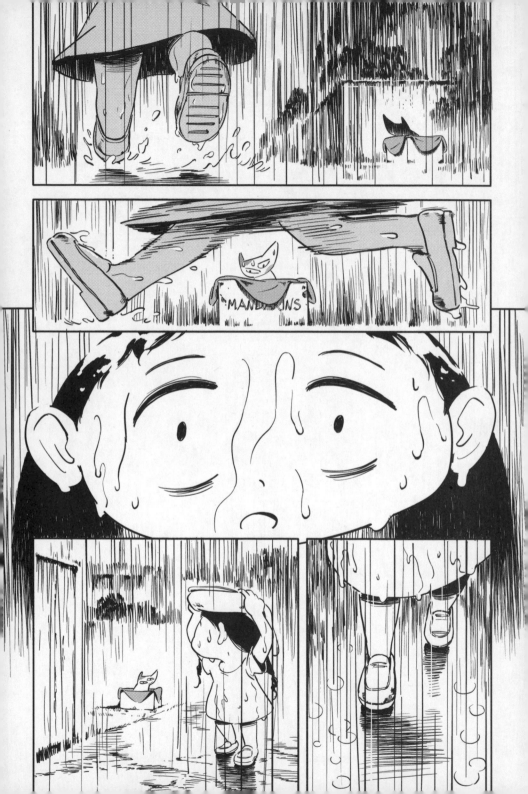

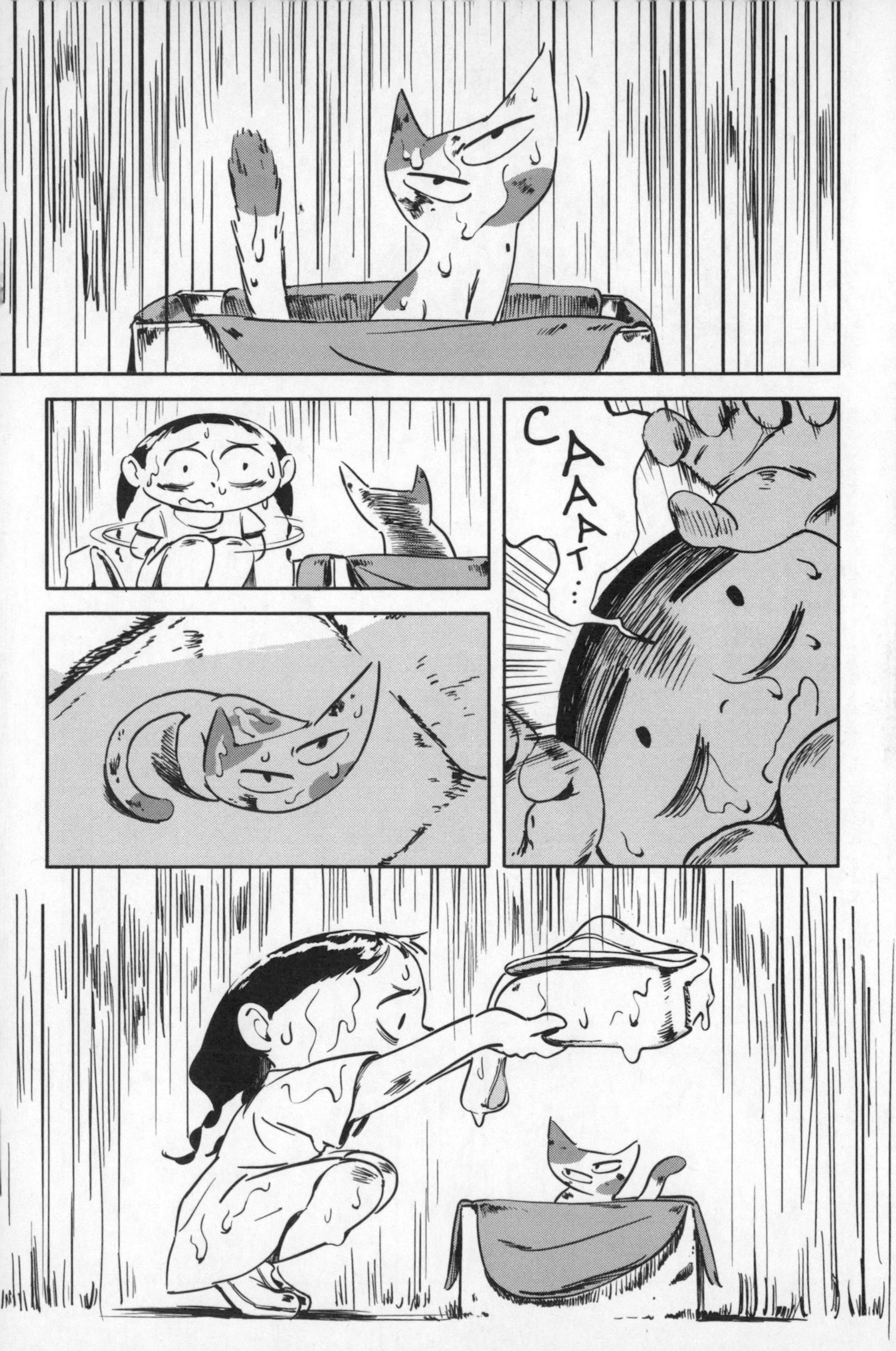
CAAAT...

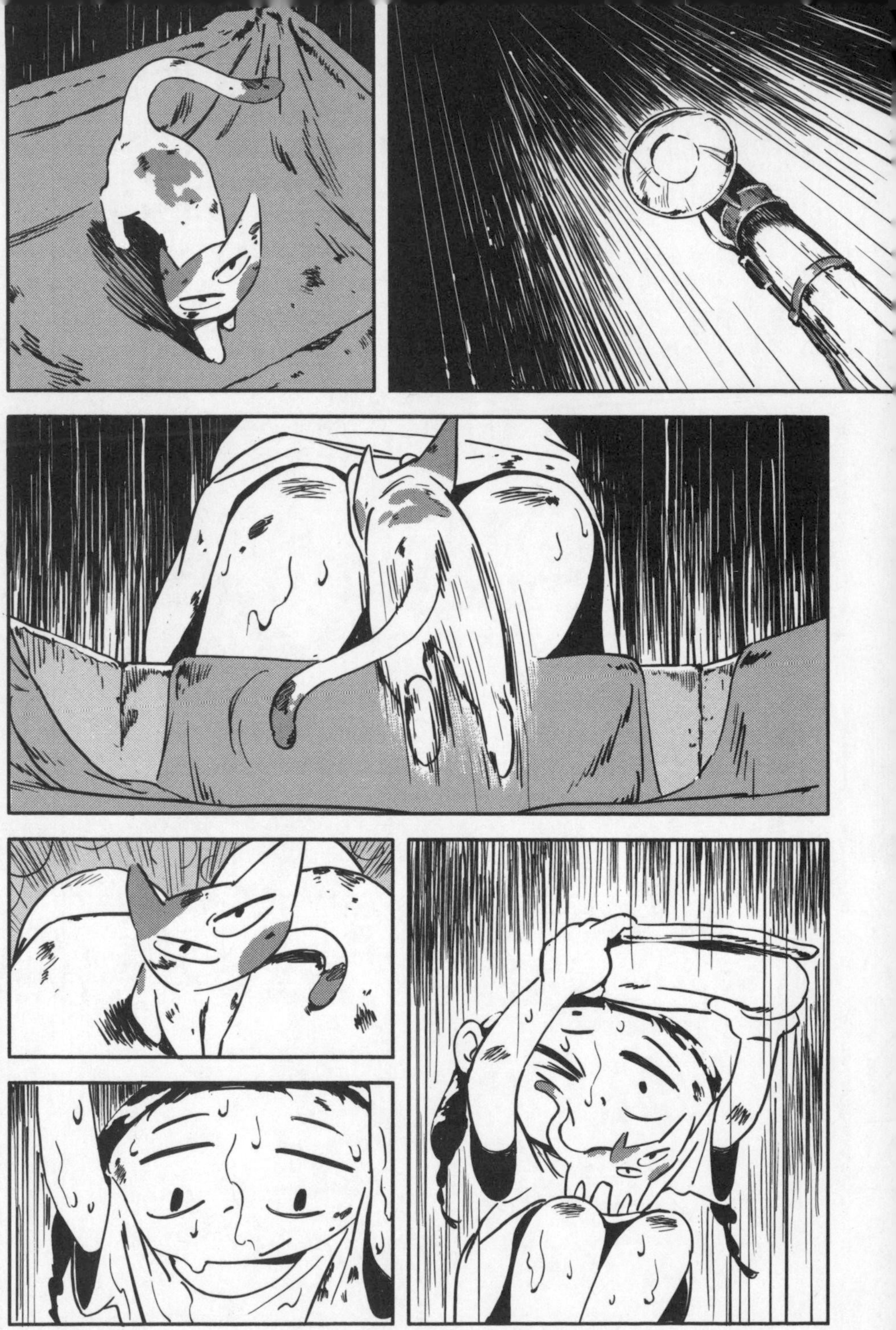

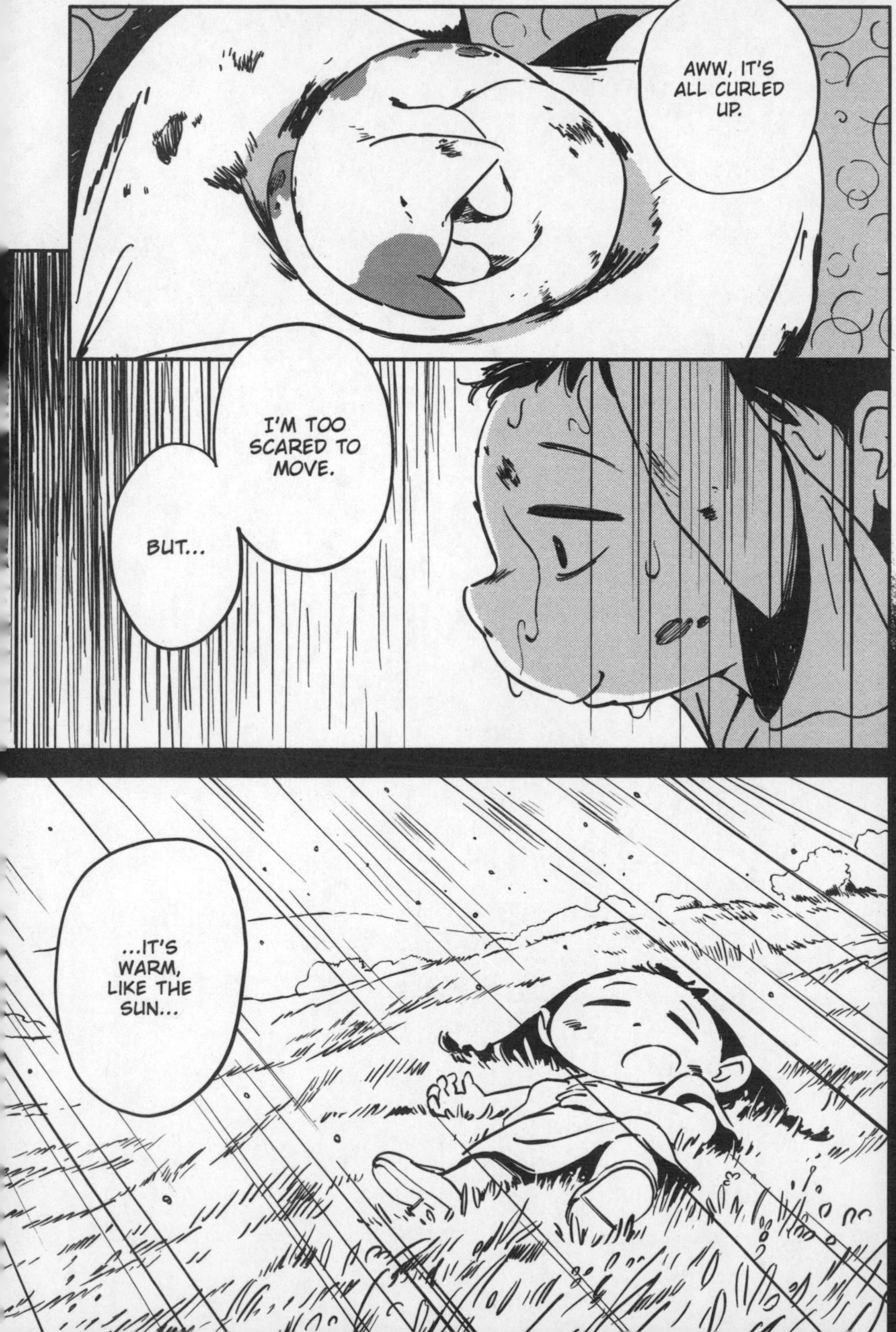
AWW, IT'S ALL CURLED UP.
I'M TOO SCARED TO MOVE.
BUT...
...IT'S WARM, LIKE THE SUN...

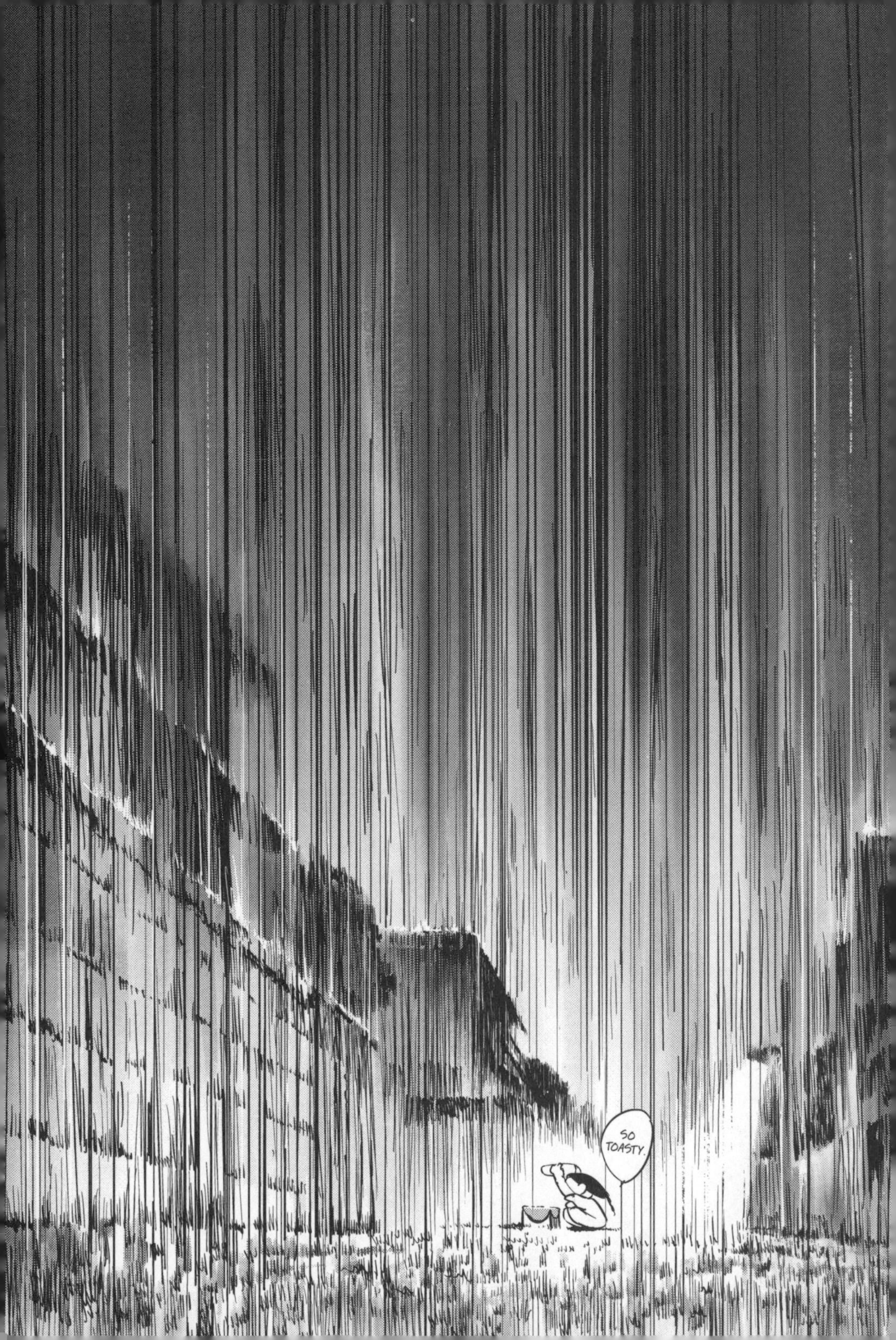
SO TOASTY.

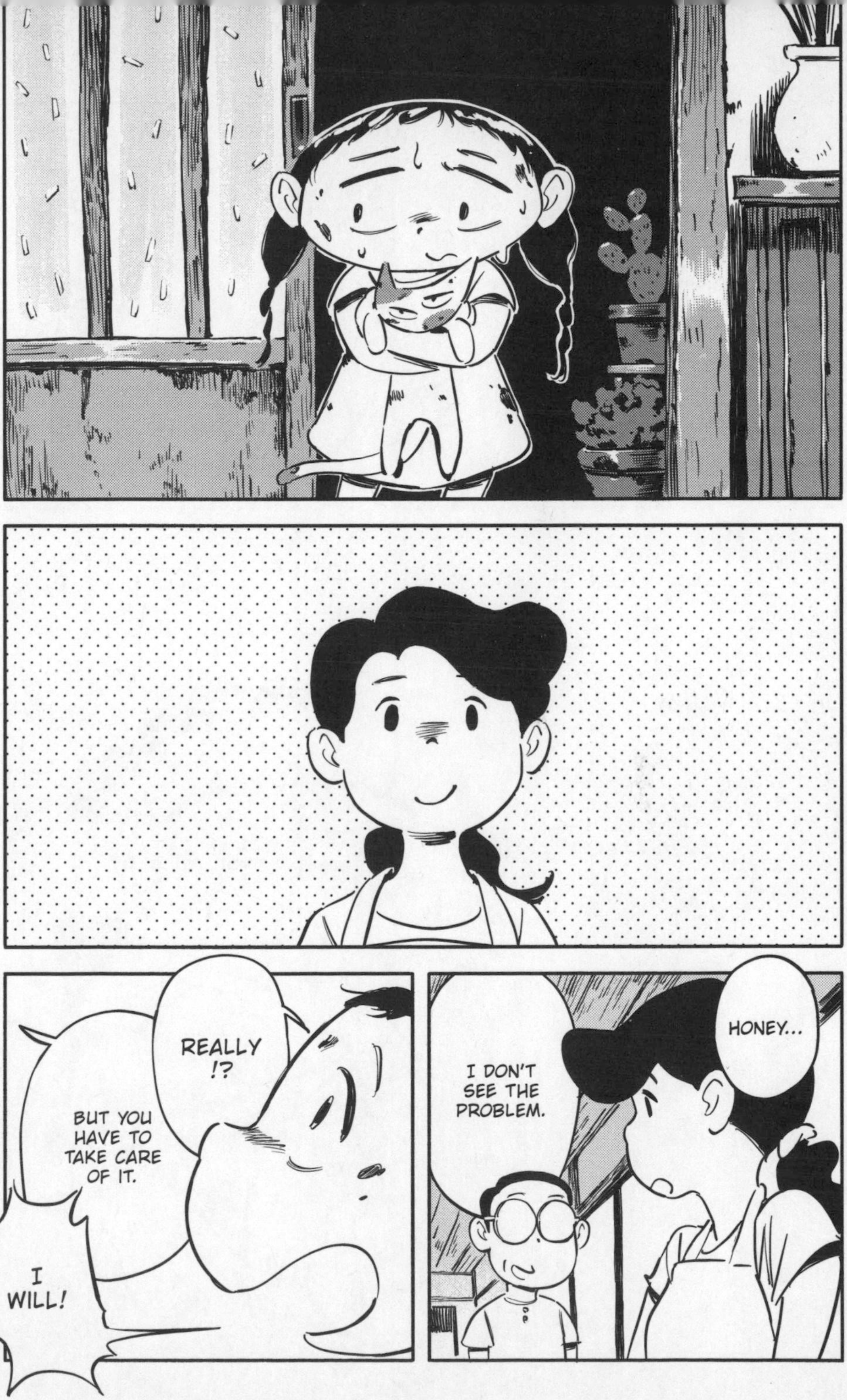
HONEY...
I DON'T SEE THE PROBLEM.
REALLY !?
BUT YOU HAVE TO TAKE CARE OF IT.
I WILL!

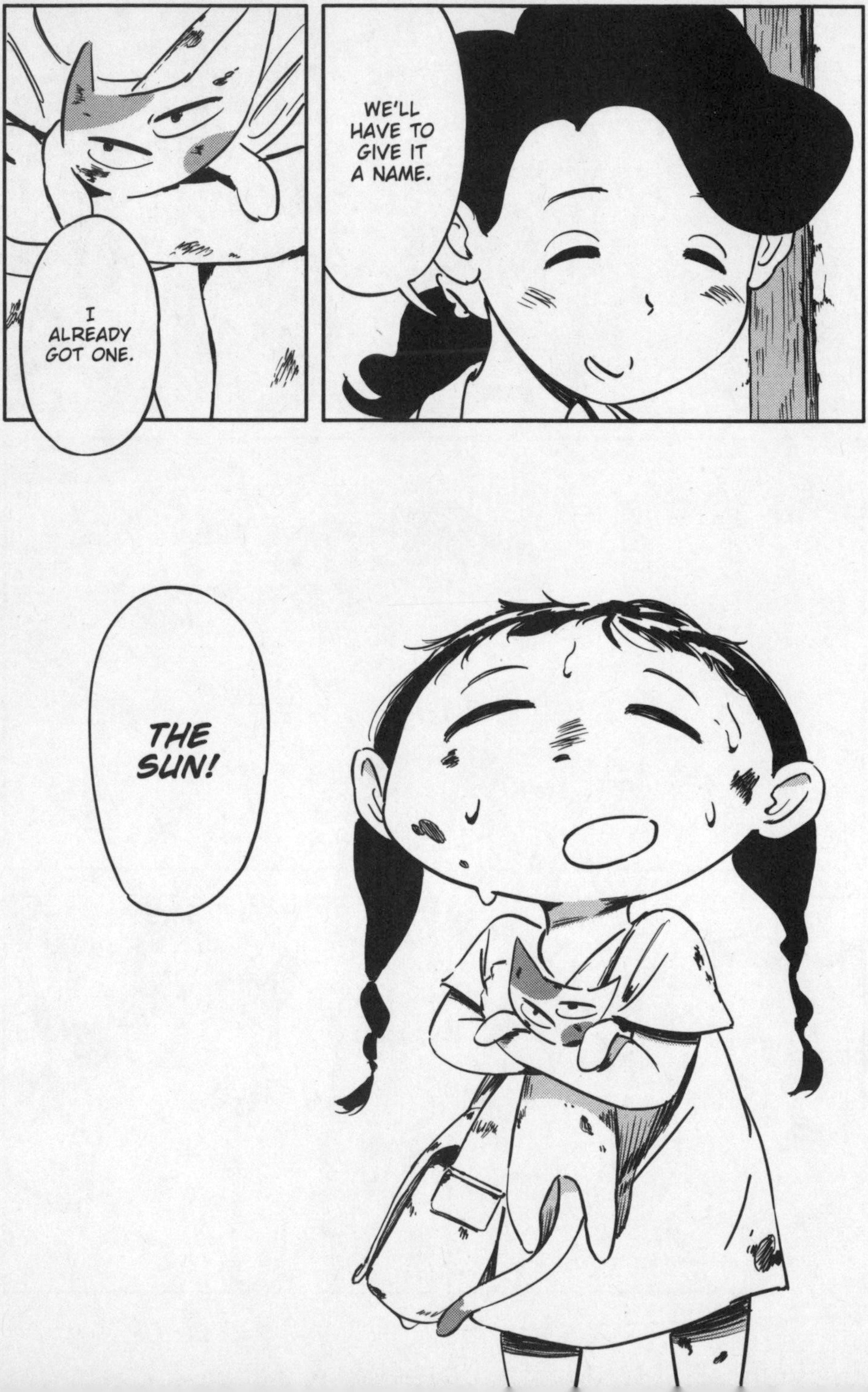
WE'LL HAVE TO GIVE IT A NAME.
I ALREADY GOT ONE.
THE SUN!

HANA-CHAN AND THE SHAPE OF THE WORLD

THE END

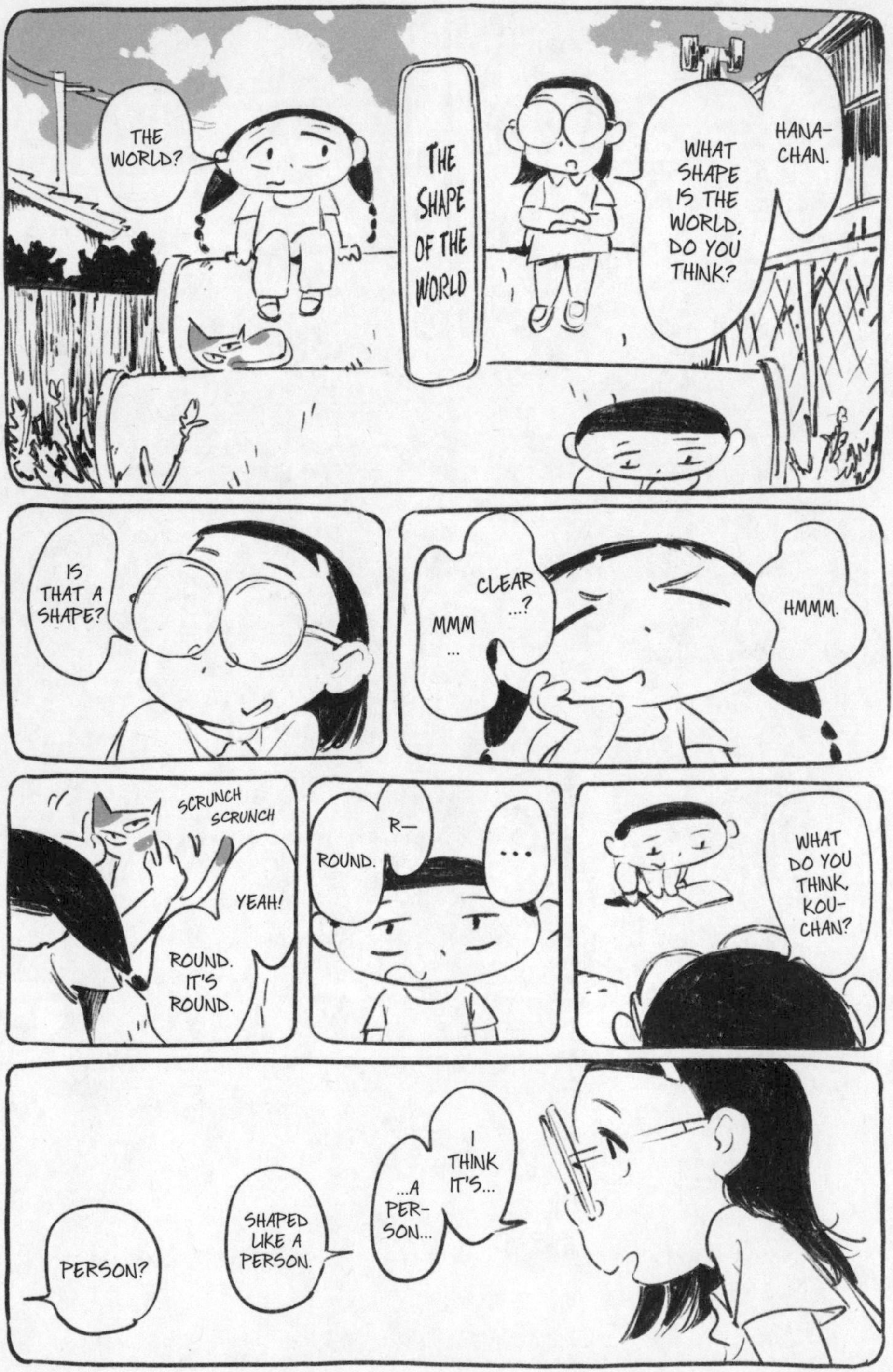
HANA-CHAN.
WHAT SHAPE IS THE WORLD, DO YOU THINK?
THE SHAPE OF THE WORLD
THE WORLD?
HMMM.
CLEAR ...?
MMM ...
IS THAT A SHAPE?
WHAT DO YOU THINK, KOU-CHAN?
...
R— ROUND.
SCRUNCH SCRUNCH
YEAH!
ROUND. IT'S ROUND.
I THINK IT'S...
...A PERSON...
SHAPED LIKE A PERSON.
PERSON?

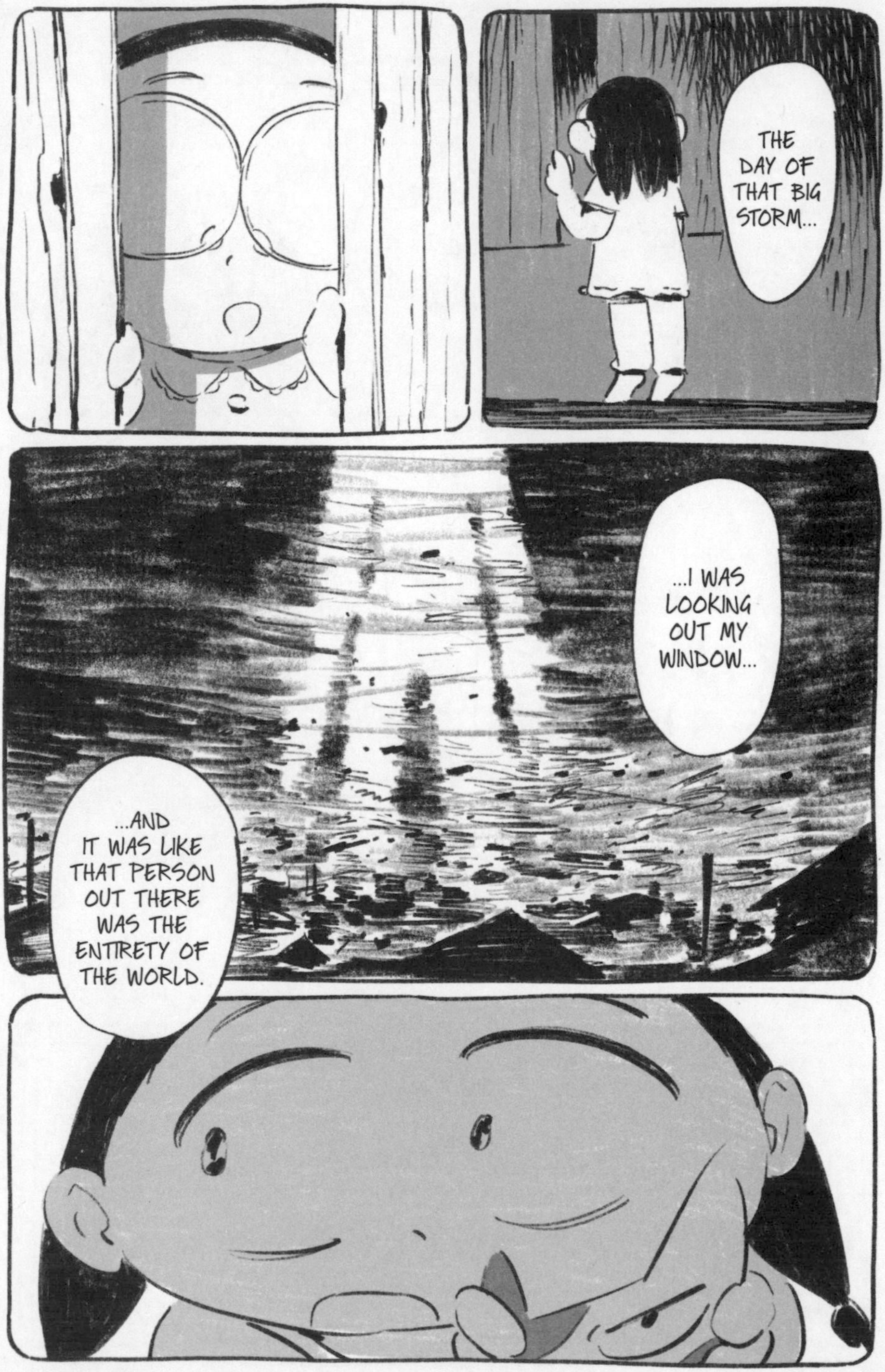
THE DAY OF THAT BIG STORM...
...I WAS LOOKING OUT MY WINDOW...
...AND IT WAS LIKE THAT PERSON OUT THERE WAS THE ENTIRETY OF THE WORLD.

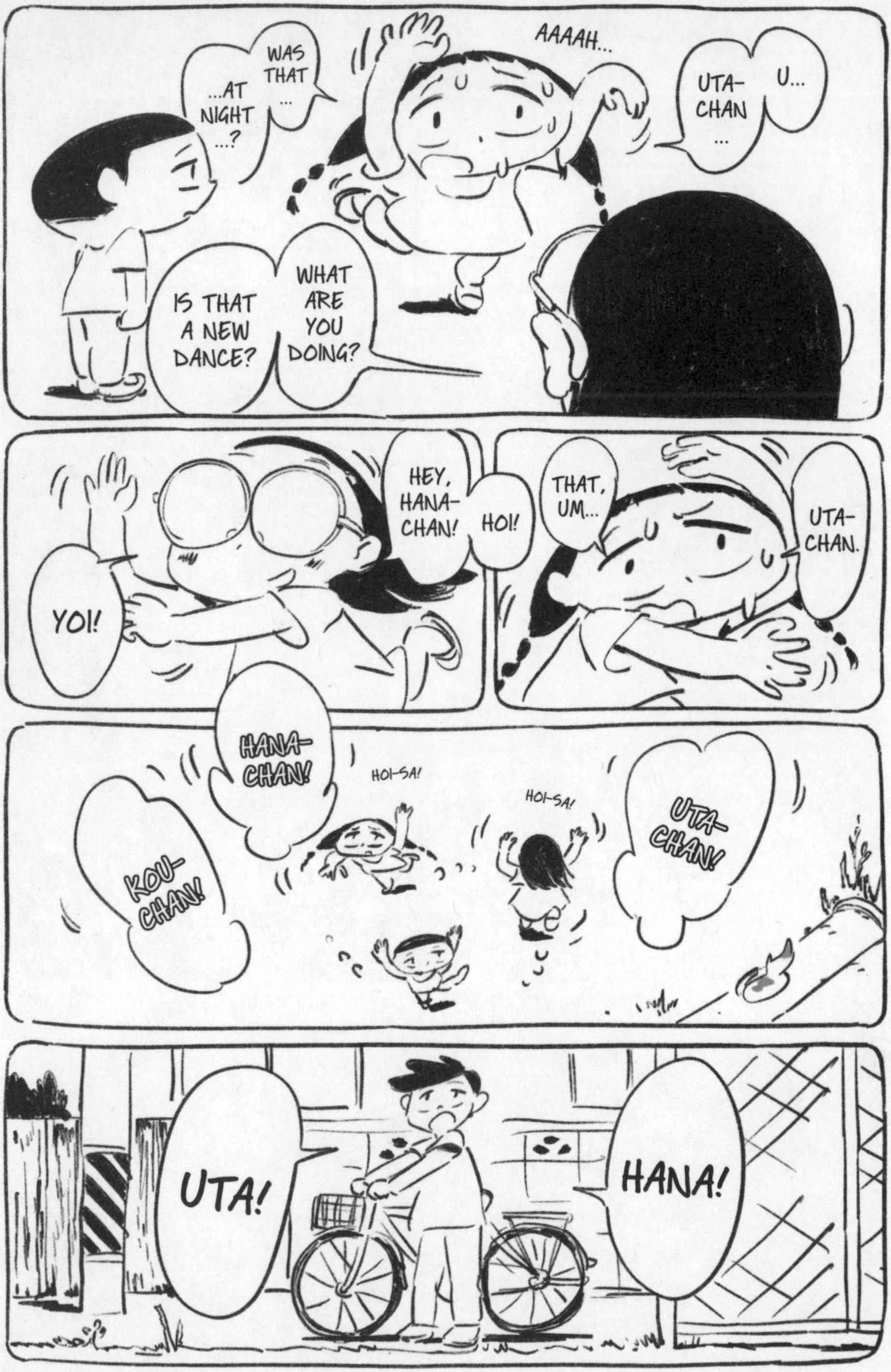
U...
UTA-CHAN...
AAAAH...
WAS THAT...
...AT NIGHT...?
WHAT ARE YOU DOING?
IS THAT A NEW DANCE?
UTA-CHAN.
THAT, UM...
HEY, HANA-CHAN!
HOI!
YOI!
UTA-CHAN!
HOI-SA!
HOI-SA!
HANA-CHAN!
KOU-CHAN!
HANA!
UTA!

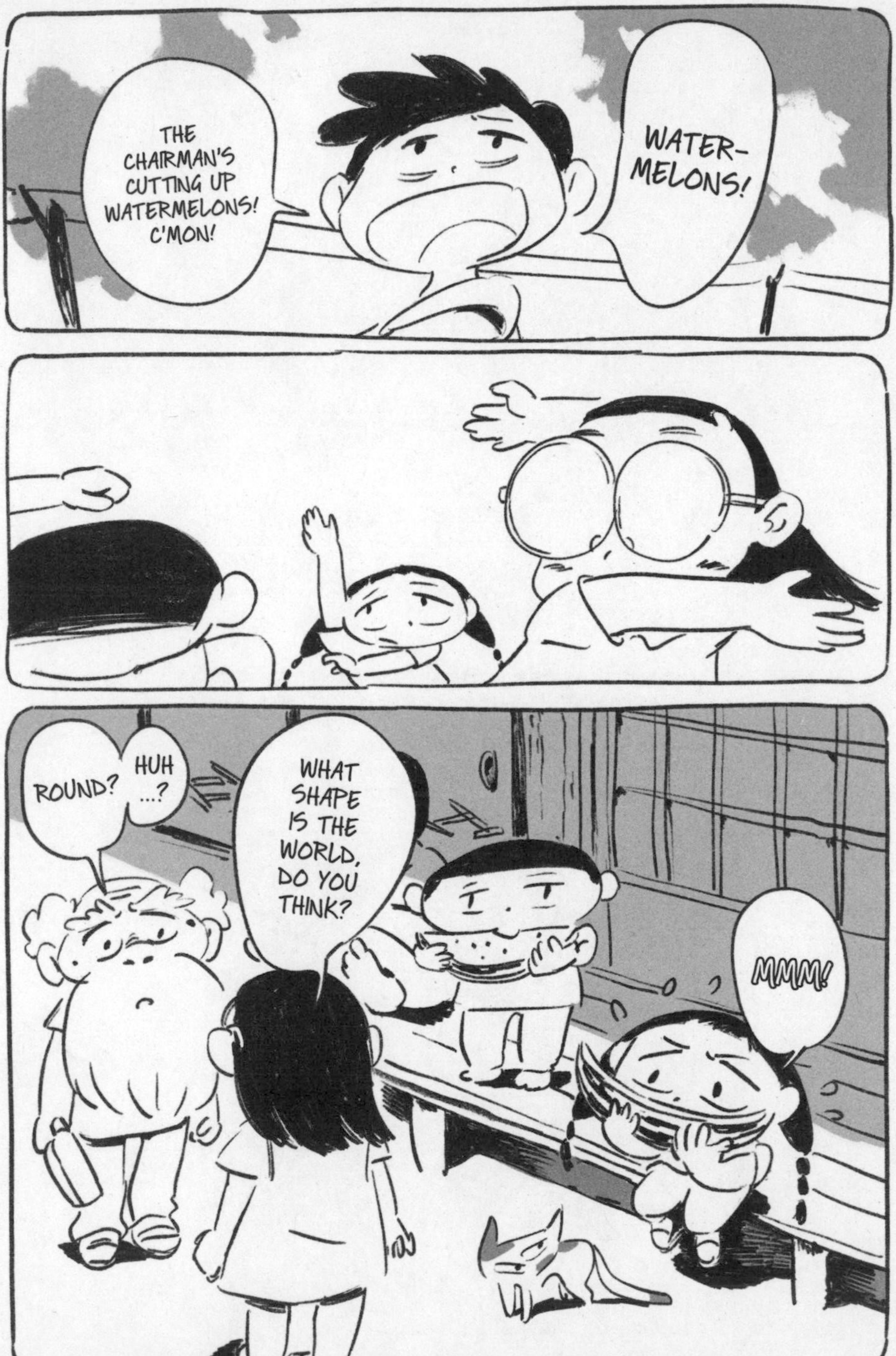
WATER-
MELONS!
THE CHAIRMAN'S CUTTING UP WATERMELONS! C'MON!
WHAT SHAPE IS THE WORLD, DO YOU THINK?
HUH ...?
ROUND?
MMM!

THE END

FIRST APPEARED IN:

THE SHAPE OF THE STORM - *MONTHLY COMIC BEAM, APRIL 2018 ISSUE*
HANA-CHAN'S DISASTER IN THE WEEDS - *MONTHLY COMIC BEAM, OCTOBER 2018 ISSUE*
PING-PONG THERAPY - *MONTHLY COMIC BEAM, FEBRUARY 2019 ISSUE*
UTA-CHAN'S HOMEWORK - *MONTHLY COMIC BEAM, JULY 2019 ISSUE*
BALLAD OF THE SUN - *MONTHLY COMIC BEAM, OCTOBER 2019 ISSUE*
THE SHAPE OF THE WORLD - NEW TO THIS EDITION

SIGN: LET'S GET ALONG

TRANSLATION NOTES

COMMON HONORIFICS

no honorific: Indicates familiarity or closeness; if used without permission or reason, addressing someone in this manner would constitute an insult.

-san: The Japanese equivalent of Mr./Mrs./Miss. If a situation calls for politeness, this is the fail-safe honorific.

-kun: Used most often when referring to boys, this indicates affection or familiarity. Occasionally used by older men among their peers, but it may also be used by anyone referring to a person of lower standing.

-chan: An affectionate honorific indicating familiarity used mostly in reference to girls; also used in reference to cute persons or animals of either gender.

-sensei: A respectful term for teachers, artists, or high-level professionals.

(o)nii-chan: An affectionate term used for older brothers or brother figures.

-senpai: An honorific used for upperclassmen and older, more knowledgable colleagues.

PAGE 9

Chocolate puffs: A Japanese candy known as *Mugi Choco*, meaning "wheat chocolate." It consists of puffed wheat kernels coated in milk chocolate. So while on the outside they might resemble treats like chocolate-covered raisins, the puffed wheat inside is much like the puffed wheat found in breakfast cereals.

PAGE 12

Kii Peninsula: On Honshu, the largest of Japan's islands, the Kii Peninsula occupies a wide stretch of land south of the center. It's considerably west of Tokyo, but is bounded on the north side by Osaka, Kyoto, and Nagoya. Although their town isn't named, the dialect spoken by Hana-chan and the other characters of the story is distinctly Kansai in flavor, the region that includes Osaka.

PAGE 159

Kikurage: A type of chewy, flat mushroom eaten regularly in Japanese cuisine. It is typically known as the "wood ear" in English because of its appearance and the fact that it grows on trees. When harvested and served, they are typically dark brown to black in color, which may explain the cat's name.

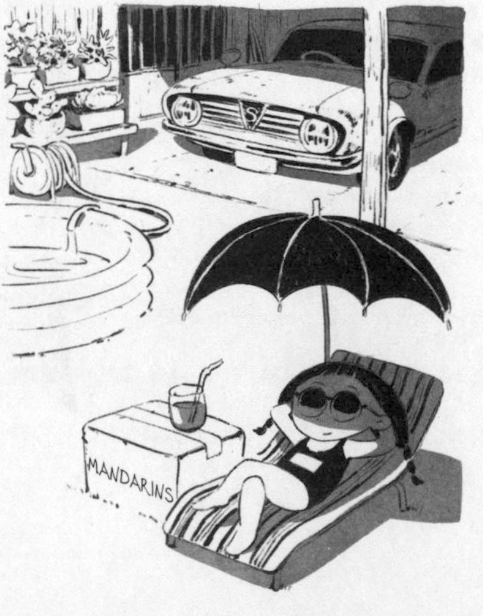
MANDARINS

JUN 2021

Hana-chan
and the Shape of the World

Ryotaro Ueda

Translation: Stephen Paul

Lettering: Bianca Pistillo

HANACHAN TO, SEKAI NO KATACHI
© Ryotaro Ueda 2019
First published in Japan in 2019 by KADOKAWA CORPORATION, Tokyo.
English translation rights arranged with KADOKAWA CORPORATION, Tokyo,
through TUTTLE-MORI AGENCY, INC., Tokyo.

English translation © 2021 by Yen Press, LLC

Yen Press
150 West 30th Street, 19th Floor
New York, NY 10001

Visit us at yenpress.com
facebook.com/yenpress
twitter.com/yenpress
yenpress.tumblr.com
instagram.com/yenpress

Yen Press is an imprint of Yen Press, LLC.
The Yen Press name and logo are trademarks of Yen Press, LLC.

The publisher is not responsible for websites
(or their content) that are not owned by the publisher.

First Yen Press Edition: March 2021

Library of Congress Control Number: 2020951853

ISBNs: 978-1-9753-1986-1 (paperback)
        978-1-9753-1985-4 (ebook)

10 9 8 7 6 5 4 3 2 1

WOR

Printed in the United States of America